The Vatican and Permanent Neutrality

The Vatican and Permanent Neutrality

Edited by Marshall J. Breger
and Herbert R. Reginbogin

LEXINGTON BOOKS
Lanham • Boulder • New York • London

Published by Lexington Books
An imprint of The Rowman & Littlefield Publishing Group, Inc.
4501 Forbes Boulevard, Suite 200, Lanham, Maryland 20706
www.rowman.com

86-90 Paul Street, London EC2A 4NE

Copyright © 2022 by The Rowman & Littlefield Publishing Group, Inc.

All rights reserved. No part of this book may be reproduced in any form or by any electronic or mechanical means, including information storage and retrieval systems, without written permission from the publisher, except by a reviewer who may quote passages in a review.

British Library Cataloguing in Publication Information Available

Library of Congress Cataloging-in-Publication Data

Names: Breger, Marshall J., editor. | Reginbogin, Herbert R., editor.
Title: The Vatican and permanent neutrality / edited by Marshall J. Breger and Herbert R. Reginbogin.
Description: Lanham : Lexington Books, [2022] | Includes bibliographical references and index. | Summary: "This book examines Vatican diplomacy from the fall of the Papal States in 1870 to the present day. The contributors focus on the concept of permanent neutrality and trace the Vatican's political transformation into a modern international institution in conjunction with its use of neutrality as a tool of diplomacy and statecraft"— Provided by publisher.
Identifiers: LCCN 2021059716 (print) | LCCN 2021059717 (ebook) | ISBN 9781793642165 (cloth) | ISBN 9781793642189 (paperback) | ISBN 9781793642172 (ebook)
Subjects: LCSH: Catholic Church—Foreign relations. | Catholic Church and world politics. | Neutrality—Vatican City. | Diplomacy—Religious aspects—Catholic Church.
Classification: LCC BX1793 .V375 2022 (print) | LCC BX1793 (ebook) | DDC 261.709456/34—dc23/eng/20220210
LC record available at https://lccn.loc.gov/2021059716
LC ebook record available at https://lccn.loc.gov/2021059717

Marshall Breger dedicates this book to his late parents Miles (Meir ben Moshe Yonah) and Beatrice (Rivka bas Yehuda Leib) Breger z'l. May their *neshamos* have an *aliyah*.

Herbert Reginbogin dedicates this book to his family.

Contents

Acknowledgments ix

Introduction xi
   Marshall J. Breger

PART I   FROM THE PAPAL STATES TO THE VATICAN: 1870–1929

1. The Holy See and Neutrality: Vatican Diplomacy 1870–1929   3
   John F. Pollard

2. The Holy See and Neutrality in the Aftermath of World War I: The Consequences of the Treaty of Versailles and Other Peace Treaties   23
   Kurt Martens

3. The Lateran Treaty and the Hermeneutics of the Holy See Neutrality: The Final Defeat of the Papal State and the Roman Question   39
   Maria d'Arienzo

PART II   THE LONG SECOND WORLD WAR: 1931–1945

4. Neutrality to the Test: The Vatican and the Fascist Wars of the 1930s   63
   Lucia Ceci

5 Vatican Diplomacy and Church Realities in the
   Philippines during World War II   83
   Pascal Lottaz

6 Pope Pius XII, Vatican Neutrality, and the Holocaust:
   Case Studies from the Newly Opened Vatican Archives   105
   Suzanne Brown-Fleming

PART III INTO THE COLD: 1950–1990

7 No Neutrality in Ideology: The Holy See and the
   Cold War   121
   Piotr H. Kosicki

8 The Holy See's Efforts to Secure the Departure of Cardinal
   Mindszenty: Diplomacy in a Cold War Context   143
   Arpad von Klimo and Margit Balogh

PART IV POST-COLD WAR: 1990–2020

9 Pope Francis and Vatican Sovereignty   161
   Massimo Faggioli

10 Neutrality as an Aid to Holy See Diplomacy:
   Iraq and Syria, 1991–2011   179
   Luke Cahill

11 The Church and the Bomb: Holy See Diplomacy
   and Nuclear Weapons   203
   Maryann Cusimano Love

12 Vatican's / Holy See's Approach to Nonproliferation:
   The United States and Japan   225
   Saho Matsumoto

13 Power and Spirituality: The Collision of Canon
   and International Law   245
   Herbert Reginbogin

Appendix   275

Index   281

About the Contributors   293

Acknowledgments

This volume arose out a workshop held on February 11, 2020, at the Catholic University of America (CUA) on "The Holy See and Vatican City (State) and Permanent Neutrality" and sponsored by the "Neutrality Working Group" of the University's Institute for Policy Research (IPR). We are grateful to the staff of IPR for every assistance.

We want to thank former vice president Madam Hsiu-lien Lu of Taiwan for a grant that supported portions of this effort.

We acknowledge an immense debt of gratitude to Steven Young, reference librarian at CUA's Kathryn J. DuFour Law Library, for research and bibliographical advice. Also, our deepest thanks to Joan Stahl, director of research and instruction at the Mullen Library of CUA, and their staff, especially Karen Stephanites, resource sharing technician, and Taras Zvir, theology, and religious studies librarian, for their endless help with acquiring books from all across the country.

Our special thanks to Dr. Pascal Lottaz, assistant professor at Waseda Institute for Advanced Study in Japan, for helping with academic and technical aspects related to the book. Lastly, we are grateful for the opportunity to have worked for countless hours with a group of brilliant scholars from different parts of the world on this project.

Introduction
Marshall J. Breger

Italy recognized the Vatican City as an independent state under the sovereignty of the Holy See in the Lateran Treaty signed February 11, 1929. This political treaty (sometimes called the Treaty of Conciliation) included a separately signed financial convention regarding financial compensation that was appended to the Conciliation Treaty as Annex 4. At the same time, Italy and the Holy See signed a Concordat regarding their religious relations. All these are referred to as the Lateran Pact or Pacts (and variously as consisting of two or more documents.

In February 2020, the neutrality working group at the Catholic University of America organized a conference on the Vatican City State and Permanent Neutrality to commemorate what was, that year, the ninety-first anniversary of the Lateran Pacts. The conference was designed to look at the evolution of the Church's foreign policy from its 1929 reemergence as an independent sovereign, evaluate its identity and institutions, and consider critically the impact the Vatican had on the world in the last ten decades. Permanent Neutrality had become an integrated feature of Vatican diplomacy, critically essential to evaluating and understanding its diplomacy. As Catholic author and activist George Weigel has trenchantly observed, "the demise of the Papal States . . . [proved] . . . to be the essential condition for the possibility of the papacy exercising politically effective moral authority in the twentieth century."[1] In that sense, the loss of the Papal States was less a tragedy than it was the liberation of the Papacy—freeing it to pursue its spiritual core. Massimo Faggioli (chapter 9) suggests that the key to understanding Pope Francis's papacy is the concept of liminality—a papacy in which the church is transforming itself across intellectual boundaries and geographical borders. In that context, both the meaning and purpose of the Vatican understanding of neutrality become particularly important to understanding the foreign policy of the Holy See.

This book will consider the interplay between two normatively disparate subjects—the concept of neutrality in international law and the concept of the Vatican as a neutral actor in international relations. To undertake the latter, we will have to briefly consider the Holy See as an international actor. The chapters herein will illuminate that interface focusing on Pontificates since World War I: Pius XI (1922–1939), Pius XII (1939–1958), through John Paul II (1978–2005) to Pope Francis (2013–). This book then is a story of the Vatican's "restoration" after the anti-clerical depredations of the French revolution[2] and the Vatican's development from a Papal State located on the Italian peninsula to the worldwide spiritual force it is today.

CONCEPTS OF NEUTRALITY

There is a rich jurisprudence of neutrality in international law starting from Vattel and Grotius[3] and other classical works of international law in the seventeenth and eighteenth centuries. An extensive caselaw on maritime neutrality developed,[4] as well as a rich literature about neutrality in international relations—including the development of wide-ranging discussion regarding the operation of neutrality in the law of war.[5]

While the term "neutrality" is anchored in the international law literature, it has been understood in a variety of ways by political scientists and in popular culture. Some of these "variants" include pacifism, even-handedness, non-alignment, isolationism, and "America First." The issue has been particularly complicated in that so many of these notions have been swept into the discussion of the Vatican and neutrality.

The "realist view" of neutrality is drawn from Thucydides. In his account of the Peloponnesian Wars, he recounts how Melios proclaimed neutrality in the war between Athens and Sparta. Athens rejected this and demanded they sign up or be destroyed—they declined, and so chose the latter. The lesson that is drawn is that "the strong do what they can, the weak suffer what they must."[6] It is this *Realpolitik* notion that must be confronted by the Vatican's efforts, discussed in this book, toward creating principles of neutrality as a positive value.

In the 1899 Peace Conference at the Hague, the concept of permanent neutrality was part of the discussion.[7] As part of conference preparations, Norway sought to have the international community recognize it as a permanent neutral, and in 1902 its representative body—the Storting—unanimously adopted neutrality.[8] In 1907, the Second Hague Conference on the Rights and Duties of Neutral Powers was held over four months,[9] and a number of the resulting Conventions were ratified by the United States in 1909.[10]

Those efforts were largely halted with World War I and the German invasion of neutral Belgium. Still, on August 31, 1935, Congress passed the first Neutrality Act prohibiting the export of "arms, ammunition, and implements of war" from the United States to foreign nations at war and requiring arms manufacturers in the United States to apply for an export license.[11] And in 1937, the United States passed the Neutrality Act of 1937.[12] This reflected a recurrent isolationist strain in American politics, particularly virulent after World War I and only allayed with the Japanese attack on Pearl Harbor[13] (although some see Trump's claims of "America First" as a twenty-first-century variant).[14]

At the same time, exhausted by the slaughter of the "Great War," a related interest in outlawing war developed. Pacifism became a force in western thinking in the 1920s and after. For example, in 1933, the Oxford Union Debating Society voted that "this House will under no circumstances fight for King or Country."[15] Furthermore, pacifism impacted diplomacy as well. The Kellogg-Briand pact[16] and other treaties to "outlaw war" were passed in the 1920s. As several articles in this book suggest, distinguishing neutrality from pacifism is often a complex analytical challenge, especially in discussions of Vatican diplomatic policy.

One cannot discuss the issue of neutrality without dealing with World War II. After WWII, academic discussion of the principles of neutrality fell off the table. There was a sense that neutrality was equivalent to complicity with the evil that is National Socialism. No Allied government wanted to be associated with giving a bye to the Nazis. For many years, there was little discussion of neutrality in the academic literature.

The problem is well explored in the exponentially growing literature on the actions of Pius XII during World War II,[17] as exemplified by Suzanne Brown Fleming's groundbreaking article (chapter 6) that makes use of evidence in the newly-opened WWII Vatican Apostolic Archive (Archivio Apostolico Vaticano) which has shed more light on this debate.[18] Her contribution also addresses Church attitudes toward neutrality and "forgiveness" during and after World War II through the story of Cardinal Aloisius Muench and the American Military government in postwar Germany.[19]

Switzerland's neutrality is well known, reaching back to the end of the Napoleonic era[20] and continuing through World War II and on into the Cold War.[21] But even elsewhere, after World War II, neutrality was a survivor, perhaps because the concept met a geopolitical need in international affairs. Austria and Finland were neutral (out of necessity) through much of the Cold War; so too for many years were Ireland and Sweden (at least de facto).[22] The "Non-aligned movement" sought to affect a species of neutrality for third-world countries.[23] Since the 1990s, we have begun to refocus on neutrality.

Turkmenistan not only declared itself permanently neutral,[24] but the UN officially ratified its status in 1995.[25]

THE VATICAN IN INTERNATIONAL AFFAIRS

The Vatican has a long history as a force in international affairs. In the early Middle Ages, it was a powerful actor on the international stage—consider the hundred years of war with the Islamic world engendered by Pope Urban II's 1095 call for a Crusade at the Council of Clermont to cries of "Deus vult!"[26] Likewise compelling were the geopolitics behind the vision of Frederic Barbarossa kneeling in the snow for three days in 1077 as he sought Pope Gregory VII's "forgiveness" at Canossa.[27]

As the head of the Papal States, the pope was of necessity a "player" in the politics of the Italian peninsula. All this ended in 1870 when Pope Pius IX lost temporal control of the surrounding Papal States and Rome—the "eternal city"—in the final act of the *Risorgimento*. Pius IX then declared himself a "prisoner of the Vatican," retreating into the Vatican itself and placing himself in internal exile.[28]

Still, the Vatican considered itself a sovereign—even when lacking a/ the formal requirement for sovereignty—territory. In 1885 Pope Leo XIII declared:

> It cannot be called in question that in the making of treaties, in the transaction of business matters, in the sending and receiving ambassadors, and in the interchange of other kinds of official dealings [temporal rulers] have been wont to treat the Church as with a supreme and legitimate power. And assuredly, all ought to hold that it was not without a singular disposition of God's providence that this power of the Church was provided with a civil sovereignty as the surest safeguard of her independence.[29]

As Maria d'Arienzo (chapter 3) makes clear, the self-understanding of the Holy See as a sovereign was a theological necessity. As she points out, "the ecclesiology that had developed since the eighteenth century within the framework of public ecclesiastical law based the independence of the Church on the concept of *societas iuridice perfecta*, which was described as possessing by right all the means to achieve it, in its self-sufficient and independent order, that is to say, fully autonomous."[30] Today, most scholars understand the Holy See (at least functionally) as a sovereign state[31] and recognize its international legal personality as well.[32] We should note that while laymen often use the terms Holy See and Vatican interchangeably, they are, in fact, conceptually distinct. Canon law defines the Holy See as the pontiff, the roman curia, and "that which appears from natural law or the context."[33] More prosaically, while the Vatican City State is a geographical entity, it is the Holy See that is the governing authority. As Martens (chapter 2) points out, a country has diplomatic relations not with the Vatican but with the Holy See.[34]

As the Duce rose to power, he sought to settle what had become known as the "Roman Question" and in 1929 succeeded in negotiating the Lateran Treaty with the Holy See, a treaty which settled many of the outstanding issues between Italy and the Holy See. As d'Arienzo (chapter 3) shows, the concept of permanent neutrality was entered into to provide the Duce "permission" to recognize Holy See sovereignty. At the same time, neutrality also assisted the Vatican in its efforts to continue to play on the international stage.

This volume will discuss the changing style and the substance of Holy See diplomacy, particularly since the creation of the Vatican City (State). The analysis will be framed in terms of the international system each pope faced, their conception of the role of the Church in the world, and the pastoral and policy vision which informed each pope's ministry into the twenty-first century. In addition, we will explore the concept of permanent neutrality both as a theoretical concept and its practical applications.

THE VATICAN VIEW OF THE CONCEPT OF NEUTRALITY

The Vatican's approach to neutrality predated the Lateran Treaty. As Pollard (chapter 1) in this volume recounts, in 1821, Cardinal Ercole Consalvi, the secretary of state, announced that the Holy Father "will maintain . . . a perfect neutrality toward all nations."[35] Pius IX reiterated this approach during the Revolution of 1848. Pollard dexterously explicates Vatican diplomacy and its approach to neutrality from the Franco-Prussian War through World War I and after. Throughout World War I, while "[b]oth the Central Powers and the Triple Entente held the belief that the Holy See was partial to the interests of the other side,"[36] the Church sought to promote peace and neutrality, as expressed by the Papal Peace Note of 1917.[37] Pope Benedict XVI explicitly opted for a neutral approach in the middle of the war, noting:

> It is, for every thinking man, abundantly clear that in this frightful conflict, the Holy See, whilst unceasingly watching it with the closest attention, must preserve the most absolute neutrality. The Roman Pontiff as, on the one hand, the Vicar of JESUS CHRIST . . . must embrace all the combatants in the same sentiment of charity.[38]

The defeat of the Central Powers in November 1918 not only put an end to World War I but also meant the collapse of the old political order in both domestic and international arenas. How did the Holy See, as the defender of the old order, react to the internal political changes in various countries? How did the Holy See fit into the new diplomacy inaugurated by Woodrow Wilson?

Immediately after the war, the Holy See adopted a pragmatic policy toward the new states seeking to establish bilateral relations. The Holy See continued to pursue the strategy adopted during World War I, undertaking multilateral actions through its diplomatic network and collaborating with nongovernment organizations on humanitarian action. Still, the position of the Holy See remained ambiguous. It was excluded from the peace conferences by Italy[39] and was openly critical of the new world order. Yet it remained concentrated on its project of re-Christianization of postwar national and international societies by way of the signing of concordats.[40]

Still, the new map of Europe obliged the Holy See to face the ecclesiastical consequences of the collapse of the "empires" and the old political order. The values of monarchy, imperial ideology, and social multi-ethnicity were destroyed in one fell swoop. The so-called Concert of Europe with its strategic concepts of balance of power accompanied by secret treaties became defunct as the lead indicator governing international relations.

These changes led to new challenges. The Holy See dramatically expanded its diplomatic activity, including the signing of concordats and the appointment of nuncios. The Vatican undertook an intense anti-Bolshevik campaign, creating and deploying a sort of Christian "Comintern."[41]

New problems came to the fore, such as the saga of diocesan geography depicted by Kurt Martens (chapter 2). After the peace treaties, the See of the archdiocese of Esztergom remained in Hungary, but the most important part of the diocese was in Czechoslovakia. At first, the Hungarian Cardinal Csernoch proposed to nominate one general vicar for the "Czechoslovak" part of his diocese and another for the Hungarians. However, Rome did not agree to this linguistic and national division. In 1922, the Holy See transformed the general vicariate in Trnava into an apostolic administration and, in 1925, entrusted it to bishop Pavol Jantausch. A similar dispute over diocesan geographical lines was the controversy over the demarcation of the dioceses following the transfer of Eupen and Malmedy from Germany to Belgium after World War I. In both instances, the state pushed for solutions that met its political purposes. However, the Church moved at its own pace, following its own values by maintaining neutrality as to temporal changes until political arrangements were finalized.

And the Palestine question raised new problems of its own. After happiness caused by the "liberation" of Jerusalem in 1917, the creation of the British mandate and the Jewish national home raised great fears in Rome; Popes Benedict XV and Pius XI frequently spoke for the rights of Christians (and against the Zionist project) in their public speeches between 1919 and 1923.[42] While these efforts pre-dated the Lateran Treaty, they have raised questions about how principles of neutrality operated in practice.

After the Cold War, the Vatican slowly adopted the approach of "positive neutrality." In the words of Cardinal Parolin, the Vatican secretary of state, "the Holy See . . . deploy[s] that positive neutrality that is typically its own, i.e., not the neutrality of one who stands at the window and watches the course of conflicts between powers, but rather that of one who, without taking part in either one or the other, takes positive action to favor the overcoming of conflict."[43] In that regard, we understand that neutrality is the very opposite of indifference for the Vatican. In his contribution to this book, Faggioli (chapter 9) helps us understand how positive neutrality is part of the liminality of Papal diplomacy and theology in the twenty-first century, as Pope Francis moves the church into the threshold of a new era.

The Lateran Treaty did not forbid the Vatican from engaging in mediation if requested. Mediation, of course, by definition requires the neutrality of the mediator. In 1895 the Holy See mediated a conflict between Spain and Germany over the Caroline Islands in the Pacific.[44] Some years later, it was asked to mediate to ward off the Spanish–American War, albeit unsuccessfully.[45] Furthermore, in 1901, the United States embassy sought the Holy See's good offices to mediate Philippine land disputes after the American occupation of the Philippines.[46] Moreover, since World War II, the Vatican has responded to such requests on numerous occasions, the foremost of which was the Beagle Channel dispute between Chile and Argentina.[47] Such mediation is considered by the Vatican among their most important activities—and is fueled, in their view, by their insistence on neutrality.

As an analytic matter, permanent neutrality has been associated with temporal neutrality—neutrality as to who owns what territory. Thus, in the 1993 Fundamental Agreement with Israel, the Holy See declared itself "a stranger to all merely temporal conflicts."[48] But neutrality as to territory has not always been understood as neutrality toward belief systems. As Piotr Kosicki (chapter 7) notes, there is "no neutrality in ideology."

Kosicki explores this approach in his discussion of the Cold War and the Holy See opposition to Communism. Lucia Ceci (chapter 4) reinforces this by discussing the challenges the Church faced in exercising neutrality in Fascist Italy. While the curia sought to maintain some autonomy from the state and distance itself from Mussolini's imperial project, the local priests and hierarchy exulted in Fascist strength and Fascist victories. Arpad von Klimo and Margit Balogh (chapter 8) make use of the (now largely forgotten) saga of Cardinal Mindszenty to show how the Vatican used pragmatism and a suggestion of neutrality to secure the Cardinal's release from the United States embassy in Budapest, where he had sought refuge for more than fifteen years.

Maryann Cusimano Love (chapter 11) describes the Church's theological commitment against nuclear weapons notwithstanding the geopolitical landscape. To this, Saho Matsumoto (chapter 12) provides a valuable counterpoint, considering different Church approaches to Just War Theory and the distinction between nonproliferation and the Zero nuclear option. Her discussion is not merely theological but discusses how the Church reacted to the Nonproliferation Treaty (NPT) in real time. Luke Cahill (chapter 10) explores how concepts of neutrality were used to allow the Vatican to reach out to Saddam Hussein and Assad to propose alternatives that might lead away from war. In that regard, neutrality is often expressed through strict adherence to protocol and evenhandedness. Cahill, in the same chapter, underscores this use of evenhandedness by the Holy See, describing how he wrote letters to both Saddam Hussein and George W. Bush before the 1991 Iraq War. He did the same with Pope John Paul II's "special envoys" before the 2003 war. Lottaz (chapter 5) explores how the Vatican threaded the needle of its relations with the Imperial Japanese Army, the Philippine National Church, and itself by adherence to protocol. Matsumoto (chapter 12) insightfully points out how, with the end of the Cold War (and thus of the Communist "menace"), the Church felt free to argue its value positions on nuclear weapons to all powers. It is this evenhandedness that has allowed its planned outreach to North Korea on the issue of nonproliferation.

Religion in the twentieth century has faced unusual challenges. In the nineteenth century, Evangelical Protestants sought to "render unto Caesar" by withdrawing from temporal matters like politics. By the time of the Reagan administration, the Evangelical community did a *volte-face*, rallying the "moral majority" to save the country for Christian values. A church so engaged in the world cannot easily be neutral, indeed, as regards ideology. The Catholic Church has also had to wend its way between the call of Caesar and that of the Spirit. Sometimes, as with the Church in Fascist Italy or the conservative Cardinals in Trump's America, reconnoitering that tension is difficult. Expanding on this point, Herbert Reginbogin (chapter 13) concludes this volume with a theoretical essay on the tensions between the dual personalities of the Holy See—a sovereign state and a spiritual pastor. This tension, he suggests, created unusual problems for the Vatican and the principle of neutrality when it comes to the Vatican's response to international law issues related to money laundering, sexual abuse and justice, and repairing historical wrongs.

One issue that seems unresolved (at least from the historical data) is the analytic relationship among territorial neutrality, ideological neutrality, and regime change. Take Communism. If, as was the case, the Holy See opposed Bolshevism but was neutral regarding territorial issues, the only way to square the circle is to have supported regime change in the Soviet Union—or was it? Indeed, there is no evidence that the Holy See sought regime change regarding National Socialism. As the study of the Vatican and neutrality develops, issues such as these will no doubt be systematically explored.

NOTES

1. George Weigel, *The Irony of Modern Catholic History: How the Church Rediscovered Itself and Challenged the Modern World to Reform* (New York: Basic Books, 2019), 48–49.

2. For the history of the Church's travails in the era of the French Revolution, see Owen Chadwick, *The Popes and European Revolution* (Oxford: Clarendon Press, 1981), 346–534.

3. For Emer de Vattel, *The Law of Nations, Or, Principles of the Law of Nature, Applied to the Conduct and Affairs of Nations and Sovereigns, with Three Early Essays on the Origin and Nature of Natural Law and on Luxury 6th American edition*, ed. Joseph Chitty (Philadelphia: T. & J. W. Johnson, Law Booksellers, 1844). For Grotius, see Hugo Grotius, *On the Law of War and Peace* (Cambridge: Cambridge University Press, 1853).

4. See Wolff Heintschel von Heinegg, "Maritime Warfare," in *The Oxford History of International Law in Armed Conflict*, edited by Andrew Clapham and Paola Gaeta, 145–81 (Oxford: Oxford University Press, 2015).

5. A good review is Paul Seger, "The Law of Neutrality," in *The Oxford History of International Law in Armed Conflict*, eds. Andrew Clapham and Paola Gaeta (Oxford: Oxford University Press, 2015), 248–70.

6. Thucydides, "The Peloponnesian War," in *The Complete Writings of Thucydides: The Peloponnesian War. the unabridged Crawley translation, with an introduction by Joseph Gavorse* (New York: The Modern Library, 1934), 332.

7. *The Proceedings of the Hague Peace Conferences: The Conference of 1899*, dir. James Brown Scott (New York: Oxford University Press, 1920), 212, accessed August 1, 2021, https://www.loc.gov/rr/frd/Military_Law/pdf/Hague-Peace-Conference_1899.pdf; Belgian "guaranteed neutrality" is discussed at *Id.* 503; see also Maartje Abbenhuis, *An Age of Neutrals: Great Power Politics, 1815–1914* (Cambridge: Cambridge University Press, 2014), 123.

8. Halvdan Koht, "Neutrality and Peace: The View of a Small Power," *Foreign Affairs* 15, no. 2 (1937): 280, accessed August 1, 2021, https://doi.org/10.2307/20028765.

9. W. F. Dodd, "The Work of the Second Hague Conference," *Michigan Law Review* 6, no. 4 (February 1908): 294, accessed August 1, 2021, https://www.jstor.org/stable/1273956.

10. Convention III (Relative to the opening of hostilities) was ratified by the United States in November 1909. See "Convention relative to the opening of hostilities: Parties," Ministry of Foreign Affairs, Government of the Netherlands, last updated February 7, 2012, accessed August 1, 2021, https://archive.ph/20130616131748/http://www.minbuza.nl/en/key-topics/treaties/search-the-treaty-database/1907/10/003318.html.

Conventions VI and VII were not ratified by the United States.

For the efforts to codify neutrality internationally from the First Hague Convention to the Second, see Abbenhuis, *An Age of Neutrals,* 178–218.

11. US, Department of State, "Neutrality Act" of August 31, 1935, 49 Stat. 1081; 22 U.S.C. 441 note, in *Peace and War: United States Foreign Policy, 1931–1941* (Washington, DC: Government Printing Office, 1943), 26671, last accessed August 31, 2021 at https://www.mtholyoke.edu/acad/intrel/interwar/neutralityact.htm.

12. *See* James Wilford Garner, "The United States Neutrality Act of 1937," *The American Journal of International Law* 31, no. 3 (July 1937): 385–97, accessed August 2, 2021, https://doi.org/10.2307/2190452. The Act outlawed most sales of arms to Spain.

13. Charles A. Kupchan, *Isolationism: A History of America's Efforts to Shield Itself from the World* (Oxford: Oxford University Press, 2020), 296–98.

14. "I'm not an isolationist. But I am American First." Maggie Haberman and David E. Sanger, "Transcript: Donald Trump expounds on his Foreign Policy Views," *New York Times,* March 25, 2016. Some see closer ties to isolationism; see Max Burns, "Donald Trump and the New Isolationism," *The Hill,* September 24, 2019, accessed August 2, 2021, https://thehill.com/opinion/international/462787-donald-trump-and-the-new-isolationism; Bill Schneider, "Isolationism Creeps back in America, as the President looks out for himself," *The Hill,* November 3, 2019, accessed August 4, 2021, https://thehill.com/opinion/international/468690-isolationism-creeps-back-over-america.

15. See Martin Ceadel, "The 'King and Country' Debate, 1933: Student Politics, Pacifism and the Dictators," *The Historical Journal* 22, no. 2 (1979): 397–422; see also the worldwide response to Erich Maria Remarque's anti-war novel *All Quiet on the Western Front* at Patrick Clardy, "All Quiet on the Western Front: Reception," Yale University Modernism Lab, accessed August 3, 2021, https://web.archive.org/web/20130615102102/http://modernism.research.yale.edu/wiki/index.php/All_Quiet_on_the_Western_Front#Reception(2010).

16. Officially styled the "General Treaty for Renunciation of War as an Instrument of National Policy," League of Nation Treaty Series, volume 94 (Registration No. 2137, 1929) 57.

17. The debate has been intense and often heated. Some examples are John Cornwell, *Hitler's Pope: The Secret History of Pius XII* (London: Penguin Books, 2008); Ronald J. Rychlak, *Hitler, the War, and the Pope* (Indiana: Our Sunday Visitor, 2010).

18. See chapter 6 of this volume written by Suzanne Brown Fleming. *See also* Elisabetta Povoledo, "Unsealed Archives Give Fresh Clues to Pope Pius XII's Response to the Holocaust," *New York Times,* August 28, 2020, accessed August 3, 2021, https://www.nytimes.com/2020/08/28/world/europe/pope-pius-xii-jews-vatican-archives.html.

19. See chapter 6 of this volume written by Suzanne Brown Fleming.

20. *See* Edgar Bonjour, *Swiss Neutrality: Its History and Meaning* (London: G. Allen & Unwin, 1952).

21. Thomas Fischer and Daniel Mockli, "The Limits of Compensation: Swiss Neutrality Policy in the Cold War," *Journal of Cold War Studies* 18, no. 4 (October 2016): 12–35.

22. Archie W. Simpson, "Realism, Small States and Neutrality," E-International Relations, February 5, 2018, accessed August 5, 2021, https://www.e-ir.info/2018/02/05/realism-small-states-and-neutrality.

23. For an explanation of the Non-Aligned Movement and its origins, see Jovan Čavoški, "Between Great Powers and Third World Neutralists," in *The Non-Aligned Movement and the Cold War*, edited by Natasa Miskovic et al., 184–206 (London and New York: Routledge, 2014).

24. Charles J. Sullivan, "Neutrality in Perpetuity: Foreign Policy Continuity in Turkmenistan," *Asian Affairs* 51, no. 4 (2020): 779–94.

25. "Permanent Neutrality of Turkmenistan," United Nations General Assembly Maintenance of International Security, A/RES/50/80, 11 January, 1996, accessed August 11, 2021, https://undocs.org/en/A/RES/50/80.

26. While the records of the Council were not preserved, several accounts of Urban's speech are provided in August. C. Krey, *The First Crusade: The Accounts of Eyewitnesses and Participants* (Princeton: Princeton University Press, 1921), 42–43, reprinted in "Medieval Sourcebook: Urban II (1088–1099): Speech at Council of Clermont, 1095, Five versions of the Speech," Fordham University (providing five such accounts from various sources), accessed August 11, 2021, https://sourcebooks.fordham.edu/source/urban2-5vers.asp.

For further illumination, see the magisterial study of the Crusades by Sir Steven Runciman, *A History of the Crusades Volume 1: The First Crusade and the Foundations of the Kingdom of Jerusalem* (Cambridge: Cambridge University Press, 1951), 106–18.

27. The entire affair is well described in I. S. Robinson, *Henry IV of Germany 1056–1106* (Cambridge: Cambridge University Press, 1999), 143–70.

28. But he maintained his Papal Court. See John Pollard, "A Court in Exile: The Vatican, 1870-1929," *The Court Historian* 12, no. 1 (2007): 35–47.

29. *Immortale Dei, Encyclical of Pope Leo XIII on the Christian Constitution of States*, Libreria Editrice Vaticana, November 1, 1885, http://kolbefoundation.org/gbookswebsite/studentlibrary/papalencyclicals/socialencyclicals/popeleo13/constitution.htm.

30. See also Roland Minnerath, *Le droit de l'Église à la liberté. Du syllabus à Vatican II*, (Paris: Beauschesne, 1982), 25–28.

31. For state status, see Hyginus Eugene Cardinale, *The Holy See and the International Order* (Canada: MacLean-Hunter Press, 1976), 123 ("The Vatican City State is known to other members of the international community as a state possessing absolute autonomy") and at 123–25 (the statehood of the Holy See is "amply attested" by the Lateran Treaty); Lassa Oppenheim, *International Law: A Treatise, Volume 1*, seventh edition, edited by H. Lauterpacht (London: Longmans, Green and

Co., 1948), 230 ("the accurate view is probably that the Lateran Treaty has created a new territorial State of the Vatican City with the incumbent of the Holy See as its head"); The United States considers the "Vatican City State, a sovereign, independent territory." *US Relations with the Holy See: Bilateral Relations Fact Sheet*, US Department of State, August 27, 2020, accessed August 19, 2021, https://www.state.gov/u-s-relations-with-the-holy-see; see also Kurt Martens, "The Position of the Holy See and Vatican City State in International Relations," *University of Detroit Mercy Law Review* 83 (Summer 2006): 732 ("Although the Pope is no longer a head of state, the various states that already had diplomatic relations with the Holy See continue these relations").

In contrast, see J. Crawford, *Brownlie's Principles of International Law*, eighth edition (Oxford: Oxford University Press, 2012), 124 (considering it as a *sui generis* entity); *but see* Yasmin Abdullah, "The Holy See at United Nations Conferences: State or Church?" *Columbia Law Review* 96 (1996): 1860–61 (the Holy See and the Vatican do not meet the criteria of statehood).

32. For further analysis of the Holy See's international personality, compare Guido Acquaviva, "Subjects of International Law: A Power Based Analysis," *Vanderbilt Journal of Transnational Law* 38, no. 2 (March 2005): 356 [hereinafter Acquaviva] (noting at 356 that it is "capable of assuming binding obligations on behalf of the Catholic Church"); Tiyanjana Maluwa, "The Holy See and the Concept of International Legal Personality: Some Reflections," *Comparative & International Law Journal of Southern Africa* 19, no. 1 (1986): 15 (arguing that the Holy See's international personality is based on a functional "societal needs" test); Horace F. Cumbo, "The Holy See and International Law," *International Law Quarterly* 2, no. 4 (Winter 1948): 607 [hereinafter Cumbo] (noting at 607 that "the most weighty arguments in favor of the personality of the See are the Concordats").

33. See Canon 360, "Chapter IV. The Roman Curia," *Code of Canon Law*, "Book II: The People of God," accessed August 11, 2021, https://www.vatican.va/archive/cod-iuris-canonici/eng/documents/cic_lib2-cann330-367_en.html.

34. Martens, "The Position of the Holy See," 729.

35. See chapter 1 of this volume written by Pollard.

36. "Which ironically helped to reaffirm the Church's papacy's neutrality." Patrick J. Houlihan, "Local Catholicism as Transnational War Experience: Everyday Religious Practice in Occupied Northern France, 1914–1918," *Central European History* 45, no. 2 (June 2012): 248.

Pollard in this volume (chapter 1) reports that after the 1917 Peace Proposal, Pope Benedict XV he was denounced in France as "la papa boche."

37. Pope Benedict XV, *Pope Benedict XV's Peace Proposal*, August 1, 1917, last modified July 7, 2009, accessed August 11, 2021, https://wwi.lib.byu.edu/index.php/Pope_Benedict_XV%27s_Peace_Proposal.

38. Pope Benedict XV, "To the Cardinals: From the Allocution to the Cardinals at the Consistory of January 22, 1915: Neutrality of the Holy See," in *His Holiness Pope Benedict XV on the Great War: A Collection of the Holy Father's Utterances in the Cause of Peace: With an Original Portrait Study of His Holiness by Gabriel Martyn* (London: Burns and Oates, 1916), 33–36; emphasis in original.

39. The 1915 "Pact of London" between the Triple Entente nations, contained a "secret" clause designed to coax Italy into World War I on the side of the Entente. The clause explicitly excluded the Holy See from any peace conference should Italy object to its inclusion. *Agreement between France, Russia, Great Britain and Italy, signed at London, April 26, 1915* (London: H. M. Stationery Office), 1920 (namely, article 15, which reads: "France, Great Britain and Russia shall support such opposition as Italy may make to any proposal in the direction of introducing a representative of the Holy See in any peace negotiations or negotiations for the settlement of questions raised by the present war.") For a discussion of the Pact of London and the circumstances surrounding Italy's eventual entry in the war see William A. Renzi, *In the Shadow of the Sword: Italy's Neutrality and Entrance into the Great War, 1914–1915* (New York: P. Lang, 1987). See also chapter 2 of this volume written by Martens.

What Italy feared was that the Vatican would raise the "Roman Question" at any peace process

40. They it did via concordats. Giuliana Chamedes, *A Twentieth Century Crusade. The Vatican's Battle to Remake Christian Europe* (Cambridge: Harvard University Press, 2019): 32, 71.

41. Ibid.

42. See Silvio Ferrari, "The Vatican, The Palestine Question and the Internationalization of Jerusalem (1918–1948)," *Rivista di Studi Politici Internazionali* 60, no. 4 (1993): 550–68.

43. By "standing at the window" is meant, colloquially translated, "standing on the sidelines," in this context with what a window provides—a safe and uninvolved view of the conflict. "Santa Sede e Stato della Città del Vaticano nel nuovo contesto internazionale (1920–2019)," *Radio Radicale*, video and transcript, 1:03:54, accessed August 10, 2021, https://www.radioradicale.it/scheda/565190/santa-sede-e-stato-della-citta-del-vaticano-nel-nuovo-contesto-internazionale-1920?i=3948723.

44. For the full translation of Pope Leo XIII's proposal as mediator for the Caroline Islands question, see "The Caroline Islands Settlement," *The Advocate* (Melbourne, Australia), March 20, 1886, accessed August 17, 2021, http://nla.gov.au/nla.news-article170442871.

45. The call for mediation came from Spain, who appealed in March 1898 "to all nations with which it had diplomatic relations." In response the Vatican sent Minnesota Archbishop John Ireland to Washington but his strenuous efforts were to no avail. *See* John Offner, "Washington Mission: Archbishop Ireland on the Eve of the Spanish-American War," *The Catholic Historical Review* 73, no. 4 (October 1987): 562, 575, accessed August 17, 2021, https://www.jstor.org/stable/25022638. It should be noted that while McKinley met with Ireland, he never accepted papal mediation, albeit due to 'mixed messages' the Vatican thought otherwise. See John L. Offner, "McKinley and the Spanish-American War," *Presidential Studies Quarterly* 34, no. 1 (March 2004): 58 accessed August 19, 2021, https://www.jstor.org/stable/27552563.

46. Simon Baldwin, "The Mission of Governor Taft to the Vatican," *Yale Law Journal* 12, no. 1 (1902): 3, accessed August 19, 2021, https://doi.org/10.2307/781304.

47. See generally M. C. Mirow, "International Law and Religion in Latin America: The Beagle Channel Dispute," *Suffolk Transnational Law Review* 24 (2004): 2.

48. *Fundamental Agreement Between the Holy See and the State of Israel Art*, article 11, sec. 2 (December 13, 1993), accessed on August 20, 2021, https://www.vatican.va/roman_curia/secretariat_state/archivio/documents/rc_seg-st_19931230_santa-sede-israele_en.html.

Part I

FROM THE PAPAL STATES TO THE VATICAN: 1870–1929

Chapter One

The Holy See and Neutrality
Vatican Diplomacy 1870–1929
John F. Pollard

The purpose of this chapter is to explore the fundamental elements of Vatican diplomacy between 1870 and 1929 and, in particular, to consider how far that diplomacy adhered to policies of neutrality and impartiality. Before Consalvi declared papal neutrality in 1821, though the pope was the Vicar of Christ, and therefore logically "The Prince of Peace," neither neutrality nor impartiality characterized the Holy See's international role. Since the popes' territorial sovereignty—the so-called Temporal Power—consisted of a medium-sized state in Central Italy, they were anxious to defend, consolidate and even extend their territory. Consequently, military alliances were formed with Italian and other European states, and in the sixteenth century, one pope, Julius II, actually led his army into battle. While these alliances were chiefly a tactical response to the political situation in the Italian peninsula-like the 1508 League of Cambrai with France, the Holy Roman Empire, and Spain against Venice—they could also be more "theological" as in the alliances against Protestantism during the Thirty Years War, and against the Muslim assault upon Europe in the sixteenth and seventeenth centuries: in these cases, neutrality was not an option for the papacy.[1]

The French Revolutionary and Napoleonic wars between 1792 and 1814 brought about the destruction of the Papal State, twice dragging the ruling pontiff—Pius VI and Pius VII—into exile. But at the Vienna Congress of 1815, Cardinal Ercole Consalvi represented the pope and, through diplomatic wheeling and dealing, managed to negotiate the restoration of the Papal State. Consequently, after that, the popes entered into alliances, some explicit and some secret, with various European powers, most notably Austria-Hungary and France, to ward off the further threat to the Temporal Power presented by rising Italian nationalism in the peninsula. Nevertheless, in 1821 Consalvi announced, "The Holy Father, because of his position as the Visible Head of the Church and as an essentially peaceful sovereign, will continue to maintain . . . a perfect neutrality toward all nations."² Pius IX (1846–1878) reiterated this position when he refused to take sides in the war of 1848 between some Italian states and the Austro-Hungarian Empire forces that occupied large parts of Italy. In his *April Allocution* of that year, Pio Nono declared that he represented "Him who is the author of peace and the lover of concord . . . who seeks after and embraces all races, peoples, and nations, with an equal devotion of paternal love."³ So, by the middle of the nineteenth century, a policy of *formal* neutrality on the part of Vatican diplomacy in a time of war had been established.

PIUS IX AND THE FRANCO-PRUSSIAN WAR

The Franco–Prussian War of 1870 posed a major problem for the Holy See. While it was undoubtedly the third of Bismarckian Prussia's wars of militaristic expansion, it was also fundamentally a war of nationalism. Even if it was ostensibly another dynastic dispute—this time over the candidature to the Spanish throne of a member of the Catholic branch of the ruling Hohenzollern dynasty of Prussia—it was really a battle between two great European nation-states, France and a Germany now firmly united behind Prussia. Germany's unification would be consummated by the proclamation of King William II of Prussia as German Kaiser in Versailles' Hall of Mirrors at the war's end.

There were two further factors that complicated the diplomatic outlook of Pius IX during the war. The Austro-Hungarian Empire was Europe's last great Catholic power, and thus a bulwark against Russian Orthodoxy: the Holy See repeatedly protested against the treatment of Catholics in the Romanov Empire throughout the nineteenth century.[4] There were also large Catholic minorities in Protestant, Prussian-dominated Germany, especially in Bavaria and neighboring south German states, and in Prussia itself, due to the territorial acquisitions already made by Prussia in the late eighteenth and early nineteenth centuries. The Catholic Church subsequently had a troubled relationship with the government of Prussia, which would culminate in the *Kulturkampf*, a serious church-state conflict lasting between 1872 and effectively 1890.[5] Last but not least, the survival of the Temporal Power was underpinned by the presence of a French garrison defending Rome against the threat of possible Italian invasion.

With difficulty, the Holy See maintained strict diplomatic neutrality during the Franco-Prussian conflict, but a war between two of Europe's greatest military powers had put the issue of how to handle competing nationalisms firmly on the agenda of papal diplomacy. Nationalism was spreading throughout

Europe and became a significant factor in the Balkans' tangled politics in the last quarter of the nineteenth century. The papacy had to remain neutral when conflicts between the powers forced Catholics into war on opposing sides.

THE POSITION OF THE HOLY SEE AFTER SEPTEMBER 1870

With the occupation of Rome by Italian troops in September 1870 and the proclamation of the city as the capital of Italy, the Holy See no longer possessed *territorial* sovereignty. However, it was, nevertheless, still regarded as a *sovereign* entity on the international plane. Thus even though both the British Empire and the American Republic had ended diplomatic relations with the Holy See by 1870,[6] several European Great Powers—the Austro-Hungarian Empire, France, Prussia (in effect, the Second German Empire after 1871) and Russia—plus a handful of medium and smaller-sized European states and a clutch of Latin American republics continued to maintain diplomatic relations with the Holy See. Henceforth it would vigorously assert the pope's sovereignty through symbolical and other means, including maintaining all the trappings of the papal court.[7] In 1871 the Italian Parliament enacted the Law of Guarantees, whereby the pope was recognized as a "sovereign," accorded the rights and honors of a sovereign, and offered a substantial annual indemnity for his loss of revenue from the Papal States.[8] Pius IX rejected this because (a) it conceded him no territorial sovereignty and (b) as a parliamentary act, it could be repealed as quickly as it had been enacted: this was a realistic judgment given the presence of a robust anticlerical faction in the Italian Parliament and the legislation which it subsequently passed circumscribing the powers, privileges, and property of the Church in Italy.[9]

LEO XIII AND RAMPOLLA

Following Pius IX's death in 1878, the Conclave chose as his successor Cardinal Vincenzo Giacchino Pecci, archbishop of Perugia, who took the name, Leo XIII. Pecci had substantial pastoral and curial experience, but limited experience in the diplomatic sphere: his tenure as nuncio in Belgium had not been a happy one.[10] Though instinctively conservative, Leo was more conciliatory in his attitudes to the modern world than his predecessor. There were to be no more fulminations condemning modernity like Pius IX's Syllabus of Errors. But as far as the "Roman Question" was concerned, he remained determined to seek a resolution that would ensure the restoration of the former Temporal Power. Despite the necessity of formal diplomatic *neutrality* in European international relations, the Vatican was not *impartial* in its dealings with the powers. Apart from anything else, there was a constant search for diplomatic allies and supporters in the conflict between the Holy See and Italy. Initially, the Third French Republic seemed the Holy See's most dependable partner, particularly in the 1870s when Leo contended with the *Kulturkampf* in Germany. Leo and his Secretary of State from 1887, Cardinal Mariano Rampolla del Tindaro, remained wary in their attitude towards the Protestant-dominated Second German Reich. Consequently, the Vatican's relationship with Catholic Austria-Hungary was regarded as the keystone of papal diplomatic strategy. Austria-Hungary was supposed to serve as both a restraint on preponderantly Protestant Germany and a counterweight to the Orthodox Tsarist Empire. For the Vatican, the Russian Orthodox were the real danger given their increasing influence over the emerging Orthodox Slav nations in the Balkans and their designs upon Constantinople. The Austrian Emperor Franz Josef did prove to be the Vatican's most consistent ally; thus, in April 1875, he observed the ban on Catholic sovereigns from visiting Rome by going instead to Venice on his state visit to be greeted there by Italian King Victor Emmanuel II.

After 1878, Leo patiently sought to eliminate the last vestiges of the *Kulturkampf* and succeeded, while henceforth relations with the Second Reich were not always very cordial, they were correct. Leo had less success with France: his promotion of the *Ralliement*, trying to persuade French Catholics to abandon monarchical nostalgia and embrace the Republic and its institutions, failed, and that failure came back to haunt the Church in the anticlerical legislation of the early 1900s.[11]

Leo suffered other defeats, like that of being unable to prevent the papacy's exclusion from the Hague conference of 1899, which partially defined international law on war and war crimes: Hans de Valk claims that "the outcome of this affair had long-ranging effects on the Vatican's international stature, as would be demonstrated clearly by its failure to mediate effectively in the two World Wars to come."[12] This is something of an overstatement because there were other reasons for the failure to successfully mediate, especially in the Second World War, but the exclusion certainly damaged Vatican diplomatic prestige in the short term. More important was the reason why the Holy See was excluded: a veto imposed by the Italian government.

Nevertheless, Leo continued to pursue a policy of an active Vatican presence on the international scene, which brought its fruits, like an understanding with the United States in 1902 over the Philippines and other former Spanish possessions acquired in the Spanish–American War of 1898,[13] and the prestige of having brokered an agreement between Germany and Spain over the disputed Caroline Islands This latter achievement was followed by mediation in other territorial disputes.[14] What is most significant about Leo's strategy was that, while re-affirming in *principle* condemnations of liberalism, secularism, freemasonry, and so on, he nevertheless conducted a conciliatory *diplomatic* policy toward liberal-democratic, secularizing, and other troublesome regimes. This patient, conciliatory approach to papal diplomacy would serve as the inspiration to Benedict and Gasparri in their peacemaking efforts during the First World War.

PIUS X AND THE FIRST WORLD WAR

The conclave which followed Leo's death in 1903 marked a clear defeat of Leonine diplomacy. After the Austro-Hungarian cardinals announced Emperor Franz Josef's objection to the candidacy of Cardinal Rampolla, Cardinal Giuseppe Sarto was elected instead. The "parish-priest pope," as Pius X is frequently described, knew nothing of diplomacy and little of the workings of the Roman Curia, having been solely engaged in pastoral roles as a parish priest, bishop of Mantua, and then as patriarch of Venice.[15] His appointment of Monsignor Rafael Merry del Val, noticeably young at thirty-eight, as his secretary of state, is the clearest proof of that. Hence, from 1903 to 1914, Pius X's pontificate may be regarded as a sort of "parenthesis" in Vatican diplomacy. During Papa Sarto's reign, the Vatican became embroiled in acrimonious church and state conflicts in Portugal, Spain, and France, which resulted in the latter case in breaking the centuries-long diplomatic relations between the Holy See and the "Elder Daughter of the Church." In 1910 Pius X also managed to thoroughly upset German Protestants and the governments of Prussia, Bavaria, and Saxony because of comments by his encyclical *Editae Saepe* describing the Lutheran reformers as "'enemies' of the cross of Christ ... they mind the things of the earth ... whose God is their belly."[16]

Count John de Salis, who was British Minister to the Holy See between 1916 and 1922, hit the nail on the head when he said that, during Pius X's reign, there occurred the "gradual estrangement of the Vatican from the political life of Europe. . . . The political situation of the Papacy, so high in the preceding century, had dropped again to nothing."[17]

Even though Pius X had reacted sharply against suggestions that he supported the Italian war against the Ottoman Empire in Libya in 1911–1912,[18] the Vatican was accused of less than "neutral" behavior during the July crisis of 1914 because of Merry del Val's pro-Austrian sentiments.[19] Furthermore, Eamon Duffy has argued that the Holy See's conclusion of a concordat with the Kingdom of Serbia in the days leading up to the outbreak of war helped to aggravate the crisis by increasing the Balkan state's diplomatic prestige.[20]

In a brief flash of Leonine diplomacy, Papa Sarto offered to mediate between Austria-Hungary and Serbia during the July Crisis, an offer that was not taken seriously.[21] During the diplomatic maneuvering that led to the First World War, the Holy See was thus reduced to the role of an impotent and irrelevant bystander.[22]

THE "GREAT NEUTRAL": BENEDICT XV (1914–1922)

Pope Benedict XV—Cardinal Giacomo Della Chiesa, archbishop of Bologna—was elected to succeed Pius X less than five weeks after the outbreak of war, and the Conclave of 1914 reflected the turmoil of those times.[23] The Austro-Hungarian, Belgian, British, French, and German cardinals represented millions of Catholics fighting on both sides. When Belgian Cardinal Mercier met German Cardinal Hartmann, the latter said, "I hope that we shall not speak of war" to which came back the sharp reply, "And I hope we shall not speak of peace."[24] Benedict owed his election to precisely the need for a cardinal from a neutral country (Italy had not yet joined in the war) with diplomatic experience. The new pope had no alternative but to proclaim the Holy See's neutrality in the conflict and its impartial treatment of all the belligerent powers, as he did in his first public statement.

Vatican diplomacy during the pontificate of Benedict XV was a reversion to that of Leo XIII since both the pope and his secretary of state, Cardinal Pietro Gasparri, had received their training in papal diplomacy in the "school" of Leo XIII and Cardinal Rampolla. Della Chiesa's early diplomatic experiences had been in Spain and Austria. Gasparri's had been in Latin America and France. Together they had also worked at the top of the Secretariat of State between 1901 and 1903 when they had come into conflict with Cardinal Merry del Val.

THE POLICY OF NEUTRALITY AND IMPARTIALITY

There has been some discussion about the origins of the policy of neutrality and impartiality and the motives for that policy.[25] However, it needs to be stressed that the Holy See was already committed to this policy before Benedict was elected because, in August 1914, the Vatican-owned newspaper *L'Osservatore Romano* had announced: "from the very beginning of the present crisis, . . . the Holy See has always wished and wishes to maintain the most absolute and complete neutrality."[26] In making that declaration, the Vatican was merely following established Vatican diplomatic practice. In any case, during the First World War, when millions of Catholics were fighting on both sides, there was no realistic alternative to neutrality and impartiality. Thus, in his apostolic exhortation, *Ubi primum* almost immediately after his election, the new pope repeated his predecessor's call for prayers to end the conflict and appealed to the powers for peace.[27] Though the statement lacked neither force nor urgency, there was still a feeling in the Vatican, as elsewhere, that the war would be over by Christmas. By November, when Benedict published his first encyclical *Ad Beatissimi*, such an illusion could no longer be maintained. In the encyclical, Benedict addressed himself to the causes of the war, as well as to its consequences. According to his analysis, the causes had their origins in the ills afflicting the whole of human society, and in his analysis of the specific causes of the war, he drew attention to the "absence in relations between men of mutual love with their fellow men."[28] Once again, condemning the horrors of the war, he urged its solution by declaring, "Surely there are other ways and means whereby violated rights can be rectified?" but as yet, he offered no clear, practical answer to his own rhetorical question.[29] *Ad Beatissimi* was to be the first of many attempts on Benedict's part to bring about an end to the war. In allocutions and encyclicals, in other public statements, and above all in careful, patient, secret diplomacy, he and Gasparri repeatedly sought first to prevent the war from spreading, as in the months leading up to both the entry of Italy into the conflict in May 1915 and that of the United States. two years later, and then to bring the two sides to the negotiating table.[30] Benedict and Gasparri also sought to preserve a stance of neutrality and impartiality for the Vatican, which the latter, in an echo of Pius IX's *April Allocution*, justified on the grounds of the "paternal-universal character of the Pope and the supreme interest of the Church."[31]

But such a policy was not without its critics and its problems. It did not go down well in any of the belligerent countries and especially among their Catholic populations. French Catholics, having entered into a *union sacrée* with their domestic political enemies in defense of the *patrie en danger*, were consistently unhappy about the Vatican's position. They and German Catholics were especially critical of Benedict's "Peace Note" of August 1917, in which he suggested to the warring powers the possible basis for a peace agreement. In France, he was denounced as "le Pape boche" (*boche* is a derogative word for Germans): even a priest in Paris's church of La Madeleine exclaimed, "Holy Father, we do not want your peace."[32] In mainly Protestant Germany, Benedict had long been seen as "Der franzoeische Papst," and in Italy, some of the more intensely patriotic elements led by a certain Benito Mussolini renamed him as "Maledetto XV" (a pun on his name: *Maledetto* means "accursed" as opposed to *Benedetto* which means "blessed" in Italian).

In Belgium, where the primate, Cardinal Desirée Mercier, was threatened with imprisonment by the German occupying authorities for his resistance to their oppressive measures, the subtleties of papal policy were not appreciated by a population almost entirely under German yoke. Indeed, Mercier became a hero to the Allied cause, and after the war, his popularity in such places as the United States outstripped that of the pope himself.[33]

In Britain, many Catholics were unhappy with papal neutrality and impartiality toward an enemy, Germany, whom they regarded as having broken all the tenets of international morality, especially by invading innocent Belgium. Father Charles Gallagher, SJ, has skillfully analyzed the difficulties that Cardinal Francis Bourne, archbishop of Westminster, the rest of the English hierarchy, and the British Catholic press faced in explaining the pope's stance of neutrality and impartiality to British Catholics.[34] The First World War demonstrated that patriotism would always trump Catholic universalism.

WAR CRIMES AND THE VATICAN

Benedict's policy also faced difficulties when allegations surfaced about the atrocities or "war crimes" being committed on both sides. Such was the increasing prestige of Vatican diplomacy that, as the war progressed, the Secretariat of State found itself in the awkward position of receiving dozens of complaints from both sides against "war crimes" allegedly committed by the others. It was not only alleged German war crimes in Belgium and France but also the brutalities inflicted by the Russians on the territories they occupied—especially to the Jews.[35] To have pronounced one way or another on alleged war crimes would inevitably have compromised the Vatican's claims to neutrality and impartiality, so in public, Benedict limited himself to generic condemnations of all atrocities.

There were other factors, primarily those inherent in the nature and composition of the Roman Curia, which undermined Benedict's policy of neutrality and impartiality. It was well-known that there was a "German lobby" inside the Roman curia with strong sympathies for the Central Powers. While virtually no biographer or serious historian doubts the underlying benevolence and humanitarianism of Benedict's motives, some historians and contemporary observers have challenged the impartiality of Vatican diplomacy during the course of the conflict and its disinterestedness. For example, Dragan Zivojinovic has argued that "although the Vatican pretended to be impartial and neutral, there is now evidence that its sympathies lay with the Central Powers, particularly Austria-Hungary."[36] These allegations echoed claims from the beginning of the conflict that the Vatican was sympathetic toward the Central

Powers. This criticism came not only from hostile, anticlerical quarters: Cardinal Aidan Gasquet, Britain's only curial cardinal in 1914, was appalled by the pro-German atmosphere which he found in the Roman Curia and among Italian Catholic clergy and laity in general. In November 1914, in a letter to British foreign secretary, Lord Grey, about the imminent return of a British diplomatic mission to the Vatican, he wrote:

> The Pope and his Secretary have been quite correct in their attitude, but the mentality of the clergy generally is astounding. . . . Germany and Austria and Bavaria have been at work for the past two years and more, and when the War started, they had the ground well-prepared. Prussia does not leave things to chance and had a good deal of wisdom of the serpent.[37]

Even allowing for Gasquet's patriotic passion, his interpretation of the situation is broadly supported by others. Matthias Erzberger, an influential German Catholic politician, confirmed the German lobby's power in the Vatican in a report on his visit to Rome in the Spring of 1915 when he sought to dissuade Italian politicians from going to war against Austria.[38] Italian historian Alberto Monticone provides an obvious and plausible explanation of the situation which Gasquet so strongly deplored. He argues that, on the one hand, there were strong German influences, political and cultural, in the Vatican due to "the gamut of German research projects, publications and conferences in Rome on theological, ecclesiological and spiritual topics," whereas, ".there was, on the other hand, a crisis in the relationship with French culture," due, no doubt, to the "Modernist"' leanings of so many French Catholic intellectuals. He also points to the influence of the Germans and Austro-Hungarians in the Jesuit headquarters in Rome, especially Wlodimir Ledechowski, who was elected father general of the Society in 1915.[39] Zivojinovic argues that Benedict was partial to the Central Powers because "he was elected with Austrian influence" and because he was dependent on Erzberger on account of his fund-raising activities on the pope's behalf: "This relieved the Pope's situation but made him, and the Curia, dependent upon Germany and on occasion ready to voice views that reflected Germany's desires and needs."[40] Zivojinovic's allegations are based on the Erzberger papers, which claim that the Vatican was almost bankrupt at Pius X's death and that his successor could hardly pay his staff. In fact, Benedict inherited a relatively strong financial position at his election.[41] In any case, while Benedict received the support of the Austro-Hungarian cardinals, their government was less than enthusiastic about him, and Cardinal Hartmann, archbishop of Cologne, made known to the conclave the German government's hostility to Benedict.[42] Again, though the war disrupted the inflow of Peter's Pence when the Vatican was spending big sums on relief work, Benedict received increasingly large sums from the

United States, but no one has suggested that he was in any way influenced in his policy toward that country as a result. Perhaps the last word should be left to J. D. Gregory, the secretary of the British Legation to the Holy See, who was otherwise highly critical of Benedict, but who said of him: "I am convinced that he is not either temperamentally or politically pro-German."[43]

What is much more convincing about Zivojinovic's claim is that Benedict and Gasparri were essentially devoted to preserving or restoring the status quo.[44] This was essential in the interests of the Holy See. Benedict and Gasparri were also incredibly aware of the threat which the disruptive forces of socialism and anarchism posed to the social and political order. They could not be indifferent to the fate of Austria-Hungary, the last Catholic great power and a bulwark against Russian Orthodoxy and Pan-Slavism. They feared the southward march of a victorious Russia, which might end in the seizure of Constantinople (present-day Istanbul). The commitments which Britain and France had given to Russia on the eventual partition of the Ottoman Empire were a constant source of anxiety in the Vatican. Sir Henry Howard, British minister to the Vatican, explained in a report to London: "The Vatican is filled with alarm and foreboding by the agreement made between H. M.'s Government and Russia, giving Russia possession of Santa Sophia, with an extraterritorial zone to which the (Russian) Holy Synod may be transferred—the erection of a rival establishment, as it were, to the Vatican on the shores of the Bosporus. This can later lead, the Vatican believes, to the Orthodox Church extending its sway to the shore of the Adriatic."[45] Gasparri confirmed these fears to Carlo Monti, the pope's intermediary with the Italian government: "the installation of the Russians in Constantinople would be a grave blow to the interests of Catholicism."[46]

Benedict and Gasparri sought only one alteration of the status quo; they obviously desired a revision of what they saw as the very unsatisfactory relationship between the Holy See and Italy. This and the broader aim of seeking to restore the Holy See's international influence and prestige were powerful influences on the Vatican's diplomatic activities between 1914 and 1920.[47] Under Benedict and Gasparri, the Vatican was not, therefore, a totally disinterested, impartial observer during the First World War.

The claims of strong German influences in the Vatican seemed to be clamorous and starkly confirmed during the Gerlach Affair of January 1917, when one of the pope's own "secret chamberlains," the Bavarian Monsignor Rudolf Gerlach was accused of espionage against Italy on behalf of the Central Powers. This affair seriously damaged Italo–Vatican relations and undermined the credibility of the pope's neutralist stance.[48]

Italy's intervention in the First World War in May 1915 also threatened to compromise the Vatican's policy of neutrality, as well as creating practical problems for the conduct of its diplomacy.[49] Hitherto, even though the Holy See was, in effect, only the "guest" of Italy, which claimed ownership and jurisdiction over the Vatican area, Italy was, at least, *neutral* in the armed conflict which was raging in Europe. Italy's entry into the war dramatically changed that situation, seeming to confirm fears in Germany and Austria-Hungary that the pope was, in fact, pro-Entente. Ironically, Italy's adherence to the Entente was bought with a secret commitment to its new allies to exclude the Holy See from any future peace conference.[50] Some Italian Catholics were ultra-patriotic, a situation which Benedict deplored,[51] and even Cardinal Gasparri succumbed to his patriotic instincts and gave a warning to Italy about an impending Austro-Hungarian offensive in 1918.[52]

Other factors that threatened the policy of neutrality and impartiality were self-inflicted. The Holy See under Benedict had its own foreign policy interests, its own "war aims," so to speak, so it could not really be entirely "neutral" and "impartial." It hoped to benefit from any subsequent peace treaty by regaining at least some of the territorial sovereignty of the popes. That, of course, assumed the defeat of Italy and its allies. As we have seen, it also had much at stake in the survival of the Austro-Hungarian Empire. The fear of a revival of Orthodoxy induced Cardinal Gasparri, presumably with Benedict's consent, to try to persuade the German High Command to make special efforts to halt the Russian advance on Constantinople, now Istanbul, the seat of the Ecumenical Orthodox Patriarch in April 1916.[53] Though the initiative was aborted halfway through, as Italian Catholic historian Roberto Morozzo della Rocca has asked, "Was this true neutrality?" Of course, it was not.[54] And as late as November 1918, Benedict and Gasparri attempted to win American support to prevent the complete military defeat and disintegration of the Austro-Hungarian Empire.[55] This was clearly a breach of "impartiality."

A "JUST WAR"?

In the First World War, Catholics on both sides invoked the "just war" theory to justify their participation in the conflict, as in the letters which Belgian, French, and German Catholics sent to the Conclave at the start of September 1914.[56] Just war theory had been developed over the centuries to ascertain whether a war was morally right or not and whether it was permissible and even necessary for Catholics to fight.[57] Catholic bishops and priests also followed just war theory in their sermons, payers, and public statements supporting their countries' war effort. Thus Cardinal Amette, archbishop of Paris, in a sermon in Notre Dame asserted that "it is therefore for victory that we pray, in praying for peace."[58] But Benedict hints in his encyclicals, in his resounding condemnations of "useless slaughter" and the "suicide of civilized Europe," that the First World War could not be "just." It has even been suggested that Benedict was a pacifist, condemning *all* wars involving aerial bombardment of civilians and submarine warfare, "total war" in other words.[59] On the other hand, there is no evidence that Benedict departed from traditional Catholic "just war theory." Pacifists condemn all wars, in whatever form and whatever their causes.

In contrast, Benedict only condemned the First World War because of its horrors and the threat it posed to European civilization's survival. It was these which shocked Catholic patriots on all sides. Nevertheless, Benedict avoided *explicitly* applying "just war theory" to the First World War. In this, he may have been influenced by the thought of Taparelli d'Azeglio, the Jesuit political philosophy, whose ideas on international relations were taught in the Gregorian University where Giacomo Della Chiesa attended lectures in the late 1870s.[60]

Benedict and his secretary of state, Cardinal Pietro Gasparri, as the heirs of Leo XIII and Rampolla, committed the Holy See to an *active* policy of neutrality and impartiality involving humanitarian aid programs to military and civilian victims of the war on both sides.[61] They also used their good offices to promote sustained peacemaking diplomacy at different times throughout the war, on several occasions endeavoring to bring the two sides to the negotiating table.[62]

Their most ambitious peace-making attempt came in in August 1917 in the "Papal Peace Note," setting out systematic proposals for bringing the war to an end and securing a just and enduring peace:

1. A simultaneous and reciprocal decrease of armaments
2. International arbitration
3. True freedom and community of the seas
4. Reciprocal renunciation of war indemnities
5. Evacuation and restoration of all occupied territories
6. An examination in a conciliatory spirit of rival territorial claims

Belgium, northern France, and the German colonies were explicitly mentioned by name under number 6, and number 7 talked equally explicitly of "territorial questions . . . pending between Italy and Austria, and between Germany and France." In addition, Benedict went beyond the *status quo ante bellum* by insisting on the need to examine "the remaining territorial and political questions, and particularly those which concern Armenia, the Balkan states, and the territories which form part of the former kingdom of Poland."[63] This was the first time during the war that any person or power had formulated a comprehensive, detailed, and practical scheme for a peace negotiation.

Did these proposals breach the policy of neutrality and impartiality? They were carefully designed not to do so, but they evinced an overwhelmingly negative reaction on the part of the warring powers, as we have already seen.

Peace eventually came, despite rather than because of the Holy See's efforts, through the prospect of Allied victory on the Western Front inducing Germany to sue for terms in November 1918. Thanks to the Italians, the Holy See was not represented at the subsequent Versailles Peace Conference. Though Benedict bitterly lamented this, it is hard to see how his policy of neutrality and impartiality could have been sustained if the Holy See had been actively involved in setting the terms of peace.

PIUS XI (1922–1939)

The Holy See's international standing was quite different at the end of Benedict's pontificate than at the beginning. Benedict's humanitarian aid programs and his peacemaking efforts had transformed the Holy See's status in the world. It now had relations with twice as many states in 1922 as in 1914, including all the European powers except the USSR and most of the "successor states" to the fallen empires. Such was the prestige of Vatican diplomacy that the Vatican had become a place for heads of state or government, including President Woodrow Wilson and King George V, to visit.[64]

At the heart of the Holy See's new diplomatic standing was its commitment to the pursuit of international peace and understanding, a policy continued by Cardinal Gasparri, who remained at the head of the Secretariat of State until his retirement in 1929, thus ensuring a general continuity between the policies of Benedict and Pius XI. Pius XI's diplomatic service had been limited to four years in Poland and the Baltic States and had been soured by his experience as the mediator between Poles and Germans during the Silesian plebiscites of 1920–1921.[65] That would at least have taught him the difficulties of maintaining neutrality and impartiality between conflicting nationalisms. The First World War had not extinguished the bitter nationalistic conflicts. On the contrary, the Versailles territorial settlement left many smoldering ethnic conflicts, especially in Eastern and Central Europe, between the empires' successor states.[66]

THE 1924 RUHR CRISIS

The most serious nation-state conflict, the one that had helped to ignite the war, that between France and Germany, was not definitively settled by Versailles, even though Alsace-Lorraine, taken from France during the

Franco–Prussian War, had now been returned. It could be said that the Allied military occupation of the Rhineland and French rule in the Saar coal basin, part of the reparation terms extracted from Germany, helped to perpetuate that conflict. Consequently, Vatican diplomacy had to navigate a complicated path between consolidating its much-improved relations with France and creating a good relationship with the new democratic government of Germany (the so-called Weimar Republic).

The Vatican's policy of neutrality and impartiality between the powers in Europe, therefore, faced its most serious challenge during the crisis which erupted over the Franco-Belgian invasion and occupation of the Ruhr in January 1923 following Germany's failure to keep up the reparations payments laid down by the Treaty of Versailles, and which lasted virtually a year.[67] The Vatican had several inter-related concerns during the crisis: a genuine fear that it could spark another war, a fear that was shared by other powers; fears for the political stability and economic viability of Germany; a concern that the separatism in the Rhineland regions encouraged by the French and Belgians threatened the Reich's territorial integrity(and the stability of ecclesiastical jurisdictions) and fear that the crisis would encourage Communism in Germany and drive its government further into the arms of Soviet Russia.[68]

Under continual pressure from both sides, the Holy See sought to play a moderating, mediatory role, avoiding condemnations of both the occupation itself and the German policy of resistance, both of which it disapproved.[69] It was even more disapproving when the "passive" resistance degenerated into violence on both sides. Its most positive achievement was the dispatch of Monsignor Gustavo Testa on a mission of "charity and pastoral care" in March 1923.[70] Through Testa, the Vatican was able to disburse practical and financial assistance to the inhabitants of the Ruhr, help in obtaining the release of German prisoners from the French, and provide itself with detailed but dispassionate knowledge of the ongoing situation. Given the very tense situation, Testa's mission could so easily have ended badly, like Monsignor Ratti's mission during the Silesian dispute between Germany and Poland two years earlier. Stehlin summarizes the outcome of the Vatican's role in the Ruhr crisis as follows: "Despite France's refusal to alter its course, the Vatican, by virtue of its moral force and influence throughout Europe, had helped to alter the thinking in some political circles and had caused Paris at least to be more cautious."[71]

The outcome of the Vatican's policy during the crisis had been broadly successful. The Holy See earned a great deal of credit with the German Reich, which would translate partly into the agreement on the Bavarian concordat, and partially into using Germany's *Ostpolitik* as the "umbrella" for talks with the Soviets.[72] The consequences for its relations with France, however, were less positive. Despite the efforts of its nuncio, Monsignor Bonaventura

Cerretti, it created a lot of suspicion and resentment toward Vatican diplomacy, which was seen as pro-German, which to a degree, it was. Gasparri had arguably underestimated both French fears for their security and their economic problems. During the Ruhr Crisis, the Vatican's role would provide ammunition for Édouard Herriot (prime minister of France) in his attempt to eliminate the French Embassy to the Vatican in 1924.[73] Such were the perils of a policy of neutrality and impartiality.

The eventual outcome of the Ruhr Crisis, that is, the Locarno Agreements of December 1925, in which French foreign minister Aristide Briand and the German Chancellor Gustav Stresemann agreed to re-affirm the territorial provisions of the Versailles Peace Treaty concerning their borders, was greeted with relief in the Vatican.

The central "foreign policy" issue that remained for the Holy See in the 1920s concerned Italy, which was, of course, also a *domestic* problem, whose development was ultimately predicated on the Vatican's attitude to the Fascist regime, which was installed a few months after the pope's election. The diplomatic and domestic political maneuvering that led to the signing of the Lateran Pacts between the Holy See and Italy does not really concern us. However, it is important to note that the Lateran Treaty would finally settle the Roman Question and restore a minuscule amount of territorial sovereignty to the Holy See. It also institutionalized the neutrality of the Holy See in international law. According to article 24: "The Holy See . . . declares that it intends to remain and will remain outside the temporal rivalries between other states. . . . In consequence of this, the territory of the Vatican City will always and in every case be considered as neutral and inviolable."[74]

CONCLUSION

A series of events—the Italian revolts of 1820–1821, the Austro–Piedmontese War of 1848, the final loss of the Temporal Power in 1870, and the outbreak of the First World War in 1914 contributed to the development and consolidation of the Holy See's policy of neutrality and impartiality in European affairs. However, certain factors and contingencies repeatedly knocked that policy off course. The spectacle of Italian Catholics fighting Austrian Catholics reminded Pius IX of the pope's fundamental, prophetic role as a force for peace and reconciliation, as the Vicar of the Prince of Peace. More materially, the loss of all territorial sovereignty in 1870 relieved the Holy See of the necessity of finding *military as* well as diplomatic allies to defend the Temporal Power. However, it still sought *diplomatic* allies against Italy in an attempt to achieve some restoration of territorial sovereignty at the latter's expense.

Leo added to the essentially "passive" policy of neutrality in international affairs, a more active one involving Vatican diplomacy in conflict resolution and peace-making processes as far as possible. This would provide a strong precedent for Benedict's efforts during the First World War and Pius XII before and during the WWII.

The pontificate of Benedict XV was undoubtedly the turning point in Vatican diplomatic development during the first great armed conflict between the European powers since the Franco–Prussian War. Vatican neutrality and impartiality were really tested in World War I, and for the multiplicity of reasons laid out here, it was frequently difficult to sustain the credibility of the policy. Despite these difficulties, Vatican diplomacy manifested the confidence to become a recognized force for international peace and reconciliation.

The Papacy after 1870 was a moral and religious power, not a secular and territorial one, but it still had its own temporal interests at odds with those of other powers and thus ultimately make it impossible to be entirely impartial. These were the urgent need to resolve the Roman Question, and consequently, for Benedict XV, a desire to be present at the eventual peace congress. These considerations weighed heavily in the formulation of Vatican diplomacy under all the popes after 1870. Only in 1929, with the restoration of the pope's Temporal Power in the form of the sovereign, independent and neutral state of the Vatican State, could these considerations be put aside, and the Holy See credibly present itself as genuinely neutral and impartial in international relations.

NOTES

1. Harry Hearder and Jonathan Morris, *Italy: A Short History* (Cambridge: Cambridge University Press, 1990), 128–31, and Eamon Duffy, *Saints and Sinners: A History of the Popes* (New Haven: Yale University Press, 1997), 177–81.

2. As quoted in Joseph H. Brady, *Rome and the Neapolitan Revolutions of 1820–1821: A Study in Papal Neutrality* (New York: Columbia University Press, 1937), 108.

3. As quoted in E. E. Y. Hales, *Pio Nono: A Study in European Politics and Religion in the Nineteenth Century* (London: Eyre & Spottiswoode, 1956), 77.

4. See Owen Chadwick, *A History of the Popes, 1830–1914* (Oxford: Oxford University Press, 1998), 417–8.

5. Ibid., 250–65 and 286–88.

6. John F. Pollard, "Anglo-Vatican Relations," in Frank Coppa (ed.), *Encyclopedia of the Vatican and Papacy*, (Westport, CT Greenwood Press, 1999), 28-31.

7. See John F. Pollard, "A Court in Exile: the Vatican 1870–1929," *The Court Historian* 12, no. 1 (June 2007): 35–37 and 44–45.

8. Carlo Arturo Jemolo, *Church and State in Italy, 1850–1950* (Oxford: Blackwell, 1960), chapter 2.

9. Ibid.

10. See Chadwick, *A History of the Popes*, 278–81.

11. See Kevin Passmore, *The Right in France from the Third Republic to Vichy* (Oxford: Oxford University Press, 2012), chapter 4.

12. Hans de Valk, "A Diplomatic Disaster: The Exclusion of the Holy See from the 1899 Hague Peace Conference," in *The Papacy and the New World Order: Vatican Diplomacy, Catholic Opinion and International Politics at the Time of Leo XIII, 1878–1903/La papauté et le nouvel ordre mondial: Diplomatie vaticane, opinion Catholique et politique internationale au temps de Léon XIII*, edited by Vincent Viane (Belgium: Leuven University Press, 2005), 435–52.

13. John F. Pollard, "Leo XIII and the United States of America, 1898–1903," in *The Papacy and the New World Order*, edited by Vincent Viane (see n12), 465–78.

14. Leo's role as a mediator/arbitrator in territorial disputes between states, a role that was continued by his successor, is thoroughly analyzed in Jean-Marc Ticchi, *Aux Frontières de la Paix: Bons Offices, Médiations, Arbitrages du Saint-Siège (1878–1922)* (Rome: École Francaise de Rome, 2002), chapter 2.

15. For an appraisal of the personality and pontificate of Pius X see Carlo Falconi, *The Popes in the Twentieth Century: From Pius X to John XXIII*, trans. Muriel Grindrod (London: Weidenfeld & Nicolson, 1967), chap. 1.

16. Claudia Carlen, IHM (ed.), *Papal Encyclicals*, volume 3 (Raleigh, NC: Pieran Press, 1992), *Editae Saepe*, May 26, 1910, 117.

17. Thomas E. Hachey (ed.), *Anglo-Vatican Relations 1914–1939: Confidential Annual Reports of the British Ministers to the Holy See* (Boston: G. K. Hall, 1972), 45.

18. John F. Pollard, *Money and the Rise of the Modern Papacy: Financing the Vatican, 1850–1950* (Cambridge: Cambridge University Press, 2005), 105.

19. Falconi, *The Popes in the Twentieth Century*, 86.

20. Duffy, *Saints and Sinners*, 250.

21. Friedrich Engel-Janosi, *Il Vaticano tra Fascismo e Nazismo* (Florence: Le Monnier, 1973), 150–51.

22. It is significant that there is no mention of pope Pius X, Merry del Val, the Holy See or even of the Catholic Church in Christopher Clark's seminal study of the July Crisis, *The Sleepwalker: How Europe Went to War in 1914* (London: Allen Lane, 2013).

23. For the circumstances surrounding the Conclave of 1914, see John F. Pollard, *Benedict XV: The Pope of Peace* (London: Continuum, 2005), chapter, 3.

24. As quoted in Ernesto Vercesi, *Il Vaticano, L'Italia la guerra* (Rome: Mondadori, 1929), 65.

25. See Charles R. Gallagher, "The Perils of Perception: British Catholics and Papal Neutrality, 1914–1918," in *The Papacy since 1500: From Italian Prince to Universal Pastor*, edited by James Corkery and Thomas Worcester (Cambridge: Cambridge University Press, 2010), 161–82.

26. As quoted in *The Tablet*, October 24, 1914.

27. Benedictis PP. XV, "Ad Universos Orbis Cattolicos," *La Civiltá Cattolica*, no. 1542, I–IV, September 19, 1914.
28. Carlen, *Papal Encyclicals*, 149
29. Ibid., 144–45
30. For an account of their peace-making efforts, see Pollard, *Benedict XV*, chapters 4 and 5.
31. ASV (Achivio Segreto Vaticano), AAES (Archivio Affari Ecclesiastici Straordinari), 1427, fasc. 569, "Imparzialitá della S. Sede," memorandum by Gasparri (n.d.).
32. As quoted by E. Serra, in Giorgio Rumi (ed.), *Benedetto XV e la pace, 1914–1918* (Brescia: Morcelliana, 1990), 63
33. On Benedict and Gasparri's attitude toward Mercier, see Roberto Morozzo Della Rocca, "Benedetto XV e il nazionalismo," *Cristianesimo nella Storia* 17, (1996): 562–65.
34. Gallagher, "The Perils of Perception," 162–81.
35. ASV, AAES, 1316, fasc. 455, "Libri diplomatici pubblicati da vari Stati belligeranti, Libro bianco tedesco sulle crudeltá delle truppe russe contro i civili e i prigionieri di guerra tedeschi." This file also includes fifteen remonstrances against the Germans by the Entente powers.
36. Dragan R. Zivojinovic, *The United States and the Vatican Policies, 1914–1918* (Boulder: Colorado Associated University Press, 1978), 4.
37. As quoted in Shane Leslie, *Cardinal Gasquet: A Memoir* (London: Burns & Oates, 1953), 214.
38. Klaus Epstein, *Matthias Erzberger and the Dilemma of German Democracy* (Princeton, NJ: Princeton University Press, 1959), 121.
39. A. Monticone, "Benedetto XV e la Germania," in *Benedetto XV e la Pace, 1918*, edited by Giorgio Rumi (Brescia: Morcelliana, 1990), 22.
40. Zivojinovic, *The United States and the Vatican Policies*, 12–13.
41. Antonio Scottà (ed.), *La Conciliazione ufficiosa: Diario del barone Carlo Monti 'incaricato d'affari' del governo italiano presso la Santa Sede (1914–1922)*, 2 vols., Vatican City, 1997 (henceforth *Diario*), *Diario*, volume 2, January 1917, where Monti says that Benedict told him the bulk of Peter's Pence came from first the United States and then from Germany.
42. M. Leibman, 'Journal secret d'un conclave', *La Revue Nouvelle* 19, no. 38 (1963): 45.
43. John D. Gregory, *On the Edge of Diplomacy: Rambles and Reflections, 1902–1928* (London: Hutchinson, n.d.), 17.
44. Zivojinovic, *The United States and the Vatican Policies*, 12.
45. Quoted in Hachey (ed.), *Anglo-Vatican Relations 1914–1939*, xx.
46. *Diario*, 416, August 9, 1916.
47. See Italo Garzia, *La Questione Romana durante la I guerra mondiale* (Naples: ESI, 1981), 68.
48. The most succinct account of the Gerlach affair is in D. Alvarez, "A German at the Vatican: The Gerlach Affair," *Intelligence and National Security* 2, no. 2 (April 1996): 443–53.
49. See Pollard, *Benedict XV*, 98–101.

50. The text is in John A.S. Grenville, *The Major International Treaties, 1914–1945: A History and Guide with Texts* (London: Methuen, n.d.), 24–27.

51. For an account of the behavior of Italian Catholics during the Intervention Crisis, see the essay by P. Scoppola, "Cattolici neutralist ed interventisti alla vigilia del conflitto," in *Benedetto XV, i cattolici e la prima Guerra Mondiale. Atti del convegno di studio tenuto a Spoleto nei giorni 7-8-9 settembre 1962*, edited by Giorgio Rossini (Rome: Edizioni 5 Lune, 1963), XLI–XLIII.

52. Francesco Margiotta-Broglio, *L'Italia e Santa Sede dalla prima Guerra Mondiale alla Conciliazione* (Bari: Editori Laterza, 1966), 40.

53. Roberto Morozzo Della Rocca, "Benedetto XV e Costantinopoli: fu vera neutralità?" *Cristianesimo nella Stori* 14 (1993): 550.

54. Ibid.

55. *Diario*, volume 2, 388, October 25, 1918.

56. Liebman "Journal secret d'un conclave,'" 37.

57. For an excellent introduction to the development of "Just war" theory, see Roland H. Bainton, *Christian Attitudes to War and Peace: An Historical Summary and Critical Re-valuation* (New York: Abingdon, 1960), especially chapters 1–2.

58. As quoted in Romain Roland, *Journal des années de guerre 1914–1919* (Paris: Albin Michel, 1952), 258; and Walter H. Peters, *The Life of Benedict XV* (Milwaukee: Bruce Publishing, 1959), 3.

59. Falconi, *The Popes in the Twentieth Century*, 116.

60. See Alfredo Verdross, "La probleme de l'organisation internationale dans la doctrine chrétienne, envisage par Fr. Suarez et développé par Luigi Taparaelli D'Azeglio," in *Miscellanea Taparelli: Raccolta di studi in onore di Luigi Taparelli D'Azeglio S.J. Nel Primo Centenario Della Morte (Analecta Gregoriana)*, edited by P. Ciprotti, et al. (Rome: Pontificia Università Gregoriana, 1964), 529–34.

61. See Pollard, *Benedict XV*, 112–16.

62. Ibid., 95–103 and 117–32.

63. For the text of the "Peace Note," see "Primary Documents—Pope Benedict XV's Peace Note of 1 August 1917," First World War, accessed January 30, 2021, https://www.firstworldwar.com/source/papalpeacenote.htm#:~:text=Primary%20Documents%20-%20Pope%20Benedi.

64. Pollard, "A Court in Exile," 45.

65. Neal Pease, *Rome's Most Faithful Daughter: The Catholic Church and Independent Poland, 1914–1939* (Athens: Ohio University Press, 2007), chapter 2.

66. For a very illuminating study of the postwar situation, see Robert Gerwarth, *The Vanquished: Why the First World War Failed to End, 1917–1923* (London: Allen Lane, 2016).

67. For an account of the Ruhr Crisis, see Conan Fischer, *The Ruhr Crisis 1923–1924* (New York: Oxford University Press, 2003).

68. It had already become evident at the Rapallo conference of 1922 in Genoa, that Germany and Russia were drawing together, though it was as yet not clear how close their cooperation was to be.

69. For the difficulties of this balancing act, see Pius XI's allocution of May 23, 1923, "Gratum Nobis," in *Tutte le encicliche e i principali documenti pontifici*

emanati dal 1740: 250 anni di sotoria visti dalla Santa Sede, edited by Ugo Bellocchi, volume 9, *Discorsi, Pius XI (1922–1929)* (Rome: Libreria Editrice Vaticana, Bellocchi, 1993), 71–72.

70. Stewart A. Stehlin, *Weimar and the Vatican, 1919–1933: German-Vatican Relations in the Inter-War Years* (Princton, NJ: Princeton University Press, 1983), 229–37.

71. Ibid., 251.

72. See John F. Pollard, *The Papacy in the Age of Totalitarianism, 1914–1958* (Oxford: Oxford University Press, 2014), 216–20.

73. Anthony Rhodes, *The Vatican in the Age of the Dictators, 1922–1945* (London: Hodder & Stoughton, 1972), 86.

74. For the text see, John F. Pollard, *The Vatican and Italian Fascism 1929–1932: A Study in Conflict* (Cambridge: Cambridge University Press, 1985), 197–203. From the translation in *Italy Today*, May, 1929; See, https://advocatetanmoy.com/2018/06/09/lateran-treaty-of-1929/ last accessed March 29, 2021.

SELECTED BIBLIOGRAPHY

Carlen, Claudia, IHM, ed. *Papal Encyclicals*. volume 3. Raleigh, NC: Pieran Press, 1992.

Chadwick, Owen. *A History of the Popes, 1846–1914*. Oxford: Oxford University Press, 1998.

Falconi, Carlo. *The Popes in the Twentieth Century: From Pius X to John XXIII*. Translated from the Italian by Muriel Grindrod. London: Weidenfeld & Nicolson, 1967.

Gallagher, Charles R. "The Perils of Perception: British Catholics and Papal Neutrality, 1914–1918." In James Corkery and Thomas Worcester (eds.), *The Papacy since 1500: From Italian Prince to Universal Pastor*, 162–81. Cambridge: Cambridge University Press, 2010.

Hales, E. E. Y., *Pio Nono: A Study in European Politics and Religion in the Nineteenth Century*. London: Eyre & Spottiswoode, 1956.

Opinion and International Politics at the Time of Leo XIII, 1878–1903/La papauté et le nouvel ordre mondial: Diplomatie vaticane, opinion Catholique et politique internationale au temps de Léon XIII. Leuven (Belgium): Leuven University Press, 2005.

Pollard, John F. *Benedict XV: The Pope of Peace*. London: Continuum, 2005.

———. *The Papacy in the Age of Totalitarianism, 1914–1958*. Oxford: Oxford University Press, 2014.

Rhodes, Anthony. *The Vatican in the Age of the Dictators 1922–1945*, London: Hodder & Stoughton, 1973.

Stehlin, Stewart A. *Weimar and the Vatican 1919–1933: German-Vatican Relations in the Inter-war Years*. Princeton, NJ: Princeton University Press, 1983.

Ticchi, Jean-Marc. *Aux Frontiéres de la Paix: Bons Offices, Médiations, Abitrages du Saint-Siége (1878–1922)*. Roma: École Francaise de Rome, 2002.

Chapter Two

The Holy See and Neutrality in the Aftermath of World War I

The Consequences of the Treaty of Versailles and Other Peace Treaties

Kurt Martens

More than nine decades ago, on February 11, 1929, Cardinal Pietro Gasparri, secretary of state of Pius XI, and Benito Mussolini, prime minister of Italy, signed two agreements in the Lateran Palace. Gasparri acted on behalf of Pope Pius XI. Mussolini represented King Vittorio Emmanuele III, the King of Italy. The two agreements—the Lateran Treaty[1] and a Concordat between Italy and the Holy See[2] (collectively referred to as The Lateran Pacts)—resolved a painful situation that began in 1870, when the Italian unification process's final steps stripped the pope of the territory of the Papal States.[3] In subsequent magisterial documents, mostly encyclicals, Pius IX and his successors lamented the Papal States' loss and labeled the occupation of the Papal States to be in opposition with Divine Providence.[4]

The Lateran Treaty would solve this "Roman Question," and the preamble to the treaty clearly states that the two parties—the Holy See and the Kingdom of Italy—wanted to guarantee absolute and visible independence to the Holy See and guarantee undisputed sovereignty of the Holy See in international affairs. That is why the Lateran Treaty created the Vatican City State, with the Holy See obtaining full ownership of, and exclusive and absolute power and sovereign jurisdiction over, Vatican City State. This principle enunciated in the preamble is further elaborated on in articles 2 and 3 of the treaty. The concordat, in turn—revised in 1984[5]—regulated the relationship between the Catholic Church in Italy and the Italian State.

It is important to note that the Holy See is the actor in international relations, not the Vatican City State.[6] Any business that the Vatican City State may have to conduct internationally is taken care of by the Secretariat of State, one of the Roman Curia's dicasteries and thus the Holy See.

Frequently, confusion is caused using the terms "Holy See," "Apostolic See," "Vatican City State," and "the Vatican." This confusion is even further increased when these terms are—incorrectly—used interchangeably. The Holy See and the Apostolic See are synonyms but are used in a different context: they refer to the Roman Pontiff, the Secretariat of State, and any of the dicasteries (departments) of the Roman Curia. The term "Holy See" is used in international affairs, while the term "Apostolic See" is preferred for internal Church use. Vatican City State then is that mini-state, created in 1929 with the Lateran Treaty, and intended to offer a sovereign jurisdiction and independence for the Holy See. Finally, "the Vatican" is just the physical location.

Article 24 of the Lateran Treaty underscores that the Holy See will not take any part in rivalries between other states and will not participate in any international congresses called to settle such temporal rivalries unless the parties make a mutual appeal to the mission of the Holy See. As a consequence, Vatican City was considered neutral and inviolable territory.

Yet, in international relations, the Holy See adopted a position of neutrality and advocated for peace among the various nations before the Lateran Treaty. During the two World Wars in the last century, Benedict XV—in World War I—and Pius XII—in World War II—both advocated for a cease-fire and an end to the hostilities without taking sides. The same neutrality is illustrated by the fact that since April 6, 1964, the Holy See has been a Permanent Observer State to the United Nations in New York. That status allows for the Holy See to participate in debates and discussions but does not let the Holy See vote on resolutions and other documents: by doing so, the Holy See does not take sides.

While the principle of neutrality is clearly accepted in the Lateran Treaty by both parties to the Treaty, the role of the Holy See in international relations after the beginning of the Roman Question and before the Lateran Treaty was not that evident, certainly not for Italy. Such was illustrated by article 15 of the 1915 Treaty of London—a secret pact between the Triple Entente (the French Republic, the United Kingdom and the Russian Empire) and the Kingdom of Italy. The article provided for the allies to support any request of Italy to exclude the Holy See in any peace negotiations or negotiations to settle questions raised by the war.[7] President Wilson would later state that the secret Treaty of London did not bind him.[8]

However, the Treaty of London would not stop the Holy See from being involved in post–World War I discussions. During these discussions, the Holy See maintained strict neutrality, as shown in what follows.

VARIOUS PEACE TREATIES

At the end of World War I, the map of Europe changed dramatically, and revolutionary forces in Russia and elsewhere threatened the established order. In this context of instability, various peace agreements were concluded with the countries that lost the war. The negotiations after the war led to five separate peace treaties: The Treaty of Versailles (with Germany, 1919), the Treaty of Saint-Germain-en-Laye (with Austria, 1919), the Treaty of Neuilly-sur-Seine (with Bulgaria, 1919), the Treaty of Trianon (with Hungary, 1920), and the Treaty of Sèvres, subsequently revised by the Treaty of Lausanne (with the Ottoman Empire, 1920, resp. Turkey, 1923). The countries that had lost the war also lost some or substantial territory or were totally dismantled, as was the case with the Austro-Hungarian Empire. While these territorial changes had first and foremost political consequences, there were, of course, also ecclesiastical consequences: what do you do with an ecclesiastical territory—a diocese or an archdiocese—that suddenly partially or entirely changes political hands?

The 1917 *Code of Canon Law*, applicable at that time, read as follows: "It is for the supreme power of the Church alone to erect or otherwise circumscribe, divide, unite [or] suppress ecclesiastical provinces, dioceses, abbeys, and prelatures *of no one*, apostolic vicariates, [or] apostolic prefectures."[9] The reality is sometimes quite different: because of changing circumstances, usually of a political nature, the Holy See has to intervene and adjust the ecclesiastical situation and hierarchy to an entirely new reality or make at least interim provisions until a final solution is sought and found.

It is not by accident that the Second Vatican Council, particularly in the decree concerning the pastoral office of bishops in the Church, *Christus Dominus*, also focuses on diocesan boundaries. The decree stipulates:

> Therefore, in what concerns the drawing up of diocesan boundaries, this synod decrees that, so far as the good of souls requires it, a prudent effort for appropriate reconstruction should be a top priority. This can be done by dividing dioceses, by cutting up some dioceses or uniting others, or by changing their boundary lines or finding a more suitable location for episcopal sees, or finally—and particularly where it is a question of dioceses containing a large proportion of big towns—by making a completely fresh internal rearrangement of them.[10]

In revising these diocesan boundaries, the fathers of the council also clearly put an emphasis on civil boundaries and suggested taking them into account as much as possible:

At the same time, attention should be given to the demographic groupings of this people together with the civil departments and social organisations which create their organic structure. Their unity must as far as possible be preserved. For this reason the geographical territory of each diocese ought to be continuous.

Where necessary, attention should also be given to the civil boundaries and the special characteristics of the people or the localities, such as psychological, economic, geographical and historical.[11]

The current legislation, the 1983 *Code of Canon Law*, stipulates that "it is only for the supreme authority to erect particular churches."[12]

The various peace treaties drawn up at the end of World War I were, of course, based on political judgments. As a result of those various peace treaties, dioceses all of a sudden not only found themselves simultaneously in two or more different countries; the church-state regimes were also often very different, thus leading to complicated pastoral situations. Moreover, the territorial changes were not always precise and unambiguous and were often questioned by political interests, populations, or even by bishops. In these difficult circumstances, the Holy See wanted to maintain absolute and strict neutrality and impartiality. What ultimately was important was the pastoral care for the people. However, often political pressure was exercised on the Holy See to recognize the new situation much faster in an attempt to incorporate the newly acquired territories in their new country.

The following three examples shall present the historical challenges and changes during this period. They are:

a) Transfer of Alsace-Lorraine from Germany to France
b) Division of prewar Hungary
c) Transfer of Eupen and Malmedy from Germany to Belgium

THE RETURN OF ALSACE-LORRAINE TO FRANCE

France's situation was seemingly the least complicated: after the German unconditional surrender, France reclaimed the territory it lost in 1871 after the Franco–Prussian War of 1870.[13] Article 51 of the Treaty of Versailles was very clear:

> The territories which were ceded to Germany in accordance with the Preliminaries of Peace signed at Versailles on 26 February 1871, and the Treaty of Frankfort of 10 May 1871, are restored to French sovereignty as from the date of the Armistice of 11 November 1918. The provisions of the Treaties establishing the delimitation of the frontiers before 1871 shall be restored.

The Versailles Peace Treaty was signed on June 28, 1919, but would not enter into force until January 10, 1920, just a few months later. France seemed to be in a hurry to reclaim its lost territory, and that also had ecclesiastical consequences, even if everything seemed to be based upon rumors as the American historian Stewart Stehlin notes:

> Even before the signing of the Versailles Treaty, reports appeared in the press stating that the German-born bishops of Metz and Strasbourg, the leading cities of Alsace-Lorraine, had resigned and were being replaced by French prelates. Berlin had not been officially informed of this and feared that the Papacy was departing from its impartiality by hastily acting to "de-Germanize" the province. The report caused even more bitterness in light of the German policy, after the absorption of Alsace-Lorraine into the Reich in 1871, of not insisting that the ordinaries be ethnic Germans. In June 1919 inquiries from German representatives to the Holy See clarified the matter. Some action had been taken, but not as stated in the newspapers. The Vatican, intent on resuming an influential position in world affairs and furthering its contacts with all the major Powers, actively sought the resumption of Vatican–French relations interrupted since 1904. Thus, anxious to strengthen its ties with France, it had begun negotiations to replace the German-speaking bishops with Frenchmen, but with the proviso that such steps could be possible only when territories in which these prelates resided had been internationally recognized as having been ceded to France.[14]

Adolf Fritzen, the bishop of Strasbourg and a German citizen, presented his resignation to the pope the day after the armistice, but his resignation was not accepted until July 31, 1919.[15] The bishop of Metz, Willibrord Benzler, OSB, likewise a German citizen, resigned the same day. Their successors, French nationals, were confirmed the next day, although their selection had taken place a few months earlier. The whole situation, although unavoidable, could have been handled much better, and the German government could have been kept informed about what was going on.

> The Holy See, however, faced enormous pressure from French clerical and political forces to recognize the transfer, and since the Curia regarded the political cession to be a foregone conclusion and did not wish to offend France at a time when it sought to renew diplomatic relations, it actually had begun discussions before the conclusion of the treaty. This situation which proved embarrassing to Rome never would have occurred had the Curia waited several months. With the signing of the treaty neither the Vatican nor Germany could raise objections to Paris' demand for the appointment of French bishops within its borders.[16]

It is interesting to point out that, when Alsace-Lorraine became German in 1871, the German government let the bishops remain in office, even though they were French citizens. Almost half a century later, the situation and reality were different.

A REDUCED HUNGARY: THE TREATY OF TRIANON

The Treaty of Trianon, signed on June 4, 1920, and effective July 31, 1920, saw the former Kingdom of Hungary reduced to less than one-third of its territory.[17] The Archdiocese of Esztergom, erected in the tenth century, underwent the same fate: after the territorial cessions to the newly erected Czechoslovakia, the city of Esztergom was suddenly situated at the border of the archdiocese and the country and was no longer more or less centrally located in the diocese.

On May 29, 1922, almost two years after the Treaty of Trianon became effective, the territory of the Archdiocese of Esztergom now located in Czechoslovakia (current-day Slovakia) was erected, albeit provisionally, as the apostolic administration of Trnava. No diocesan bishop was appointed, but only an apostolic administrator, who would govern the territory in the name of the Holy See until a final solution was found. Meanwhile, János Cardinal Csernoch remained archbishop of Esztergom (1912–1927), as did his two immediate successors, Jusztinián Györg Cardinal Serédi, OSB (1927–1945) and József Cardinal Mindszenty (1945–1973). While the Archdiocese of Esztergom had been declared vacant by Paul VI on December 19, 1973, László Lékai was appointed apostolic administrator on February 5, 1974, and only became archbishop of Esztergom on February 12, 1976, after József Cardinal Mindszenty, his predecessor, had passed away on May 6, 1975. The apostolic administration of Trnava was separated from the Archdiocese of Esztergom[18] and elevated to archdiocese only on December 30, 1977, almost sixty years after the end of the war.[19] In other words, six decades after the war, and after the passing of one of the significant figures of Hungarian ecclesiastical history, the Holy See finally recognized the countries' new boundaries as definitive and made the ecclesiastical circumscriptions final. To some extent, of course, this extended timing reflected the unique situation involving Cardinal Mindszenty.[20]

On March 31, 1995, the name of the Archdiocese of Trnava changed to the Archdiocese of Bratislava-Trnava.[21] The archdiocese of Bratislava-Trnava lost territory to the Diocese of Nitra and was split into the Archdiocese of Bratislava and the Archdiocese of Trnava on February 14, 2008, ninety years after the end of World War I.[22] On the Hungarian side of the border, on May 31, 1993, the name of the Archdiocese of Esztergom was changed into Esztergom-Budapest.[23] It took thus almost a century to more or less completely adjust to the new political situation.

Such is, of course, an example of the vision of the Holy See to be extremely cautious and not to take sides, but to maintain absolute and strict neutrality and impartiality. After all, the main concern is the salvation of souls and the pastoral solicitude for the flock entrusted to the Church.

TRANSFERRING OF EUPEN-MALMEDY FROM GERMANY TO BELGIUM

The transfer of Eupen and Malmedy from Germany to Belgium was somewhat more complicated, if only because of the different language used in the Versailles Treaty compared to other territorial cessions: the population was to be consulted before the League of Nations would recognize the transfer as final.[24] The Belgian government appointed a Belgian military officer, Herman Baltia (1863–1938), as royal high commissioner (*Haut-Commissaire Royal*), only accountable to the prime minister, to govern the territories from January 10, 1920, until June 1, 1925.[25]

At the Peace Conference in Versailles, the territorial claims of Belgium were explicit: Belgium wanted a revision of the three treaties of 1839 and the territorial limits of Belgium. Although it was never stated explicitly, these claims amounted, in fact, to the transfer of sovereignty over Zeeland and other parts of the Netherlands and claims on the Grand Duchy of Luxembourg.[26] But these claims failed. Belgium got much less than it had demanded. The Treaty of Versailles gave full sovereignty over the contested territory of Moresnet[27] and Prussian Moresnet[28] to Belgium and likewise transferred all rights and title over the territory of Eupen and Malmedy to Belgium.[29] Yet, in the latter case, within six months after the treaty came into force, a referendum about this change of sovereignty had to be held among the population; the results of the referendum were to be communicated to the League of Nations, and the League of Nations was to make a final decision about the sovereignty over this territory of Eupen and Malmedy. The use of the term "referendum," especially when understood in its present-day meaning, is actually incorrect: the Treaty of Versailles called for a public expression of opinion by having a preference registered in registers held in Eupen and Malmedy. While the transfer of this small territory seemed to be of minor importance, the economic, ethnic, historical, and above all, military arguments all pointed in favor of a transfer of the area to Belgium.[30]

For the Holy See, it was clear from the beginning that article 34 of the Peace Treaty of Versailles called for the territories of Eupen and Malmedy to be annexed by Belgium, but that there were two opposing positions: the Belgian government wanted the territories to be added to the ecclesiastical jurisdictions of the dioceses of Liège and Namur. In contrast, the archbishop of Cologne and his metropolitan chapter wanted these same territories to remain within the Archdiocese of Cologne. The Holy See chose to wait for a decision of the League of Nations, and in the meantime, appointed the apostolic nuncio in Belgium as apostolic administrator of the two territories. It was nothing but a temporary solution to the problem.

That the battle for this small piece of territory began almost at once is proven by the intense diplomatic activity of the Belgian legation to the Holy See. The activity started at least as early as May of 1919, thus before the Treaty of Versailles was signed. From the very beginning, the Belgian government wanted to transfer the territory of Eupen and Malmedy from the Archdiocese of Cologne to the Diocese of Liège to be materialized as soon as possible. The Belgian Ministry of Foreign Affairs gave instructions to the Belgian ambassador to the Holy See to obtain at the earliest an agreement in principle from the Holy See to achieve this transfer. The diplomatic exchange between Belgium and the Holy See highlights the position of the Holy See, expressed by Cardinal Gasparri, then-cardinal secretary of state. An immediate transfer of Eupen and Malmedy was impossible since the territory did not belong yet to Belgium, and the constant attitude of the Holy See in such circumstances was to maintain absolute neutrality and total impartiality. Nevertheless, he understood the Belgian government's concern about German propaganda on the part of the clergy, particularly from the cardinal of Cologne. He asked the Belgian government to suggest a solution that would reach that goal and safeguard the Holy See's absolute impartiality. The answer would be the appointment of an apostolic administrator who would govern these territories until clarity about their fate was reached.

When it became increasingly clear that the population's public consultation would confirm the definitive transfer of Eupen and Malmedy to Belgium, a new discussion emerged: what would be the ecclesiastical status of these territories? The Belgian government wanted to incorporate the territories in existing Belgian dioceses, but the archbishop of Cologne wanted his former territory to be erected as a separate entity. On September 20, 1920, the Council of the League of Nations recognized the definitive transfer of the districts of Eupen and Malmedy under the sovereignty of Belgium.[31] The council pointed out that the terms of article 34 of the Treaty of Versailles left the establishment of the conditions for the public expression of opinion to the Belgian government and recognized that the requirements established by the Belgian authorities were in harmony with the letter and the spirit of the treaty. After much diplomatic wrangling, the Holy See made it clear that the new Belgian territory would be established as a new and separate diocese, a decision confirmed by Pope Benedict XV: the territory of Eupen and Malmedy was taken away from the Archdiocese of Cologne and erected on July 30, 1921, as the Diocese of Eupen-Malmedy. At the same time, a personal union between the new diocese and the Diocese of Liège was created.[32] Interestingly enough, the apostolic constitution did not mention if the newly created diocese would belong to the ecclesiastical province of Mechelen or the ecclesiastical province of Cologne. Civil authorities recognized the decision of the supreme authority of the Church to erect the territory of Eupen-Malmedy as a new diocese in a somewhat unusual way: article 2-II of the budget law for the department of justice stipulated that the territory of Eupen-Malmedy for the time being, as far as the exercise of the Catholic religion is concerned, was entrusted to the Diocese of Liège and that the bishop of Liège would have the title of bishop of Liège, Eupen and Malmedy.[33]

Soon after this ecclesiastical decision was made, it became clear that acquiring sovereignty and establishing a new diocese was not enough to "Belgicize" the new territories. The publication of the directory for the newly created diocese became fairly quickly problematic: the holy days of obligation in the new diocese were different from the other dioceses in Belgium. Furthermore, it was unclear what type of civil legislation would apply to the newly acquired territories: would one maintain the German concordat system, or would the Belgian system of church-state relations be applicable?

The Belgian government's ultimate goal was to incorporate the newly acquired territory into existing Belgian (church) structures facilitating the territories' incorporation in and assimilation with Belgium. But the Holy See wanted to keep absolute neutrality and guarantee equal treatment for similar situations. Yet, on April 15, 1925, Pius XI suppressed the Diocese of Eupen-Malmedy and added the three deaneries (Eupen, Malmedy, and Sankt-Vith) to the Diocese of Liège. The canonical document suppressing the Diocese of Eupen-Malmedy and incorporating it into the Diocese of Liège was never published in the *Acta Apostolicae Sedis*. Less than ten years after the end of the First World War, the territory of Eupen-Malmedy was not only definitively transferred to Belgium, also ecclesiastically. A final solution was reached by ultimately incorporating the newly acquired territory into the existing diocese of Liège.

CONCLUSION

The Church rightly claims that it is for the competent ecclesiastical authority to erect and suppress particular churches, change boundaries, and make any decisions pertaining to the organization of these particular churches. Yet, one cannot forget that there is also the reality of life: *Ecclesia vivit in mundo*.

Circumstances, especially of a political nature, may prevent the competent ecclesiastical authority from acting, or at least to make any final decisions until the civil situation has been resolved. This illustrates how canonical norms and their application are at least influenced and conditioned by politics and civil law.

While article 24 of the Lateran Treaty requires the Holy See to remain neutral in international conflicts, this neutrality was not a new phenomenon in 1929: the same neutrality was already operative before the Lateran Treaty, as was illustrated by some of the situations following the peace treaties after World War I. For instance, this absolute neutrality is clearly visible in the case of the post–World War I transfer of the territory of Eupen and Malmedy from Germany to Belgium: if no final decision was made in virtue of the Treaty of Versailles, the Holy See waited, and took at most protective measures, among others by appointing an apostolic administrator to govern the territory temporarily. The choice made by the Holy See was undoubtedly not easy, as a lot of political and diplomatic pressure was exercised. This prudential approach can best be compared with the situation of a *sede vacante*, where the principle *sede vacante nihil innovetur* always applies. No changes were made until the dust finally settled and the political reality had stabilized. It was and is the only way for the Holy See to maintain its neutrality and impartiality and, above all, in the long run.

This neutrality is permanent: it was there before 1929 and continues to be present after 1929, as has been illustrated by the mediation of the Holy See in other international conflicts at the request of the parties concerned. An example that comes to mind is the Holy See's mediation between Argentina and Chili in their dispute about the Beagle Channel. A more recent example is the mediation by the Holy See between the United States and Cuba.[34]

Perhaps, this permanent neutrality has best been summarized by Pope John Paul I, the pope of only thirty-three days, in his first and only address to the diplomatic corps accredited to the Holy See, on August 31, 1978, when he said:

> Certainly, among the various diplomatic posts, the function which is yours here is "sui generis", as are the mission and competence of the Holy See. We have evidently no temporal goods to exchange, no economic interest to discuss, as your States have. Our possibilities of diplomatic interventions are restricted and particular. They do not interfere in the purely temporal, technical and political affairs, which are reserved to your Governments. In this sense, our diplomatic representatives to the highest civil Authorities, far from being a relic of the past, witness at the same time our respect for the legitimate temporal power, and the very lively interest in human interests which this power is intended to promote. Also, you are here the spokespersons of your Governments and the vigilant witnesses of the spiritual work of the Holy See. On both sides, there is presence, respect, exchange, collaboration, without confusion of competencies.[35]

NOTES

1. *Trattato fra la Santa Sede e l'Italia*, February 11, 1929, *AAS* 21 (1929): 209–74.
2. *Concordato fra la Santa Sede e l'Italia*, February 11, 1929, *AAS* 21 (1929): 275–94.
3. David Gilmour, *The Pursuit of Italy: A History of a Land, Its Regions, and Their Peoples* (New York: Farrar, Straus and Giroux, 2012).
4. Kurt Martens, "The Position of the Holy See and Vatican City State in International Relations," *University of Detroit Mercy Law Review* 83 (2006): 729–60, here at 733–40.
5. Accordo tra la Santa Sede e la Repubblica italiana che apporta modificazioni al Concordato lateranense, *AAS* 77 (1985): 521–46.
6. See, on this matter, Kurt Martens, "The Position of the Holy See and Vatican City State in International Relations," *University of Detroit Mercy Law Review* 83 (2006): 729–60.
7. Treaty of London, article 15: "France, Great Britain and Russia pledge themselves to support Italy in not allowing the representatives of the Holy See to undertake any diplomatic steps having for their object the conclusion of peace or the settlement of questions connected with the present war." Gordon–Smith, Gordon, "Genesis of the Secret Treaty of London," Current History (1916–1940) 11, no. 2 (1919): 253.
8. *The American Journal of International Law* 15 (1921): 253.
9. *Codex Iuris Canonici Pii X Pontificis Maximi iussu digestus Benedicti Papae XV auctoritate promulgatus* (Rome: Typis Polyglottis Vaticanis, 1917), c. 215 §1: "Unius supremae ecclesiasticae potestatis est provincias ecclesiasticas dioeceses, abbatias vel praelaturas *nullius*, vicariatus apostolicos, praefecturas apostolicas erigere, aliter circumscribere dividere, unire, supprimere." English translation from Edward N. Peters, curator, *The 1917 or Pio-Benedictine Code of Canon Law in English Translation with Extensive Scholarly Apparatus* (San Francisco: Ignatius Press, 2001); all subsequent English translations of canons from this code will be taken from this source unless otherwise indicated.
10. Vatican II, decree *Christus Dominus* 22, October 28, 1965: *AAS* 58 (1966): 683–84: "Itaque, ad dioecesium circumscriptiones quod attinet, decernit Sacrosancta Synodus ut, quatenus animarum bonum id exigat, quamprimum ad congruam recognitionem prudenter deveniatur, eas dividendo vel dismembrando vel uniendo, aut ipsarum fines mutando vel episcopalium sedium aptiorem locum determinando, aut denique, praesertim si de dioecesibus agatur quae ex maioribus urbibus constant, eas nova interna ordinatione disponendo"; English translation in *Decrees of the Ecumenical Councils*, edited by Norman P. Tanner, 2 volumes (London and Washington: Sheed & Ward and Georgetown University Press, 1990), 2: 929; hereafter Tanner.
11. *Christus Dominus* 23: "simulque curetur ut huius populi conglobationes demographicae, cum civilibus officiis institutisque socialibus quae structuram ipsius organicam efficiunt, in unum, quantum fieri poterit, serventur. Qua de causa uniuscuiusque dioecesis territorium nonnisi continuum pateat. Attendatur etiam, si casus ferat, ad fines circumscriptionum civilium, atque ad peculiaria personarum locorumve

adiuncta, v. g. psychologica, oeconomica, geographica, historica." *AAS* 58 (1966) : 684; Tanner, 2: 929.

12. *Codex Iuris Canonici auctoritate Ioannis Pauli PP. II promulgatus* (Vatican City: Libreria Editrice Vaticana, 1983), c. 373: "Unius supremae auctoritatis est Ecclesias particulares erigere" ; English translation from *Code of Canon Law, Latin-English Edition: New English Translation* (Washington, DC: CLSA, 1998); all subsequent English translations of canons from this code will be taken from this source unless otherwise indicated.

13. G. J. Meyer, *A World Undone: The Story of the Great War, 1914–1918* (New York: Bantam, 2015), 710.

14. Stewart A. Stehlin, *Weimar and the Vatican, 1919–1933: German–Vatican Diplomatic Relations in the Interwar Years* (Princeton, NJ: Princeton University Press, 1983), 162.

15. Just before the armistice of November 11, 1918, Bishop Fritzen wrote to Benedict XV and asked him to use his influence to maintain the concordatarian regime in Alsace-Lorraine once the territory would become French again. See, C. Muller, "Les démarches de Mgr. Adolphe Fritzen auprès du Saint–Siège concernant le maintien du statu quo du diocèse lors du retour de l'Alsace à la France (1918–1919)," *Archives de l'Église d'Alsace* 41 (1982) : 315–17.

16. Stehlin, *Weimar and the Vatican, 1919–1933*, 163.

17. Count László Széchényi, "Hungary since the Armistice," *The North American Review* 218, no. 812 (1923): 23–36, in particular 36; Harold Temperley, "How the Hungarian Frontiers Were Drawn," *Foreign Affairs* 6 (1928): 432–47; István Deák, "Hungary," *The American Historical Review* 97 (1992): 1050; Wesley J. Reisser, "Self–Determination and the Difficulty of Creating Nation–States: The Transylvania Case," *Geographical Review* 99, no. 2 (2009): 231–47. In addition to the loss of two thirds of its prewar territory, Hungary also lost nearly 60 percent of its prewar population, more than three million of whom were ethnic Hungarians, Miklós Molnár, *A Concise History of Hungary* (Cambridge: Cambridge University Press, 2014), 262; see also Margaret MacMillan, *Paris 1919: Six Months that Changed the World* (New York: Random House, 2003), 269. At the peace conference in Versailles, the leader of the Hungarian delegation, Count Albert Apponyi, pointed out that Hungary was being punished more severely than any other of the defeated nations. Further on the end of the Habsburg Empire, Pieter M. Judson, The Habsburg Empire. A New History (Cambridge, MA and London, England: The Belknap Press of Harvard University Press, 2016).

18. Paul VI, apostolic constitution *Praescriptionum sacrosancti Concilii*, December 30, 1977, *AAS* 70 (1978): 273–74.

19. Paul VI, apostolic constitution *Qui divino consilio*, December 30, 1977, *AAS* 70 (1978): 275–76.

20. See chapter 8 of this book, titled "The Holy See's Efforts to Secure the Departure of Cardinal Mindszenty: Diplomacy in a Cold War Context," by Arpad von Klimo and Margit Balogh.

21. Congregation for Bishops, decree *Cum intra fines*, March 31, 1995, *AAS* 87 (1995): 1164–65.

22. Benedict XVI, apostolic constitution *Slovachiae sacrorum Antistites*, February 14, 2008, *AAS* 100 (2008): 125–28.

23. John Paul II, decree *Hungarorum gens*, May 31, 1993, *AAS* 85 (1993): 871–76.

24. A detailed analysis of this particular case of the transfer of Eupen–Malmedy from Germany to Belgium with references to archival materials can be found in Kurt Martens, "Pastoral Solicitude and New National Interests after Post-War Territorial Changes: The Annexation of Eupen–Malmedy by Belgium after World War I," in *A Service Beyond All Recompense: Essays in Honor of Monsignor Thomas J. Green* (Institutiones Iuris Ecclesiae 2), edited by Kurt Martens (Washington, DC: The Catholic University of America Press, 2018), 85–114.

25. The Royal High Commissioner was given extraordinary powers by the law of September 15, 1919.

26. Theo Luykx and Marc Platel, *Politieke Geschiedenis van België. 1. Van 1789 tot 1944* (Antwerp: Kluwer Rechtswetenschappen, 1985), 1: 276–77; Rik Coolsaet, *België en zijn buitenlandse politiek 1830–1990* (Leuven: Van Halewyck, 1998), 223 and 227.

27. Article 32 of the Treaty of Versailles: "Germany recognises the full sovereignty of Belgium over the whole of the contested territory of Moresnet (called *Moresnet neutre*)."

28. Article 33 of the Treaty of Versailles: "Germany renounces in favour of Belgium all rights and title over the territory of Prussian Moresnet situated on the west of the road from Liège to Aix–la–Chapelle; the road will belong to Belgium where it bounds this territory."

29. Article 34 of the Treaty of Versailles:

Germany renounces in favour of Belgium all rights and title over the territory comprising the whole of the *Kreise* of Eupen and of Malmédy. During the six months after the coming into force of this Treaty, registers will be opened by the Belgian authority at Eupen and Malmédy in which the inhabitants of the above territory will be entitled to record in writing a desire to see the whole or part of it remain under German sovereignty. The results of this public expression of opinion will be communicated by the Belgian Government to the League of Nations, and Belgium undertakes to accept the decision of the League.

30. Robert H. George, "Eupen and Malmedy," *Foreign Affairs* 5 (1927) 332.

31. *League of Nations Official Journal* 1 (1920): 404–9, here at 408–9:

The Council of the League of Nations, Considering: That, inasmuch as full effective sovereignty over the districts of Eupen and Malmedy was exercised by Belgium, the establishment of the conditions for the public expression of opinion provided for on Article 34, appertained to the Belgian Government; That the conditions established by the Belgian authorities are in harmony with the letter and the spirit of the Treaty;

That the results of the public expression of opinion were brought to the knowledge of the League of Nations on 19th August, 1920, by the Belgian Government, together with the Registers on which the protest were recorded;

That these protests are 271 in number out of a total population of more than 63,000 inhabitants;

That these results show that among the inhabitants of Eupen and Malmedy the opposition to the cession of these districts is not sufficiently strong to outweigh, in the opinion of the League, all the considerations which form the basis of the provisions of the Treaty;

That under these conditions the cession of the districts to Belgium is, according to the terms of the Treaty of Versailles, to remain effective and valid;

That no other decision can be taken unless it was demonstrated by definite and concordant proofs that the result of the public expression of opinion had been determined by means of intimidation and pressure, by abuse of authority and threat of reprisals which had prevented the free expression of the will of the inhabitants;

That the documents brought forward with a view of proving such abuses or manoeuvres are not pertinent nor definite;

That, finally, the circular which forms the subject of a charge against a Belgian official, and which threatened reprisals against persons of three communes of the district of Malmedy, who protested, was immediately disclaimed by the High Commissioner of the Belgian Government and was not applied;

Recognises:

The definitive transfer of the districts of Eupen and Malmedy under the sovereignty of Belgium.

32. Benedict XV, apostolic constitution *Ecclesiae universae*, July 30, 1921, *AAS* 13 (1921): 467–69.

33. Loi 27 juin 1922 contenant le budget du ministère de la justice pour l'exercice 1922, *Moniteur* belge 1er juillet 1922: "Art. 2–II—Les territoires d'Eupen et de Malmédy sont, en ce qui concerne l'exercice cu culte catholique, attachés provisoirement à l'évêché de Liège. M. l'Évêque de Liège portera le titre d'Évêque de Liège, d'Eupen et Malmédy." When proposing this article, the government explicitly referenced the apostolic constitution of July 30, 1921, and added: "Le Gouvernement estime qu'il est opportun que la disposition légale qui consacre provisoirement cette solution, et qui fait l'objet de l'article 2 (nouveau) ci–dessus, rende en même temps les lois relatives aux cultes applicables dans ces territoires. Si le Gouvernement propose d'insérer dans la loi budgétaire la disposition dont il s'agit, plutôt que d'en faire l'objet d'un projet de loi spécial, c'est qu'elle justifie l'inscription au Budget des crédits nécessaires."

34. Ben Rhodes, *The World as It Is. A Memoir of the Obama White House* (New York: Random House, 2018), 283–87, 289, and 300–304.

35. John Paul I, Allocution to the Diplomatic Corps accredited to the Holy See, August 31, 1978, *Acta Apostolicae Sedis* 70 (1978) : 706–7:

> Certes, dans l'éventail des postes de diplomates, la fonction qui est ici la vôtre est «sui generis», comme le sont la mission et la compétence du Saint–Siège. Nous n'avons évidemment aucun bien temporel à échanger, aucun intérêt économique à discuter, comme en ont vos États. Nos possibilités d'interventions diplomatiques sont limitées et particulières. Elles ne s'immiscent pas dans les affaires purement temporelles, techniques et politiques, qui relèvent de vos Gouvernements. En ce sens, nos Représentations diplomatiques auprès des plus hautes Autorités civiles, bien loin d'être une survivance du passé, témoignent à la fois de notre respect pour le pouvoir temporel légitime, et de l'intérêt très vif porté aux causes humaines que ce pouvoir est destiné à promouvoir. De même, vous êtes ici les porte–parole de vos Gouvernements et les témoins vigilants de l'oeuvre spirituelle du Saint–Siège. Des deux côtés, il y a présence, respect, échange, collaboration, sans confusion des compétences.

SELECTED BIBLIOGRAPHY

MacMillan, Margaret. *Paris 1919. Six Months that Changed the World*. New York: Random House, 2003.

Martens, Kurt. "Pastoral Solicitude and New National Interests after Post-War Territorial Changes: The Annexation of Eupen-Malmedy by Belgium after World War I." In *A Service Beyond All Recompense. Essays in Honor of Monsignor Thomas J. Green*, edited by Kurt Martens, 85–114 (Washington, DC: The Catholic University of America Press, 2018).

———. "The Position of the Holy See and Vatican City State in International Relations." *University of Detroit Mercy Law Review* 83 (2006): 729–60.

Meyer, G. J. *A World Undone: The Story of the Great War, 1914–1918*. New York: Bantam, 2015.

Stehlin, Stewart A. *Weimar and the Vatican, 1919–1933: German-Vatican Diplomatic Relations in the Interwar Years*. Princeton, NJ: Princeton University Press, 1983.

Chapter Three

The Lateran Treaty and the Hermeneutics of the Holy See Neutrality

The Final Defeat of the Papal State and the Roman Question

Maria d'Arienzo

On September 20, 1870, with the entry of the army of the Italian Kingdom into the city of Rome, the defeat of the Papal State was completed.[1] For centuries, Rome had been the inseparable center of power of the Chair of Saint Peter.[2] Therefore, when the Kingdom of Italy proclaimed Rome its capital city the following year, it marked the beginning of a bitter political, diplomatic, and legal dispute between the Italian State and the Holy See. History remembers this issue as the "Roman Question."

The vehement protest of the Pontiff Pius IX, who declared himself a political prisoner, found its highest expression in the ex-communication launched in the "Rescipicientes ea omnia" encyclical against the "usurpers" and "invaders." Although territoriality was considered an indispensable element for sovereignty, according to the theories of international law of the time, the inalienability of Peter's patrimony arose from intrinsically ecclesiological reasons, enclosed in the triple oath taken by the popes at the time of election to preserve the integrity of the Papal State, to defend it, and to pass it onto successors.[3] The commitments incurred by the pope's oaths to preserve the "traditio" and to transmit all the Church's assets intact to his successor were linked to the general principles of canon law regarding ecclesiastical assets. The pontiff was merely the "custodian" and not the owner. For this reason, Pius IX disdainfully rejected any discussion of territory during negotiations after Italian troops captured Rome in 1870 as it was impossible for him to dispose of territory belonging to the Holy See, that he had inherited as administrator,[4] which belongs exclusively to God and the people of the faithful. In addition, the ecclesiology that had developed since the eighteenth century within the framework of public ecclesiastical law based the independence of the Church on the concept of "societas iuridice perfecta," which was described as possessing by right all the means to achieve it, in its self-sufficient and independent order, that is to say, fully autonomous.[5]

While Pope Pius IX rejected any peaceful solution offered, his Secretariat of State Giacomo Antonelli was actively protesting and denouncing the Italian usurpation of Rome. His aim was to obtain a concrete response by foreign powers in the form of diplomatic and military intervention to restore the sovereignty of the Papal State, whose "sacredness" had been violated. In this way, the "Roman Question" could no longer be considered at the level of church and state relations in Italy. However, it would be "internationalized" posing an impending danger of possible conflicts hanging over the recently unified Kingdom of Italy.

The reconciliation between the needs of domestic politics and the internationalist implications posed by the legal status of the Holy See represented the main problem. The new Italian State tried to give a unilateral solution through the Law of Guarantees issued by the Italian Parliament in 1871. It was meant to guarantee the freedom of the Holy See to carry out its universal mission, assimilating it to the condition of a sovereign body, albeit "sui generis." The Law of 1871, however, was rejected by the pontiff through his encyclical "Ubi nos."[6]

THE TERRITORIAL SOVEREIGNTY OF THE HOLY SEE AND THE GENESIS OF THE NEUTRALITY CLAUSE IN THE LATERAN TREATY OF 1929

The non-acceptance of the Law of 1871 by the pontiff and his successors was essentially grounded in the failure to recognize the full sovereignty of the Holy See. For the Holy See, this was necessary to ensure its independence, but above all to ensure its position of neutrality concerning the conflicts between states, arising from the juridical dimension of ecclesial society in the international community. But it was also necessary—for theological reasons—stemming from its nature as a moral and spiritual power following the canonical doctrine of the "potestas indirecta Ecclesiae in temporalibus" was to be considered superior precisely for its temporal purposes proper to civil and state-based societies.[7] As such, the juridical status of the Holy See was not a problem that could be solved by defining institutional relations exclusively with bilateral agreement within the Italian legal system, but necessarily with an agreement of an international nature.

In the absence of a successful negotiated outcome with the Holy See, the Law of Guarantees failed to resolve the "Roman Question." Nevertheless, it constituted the legal basis for relations with the Catholic Church from 1871 until the signing of the Lateran Pacts between the Holy See and the Italian government on February 11, 1929,[8] in which the question of sovereignty is linked to the establishment of the Vatican City State, as expressly stated already in the preamble of the Lateran Treaty.[9]

The documentation of the secret negotiations leading to the Conciliation Treaty of 1929 clarifies that the establishment of a territorial State of the Holy See was a significant question from the first unofficial conversations[10] between the councilor of state, Professor Domenico Barone, and the Vatican's lawyer Francesco Pacelli.[11] They were tasked with conducting the negotiations respectively by Benito Mussolini, head of the Italian government, in a letter dated October 4, 1926, and Cardinal Pietro Gasparri, secretary of state, in a letter dated October 6, 1926.[12]

The Holy See response was to claim full and exclusive ownership and sovereignty over a territory (as small as it could be) to be recognized internationally as a territorial state to exercise its spiritual ministry with complete independence.[13]

However, the request for territorial sovereignty by the Holy See in the Italian State initially met with strong opposition from Mussolini. As can be read in the annotations to the first draft of the treaty published by Francesco Pacelli, the government wanted the Holy See not to be a: "true State properly so-called in the sense of being able to take part in all competitions of an international nature, and that it should instead limit its activity to religious, moral, civilizational problems, etc."[14] In order to overcome the deadlocked negotiations, the Holy See decided on its own initiative to propose the inclusion in the treaty of a solemn declaration specifying that the establishment of a State of the Holy See did not aspire to territorial aims but was exclusively aimed at the visibility of its own independence. As reported by Francesco Pacelli, the first draft of the Treaty signed on November 24, 1926, declared in the preamble: "That the Holy See, since political sovereignty is to be used only as a means for the free exercise of its spiritual power, has manifested its firm intention never to take part in temporal competitions between states, nor to be urged by them to intervene; and that, therefore, the territory assigned to the Holy See must always be treated as neutral and inviolable."[15] Article 12 of that first draft notes as follows:

> In accepting the above, the Holy See declares, in relation to the sovereignty that belongs to it in the international field as well, that it intends to continue to remain extraneous to the competitions between States directed to temporal ends, and that, therefore, while reserving the right to assert its moral and

spiritual influence, it will not participate in international congresses in which political or economic (or territorial or temporal) questions are agitated, and that it does not wish to be solicited into such participations. Because of this, the territory assigned to the Holy See will in any case be considered neutral and inviolable.[16]

The Italian government was guaranteed, therefore, the specific nature of the Holy See's territorial sovereignty as instrumental only to the exercise of its free spiritual power, with the explicitly stated commitment neither to interfere in temporal competitions between states nor to participate in international congresses on secular issues or be "urged" or "solicited" to intervene in them.[17] As is evident from the reports of the negotiations, which shed light on the genesis of the declaration of extraneousness contained in the current article 24 of the treaty, this commitment did not derive, as earlier stated, from a request by the Italian government, but on the contrary, was inserted on the initiative of the Holy See to unblock the initial stalemate in the negotiations.[18]

In the last text submitted for revision by Pius XI, the December 2, 1928, draft,[19] the references to "political sovereignty" and the "declaration of extraneousness of the Holy See to temporal competitions" are no longer present in the preamble. Although initially proposed by the Holy See, they were nevertheless probably deemed to be absorbed by the formulation of, or contained in, what became article 24 of the treaty. In the same way, the denomination Vatican City as a "State" appeared for the first time only in the last draft before the signature of January 31, 1929, as can be seen from previous drafts, in which the expression used was "Vatican City," without the explicit reference to statehood.[20]

The initial opposition of the Italian government to express recognition of the sovereignty of the Holy See as a "State" sovereignty within the Italian State was thus formally overcome.[21] The consent of the Italian government to add the term "State" just before the signing of the pacts could be considered to be connected with the solemn declarations of the Holy See on the relationship between sovereignty and neutrality that guaranteed Italy that any new Papal State would not seek to return to the legal and political situation before 1870.[22] Nevertheless, it was essential to Mussolini that the pacts were to appear as bilateral in nature, as can be seen from the authorization given to the Italian ambassadors to communicate "as a simple courtesy" the signing of the treaty by foreign ministers in the countries in which they were accredited,[23] while firmly opposing the registration of the treaty with the League of Nations, as stated in the diplomatic documents of the Italian Ministry of Foreign Affairs.[24]

THE LATERAN PACTS IMPACT ON THE CATHOLIC CHURCH'S EXTERNAL RELATIONS

The strenuous diplomatic activity of the Holy See since the pontificate of Pope Dalla Chiesa[25] to internationalize the solution of the so-called "Roman Question" had found strong opposition from Italian governments in the years preceding the negotiations for the conciliation. Consider the 1915 Treaty of London, which set the conditions for Italy's entry into the war alongside the Allied Powers. Under intense pressure from Italy,[26] France, Great Britain, and Russia committed in article 15 to excluding the Holy See from participating in the negotiations for peace and the regulation of issues that would arise after the First World War concluded, Italy feared that secret negotiations by Germany, the Austro-Hungarian Empire, and the Holy See[27] would eventually provide, an opportunity in finding a solution to the "Roman Question" in the Holy See's favor after an eventual German victory.[28]

The new scenario of relations between the Holy See and the Italian State, which led to the signing of the Lateran Pacts—consisting of the treaty, the concordat, and the financial convention—entailed the beginning of a different political direction in the regulation of the religious factor, characterized by substantial downsizing of the state-centric ideology that had characterized the Italian legal reality until then. The creation of the Vatican City State marked a reversal of the trend compared to the previous period in relations with the Holy See as regards the recognition through the treaty of its complete international subjectivity, which found its implication on the domestic level in the commitment of the state to implement a new ecclesiastical policy whose rules arose from the agreement provided for in the concordat. An ecclesiastical policy that recognized a new juridical importance to the religious feature was one through which the ideology of the state as a person of the liberal and secular period had in fact conculcated from the public sphere. In the regulation of the institutions on which the interests of both the state and the Church insisted—in matrimonial matters, in recognition of ecclesiastical bodies, in religious instruction in public schools, in the free exercise of ecclesiastical jurisdiction—the doctrine and the jurisprudence adopt the categories proper to legal relations established between foreign legal systems, such as the formal and receptive reference or the deliberation of matrimonial sentences, in the attempt to preserve in this way, from a formal point of view, the state-centric approach to legal reality. Nevertheless, the concordat marked a new confessionalization of the public sphere. Just think of the compulsory nature of Catholic religious instruction in schools, which continued until 1984 with the amendments to the Lateran Concordat, which introduced the freedom to choose whether to take advantage of the Catholic religious class in public schools or not.[29]

In addition to the regulation of "res mixtae" from an inter-legislative perspective, the recourse to the stipulation of the concordat took on a particular value in the peculiar historical and political context of fascist Italy, by now increasingly reluctant to recognize spaces of freedom for individuals and intermediate social formations. Through the instrument of the concordat, in other words, the Holy See succeeded in exerting a form of pressure on totalitarian states,[30] and the "Italian Concordat became the model of reference for similar agreements with other non-democratic states."[31] The claim to "libertas Ecclesiae", entrusted especially to the concordat, was thus translated into a correlated guarantee of freedom for the faithful within the totalitarian systems.

Ultimately, the Lateran Pacts of 1929 as authoritatively affirmed by His Eminence Card. Pietro Parolin soon took on the role of "wise midwife" with regard to the subsequent international action that the Holy See, also in the wake of the conciliar results of Vatican II, in which it would engage in, on a global scale, to protect the freedom and dignity of man.[32] This commitment was made possible thanks to the enhancement of the ductility and flexibility of the pact which, from a perspective of the protection of religious freedom as a fundamental right of every man, and not only of Catholics, included new instruments in the group of "res mixtae," such as bioethics, cultural heritage, means of social communication, protection of privacy,[33] and even new juridical forms.

ARTICLE 24 OF THE LATERAN TREATY: NEUTRALITY AND INVIOLABILITY OF THE VATICAN CITY STATE AND EXTRANEOUSNESS TO THE TEMPORAL COMPETITIONS OF THE HOLY SEE

The creation of the Vatican City State highlights the peculiarity that distinguishes the relationship between the Holy See and the Vatican State on the international level. As stated, after 1929, the Holy See was a state, but not a state in the traditional sense of international law.[34] The birth of the State of Vatican City delineates a new reality both from a historical perspective, about the Papal State that ceased to exist due to "final defeat" in 1870, and from a political-institutional point of view, due to the peculiarity that distinguishes the nature of the new State on the international level.[35] The constitutive character of the State of Vatican City is its instrumental function "to the full and visible sovereignty and independence of the Holy See" in temporal spheres. As Pope Pius XI declared on the day of signing of the pacts, the new state created by the Lateran Treaty represented "just enough of a body to keep its soul united."[36] An essential element distinguishes it from nation-states being a state entity devoid of the prerogatives proper of international sovereignty. Its nature as a state-apparatus and not as a state-community is functional to the independent exercise of the universal mission of the Apostolic See.[37] It follows that its sovereignty and international subjectivity cannot be disjointed. On the contrary, it is conditioned, and subordinate to the Holy See as a territorial entity subject to the full ownership and exclusive sovereign power and jurisdiction of the Apostolic See.[38]

There have been various doctrinal positions regarding the complex reality that characterizes the atypical nature of the new institutional reality determined by the creation of the Vatican City State, which can be classified in theory as monist, dualist, and mixed.[39] These doctrinaire reflections derive from the international activity of the Vatican City State, which has signed agreements in the specific interest of the territorial entity. Suffice it to think of the agreements between the Vatican City State and Italy for relations in judicial matters that are carried out according to international law procedures, and participation of the Vatican City State in various agreements with international organizations about issues of a technical nature concerning the functioning of the territorial entity.[40]

The complex reality that characterizes the relationship between the Vatican City State and the Holy See emerges from the connection between the second paragraph of article 24 of the Lateran Treaty—which affirms the neutrality and inviolability of the territorial entity—and the first paragraph declares the Holy See's extraneousness to questions of a temporal nature. The constitution of a state entity with complete international subjectivity, but with a juridical capacity limited by the condition of permanent neutrality,[41] undoubtedly appears to be the direct consequence of the declaration of the Holy See's extraneousness with the temporal competitions of the Holy See since extraneousness does not always take on the meaning of disinterest, political or ideological indifference in relation to temporal questions, unlike what could be understood in the negative meaning of neutrality. As is specified in the declaration of the first paragraph of article 24 of the treaty, the Holy See obliged itself not to act in favor of any of the competing parties, but without renouncing its role of mediation and arbitration should it be required. In other words, the Holy See does not renounce the exercise of its moral authority to find a "political" solution to conflicts of a temporal nature. However, the connection between the two paragraphs of article 24 makes it possible to specify the imperfect overlapping of the concepts of neutrality and extraneousness with the temporal competitions of the Holy See, since extraneousness does not always take on the meaning of disinterest or political or ideological indifference in relation to temporal questions, unlike what could be understood in the negative meaning of neutrality. Therefore, the concept of "extraneousness" acquires a broader meaning than that of "neutrality," besides taking on different nuances regarding the meaning of impartiality that could be assigned to the term.[42] Compared to the meaning that neutrality has historically acquired in so-called international law in time of war,[43] extraneousness to temporal competitions represents an evolution, in that it refers to a condition no longer transitory, linked to the state of war,[44] but permanent, and therefore to conduct equidistant between the competitions among sovereign entities; this condition does not necessarily translate into the ideological neutrality of the policy of a state, or in aseptic impartiality.

The policy of impartiality with regard to temporal competition between states allows the Holy See to be free to actively assert its moral and spiritual power in its role of moral authority "super partes"[45] in defense of the higher values of justice and the search for peace. As a category of international law, "neutrality" could be adopted regarding the Papal State but appears inadequate to encompass the Universal Church's activities after the Lateran Treaty.[46] Ideological neutrality concerning the different opposing positions of sovereign entities, consisting in an abstention from taking sides in favor of one party or in condemning the other party required of neutral states, is hardly adaptable to the exercise of the magisterial function, as a right-duty in which the moral and spiritual power of the pontiff is concretely embodied. While refraining from intervening directly in temporal competitions, the pontiff is free to pronounce himself on concrete questions relating to the defense of rights incorporating exceedingly high values.

Even before the Treaty of the Lateran, during the Great War of 1914 to 1918, the Holy See committed itself to put an end to the tragedy of the war.[47] However, the attempts for peace were doomed to failure, as the position of the Holy See, though formally neutral, did not appear equidistant, but on the contrary biased in favor of the supranational empires, and therefore more interested in the consolidation of the old central European order than in the new nationalisms supported by the Western powers.[48] Thus the Great War in Europe offered the opportunity to reverse the diplomatic isolation of the Holy See recorded during the pontificate of Pius X, as evidenced by the documented report drawn up in 1914 by the Congregation for Extraordinary Ecclesiastical Affairs.[49] For Benedict XV, the limitations of this isolation were to be overcome by repositioning the Church's mission concerning the new geopolitical balances emerging in international society.

The affirmation and defense of the impartiality of the Holy See had its important "testing ground" during the Second World War in respect to the Nazi and Communist regimes. Pius XII's attitude was strictly equidistant from the warring parties, but with intense and incessant diplomatic activity in favor of a possible mediation and a political solution to the war. Since 1939, Pope Pacelli reiterated the moral condemnation of the war. He often intervened to support victims due to the violence of war and in defense of the persecuted victims due to the violence of war and in defense of the persecuted.[50] While it has been widely emphasized and discussed, the reasons for political prudence were prevalent, in the well-founded fear of retaliatory reactions and escalation of violence, compared to a public denunciation of violations of international law by the Nazi army and a firm stance regarding the extermination of Jews.[51]

IMPARTIALITY AND PARTICIPATION OF THE HOLY SEE IN INTERNATIONAL ORGANIZATIONS AFTER THE SECOND VATICAN COUNCIL

The need to rebuild the conditions for lasting peace among peoples after the material, social, and economic devastation of the Second World War marked a decisive evolution in the Holy See's diplomatic action in the international context and in its role of impartial condemnation of all violations of human rights, which was to find its magisterial expression in the Second Vatican Council. The Pastoral Constitution "Gaudium et Spes" as well as the Declaration on Religious Freedom, "Dignitatis Humanae," outline, in the wake of the teachings of the previous magisterium,[52] the guidelines on which the Church's commitment in defense of the dignity of the person, the inviolable rights of man and the promotion of cooperation and peace among peoples, will be based. The council condemned war as an instrument of conquest and domination over peoples that had characterized nineteenth-century imperialism, and Pope Paul VI's encyclical "Populorum Progressio" condemned European colonialism and the exploitation of peoples, asserting the Church's right to speak out even in temporal matters to defend the fundamental rights of peoples. The new international scenario characterized by the end of Eurocentrism, by the birth of new states in the postcolonial age, the expression of diversified cultures, including those of a religious matrix, hence with different demands compared to the old order of international relations, by the intensification of the phenomenon of migration and multicultural social realities, with an ever more consistent gap between developed countries and underdeveloped areas, sees the commitment of the Holy See increasingly aligned in support of the countries of the so-called Third World. As is well known, this terminology refers in geopolitical and economic language to countries that do not belong to the division into ideological and economic blocs that characterized the period of the Cold War.

With regard to this political-military contrast between the East and West, the Holy See, even if it initially held a position of open hostility toward the atheistic ideology of Marxist communism, began with Pope John XXIII and Pope Paul VI. They started a series of dialogues and mediations that culminated under the pontificate of John Paul II with the Holy See's *Ostpolitik*, which contributed to the dissolution of the Soviet Union and the Communist Bloc in Europe.

Since the end of the Second World War, the Holy See has significantly developed its presence in the international field by sending representatives to International Conferences[53] and participating in international governmental and nongovernmental organizations. Since 1949, a permanent observer has been accredited to the Food and Agriculture Organization (FAO); in 1951, the Holy See became a "pleno iure" member of the Advisory Committee of the High Commission for Refugees (UNHCR); in 1952, a permanent observer was accredited to United Nations Educational, Scientific, and Cultural Organization (UNESCO) and in 1957 the Holy See became a founding member of the International Atomic Energy Agency (IAEA), where an apostolic delegate is accredited. On March 21, 1964, the Holy See accredited its own permanent observer to the UN, and from 1967 also to the UN Office in Geneva,[54] which entails the right of the Holy See participation in the UN General Assembly debate. With UN resolution no. 58/314 of July 1, 2004, the Holy See became a "qualified" permanent observer, which entails the right of Holy See to register in the list of speakers and participation in the assembly debates; generally, the right of reply, the right to publish and circulate its communications as official, to raise motions order and to co-sponsor draft resolutions that rightly refer to his work.[55] On May 31, 2021, the World Health Assembly adopted, by consensus, resolution "Participation of the Holy See in the World Health Organization" presented by Italy, which "formalizes the participation of the Holy See in the work of the World Health Organization as a non-Member State Observer."[56]

It is necessary to specify that the Holy See has never requested to be a "pleno iure" member of the United Nations, precisely because of the unique character of the international subjectivity of the Holy See, which obliges it "ex ipsa natura," due to the religious aims of the mission of the Universal Church, not to participate in the resolution of political, economic, and commercial conflicts between states, nor to commit itself, as is the case for all states adhering to the UN, to juridical and political interventions against the member state that has violated the pact stipulated with the organization.[57]

As to regionally-based international bodies, the Holy See appointed an observer to the Council of Europe in Strasbourg in 1970 and a permanent observer to the Organization of American States in 1978; it sent a permanent representative to the Organization for Security and Cooperation in Europe (OSCE) in 1994 and appointed permanent observers to the Organization of the Arab League and the African Union in 2000. The papal representative to the European Union has the title of apostolic nuncio.

In addition, the Holy See is a party to numerous international agreements, ranging from those relating to arms limitations to conventions on humanitarian law and human rights and those concerning cultural heritage, commercial law, maritime law, and the fight against terrorism.[58]

Some of these conventions have explicitly recognized the Holy See's international juridical personality, such as the Concordat with the Dominican Republic of 1954[59] and the Convention with Venezuela of 1964.[60] However, the recognized international sovereignty of the Vatican City State is not separate from that of the Holy See precisely because it is an instrument of the pontiff's independence. Interestingly, since January 18, 1960, the Vatican City State has been registered by UNESCO as a world heritage site with special protection in case of armed conflict, according to the Hague Convention of 1954.[61]

NEUTRALITY OR IMPARTIALITY? ARTICLE 24 OF THE LATERAN TREATY AND THE "POLICY" OF THE HOLY SEE IN THE POST-WWII INTERNATIONAL LEGAL SYSTEM

With the increase in active participation by the Holy See in international organizations, the clause of extraneousness to temporal competitions established in article 24 of the Lateran Treaty has been enriched with interpretative profiles that determine more precisely the definition of the relationship between "neutrality" and "impartiality" in a changed international political context compared to the one existing in 1929.

In formal terms, the question of the compatibility of the Holy See's presence in bodies of a political nature arose at the time of the invitation by the countries of the Warsaw Pact to participate in the 1975 Helsinki Conference on Security and Cooperation in Europe (CSCE).[62] After some initial reservations, because it was a meeting of states in a situation of extreme delicacy for international balance, the Holy See decided to participate "pleno iure," with the clarification, however, that it would intervene as a spiritual and religious institution, and therefore abstain in the case of decisions of a strictly political nature, to contribute to detente in the name of the primacy of the moral and political value of peace.[63]

Moreover, the delegation of Italy informally clarified that the participation of the Holy See in the 1975 Helsinki Conference did not constitute a violation of article 24.1 of the treaty, since it dealt with "general political affairs."[64] The invitation extended to the Holy See undoubtedly represented the recognition of its moral prestige and offered the opportunity for its international presence without the possibility of Western labeling. The specification of the active role of the Holy See in promoting ethics in relations between subjects of the international community was reiterated in 1992, when the conference became a supranational entity with powers of intervention. In the memorandum sent to all delegates, the Holy See specifies that its participation can continue only "in a way that takes into account the particular condition conferred on it by its spiritual nature, its universal mission and its humanitarian duty."[65] The decision to continue full participation in the body of a political and military nature (since 1994 transformed into OSCE) allows for a broadening of perspective on the juris political notion of extraneousness in the temporal competitions of the Holy See. The "extraneousness" appears to be declined more and more in the sense not of aseptic neutrality, but as an expression of an active role of intermediation between international subjects in the name of the pursuit of non-partisan interests, but common to all, as values and principles aimed at the pursuit of peace and based on the primacy of human rights.

The turning point in the experience of diplomatic activity in the new international context is undoubtedly marked by Paul VI's 1965 speech to the United Nations in 1965, in which he presented the Holy See as an "expert in humanity" and outlined the essential lines of a new theory of relations between the Church and the political community.[66] Recognizing the UN as the institution that "represents in some way, in the temporal sphere, what our Universal Church wants to be in the spiritual sphere: unique and universal,"[67] Paul VI's speech reiterated the conciliar principle expressed in "Gaudium et Spes" of healthy collaboration with civil institutions.[68] A conciliar doctrine that laid the foundations for an evolution of neutrality toward more decisive impartiality and "super partes" role of the Holy See and would inspire Vatican policy in the following decades.

It will be precisely in his second speech to the United Nations that John Paul II will claim the need to protect the inviolable rights of man as well as those of nations:[69] impartiality that is not antithetical to an "active political action" in defense of the human rights and peoples that form during the pontificate of John Paul II the two poles of oscillation of Vatican diplomacy.[70] Concerning the relationship between the conciliar doctrine of just war and the Holy See's neutrality, international crises have highlighted the problematic nature of defending rights and authentic equidistance from the parties in conflict. If, in fact, on occasion, the military intervention decided by the UN to liberate Kuwait, the pontiff bitterly condemned the armed conflict, judging it to be inspired by the "firm logic of retaliation and revenge."[71] Concerning the war in the Balkans, on the contrary, he invokes the intervention of the international community to stop Serbian aggression and violence against populations and ethnic groups.[72]

The support given by the Holy See to the recognition of the independence of Slovenia and Croatia, as exemplified at the meeting of OECD foreign ministers in January 1992, was, however, "conditioned by the solemn commitment of the two parties to contribute to the construction of a Europe of rights and democracy," considered as "aims extraneous to the logic of political-temporal interest."[73] The "Charter of Paris for a New Europe" was adopted by a summit meeting of most European governments and those of Canada, the United States, and the Soviet Union, in Paris, from November 19 to 21, 1990. It was established on the foundation of the 1975 Helsinki Accords. Paragraph 1 of chapter 1 emphasizes that protection and promotion of human rights was one of the fundamental purposes of government. During the next two years at different summits, human rights were reaffirmed. By the time of the Helsinki Conference in 1992, the Soviet Union had dissolved, and the political climate in Eastern Europe had changed. Establishing democratic regimes increased while all fifty participants were strongly reaffirming the principles in the charter as well as the human dimension commitments made at the Moscow Human Dimension Meeting in 1991 to address the full range of human rights and humanitarian concerns associated with the Helsinki process within the scope of the Council of Security and Cooperation in Europe.[74]

As regards the international crises of the following years, the Holy See, regarding the humanitarian interference of the international community, as in the intervention to liberate Kosovo, the case of East Timor, and the war in Afghanistan, recalled the conciliar doctrine of the just war theory, the lawfulness of the right of defense against armed aggression as long as it is proportional and temporary, condemning any war motivated by revenge or domination, and reiterated that for war to be just, it must be the "extrema ratio."

The defense of the global common good appears even more dilated in the international diplomatic action under the pontificate of Pope Francis. Aimed at implementing the role of the Church in overcoming the "globalization of indifference" and the "culture of waste,"[75] diplomatic action is implemented through multilateral action, in which cooperation with the international political community is combined with the development of specific forms of interreligious dialogue as an expression of common brotherhood rooted in the very foundation of supranational institutions against the environmental, economic and humanitarian crisis in favor of the rights of the weakest and the vulnerable.

An action in protecting human rights that is at the same time the goal of the international activity of the Holy See, but also a means, insofar as it is a condition through which the mission of the Church, representing the people of God in civil society can be more effective. A paradigmatic example[76] in the Letter to Chinese Catholics by Benedict XVI of May 27, 2007,[77] which urged that enhancement of the Christian's responsibility to promote the common good and contribute to the development of the social realities in which one operates constitutes a broadening of the perspective of analysis of the "ius publicum ecclesiasticum," not only in the relations between the Holy See and political communities, but also between the Church and civil community.

CONCLUDING REMARKS

The neutrality of the Vatican City State, in its original form, had the specific intent of reassuring the Italian Fascist regime on the risk of possible interference by foreign powers in bilateral relations with the Holy See.

Following the Holy See's participation in the Helsinki Conference, however, the Holy See concept of neutrality would take on new weight and new purposes, evidencing a clear commitment to the need for cooperation at the international level for security and social justice. Adhesion to the conference implied the abandonment of a position limited to the sole function of the arbitrator in international disputes.

It is no coincidence that, especially in recent decades, there has been a notable intensification of the activities of the Vatican City State, as well as of the Holy See, for international cooperation, which at times has also required conforming the Vatican system to the international order in combating the financing of criminal activities and money laundering.[78]

The most recent reforms promoted by Pope Francis are moving in this direction. On November 25, 2018, Pope Francis issued the "motu proprio" "Fin dall'inizio" promulgating a new law on the governance of the Vatican City State to continue "the process of review of the institutions of the Vatican City State and a progressive replacement of the initial laws of 1929 contextual to its creation,"[79] a process that began in 2000 with the promulgation of the fundamental law of the state by John Paul II.[80] In the chirography with which the pope delegated to the president of the Governorate of Vatican City State the power to draw up new law and related regulations, it is stated that there is now a pressing need "to reorganize the structure of the State and make it responsive to today's needs" with the intent to "make even clearer the particular institutional purpose of the Vatican City State called upon by its nature to guarantee the absolute and visible independence of the See of Peter."[81]

In the same vein, the "motu proprio" of May 19, 2020, on transparency, control, and competition in the procedures for the awarding of public contracts by the Holy See and the Vatican State is promulgated because there is a "perceived urgent need for faithful and honest administration," a need that has fostered "a specific and coherent regulation within the international community, which now has principles and rules that inspire the conduct and demonstrate the experience of the various states. It is useful to refer to this normative patrimony, with its connected 'good practices,' while keeping in mind the fundamental principles and aims specifically to the canonical system and the peculiarity of the Vatican City State."[82]

Therefore, the reforming action of the current pontiff comes in the wake of a total enhancement of the instrumental function of the Vatican City State vis-à-vis the new challenges of collaboration and cooperation that are imposed on a planetary scale. Precisely the intensification of reciprocal relations between states, including those of an economic and financial nature, postulate a necessary cooperation in the global arena, which even the Vatican City State cannot escape in the name of the common good.

NOTES

1. For an accurate reconstruction, cf. Vittorio Vidotto, *20 settembre 1870* (Roma-Bari: Laterza, 2020); Giuseppe Dalla Torre, "XX settembre 1870," *Diritto e Religioni* 2 (2020): 191–96.

2. Giovanni Battista Varnier, "La Santa Sede, il potere temporale e la specificità del caso italiano," in S*anta Sede e Stato della Città del Vaticano nel nuovo contesto internazionale (1929–2019): Atti del Convegno, Roma, Università LUMSA, 7 febbraio 2019*, edited by Matteo Carnì (Roma: Studium, 2019), 176ff.

3. On this point, see Giacomo Martina, "Pio IX", in *Enciclopedia dei Papi*, vol. 3 (Roma: Istituto della Enciclopedia Italiana, 2000), 567.

4. Saretta Marotta, "La questione romana," in *Cristiani d'Italia. Chiese, Società Stato, 1861–2011*, edited by Alberto Melloni (Roma: Istituto della Enciclopedia Italiana, 2011), 641–54; Giuseppe Dalla Torre, *Lezioni di Diritto Vaticano* (Torino: Giappichelli, 2020): 4ff; Dalla Torre, "XX settembre 1870," 194.

5. Roland Minnerath, *Le droit de l'Église à la liberté. Du Syllabus à Vatican II* (Paris: Beauschesne, 1982), 25–60.

6. Pio IX, "Lettera Enciclica *Ubi Nos* (15 Maggio1871)," *Acta Sanctae Sedis* 6 (1871): 257–63.

7. On the different doctrinaire positions relating to the international juridical subjectivity of the Holy See before the Lateran Pacts, cf. Jean Pierre Schouppe, *Diritto dei rapporti tra Chiesa e Comunità politica: Profili dottrinali e giuridic*i (Roma: Edusc, 2018), 259ff.

8. Cf. Dalla Torre, *Lezioni di Diritto Vaticano*, 7.

9. "Preamble" of Lateran Treaty, available at www.vatican.va.

10. Carlo Alberto Biggini, *Storia inedita della Conciliazione* (Milano: Garzanti, 1942), 72–73; Giovanni Barberini, "Riflessioni sull'origine e sul significato dell'art. 24 del Trattato lateranense," *Stato, Chiese e pluralismo confessionale*, Rivista telematica (www.statoechiese.it) dicembre (2010), 3ff.

11. Brother of Eugenio Pacelli, who would later become Pope Pius XII, Francesco Pacelli acted as a legal advisor to Pope Pius XI. See, Michele Maccarrone, "Pacelli Francesco," *Enciclopedia Cattolica* (IX, Città del Vaticano, 1953), 502; Giovanni Sale, "La conciliazione tra Santa Sede e Italia. Il ruolo dell'avv. Francesco Pacelli," *Civiltà Cattolica* 3 (2011): 29–41.

12. Biggini, *Storia inedita della Conciliazione*, 93–94.

13. Francesco Pacelli, *Diario della Conciliazione con verbali e appendice di documenti*, edited by M. Maccarrone (Città del Vaticano: Libreria Editrice Vaticana, 1959), 12.

14. Pacelli, *Diario della Conciliazione con verbali e appendice di documenti*, 14.

15. Ivi, 210ff.

16. Ibid.

17. Ibid.

18. Barberini, "Riflessioni sull'origine e sul significato dell'art. 24 del Trattato lateranense", 6.

19. Pacelli, *Diario della Conciliazione con verbali e appendice di documenti*, 384.

20. Ivi, 484.

21. Ivi, 14.

22. Barberini, "Riflessioni sull'origine e sul significato dell'art. 24 del Trattato lateranense," 7.

23. Ministero degli Affari Esteri, *Commissione per la pubblicazione dei documenti diplomatici, I documenti diplomatici italiani*, VII serie, vol. VII, (Roma: Istituto poligrafico dello Stato, 1970), document 240.

24. To the dispatch of Ambassador Paolucci de' Calboli Barone, undersecretary general of the League of Nations, who reported the favor of the leaders of the League of Nations to the registration of the Treaty, while excluding the possibility of participation by the Holy See, Mussolini replied with the following dispatch of February 16, 1929: «Il Governo Italiano non desidera (dico non) che l'accordo lateranense sia registrato alla S.d.N. La S.d.N. non c'entra . . . Nel Trattato fra l'Italia e la Santa Sede Ginevra non c'entra né ci deve entrare. . . . La cosa è importante e delicata», Ministero degli Affari Esteri, *Commissione per la pubblicazione dei documenti diplomatici*, documents 253 and 258. On the relationship between Holy See and League of Nations, see Vincenzo Bonomo, "L'attività diplomatica della Santa Sede alla vigilia dei Patti Lateranensi: il caso della Società delle Nazioni," in *I Patti lateranensi in occasione del CX anniversario (1929–2019)*, edited by Bernard Ardura (Città del Vaticano: Libreria Editrice Vaticana, 2019), 41–78.

25. Giovanni Battista Varnier, «Una guerra ingiusta». "La Santa Sede e l'Italia tra neutralità e intervento (1914–1915)," *Anuario de historia de La Iglesia* 23 (2014): 17–39; Roberto Regoli, Paolo Valvo, *Tra Pio X e Benedetto XV. La diplomazia pontificia in Europa e America Latina nel 1914* (Roma: Studium, 2018); Gabriele Rigano, "'La nostra neutralità ci rende tutti nemici!' La Santa Sede e i cattolici italiani:

universalismo e nazionalismo durante la Prima guerra mondiale," *Storia e Politica. Annali della Fondazione Ugo La Malfa* 31 (2018): 315–36.

26. Italo Garzia, "La genesi dell'art. 15 del Patto di Londra," *Storia e Politica* 4 (1974): 523–49.

27. Ruffini, "Il potere temporale negli scopi di guerra degli ex imperi centrali;" Ruffini, "Progetti e propositi germanici per risolvere la questione romana," in Francesco Ruffini, *Scritti giuridici minori*, vol. 1, *Scritti di diritto ecclesiastico* (Torino: Gappichelli, 1936), respectively to 199–218 and 221–48.

28. Italo Garzia, *La Questione romana durante la prima guerra mondiale* (Napoli: ESI, 1981); Gabriele Rigano, "Un così necessario dissidio," La Santa Sede e la Conferenza per la Pace: politica religiosa, questione romana e diplomazia internazionale (1914–1919), *Storia e Politica. Annali della Fondazione Ugo La Malfa* 32 (2017): 104–38.

29. Roberto Pertici, *Chiesa e Stato in Italia. Dalla Grande Guerra al nuovo Concordato (1914–1984)* (Bologna: Il Mulino, 2009).

30. On the attitude of Pius XI toward totalitarianism, cf. Yves Chiron, *Pio XI: Il papa dei Patti Lateranensi e dell'opposizione ai totalitarismi* (Cinisello Balsamo: San Paolo, 2006).

31. Thus Pietro Parolin, "Chiesa e comunità politica. Dinamiche giuridiche delle relazioni internazionali della Santa Sede," in *1929–2019 Novant'anni di rapporti tra Stato e confessioni religiose: Attualità e prospettive*, edited by Maria d'Arienzo, Quaderno monografico n. 1. Supplement to the Review *Diritto e Religioni* (Cosenza: Pellegrini Editore, 2020), 130.

32. Ibid.

33. Mario Tedeschi, "Chiesa e Stato," *Novissimo Digesto Italiano, Appendice A-COD*, (Torino: Utet, 1980), 1445ff.; Tedeschi, "La parabola dei Concordati," in Mario Tedeschi, *Studi di diritto ecclesiastico* (Napoli: Jovene, 2002), 49–59; Tedeschi, "Attualità e caducità del Concordato," in Mario Tedeschi, *Studi di diritto ecclesiastico*, vol. 2 (Napoli: Jovene, 2004), 69–75; Giuseppe Dalla Torre, *La Chiesa e gli Stati. Percorsi giuridici del Novecento*, (Roma: Studium, 2017), 107ff.; Marco Ventura, "La diplomazia religiosa. Una nuova prospettiva," *1929–2019 Novant'anni di rapporti tra Stato e confessioni religiose. Attualità e prospettive*, 39–47.

34. See Robert John Araujo, "The International Personality and Sovereignty of the Holy See," *Catholic University Law Review* (2001): 291–360; Dalla Torre, *Lezioni di Diritto Vaticano*, 10 and bibliography ivi quoted.

35. See Francesco Bonini, "Uno Stato nuovo," in *Santa Sede e Stato della Città del Vaticano nel nuovo contesto internazionale (1929–2019)*, 19ff.

36. Pio XI, Allocuzione *"Il nostro benvenuto"* (11 febbraio 1929), *Acta Apostolicae Sedis* 21 (1929): 103–10, see 108.

37. Cf. Carlo Cardia, *Ordinamenti religiosi e ordinamenti dello Stato: Profili giurisdizionali* (Bologna: Il Mulino, 2003), 39ff., specially 41.

38. According to canon 113 Codex iuris canonici of 1983, the Church and the Holy See have autonomous juridical personality; cf. Vincenzo Bonuomo, "Considerazioni sul rapporto tra diritto canonico e diritto internazionale," *Anuario de Derecho Canónico* 4 (2015): 13–70.

39. Cf. Mario Tedeschi, "Santa Sede (diritto ecclesiastico)," *Enciclopedia del diritto*, vol. XLI (Milano: Giuffré,1989), 288ff.; Tedeschi, "Vaticano (Stato della Città del)," *Enciclopedia del diritto*, XLVI (Milano: Giuffré, 1993), 284–96.

40. Fabio Vecchi, "L'affievolimento di sovranità dello Stato Città del Vaticano per assorbimento nell'area monetaria dell'euro," *Diritto ecclesiastico* 109 (2002): 1045; David Durisotto, "I rapporti internazionali dello Stato Città del Vaticano alla luce degli interventi normativi in materia finanziaria," *Stato, Chiese e pluralismo confessionale*, Rivista telematica, (www.statoechiese.it) 24 (2017).

41. Barberini, "Riflessioni sull'origine e sul significato dell'art. 24 del trattato lateranense," 16.

42. Ivi, 14.

43. Luigi Sico, "Neutralità," *Enciclopedia del diritto*, XXVIII (Milano: Giuffré, 1978), 181.

44. Sico, "Neutralità," 166; Alberto Miele, *L'estraneità ai conflitti armati, vol. I, Origine ed evoluzione del diritto di neutralità* (Padova: Cedam, 1970), 52ff.; Sara Tonolo, "Neutralità e non intervento nel diritto internazionale attuale," in *Attraverso i conflitti. Neutralità e commercio fra età moderna ed età contemporanea*," edited by Daniele Andreozzi (Trieste: Edizioni Università di Trieste, 2017), 131–45. On the evolution of the concept of neutrality, see Rita Benigni, "La neutralità della Santa Sede (Percorsi teorici e ipotesi ricostruttive)," *Archivio Giuridico* 222 (2002/II): 252–53; Enrico Giarnieri, *Lo Status della Santa Sede e della Svizzera presso l'Onu. Una neutralità differenziata* (Torino: Giappichelli, 2008).

45. Barberini, "Riflessioni sull'origine e sul significato dell'art. 24 del trattato lateranense," 12.

46. Carlo Cardia, *Principi di diritto ecclesiastico. Tradizione europea legislazione italiana* (Torino: Giappichelli, 2019), 236.

47. Condemned by Benedict XV as an "unjust war" and defined as "useless slaughter" in the Peace Note of 1917. For the two citations, see respectively, *Acta Apostolicae Sedis* 91 (1917), 423 and 8 (1916), 59.

48. Cf. Francesco Margiotta Broglio, *Italia e Santa Sede dalla grande guerra alla Conciliazione* (Bari: Laterza, 1966); Giovanni Battista Varnier, *Gli ultimi governi liberali e questione romana, 1918–1922* (Milano: Giuffrè, 1976).

49. Archivio Segreto Vaticano, Sacra Congregazione degli Affari Ecclesiastici Straordinari, *Stati Ecclesiastici*, position n. 1350. *Italia anno 1915–1924, Situazione della S. Sede in Italia. «Questione romana»*. The document is also indicated in "Segreteria di Stato. Guerra 1914–1918," rubr. 244, p. inventario 14, reproduced in Varnier, "'Una guerra ingiusta'": La Santa Sede e L'Italia tra neutralità e intervento," 29ff.

50. See archival documents published in *L'Archivio della Commissione Soccorsi (1939–1958): Inventario, I–II* edited by Francesca Di Giovanni and Giuseppina Roselli, (Città del Vaticano: Archivio Segreto Vaticano, 2019).

51. Iohan Ickx, *Pio XII e gli ebrei: L'archivista del Vaticano rivela finalmente il ruolo di Papa Pacelli durante la Seconda guerra mondiale* (Rizzoli: Milano, 2021).

52. See the Radiomessage of the Pope Pacelli, August 24 1939: "Nulla è perduto con la pace. Tutto può essere perduto con la guerra" (cf. *Discorsi e Radiomessaggi*

di Pio XII 1 (Città del Vaticano: Ed. Poliglotta Vaticana, 1939), 306 and the *Encyclical Pacem in terris* of Pope John XXIII (April 11, 1963), *Acta Apostolicae Sedis* 55 (1963): 257–304.

53. Sergio Ferlito, *L'attività internazionale della Santa Sede* (Milano: Giuffré, 1988); Giovanni Barberini, *Chiesa e Santa Sede nell'ordinamento internazionale* (Turin: Giappichelli, 1996); Barberini, *Le Saint-Siège sujet souverain de droit international* (Paris: Ed. du Cerf, 2003), 21ff.

54. As is well known, according to the norms of canon 363 § 2 of the Codex iuris canonici in force, the Legates of the Apostolic See to international organizations can have the title of delegates or observers. They have the title of apostolic delegates if the Holy See is a member of the organization, or observer, if it is not a member.

55. Cf. Giarnieri, *Lo Status della Santa Sede e della Svizzera presso l'Onu*, 104ff.; Francesco Margiotta Broglio, "Sul nuovo ruolo dell'Osservatore della Santa Sede alle Nazioni Unite," *Rivista di Studi politici Internazionali* 4 (2004): 555–66.

56. Holy See Press Office, *Communiqué*, June 1, 2021, available at https://press.vatican.va/content/salastampa/en/bollettino.html.

57. Carlo Cardia, "La soggettività internazionale della Santa Sede e i processi di integrazione europea," *Ius Ecclesiae* 11 (1999): 301–43.

58. On the evolutionary features of the international activity of the Holy See, cf. Luca Caveada, *Questioni aperte sulla presenza della Santa Sede nel diritto internazionale* (Padova: Cedam, 2018).

59. *Acta Apostolicae Sedis* 46 (1954): 433–57, art. II.1.

60. *Acta Apostolicae Sedis* 56 (1964): 925–32.

61. UN Educational, Scientific and Cultural Organisation (UNESCO), Convention for the Protection of Cultural Property in the Event of Armed Conflict, May 14, 1954, available at https://www.refworld.org/docid/40422c914.html.

62. Barberini, "La partecipazione della Santa Sede alla Conferenza di Helsinki," in, *La tutela della libertà di religione: Ordinamento internazionale e normative confessionali*, edited by Silvio Ferrari and Andrea Scovazzi (Padova: Cedam, 1988), 149ff.; Barberini, *Pagine di storia contemporanea: La Santa Sede alla Conferenza di Helsinki* (Siena: Cantagalli, 2010).

63. *L'Osservatore Romano*, December 4–5, 1972.

64. Barberini, "La partecipazione della Santa Sede alla Conferenza di Helsinki," 168.

65. *L'Osservatore Romano*, July 27–28, 1992.

66. Cf. "Summi Pontificis allocutio in Consilio Nationum Unitarum," *Acta Apostolicae Sedis* 57 (1965): 877ff.

67. Ibid.

68. "The fiftieth general Assembly of the United Nations organization Address of his holiness John Paul II, 5 october 1995," at www.vatican.va.

69. *Gaudium et Spes*, n. 76.

70. Cardia, *Principi di diritto ecclesiastico: Tradizione europea, legislazione italiana*, 259ff.

71. On the position of John Paul II with respect to the intervention for the liberation of Kuwait, cf. *La pace sprecata: Il Papa, la Chiesa e la guerra nel Golfo*, edited by Domenico del Rio, (Casale Monferrato: Piemme, 1991).

72. Charles de Montclos, *Le Vatican et l'éclatement de la Yougoslavie* (Paris: Puf, 1999), 123–36.

73. Pasquale Ferrara, *Il mondo di Francesco: Bergoglio e la politica internazionale*, presentation of Paolo Gentiloni (Cinisello Balsamo: San Paolo, 2016).

74. See Malcolm N. Shaw, *International Law* (Cambridge: Cambridge University Press, 2008), 374–75.

75. On Francis' "diplomacy of Mercy," see Gianni La Bella, "Santa Sede e ONU," *Nazioni Unite e sistema internazionale*, edited by Marco Mugnaini (Milano: Franco Angeli, 2018), 174ff.

76. Dalla Torre, *La Chiesa e gli Stati: Percorsi giuridici del Novecento*, 111.

77. *Lettera del Santo Padre Benedetto XVI ai Vescovi, ai presbiteri, alle persone consacrate e ai fedeli laici della Chiesa cattolica nella Repubblica Popolare Cinese*, May 17 2007 at www.vatican.va.

78. *Legge XVIII*, October 8, 2013, and *Decreto* n. CCCLXXII, October 10, 2020.

79. Francesco, "'Motu proprio'" of the Holy Father on the approval of the New Law on the Governance of Vatican City State," June 12, 2018, *Bulletin Holy See Press Office* available at https://press.vatican.va/content/salastampa/en/bollettino/pubblico/2018/12/06/181207i.html; Buonomo, "Annotazioni sulla nuova Legge sul governo dello Stato della Città del Vaticano," *Ius Ecclesiae* 81 (2019): 647–59; Alessio Sarais, "Brevi considerazioni sulla nuova legge sul governo dello Stato della Città del Vaticano," *Monitor Ecclesiasticus* 123 (2018): 237–58.

80. "Legge fondamentale dello Stato della Città del Vaticano, 26 novembre 2000," Proemio, *Acta Apostolicae Sedis*, Suppl. 71 (2000): 75–80.

81. See "Explanatory note of the Presidency of the Governorate on the New Law on the Governance of Vatican City State," June 12, 2018, *Bulletin Holy See Press Office* available at https://press.vatican.va/content/salastampa/en/bollettino/pubblico/2018/12/06/181207i.html.

82. http://www.vatican.va/content/francesco/it/motu_proprio/documents/papa-francesco-motu-proprio-20200519_procedure-aggiudicazione-contrattipubblici.html.

SELECTED BIBLIOGRAPHY

Araujo, Robert John, SJ, and John A. Lucal, SJ. *Papal Diplomacy and the Quest for Peace: The Vatican and International Organization from the Early Years to the League of Nations*. Naples, FL: Sapientia Press, 2004.

Falco, Mario. *The Legal Position of the Holy See before and after the Lateran Agreements: Two Lectures Delivered at the University of Oxford by Mario Falco*. Translation by Archibald Hunter Campbell. London: Oxford University Press, 1935.

Kent, Peter C. *The Pope and the Duce: The International Impact of the Lateran Agreements*. London: Macmillan, 1981.

Lottaz, Pascal, and Reginbogin, Herbert R., eds. *Notions of Neutralities*. Lanham, MD: Lexington Books, 2019.

Tomasi, Silvano Maria. *The Vatican in the Family of Nations. Diplomatic Actions of the Holy See at the UN and Other International Organizations in Geneva*. Cambridge: Cambridge University Press, 2017.

Part II

THE LONG SECOND WORLD WAR: 1931–1945

Chapter Four

Neutrality to the Test

The Vatican and the Fascist Wars of the 1930s

Lucia Ceci

Thanks to the Lateran Treaty, Italy finally recognized the sovereignty of the Holy See and its jurisdiction over Vatican City. This ended decades of dispute between successive popes and the leaders of the Italian state, and for the first time, the Kingdom of Italy renounced two principles of its liberal vision of the state: the idea of religion as a private matter and the exclusive sovereignty of the state. Importantly, the treaty also was an agreement signed with an authoritarian government with totalitarian ambitions.[1] The presence of the Vatican City State in the capital of the Kingdom, as well as the privileges recognized to the Catholic Church through the concordat and the reality of the dictatorship put to the test the determination of the Vatican to maintain a position of neutrality in the international conflicts of fascist Italy.

This chapter asks about Pope Pius XI's role in this dynamic and investigates the Holy See's choices. Concretely, did the Vatican manage to remain neutral with respect to the wars that Mussolini waged in the 1930s, a few years after the Conciliation? To answer these questions, in the following pages, the impact of the Lateran Treaty is first examined as it opened up areas for closer cooperation with the Italian government at an international level. The Vatican's efforts are then analyzed in terms of seeking a position of neutrality in the face of the war in Ethiopia[2] (1935–1936) and the Spanish Civil War (1936–1939). The analysis finally considers Mussolini's pressure to obtain the Holy See's support for his government's aggressive foreign policy and the consequences of the mobilization of the Italian Catholic world on Vatican strategies.

THE LATERAN TREATY: OPPORTUNITIES AND LIMITS OF VATICAN SOVEREIGNTY VIS-A-VIS FASCIST ITALY

On March 14, 1933, the Italian ambassador to the Holy See, Cesare Maria De Vecchi, reported to Mussolini about an interview he had had that morning with the secretary of state, Cardinal Eugenio Pacelli. Four years had passed since the signing of the Lateran Treaty and barely a month since Hitler's appointment as Reich chancellor. Pacelli appeared to De Vecchi inclined to trust the Duce and align himself with the policy of the Italian government. "In the Holy See," he wrote in his report to Mussolini, "we now have friends. They are trusted friends you can rely on. If war is our destiny, you will realize that."[3] According to the ambassador, the Vatican secretary of state and Pope Pius XI had been definitively "conquered" by the fascist regime and would support its foreign policy.

In the following two years, until the first half of 1935, there was no lack of tangible signs of a retreat of Vatican diplomacy toward the positions of fascist Italy. On the one hand, Mussolini's pro-Soviet policy of the early 1930s appeared "very deplorable" to the pontiff.[4] In 1933, the Duce had signed an agreement of friendship and non-aggression between Italy and the USSR. However, the head of the Italian government managed to recover, in the eyes of the Vatican, when he acted as a guarantor of European peace by defending Catholic Austria, in July 1934, from the expansionist aims of the pagan Nazi regime and for promoting, in April 1935, the Stresa Front, thus getting closer to the France of the conservative Laval government. As a guarantor of the *Pax Romana*, Mussolini once again appeared, as it had been said in the aftermath of the Lateran Treaty, as a man sent by providence—a modern reinterpretation of the emperors Augustus and Constantine.[5] These juxtapositions corroborated not only the idea that Providence had assigned Rome an outsized destiny in history and Italy, as Vincenzo Gioberti wrote, "primacy among states," but also strengthened the image of fascist Rome as heir to the Rome of the emperors and the popes.[6]

To gain legitimacy in the eyes of Catholics, Mussolini had carefully built the public image of the new Constantine even through choices in his personal and familial spheres (i.e., the religious marriage with Rachele Guidi and the baptism of his children), but above all through religious policies very favorable to the Catholic Church. The Lateran Treaty had, in fact, been preceded by a series of measures: the obligation of displaying the crucifix in the classrooms, the dissolution of Freemasonry, the rescue of the Banca Romana, and the introduction of the Catholic religion in elementary school.

Still, in the aftermath of the historic signing of the Lateran Treaty, on February 11, 1929, there was no lack of tension between the Palazzo Venezia and the Vatican. The discussions for the ratification of the treaty revealed, in fact, a tug of war between two centers of power. Both were determined to appear as the winners of the Conciliation. Mussolini, seeing himself in the historical role as solver of the Roman Question, was convinced that the Conciliation would make Catholicism a pillar of his regime. On the other hand, Pius XI decided to advocate the inseparability between the international treaty and the concordat ("simul stabunt, simul cadent").[7] Mussolini had focused above all on the Treaty that recognized the Holy See's sovereignty over a territory called Vatican City and had granted in the concordat ample concessions that diminished the sovereignty of the State in many sectors (marriage, teaching). Pius XI, too had made concessions. He had definitively given up temporal power over Rome. But only on the condition that the Italian State would accept the concordat that was stipulated simultaneously without any modification, as if the concordat and the treaty were two inseparable parts of the same agreement. Not only was the concordat particularly favorable to the Catholic Church in Italy, but the pontiff interpreted it as a platform from which to guarantee additional spaces for action for the ecclesiastical institution. For instance, in the fields of youth education and religious freedom. This is testified by the publication of the encyclical *Divini Illius Magistris* on December 31, 1929, in which the traditional principle of the family's primacy over the State in children's education was proclaimed. The Vatican also promulgated through the encyclical its discontent with the "Law on admitted cults" (enacted 1930), which the Holy See considered too soft with regard to Protestant proselytism.[8]

In the shadows of the concordat, the ecclesiastical project of a "Catholic nation" had taken shape and form in Italy. It aimed at creating a leading and competitive presence for the Church in an authoritarian and confessional regime. Nonetheless, despite the undeniable advantages that the two sides gained from the Lateran Treaty, contradictions arose from the clash of two exclusive faiths, not least because fascism itself was taking on the characteristics of a new religion, with myths, rituals, symbols, and codified dogmas: a political and secular religion, demanding obedience to its infallible chief, who at the end of the 1920s, had already codified some of these features. Mussolini and a part of the fascist organizations, especially the ones at universities, as expressed by the Gruppi Universitari Fascisti (Fascist Groups in Italian Universities), showed more and more intolerance toward the associative network of Azione Cattolica (Catholic Action)[9]—especially from the moment when that network started intensifying its work for propaganda and the penetration of society, by taking advantage of the space and means that the concordat guaranteed.[10]

Still, fundamentally, the Vatican thought that fascism was "catholicizable" but that it would be necessary to carry out a long "war of attrition" to consolidate the elements that it considered positive while marginalizing others. The return to an image of a consensus that Mussolini's regime had expected from the conciliation would, in the short term, be clouded by a conflict that reached its peak in 1931.

The tension reached its highest point on June 29, 1931, with the promulgation of the encyclical of Pius XI *Non Abbiamo Bisogno* (We have no need), made public on July 5, after it had already been circulated abroad as a precaution. It was sent directly from the pope to the nuncios of various countries. The tone of the encyclical was unusually harsh. While the Holy See previously used to distinguish within Fascism the good intentions of the government and its leader from the (regrettable) actions that were carried out in the provinces, this differentiation disappeared.[11] The condemnation of this document aimed not at individual instances of oppression (which is also mentioned and meticulously described) but at the fascist conception of the State, which it described as pushing the government to monopolize education and display "religiosity" that was antagonistic to the Catholic faith. It defined this aspect as irreconcilable with the Catholic doctrine and the natural law of families. Indeed, the stakes had risen.

After some moments of sharp tension, Pius XI chose to negotiate. The discussions ended with an agreement on September 2, which stated that the Azione Cattolica would not get involved in political or trade union tasks and affirmed its direct supervision by the bishops. It also renounced the organizing of sporting activities and confirmed the prohibition of former members of the Partito Popolare to hold managerial positions in the organization. However, accepting the dismantling of the Catholic laity would have signified the complete renunciation of the fight for ideological supremacy over the following generations. Besides, Azione Cattolica also had an international spread, unlike other lay associations. Its suppression, consequently, would have set a dangerous precedent.[12]

The new pact seemed to offer the most significant advantages to the regime for the definitive elimination of what was left of the Partito Popolare. However, the "reconciliation" with the government allowed the Church to carry out subversion and coordination from within the fascist state. After the reopening of youth clubs, Azione Cattolica emerged from the conflict strengthened by its consistency and ability to promote organizational initiatives and proselytism. Of course, for Pius XI and most Italian Catholics, this was not a question of finding spaces to act against the regime but of working toward transforming the fascist state into one that would adhere as closely as possible to the ideals of a Catholic state.

THE TEST OF VATICAN NEUTRALITY IN THE FIRST FASCIST WAR AFTER THE CONCILIATION (1935–1936)

Hitler's ascent to power and the international environment, including fears about a new European conflict, pushed Pius XI to take risks concerning Italy's potential for peacemaking. The pope thought it wise to smooth out his reservations toward Mussolini, believing that he could count on his role as an arbiter of the European equilibrium, especially in the face of the rifts between Berlin and Moscow. Mussolini's reaction to the Nazi putsch in Vienna, with the mobilization of Italian troops on the border with Austria, and the Duce's role in the Stresa Front to stop German rearmament seemed to confirm this belief. But there was more. Mussolini had discreetly favored in 1933 the signing of a concordat between the Holy See and Hitler's Third Reich to later personally intervene to defend the cause of Catholicism in Germany. The idea of a fruitful collaboration, on an international level, between the Vatican and the Italian government also seemed confirmed by the results obtained in Eastern Europe, where the Duce had supported the diplomatic actions of the Holy See, collaborating to maintain Catholic practice in Soviet Russia. Furthermore, in the Balkans, in the autumn of 1934, Italian diplomacy moved to protect the rights of the Catholic minority in Albania.[13] In nationalist China, relations between the Italian diplomatic authorities and the apostolic delegation proceeded in lockstep collaboration.[14]

However, in the still reserved relationship between the Holy See and the Italian government, this equilibrium suffered a crack in the second half of 1935, during the diplomatic negotiations preceding Italy's invasion of Ethiopia (1935–1936). In his war against the centuries-old Ethiopian Empire, Mussolini mobilized all the forces of the regime. It became the greatest of Italy's colonial wars: half a million Italians were sent to East Africa within a few months.

It was also the last of the classic colonial wars: Italy's extreme war effort and the involvement of national public opinion, in addition to the vigor of international protests, anticipated aspects of the subsequent French and US wars in Algeria and Indochina. However, there were also substantial differences: in the post-1945 wars of liberation, the Algerians, Laotians, Cambodians, and Vietnamese had a modern political organization, international support, and mostly adequate weapons.

In contrast, in 1935, the Ethiopian Empire was a backward state, suffering from an overwhelming military and technological inferiority to Italy. In addition, Italy waged "total" war with enormous use of resources, men, and even toxic chemicals banned under international treaties. The Italian occupation lasted until 1941. Marked by massacres, deportations, and incarcerations in concentration camps, it caused the deaths of more than three hundred thousand Ethiopian soldiers and civilians.[15]

The war was vehemently opposed throughout the world. To legitimize it, Mussolini needed, if not the spontaneous and benevolent support of the Holy See, at least its silence. Pius XI's attitude toward this war of fascist aggression captured the interest of world public opinion, diplomats, and Christian churches. It was the first time that the world community would wonder if the Lateran Treaty had made the pope a prisoner of Mussolini?

However, the Vatican papers confirm Pius XI's absolute opposition to the Italian war of conquest.[16] In confidential talks with members of the curia and diplomacy, Pope Achille Ratti disapproved of the attack on Ethiopia, in quiet. He, along with many other observers, feared that the conflict would spread to Europe. He also knew that aggression against a sovereign state present in the League of Nations would push Mussolini closer to Hitler. Finally, "the pope of the missions" was very concerned about the inevitable consequences that the clash between Italy and the other colonial powers would have on the organizational development of the propagation of the faith—that is, on the Vatican's own missionaries.

Pius XI condemned the fascist war of conquest most strongly in a speech at Castel Gandolfo on August 27, 1935.[17] That became the start of a deep crisis with the government of Rome. The reaction of Italian diplomacy, moving on to the personal orders of Mussolini, was aggressive. It aimed at taming future public stances of the pontiff on the conflict, under the threat of destroying the good relations between State and Church in Italy after the conciliation. The pope bowed to this blackmail—a choice to which his closest confidants agreed.[18]

To get an idea of how much Pius XI had received a diktat of silence on the fascist war of conquest, we can recall the following episode (of which there were others). In December 1935, Pius XI wanted to publicly express hope for peace in a consistorial address on December 16, or his Christmas speech. The overspilling of the Italo-Ethiopian conflict to Europe has been averted. However, the League of Nations' sanctions caused financial disruption spawning a catalytic reaction in the form of an Italian national movement to mobilize gold from private households to be donated to the Italian government for the war against Abyssinia. In this spectacular event of propaganda and mobilization against the "unfair sanctions" decreed by the League of Nations, bishops, and cardinals from all over Italy handed over valuables such as episcopal necklaces, rings, precious objects, and family heirlooms to Fascist Party delegates, who represented the "Nation at war" against the "Geneva aggression." The prelates encouraged the faithful, even the humblest, to do the same with blatant gestures highlighted by the media.[19]

The pope's prudence reached the point that he tested the waters through the office of Cadinal Pacelli, who met the new Italian ambassador to the Holy See, Bonifacio Pignatti, on December 14. From him, Pacelli received a very harsh response: a public encouragement from the pope for a truce "would have been considered by the fascist government and the country as an act of enmity."[20] Pacelli reassured Pignatti that, in this case, the pope would not intervene. The following day the Jesuit Pietro Tacchi Venturi, who, since 1923, had been the link between the Vatican and Palazzo Venezia,[21] reiterated the decision to Mussolini at the request of Pius XI: "The Holy Father, aware of the conversation between the Ambassador and the Cardinal Secretary of State, would not even mention the Italo-Ethiopian conflict in the next Papal Consistory, as if *tamquam non esset* [as if it did not exist]."[22] True to his word, in the consistorial address of December 16, Pius XI made no mention of the Italo-Ethiopian war, nor on Christmas day.

Furthermore, at the beginning of December, two months after the start of military operations in Ethiopia, Monsignor Domenico Tardini, Undersecretary of the Congregation for Extraordinary Ecclesiastical Affairs, wrote in his notes on the Italo-Ethiopian conflict whether or not the pope should publicly intervene in the war but concluded that only the pope's silence would allow for "his pacifying action."[23]

Tardini forcefully posed the question of the pope's silence on the fascist war because the blatant mobilization of the clergy, bishops, and many Italian cardinals offered the image of a total alignment of Catholicism, starting from its leaders, to Mussolini government's war of conquest. The broad support offered by Catholics to the regime on the occasion of the Italo-Ethiopian conflict is a fact that stands out as in few other circumstances of Italian political life. In numerous public positions, the bishops expressed their most fervent support for government initiatives in Ethiopia. High prelates blessed the troops and ships leaving for East Africa, and the national president of Azione Cattolica adopted a line of open support for the war. Political praise for the government also came from different branches of the Catholic Youth (of Azione Cattolica). Furthermore, the group of priests from Italia e Fede, which had a central role in guiding the local clergy, reaffirmed their support for the imperial and autarchic goals of the Duce. Catholic missionary press, church press, cinema, and even theater contributed to spreading colonial enthusiasm among the Italian population and the image of the war as a Catholic missionary crusade in a heretical country.

Amplified by the Fascist press, the image of an Italian Catholic world aligned with the regime's policy in Ethiopia, made headlines around the world. It was reported to the European governments by diplomats stationed in Italy and the Holy See. The same was pointed out in the reports of the League of Nations—the anti-fascists highlighted it. Vatican leaders were perfectly aware of that and sometimes embarrassed by it.

The ostentatious and blanket support for the government's propaganda was by far the most dominant element of the discussion, but from a more detailed analysis, it appears that the propaganda went through phases. A diversified attitude, made up of caution, silence, and support, accompanied the political-diplomatic negotiations. A massive response in support of the war was given to the general mobilization of October 2, 1935. But it was the entry into force of the sanctions imposed on Italy by the League of Nations for the aggression against Ethiopia (November 18, 1935) that generated the almost total support of Catholics to the African war. The support reached its maximum in the mobilization for the Gold to the Fatherland and culminated in the Day of Faith (December 18, 1935). It manifested most blatantly again when the Empire was proclaimed (May 9, 1936) but then faded away, as the Spanish Civil War—perceived as a "Crusade" for the defense of Christianity—stole the international attention away from Ethiopia.[24]

Starting from the mobilization of the anti-sanctionists, the participation of Catholics in the war became absolute. Anti-sanctionists mystified the Ethiopian war of conquest, thus transforming it into a battle to defend Italy from the corporate aggression of the plutocratic democracies. To many, the situation seemed to offer an excellent opportunity to demonstrate the loyalty of Catholics to their homeland, which was now reconciled through the Lateran Treaty with the Church of Rome, and to the leader of fascism, who seemed to be the architect of this reconciliation. The most widespread and theatrical moment of the exaltation of Italian Catholicism coincided with the mobilization of gold for the homeland.[25]

The line held publicly by the Holy See was not much removed from the bellicose and clerical-imperial enthusiasm of Italian Catholics. After the diplomatic incident between the Vatican and Mussolini's government at the end of August 1935, following the words of condemnation pronounced by Pius XI on August 27, there were no further public interventions by the pontiff to denounce Italy's war of aggression. The silence was essentially interpreted by the episcopate as a form of adherence to the regime's colonial policy. The Italian bishops had a broad consensus concerning the line followed by the Holy See.[26] Consequently, while, on the one hand, for reasons of cultural poverty, they were unable to discuss and counter the clichés of fascist propaganda, it was, on the other hand, unthinkable that they would take positions considered to conflict with those of the pope.

By not intervening publicly in a different direction from that of the high clergy, the pope signaled to the episcopate, priests, believers, and the national and international public that there was substantial approval by the Holy See for the African War and the Italian Catholic world overall. This seemed moreover confirmed by the guidelines of the *L'Osservatore Romano*, which, for the whole duration of the conflict, legitimized the imperial enterprises of fascist Italy. Albeit, it avoided reporting the most heated interventions of the episcopate and, from time to time, allowed some space to the *Acta Diurna* (a column in the *L'Osservatore*) by Guido Gonella to make distinctions with respect to the government press campaign.

The pro-imperialist and pro-fascist declarations of Italian Catholics aroused reactions in many parts of the world. Dozens of letters from individual believers, Catholic associations, Protestant associations, and Catholic parties came to the Vatican from various countries of the world to ask for dissociation from the colonialist and bellicose declarations of the Italian bishops. Besides, protests were made to the Vatican by the British government for the anti-British tirades, which had manifested in many interventions of the Italian episcopate and were widely publicized by the press.

No less embarrassing for the Holy See was what had been claimed in Germany by the National Socialist newspapers. According to those, the various statements by the Italian high clergy were proof that the Holy See had left to the national clergy the choice of full adhesion to the fascist war, which, for political wisdom, the pope did not interfere with.[27] Likewise, the NS press claimed that it would be unthinkable if these statements had been made without the Vatican's consent.

We need to understand Monsignor Tardini's question about the pope's silence in this context. He judged the Italian clergy and bishops to be "tumultuous, exalted, warmongers, deranged." Hence, his concern about how the pro-Italian and pro-imperial demonstrations of the episcopate would reflect on the international image of the Holy See, which by now was accused "of being in one league with Fascism."[28] The risk of a fall in the Holy See's international prestige led Tardini to formulate a very negative opinion on the consequences of the Lateran Treaty. This was not unimportant, as he was one of the main architects of the Holy See's diplomatic action. He was considered among the "most influential" personalities of the Church of the twentieth century.[29]

In 1929, Tardini was enthusiastic about the restructuring of the conflict between Church and State in Italy. However, five years later, in February 1934, he noted in the pages of his personal diary more than one reservation about the pacts' effectiveness. His doubts included that in the international field, the friendship between the pope and Italy was "instead of a help, a stumbling block not always easy to overcome. So much so that from 1870 onward, the strongest guarantee for the pope's independence abroad would be the break with Italy."[30] In the eyes of the undersecretary, the international crisis opened by the conflict was a complete confirmation of his previous reservations. In his view, it was, in fact, from the Conciliation that the discredit explicitly derived in which the Holy See found itself before the eyes of the world. While vice versa, a "quarrel" with Italy would have constituted "the best guarantee" for its independence. Without the Conciliation, Tardini stated, "the clergy would not have taken today's attitude. And the difficulty would not have arisen. Moreover, it is historically certain that the disagreement with Italy was the best guarantee of the independence of the Holy See."[31] If, until 1929, the conflict with the Kingdom of Italy had guaranteed the irreconcilability of the See of Rome and the pontifical authority with the nationalistic logic of Mussolini's Italy, once that conflict was resolved, the nationalism of the Italian clergy—above all of the high clergy—ended up investing and incorporating the Holy See into that nationalistic enterprise. After all, the Holy See was the historical and institutional pinnacle of the national-Catholic identity of Italians.

A few days after the end of military operations in Ethiopia and the proclamation of the Empire of Italian East Africa (May 9, 1936) Pius XI, intervened at the inauguration of the World Exhibition of the Catholic Press (May 12). Speaking in front of many diplomatic representatives, he rejoiced in the "triumphal happiness" of the "great and good people" of Italy and celebrated the "fortunate" coincidence of the opening of the Exposition with the "favorable general climate." The speech was not without ambiguity because, on the one hand, the pope recalled the triumphal joy of the Italian people, in reference to the grandiose gathering three days earlier in which Mussolini had proclaimed the return of the empire to the providential hills of Rome. On the other hand, Pius XI, who had never evoked the link (so often recalled by Catholic propaganda) between fascist imperialism and the expansion of Catholicism, greeted not the empire's proclamation but the advent of peace.[32] On March 24, 1937, the Holy See decreed the complete Italianization of the Catholic missions present in Italian East Africa (Mussolini had already driven out French Lazarists and Swedish Protestants). Those were the weeks when viceroy Rodolfo Graziani unleashed massive repression after Italian forces suffered an attack in Ethiopia (February 19, 1937). In the first three days alone, more than three thousand people were summarily executed in Addis Ababa. Villages were destroyed, and between May 19 and 20, the Coptic convent of Debra Libanos was massacred. About two thousand people died, including priests, monks, pilgrims, and two hundred very young deacons.[33] Even in the face of such massacres, the Vatican did not intervene. Instead, it allowed the missionaries to support the first fascist interventions in defense of the superiority of the "Italic race," punishing marital unions between Italian citizens and colonial subjects.[34]

In contrast, in October 1938, the Holy See used the concordat of 1929 to protest against the Italian government for the consequences of the anti-Jewish legislation on mixed marriages. This position of the elderly Pius XI remained isolated, however, as he would have liked to extend the Vatican's intervention to the question of the Jews as a whole. Faced with the regime's intransigence on race, the pope profoundly grasped the limits that the concordat offered to the Church in the totalitarian state. During an audience with Tacchi Venturi, the unofficial liaison between Mussolini and the pontiff, on October 24, Pius XI even said that he was willing to give up the negotiations with the government because, more than the concordat, he cared about his conscience:

> But this is enormous! And I am ashamed . . . ashamed to be Italian. And tell that, father, to Mussolini himself! I am ashamed not as pope but as an Italian! The Italian people have become a herd of stupid sheep. I will speak out, without fear. I am forced to by the Concordat, but even more so by my conscience. I have no fear! I would prefer to beg in the streets. I will not even ask Mussolini to defend the Vatican. And even if the piazza fills with people, I will not be afraid! . . . I am truly discouraged, both as pope and as an Italian.[35]

However, the dispute over anti-Jewish laws remained limited to the question of marriages between Italian Jews and Italian non-Jews, as the aim of safeguarding the relationship between the Holy See and the government prevailed.[36] Simultaneously, the massive demonstrations of (popular) consent that followed Mussolini's return from the Munich Conference, and that lasted for a few weeks, had the effect of further diminishing the scope of the Vatican protests. Hierarchy, clergy, and faithful contributed actively to spread the image of the Duce as a protagonist of the agreements in Munich and as a bulwark for European peace.[37] In the aftermath of those agreements, Father Agostino Gemelli promoted Mussolini's version of a "pax romana." He stated that the Duce, with his "political wisdom," had succeeded in one of the darkest moments in history, entrusting the very young "Italian Empire" with the task of ensuring "the victory of peace" and the "salvation of European civilization."[38]

GLOBAL THREAT AND THE STRUGGLE FOR CIVILIZATION: THE SPANISH CIVIL WAR

The affirmation of a theoretical indifference to the nature of political regimes and the tendency to judge a government or a political movement based on its attitude toward Catholicism has given the Vatican a malleability that lent itself to frequent fluctuations. It enabled a form of pragmatism which, in political action, valued the "hypothesis" more than the "thesis" and the search for a modus vivendi with governments over condemnations as the last resort. A break to this long-term strategy occurred in the aftermath of the seventh Congress of the Comintern (1935) and, more importantly, in response to the Spanish Civil War. It was in this period that in the Holy See, a sense of isolation was accentuated. It was fueled by a perception of threat from global communism that was itself based on fears of the growing connection between the Soviet state and the communist movement.[39]

Suffice it to recall a few elements briefly. In 1934, with the approval of the Holy See, but on the initiative of the leader of the Society of Jesus, Wladimir Ledóchowski, the Secretariat on Modern Atheism, and the magazine *Lettres de Rome* were born. The two structures had the specific purpose of educating priests and militants of Azione Cattolica on the actions of international communism and of becoming "the center of the Catholic International," countering the propaganda of the Comintern and influencing the press on a global level.[40] The periodical, which in 1937 was transformed from a monthly to a biweekly publication, appeared in five languages and quickly became a point of reference for the European clergy. It counted among its subscribers all the editorial offices of the foremost Catholic magazines. It was directed by Joseph Ledit, an American Jesuit of French origin, and by his German brother, Friedrich Muckerman. Also, Tacchi Venturi actively collaborated on it. Through his proximity to government circles, he managed to access foreign press materials that otherwise would not have passed the censorship. From 1935 to 1939, the Secretariat and the magazine were the directing centers of a global network of information and political analysis based on the structure of the Society of Jesus.[41] The fight against communism spread across the board and involved literary, social, economic, and ideological issues. "At the present time," stated Ledóchowski in a letter addressed to the entire Company on June 19, 1936, "nothing is more to the point, nothing is more necessary, than this war against atheistic communism."[42]

In this "war," the Holy See, which until 1933 had left open the prospects of a diplomatic link with Moscow, now grasped the transnational connection between the USSR and the international communist movement. This became evident from a global inquiry into the propaganda efforts of communism, which the Secretariat of State launched through a circular letter on February 20, 1936. It was sent to all the nuncios and apostolic delegates on the four continents, asking them to provide Rome with information about communist propaganda. In a second letter, the Vatican focused explicitly on the USSR, drawing attention to the harsh treatment of Catholics and the two essential and original political aspects of communism: namely, its global dimension on the one hand, and the link between the Soviet state and the communist movement, on the other.⁴³ This vision is reflected in an article that appeared in October 1936 on the pages of *Civiltà Cattolica* (a Jesuit magazine considered to express the opinions of the Vatican Secretariat of State and publishing articles on the most delicate issues). It presented an initial assessment of the work carried out by the Secretariat and the *Lettres de Rome*, describing the findings in terms of a "review of the diabolic" nature of "Communist propaganda in the world."⁴⁴ There were two elements which the magazine emphasized: the global spread of communism, whose geographical expansion it described, and the essential centrality of the Soviet leadership—the "brain" of the "gigantic and monstrous spider that spreads its web through its enormous legs on all classes of people," by way of financial aid and the organizational apparatus of the Comintern. The Spanish events constituted the historical scenario that dramatically demonstrated this interpretation.

Faced with the military uprising of Francisco Franco of July 17 and 18, 1936, the Holy See initially maintained a cautious line despite news reaching the Vatican almost in real-time about the violent anti-religious movements that accompanied the extension of the civil war following the *alzamiento*. Pius XI's first intervention in favor of Franco's insurgents came after almost two months, on September 14, 1936, on the occasion of an audience granted in Castel Gandolfo to a group of Spanish refugees, about five hundred priests and believers, mostly Catalan, led by the bishops of Cartagena, Vich, Tortosa, and La Seu d'Urgell.⁴⁵ His speech had the significance of an official position taken by the Holy See for two reasons. First, it was carefully prepared with the cardinal secretary of state and delivered in Spanish to those present at the audience and broadcast worldwide by Vatican Radio. Second, the pope took an unequivocal position on Spanish affairs, which the Holy See would maintain from that moment on. It represented the culmination of a process of elaboration that had grown in the Vatican as more and more dramatic news arrived about the killings of ecclesiastics, burned churches, and corpses of nuns removed from convents transformed into socialist circles under the indifferent eyes of the Madrid government.⁴⁶ The information came from the reports sent by the Cardinal Primate of the Spanish Church, Isidro Gomá, and from the ecclesiastics who had escaped the anti-clerical violence. This news was already packaged in an interpretative framework that counterposed, on the one hand, the revival of religious life in the backyard of the nationalist camp (and the fervor of its fighters) with, on the other hand, the acts of barbarism committed with Madrid's approval by armed communists from Moscow. It was the failure of the republican authorities to disassociate themselves from the most brutal acts committed against men, women, and property of the Church that determined the Holy See's turn in favor of the insurgents.⁴⁷

In the second half of August, Pius XI considered the possibility of dedicating a pontifical letter to the Spanish question and, together with Pacelli, drew up a draft. That project was abandoned in early September in favor of a speech. Beyond the form, however, the most significant shift concerned the content: the pontiff chose aside. Pius XI denounced "the devastation, massacres, desecrations, [and] slaughters" that had befallen people and property. Second, he defined the fate suffered by the victims of that violence as martyrdom and described that violence as programmatic and "satanic," alluding to the evident plots of international communism. Third, he gave a special blessing to those in Spain who had taken on "the difficult and dangerous task" of defending and restoring the "rights of God and of religion." Finally, he stopped asking for an end to hostilities, as he had been doing until the end of August.

Nonetheless, the Vatican continued to maintain diplomatic relations with the legal government of Madrid. It intervened to prevent a few prelates, such as Cardinal Vidal I Barraquer, from being obliged to sign the "Letter of the Spanish Bishops to the Bishops of the Whole World Concerning the War in Spain" of July 1937.[48] While denouncing the brutal violence to which men and property of the Church had been subjected, Pius XI himself avoided the interpretation that the conflict was a crusade to defend Christianity from the attack of Bolshevism, as had been proposed from the earliest stages, by the clergy and episcopate of Spain, first of all by Cardinal Gomá.[49] His contribution to the religion of the war, which he advanced both in public discourse and in the reports that he sent to Romel, was of significant influence. He also sent many circulars in which he repeatedly requested the Spanish bishops to postpone the publication of the *Mit brennender Sorge*, which was sent to the officials of the Secretariat of State with a provision (dated March 10, 1937) asking that Catholics be made aware of its content as soon as possible.[50] In the same months in which Vatican diplomacy was busy trying to contain the infiltration of Nazi ideology on Spain through concrete interventions toward Franco's authorities, Gomá tried to explain to Pacelli that the publication of *Mit brennender Sorge* risked appearing like censorship of Hitlerian components of the Falange, which would undermine their unity and strength. Thus, in Spain, the encyclical appeared in ecclesiastical bulletins only starting from January 15, 1938. The *Divini Redemptoris*, on the other hand, had been published there since April 1937.[51]

Almost all components of the meaning of the radical and universal clash that the Spanish Civil War was, came to be reflected upon by the Italian Catholic world exclusively from Franco's side. This was a level of support that even went beyond the consent for Mussolini's regime and was anchored in an interpretation of the conflict as a crusade—a final clash for the destiny not only of Spain but of the Church and Western civilization and, therefore, of humanity. The images of places and holy objects desecrated in the regions that had remained faithful to the Republic went around the world and had a symbolic impact far stronger than political reasoning. Therefore, it is not surprising that, generally, the topic of anti-religious persecution is given a central place in the analysis of the civil war. Just as in the Ethiopian case, this purely fascist war with precise ideological characteristics was presented to—and experienced by—Italy's collective imagination as a religious conflict.[52] On the pages of *Civiltà Cattolica*, Father Enrico Rosa wrote, in September 1937, that the struggle fought in Spain against the enemies of religion was even more crucial than the one of the "ancient crusades," since it was "a campaign against foreign subversives and common criminals, men much worse than Muslims or Moors, like the present invaders, in which the perversity of the apostate and the ingenuity of modern man are 'added to malevolence and power.'"[53] In other articles the magazine held that the Spanish republican revolution was not due to "intrinsic causes," but to "extrinsic" ones, namely to the work of the Communist International—a manifestation of "Russian Sovietism."[54] And if this were to triumph in Spain, the magazine portrayed in apocalyptic tones would spread to Portugal, France, North Africa, and South America.[55] There were no references to priests and militant Catholics in the Basque Nationalist Party and the Catholic trade union, who were killed by Franco's nationalist troops because they worked alongside the Popular Front. Not that *Civiltà Cattolica* intended to identify the causes of Francoism appropriately. Probably also to avoid this risk, the analysis of the Spanish reality was conducted on meta-historical and pre-political levels, at times in elusive ways. But the Iberian crisis engraved on the anti-communist struggle (the most important topic to Roman Jesuits since the 1920s) the characteristics of an irreducible antithesis between Rome and Moscow: the communist "devil" was now perceived as omnipresent and, compared to the insurgents, undoubtedly represented the greater of two evils.

In the meantime, the Holy See, too, had moved to Franco's side without rejecting active diplomacy to negotiate peace. First, by recognizing, on August 28, 1937, the Burgos regime as a de facto government. Subsequently, during 1938, by taking a stand against Catholic intellectuals such as Jacques Maritain, Alfred Mendizábal, and Luigi Sturzo. These intellectuals actively opposed the sacralizing reading of the conflict in international public opinion, denounced the bombings of cities and civilian populations, and encouraged committees for peace in Spain. In the columns of *Civiltà Cattolica* of July 1938, Rosa even accused them of "colluding" with the "new barbarians" of the republican government. In the same weeks in which Italy was gearing up to become an anti-Semitic country officially, and when the magazine boasted its foresight in having previously deplored the acquisition of equal civil rights for Jews, Father Rosa offered Madrid's "new barbarians" a dehumanized and global definition: "enemies of religion, indeed of every human order and civilization."[56]

On April 1, 1939, Franco's headquarters issued a statement that the war was over. Within two weeks, a new pontiff, Pius XII, addressed in a radio message the beloved children of Spain, presenting Franco's victory as the result of Providence, invoking divine blessings on the generalissimo, on his government, and the Iberian episcopate. Although Rome had never described the civil war in terms of an anti-communist crusade nor explicitly condemned the choice of Basque Catholics to remain loyal to the Madrid government, Pius XII's appreciation for the Spanish political authorities and bishops who had interpreted the civil war like a crusade represented an indirect legitimation of the concept they had proposed. The nuncio in Madrid, Monsignor Giovanni Cicognani confirmed this. He was delighted in his relations with the Francoist government because the crusade had resulted in a victory for Franco.[57]

Shortly after that, following the aggression of the Axis powers against the USSR, the Italian government would try to exploit the Roman position on the anti-Bolshevik "crusade." It backed the request of the German Reich toward the Vatican for its support of the Nazi crusade against Soviet communism. However, without openly disavowing Operation Barbarossa, the Holy See did not accept to sanctify the attack, nor did it embrace the thesis of the fascist press that this war was aimed at the triumph of Christian principles. To the Holy See, the total war between opposing worldviews, with its combination of death, destruction, genocide, forced displacement of peoples, and civil wars, posed new, dramatic dilemmas. With respect to this, its neutrality, although difficult to pursue, would this time remain the only possible option.

CONCLUSION

In the years following the Conciliation, the Vatican leaders adopted a political strategy toward the fascist regime that played out on two levels. One was open support for the government of Mussolini, manifested or endorsed in public messages. The other was a commitment to neutrality and peacemaking, resulting in a passive confrontation with political powers. The escalation of tensions that swept Europe from the mid-thirties, with the German rearmament, the Italo-Ethiopian conflict, and the Spanish Civil War, showed the limits of this strategy in the context of a totalitarian state. The cautious approaches of the Vatican were presented by the media—in Italy and abroad—substantially as agreeing with the foreign policy lines of the Italian government. This was also possible thanks to the fervent contributions of the upper clergy, who succeeded in sacralizing and conceptualizing Italy's wars as crusades: to expand the Catholic faith in Ethiopia and for the defense of civilization in Spain.

NOTES

1. Refer to articles 2 and 3 of the Lateran Treaty, see http://www.uniset.ca/nold/lateran.htm.

2. Ethiopia also formerly known by the exonym Abyssinia, which was a monarchy that spanned a geographical area in the current states of Ethiopia and Eritrea.

3. Cesare Maria De Vecchi, *Tra papa, duce e re: il conflitto tra Chiesa cattolica e Stato fascista nel diario 1930–1931 del primo ambasciatore del Regno d'Italia presso la Santa Sede* (Roma: Jouvence, 1998), 56.

4. Giovanni Coco, *Il labirinto romano: Il filo delle relazioni Chiesa-Stato tra Pio XI, Pacelli e Mussolini (1929–1939)* (Archivio Segreto Vaticano: Città del Vaticano, 2019), 410.

5. Alberto Guasco, *Il "nuovo Costantino" fascista: Immagini e utilizzi dell'imperatore tra chiesa cattolica e regime*, in *Costantino I. Enciclopedia costantiniana sulla figura e l'immagine dell'imperatore del cosiddetto Editto di Milano 313–2013* (Roma: Treccani, 2013), 3, 469–80.

6. Lucia Ceci, *The Vatican and Mussolini's Italy* (Boston-Leiden: Brill, 2016), 164–71.

7. Pio XI, in *Acta Apostolicae Sedis*, XXI (1929), 113.

8. Roberto Pertici, *Chiesa e Stato in Italia: Dalla Grande Guerra al nuovo Concordato (1914–1984)*. Bologna: Il Mulino, 2009), 152–240.

9. Article 43 of the Concordat recognized the full legitimacy of Italian Catholic Action, providing that it remained outside the political sphere. Nevertheless, Mussolini attempted to reduce the proportions of what appeared to be a *vulnus* of the regime totalitarian claim: Catholic Action, like fascism, had in effect the ambition to shape the soul of youth. This is the reason why tensions occurred in 1931 and 1938. With the exception of these two moments, in the 1930s the Catholic organization traced a path of explicit consent to the fascist State. D. Menozzi and R. Moro (eds.), *Cattolicesimo e totalitarismo: Chiese e culture religiose tra le due guerre mondiali* (Brescia: Morcelliana, 2004).

10. Ceci, *The Vatican and Mussolini's Italy*, 172–78.

11. Alberto Guasco, *Cattolici e fascisti: La Santa Sede e la politica italiana all'alba del regime (1919–1925)* (Bologna: Il Mulino, 2013).

12. John Pollard, *The Vatican and Italian Fascism, 1929–1932: A Study in Conflict* (Cambridge: Cambridge University Press, 1985).

13. Coco, *Il labirinto romano*, 389.

14. Chiara D'Auria, *Fascismo, Santa Sede e Cina nazionalista nella documentazione diplomatica vaticana (1922–1933)* (Soveria Mannelli: Rubbettino, 2018), 244.

15. See, among the most recent studies, Robert Mallet, *Mussolini in Ethiopia, 1919–1935, The Origins of Fascist Italy's African War* (Cambridge: Cambridge University Press, 2015) and Nicola Labanca, *La guerra d'Etiopia 1935–1941* (Bologna: Il Mulino, 2015).

16. Lucia Ceci, *Il papa non deve parlare: Chiesa, fascismo e guerra d'Etiopia* (Roma-Bari: Laterza, 2010).

17. The official version of the speech, revised and edited, was published in the *L'Osservatore Romano* on August 29, 1935. A synoptic edition of the two versions in Lucia Ceci, *La guerra di Etiopia fuori dall'Italia: Le posizioni dei vescovi cattolici europei*, in *L'Impero fascista. Italia ed Etiopia (1935–1941)*, edited by Riccardo Bottoni (Bologna: Il Mulino, 2008), 117–43.

18. Carlo Felice Casula, *Domenico Tardini (1888–1961): L'azione della Santa Sede nella crisi fra le due guerre* (Roma: Studium, 1988), 291–390.

19. Ceci, *Il papa non deve parlare*, 94–107.

20. The Report of Bonifacio Pignatti Morano di Custoza to the head of the government (December 14, 1935), in *Documenti diplomatici italiani*, eighth series, 1935–1939, II, Roma 1991, 836–37.

21. About the Jesuit Pietro Tacchi Venturi, see David I. Kertzer, *The Pope and Mussolini: The Secret History of Pius XI and the Rise of Fascism in Italy* (Random House: New York, 2014), 63–66.

22. S.RR.SS., AA.EE.SS., Italia, pos. 967, vol. II, fols. 260r–262v, P. Tacchi Venturi to Pio XI, Report of the hearing held with H. E. Mussolini on the afternoon of Saturday, December 14, 1935, at 5:30 p.m., at Palazzo di Venezia.

23. The document, entitled *Previsioni e giudizi di Mons. Tardini sul conflitto tra l'Italia e l'Etiopia*, in S.RR.SS., AA.EE.SS., Italia, pos. 967, vol. I bis, fols. 1r–71r. It was published in full in Lucia Ceci, "«Il Fascismo manda l'Italia in rovina». Le note inedite di monsignor Domenico Tardini (September 23–December 13, 1935)," *Rivista storica italiana* (2008): 313–67, notes of December 3, 1935, 342–44.

24. Ceci, *Il papa non deve parlare*, 67–108. The importance of the reference to the crusade in contemporary history: Daniele Menozzi, *"Crociata." Storia di un'ideologia dalla Rivoluzione francese a Bergoglio* (Roma: Carocci, 2020).

25. Petra Terhoeven, *Liebespfand fürs Vaterland. Krieg, Geschlecht und faschistiche Nation in der italianischen Gold und Eheringsammlung, 1935–1936* (Max Niemeyer Verlag: Tübingen, 2003).

26. Giacomo Martina, *I Cattolici di fronte al fascismo*, in "Rassegna di teologia," no. 17 (1976), 175–94.

27. Segreteria di Stato, Sezione per i Rapporti con gli Stati, Archivio Storico, Congregazione degli Affari Ecclesiastici Straordinari (d'ora in poi: S.RR.SS., AA.EE. SS.), Italia, pos. 967, vol. III, 91r, Rassegna stampa del 2 novembre 1935.

28. Ceci, "«Il Fascismo manda l'Italia in rovina». Le note inedite di monsignor Domenico Tardini," 344–45.

29. Andrea Riccardi, *Tardini Domenico*, in *Dizionario storico del movimento cattolico in Italia, 1860–1980*, Francesco Traniello-Giorgio Campanini eds, III/1 (Marietti: Casale Monferrato, 1982), 832–34.

30. Casula, *Domenico Tardini*, 74–80.

31. Ceci, "«Il Fascismo manda l'Italia in rovina». Le note inedite di monsignor Domenico Tardini," 343.

32. *Discorsi di Pio XI* (ed.), italiana a cura di Domenico Bertetto, 3, *1934–1939* (SEI: Torino, 1961), 386–90.

33. Ian Campbell, *The Massacre of Debre Libanos. Ethiopia 1937. The Story of one of Fascism's most Shocking Atrocities* (Addis Ababa: Addis Ababa University Press, 2014).

34. Ceci, *Il papa non deve parlare*, 160–69.

35. Emma Fattorini, *Mussolini and the Vatican. Pope Pius XI and the Speech never made* (Cambridge: Malden Polity, 2011), 163.

36. Raffaella Perin, "Pio XI, l'antisemitismo e le leggi razziste," in *La svolta del 1938. Fascismo, cattolicesimo e antisemitismo*, edited by Andrea Riccardi and Gabriele Rigano (Milano: Guerini e Associati, 2020), 63–76.

37. Giovanni Miccoli, *Santa Sede e Chiesa italiana di fronte alle leggi antiebraiche del 1938*, in *La legislazione antiebraica in Italia e in Europa* (Roma: Camera dei Deputati, 1989), 163–274.

38. Agostino Gemelli, "Per gli uomini di buona volontà," *Vita e Pensiero*, October 1938, 453–54.

39. Laura, Pettinaroli, *La politique russe du Saint-Siège (1905–1939)* (Rome: École française de Rome, 2015), new edition open access http://books.openedition.org/efr/2933.

40. Filippo Frangioni, *Unione Sovietica e guerra di Spagna: comunismo e Santa Sede*, in *Diplomazia senza eserciti. Le relazioni internazionali della Chiesa di Pio XI*, edited by Emma Fattorini (Roma: Carocci, 2013), 19–54.

41. Giorgio Petracchi, *I gesuiti e il comunismo tra le due guerre*, La Chiesa cattolica e il totalitarismo, ed. Vincenzo Ferrone ed. (Firenze: Olschki, 2004), 123–52.

42. "On Furthering the fight against Atheism. A letter addressed to Whole Society, June 19, 1936," *Selected Writings of Father Ledóchowski*, Chicago 1945, p. 610.

43. Elisa Giunipero, *Le inchieste sul comunismo,* in *Gouvernement pontifical sous Pie XI. Pratiques romaines et gestion de l'universel*, edited by Laura Pettinaroli (École française de Rome: Rome 2013), 91–202.

44. "Rassegna infernale. La propaganda comunista mondiale," *La Civiltà Cattolica* 84, no. 4 (1936), 89–98; italics are in the original text.

45. *Discorsi di Pio XI*, 3, 554–62.

46. Alfonso Botti, *Con la Tercera España: Luigi Sturzo, la Iglesia y la Guerra Civil Española* (Alianza Editorial: Madrid, 2020), 111–16.

47. Ibid., 116–18.

48. The famous "Letter of the Spanish Bishops to the Bishops of the Whole World Concerning the War in Spain" supported nationalist movement of Francisco Franco and sacralized the conflict as a war in defense of Western civilization, giving it a universalistic significance. The text was dated July 1, 1937, but it was sent to the Franco press on August 5, and published on August 15, 1937. It is known that the Letter was drafted by the Archbishop of Toledo and subsequently signed by all the Spanish bishops except for Cardinal Francisco Vidal i Barraquer, the metropolitan archbishop of Tarragona. Hilari Raguer, *Gunpowder and Incense: The Catholic Church and the Spanish Civil War* (London and New York: Routledge, 2007), 106–25.

49. Alfonso Álvarez Bolado, *Para ganar la guerra, para ganar la paz* (Madrid: Universidad Pontificia Comillas, 1995).

50. Alfonso Botti, *Santa Sede e influenza nazista nella Spagna della guerra civile, Pio XI: Keywords. International Conference Milan 2009*, edited by Alberto Guasco and Raffaella Perin (Berlin: Lit, 2010), 107–29.

51. Ibid., 124.

52. Javier Rodrigo, "Guerreros y teólogos. Guerra santa y martirio fascista en la literatura de la cruzada del 36," *Hispania*, no. 74 (2014): 555–86.

53. Enrico Rosa, "Il martirio della Spagna e la lettera collettiva dei suoi vescovi," *La Civiltà Cattolica* 88, no. 3 (1937): 481–91 and 486.

54. Petracchi, *I gesuiti e il comunismo tra le due guerre*, 123–52.

55. Leo Lestingi, "Questione del comunismo e difesa della 'civiltà cristiana' nei commenti della 'Civiltà Cattolica' sulla guerra di Spagna (1936–1939)," in *I cattolici italiani e la guerra di Spagna. Studi e ricerche*, edited by Giorgio Campanini (Morcelliana: Brescia, 1987), 99–125.

56. Enrico Rosa, "Grandezza cristiana della Spagna nella sua tragedia religiosa e sociale," *La Civiltà Cattolica* 89, no. 3 (1938): 481–91.

57. José Andrés-Gallego and Antón Martín Pazos (eds.), *Archivo Gomá. Documentos de la Guerra Civil*, XIII (Madrid: Consejo Superior de Investigaciones Científicas, 2010), 350.

SELECTED BIBLIOGRAPHY

Botti, Alfonso. *Con la Tercera España: Luigi Sturzo, la Iglesia y la Guerra Civil Española.* Madrid: Alianza Editorial, 2020.

Ceci, Lucia. *Il papa non deve parlare. Chiesa, fascismo e guerra d'Etiopia.* Roma-Bari: Laterza, 2010.

———. *The Vatican and Mussolini's Italy.* Boston-Leiden: Brill, 2016.

Chamedes, Giuliana. *A Twentieth-Century Crusade. The Vatican Battle to Remake Christian Europe.* Cambridge and London: Harvard University Press, 2019.

Coco, Giovanni. *Il labirinto romano. Il filo delle relazioni Chiesa-Stato tra Pio XI, Pacelli e Mussolini (1929–1939).* Archivio Segreto Vaticano: Città del Vaticano, 2019.

Fattorini, Emma. *Mussolini and the Vatican: Pope Pius XI and the Speech Never Made.* Cambridge: Malden Polity, 2011.

Guasco, Alberto, and Raffaella Perin, eds. *Pio XI: Keywords. International Conference Milan 2009.* Berlin: Lit, 2010.

Kertzer, David I. *The Pope and Mussolini: The Secret History of Pius XI and the Rise of Fascism in Italy.* New York: Random House, 2014.

Pertici, Roberto. *Chiesa e Stato in Italia. Dalla Grande Guerra al nuovo Concordato (1914–1984).* Bologna: Il Mulino, 2009.

Pollard, John. *The Papacy in the Age of Totalitarianism, 1914–1958.* Oxford: Oxford University Press, 2014.

Chapter Five

Vatican Diplomacy and Church Realities in the Philippines during World War II

Pascal Lottaz

On the death[1] of Pope Pius XI in 1939, Manuel L. Quezon wrote a letter of condolence on behalf of the Philippine nation, which he signed as "President of the Philippines."[2] Three days later, he received a warm response from the Vatican's secretary of state, Cardinal Eugenio Pacelli—soon to be Pope Pius XII—thanking the "President of the Philippine Commonwealth" for his expression of sympathy.[3] The marginal difference in Quezon's title was a subtle nuance but characteristic of Pacelli's sense of diplomatic etiquette. The Commonwealth was the Philippines' civil administration, which had been governing the island's internal matters since 1935, in preparation for independence, which the US Congress had already granted, but that awaited the end of a ten-year transitional period. A diplomat for forty years, Pacelli was keenly aware of the importance of diplomatic accuracy. The exchange with Quezon stands in stark contrast to Pacelli's rejection of correspondence with José P. Laurel, who became the president of the Second Republic of the Philippines, 1943 through 1945.[4] The republic was a Japanese satellite state, which was reliant on and allied with the Japanese Empire. The Holy See (HS) never recognized it.

When the Japanese occupation started in early 1942, the Catholic Church did not pack up and leave the Philippines. That was out of the question. The Philippines was the most Christian nation in all of East Asia, with nearly four hundred years of Catholic history, hundreds of churches, parishes, monasteries, and all kinds of Catholic institutions. In 1939, it had a population of sixteen million people, of whom 78.8 percent were Roman Catholic. Including other denominations, the population was 91 percent Christian.[5] Therefore, unlike other European neutrals during the war in the Pacific, the Vatican never had the option of evacuating.[6] The question about a war in Southeast Asia was not if HS diplomacy would be involved, but to what degree? The situation

83

was complex, and despite the Vatican's refusal to legitimize Japanese actions, we find various examples of Catholic support for the occupation of the archipelago. Not only was there a "Religious Section" of the occupation forces, staffed with Japanese priests, laypeople, and even a Japanese bishop, but there were also Filipino priests who, in words and deeds, welcomed Japan.[7]

Nothing exemplifies the delicate relationship between Filipinos, Japanese, and the various layers of the Catholic Church quite as well as figure 5.1. Appearing in a Japanese propaganda magazine in the Philippines, in 1943, the *Shin Seiki* ("New Era") printed a photograph of the Archbishop of Manilla, Michael O'Doherty, together with the Apostolic Delegate to the Philippines, Guglielmo Piani, and the Japanese Bishop of Osaka, Taguchi Yoshigoro. The three men are depicted in conversation right beneath the watchful eyes of Pius XII, hanging over them as a portrait. The caption explained that this was "the date of the founding of the Japanese and Philippine Catholic Churches in the rebuilding of the New Order"—never mind that there was no special "bilateral Catholic body." The example shows how the Japanese tried to use Catholicism to pacify and govern the Philippines strategically. They propagandistically suggested to the Filipinos that Japan embraced the Catholic faith and, vice versa, that Japanese actions were embraced by the entirety of the Catholic Church, from Rome via Tokyo to Manila.

Figure 5.1. Photo of Bishops Talking in Manila, by H. Abe.
Source: Shin Seiki, "A Brief History of Japan–Philippines Catholic Amity for more than 400 Years," no. 3, December 1942, 73 (From the Collection of Hunter Library, Western Carolina University).

The Philippines was the only country in which Japanese propaganda through the Church made sense because of the size of the Catholic flock. For the same reason, the Vatican was considerably attached to the archipelago. Furthermore, the Philippines presents a special case of the Vatican's Second World War diplomacy because of the relative isolation of its church during the Japanese period, which resulted from a mix of Vatican and Japanese policies.

On the one hand, the HS took the firm stance in Asia that it did not recognize political changes that had come about through military force. This non-recognition principle first took shape as a response to Japan's chipping away of Manchuria from China, which, in 1932, was transformed into Japan's first satellite state under the name "Manchukuo." There, like in the Philippines, the Vatican would refuse to deal diplomatically with the governing regime while maintaining a network of Church representatives for the sake of communication and caretaking of local Catholics. This formula was the most beneficial option for a neutral city-state that had to remain impartial between belligerents without passively lending support to aggressor regimes or completely giving up on the local members of its Church.[8] This stood in stark contrast to the Vatican's diplomatic actions toward Fascist Italy and its war in Abyssinia (today's Ethiopia) around the same time.[9]

The situation ten years later in the Philippines was a balancing act of exceptional sensitivity. For instance, after the Japanese had entered Manila, the US requested that the Holy See withdraw its apostolic delegate, Piani, not to lend diplomatic legitimacy to Japan's occupation. However, doing so would have eliminated a potential communication channel and hurt the Vatican's standing in the capital. The HS had to clarify to the United States that it had been its "constant desire that the apostolic delegates remain in their place since their task is all the more useful, the more difficult and delicate the circumstances are."[10] Eventually, Piani stayed. However, he did so only for the purpose of protecting the local flock of Catholics, not as a diplomatic representative to the Japanese authorities.

On the other hand, the Japanese occupation forces did not allow direct contact between the HS and its Church in the Philippines for reasons illustrated in this chapter. Piani was only allowed to communicate with Rome through the office of the apostolic delegate in Tokyo, Archbishop Paolo Marella, and even then, only in the Japanese language, which naturally meant that no private or even secret communication was possible. The State Secretariat was aware of this and resented the lack of a secure and confidential channel to the Philippines.[11] This made the Philippine case considerably different from the Japanese Empire (which included Korea and Taiwan). Apostolic Delegate Marella, in Tokyo, could always directly contact the State Secretariat.

Furthermore, in 1942, the first Japanese ambassador was appointed to the Vatican. That affair was itself a diplomatic tightrope act because the Allies interpreted the Vatican's acceptance of a Japanese ambassador to the Holy See right after Pearl Harbor as an insult. However, for the Vatican, the elevation of diplomatic relations was a blessing. Ambassador Harada Ken's presence inside the walls of the Holy City strengthened the communication channels with Japan.[12] For instance, it allowed for soliciting the help of the ambassador in petitioning Japan for a direct communication channel with Piani—albeit without success.[13] Hence, with Japan, the normal vertical integration of the local Church and Vatican diplomacy was guaranteed. The situation was different for Southeast Asia.

The historical events surrounding the occupation of the Philippines and the actions of the Church have been researched to various degrees from the sides of Japan,[14] the Allies,[15] the Philippines,[16] and even the Vatican.[17] What is lacking, however, is an assessment of the occurrences in the light of diplomacy and policy. To what extent were specific actions part of an HS strategy, and what followed from these policies? How far did institutional influence go, and at what point did personal decisions make a difference? And, lastly, what does this reveal about the neutrality of the Vatican?

In the absence of direct diplomatic engagement, the Church's fate in the Philippines was mainly in the hands of Catholic clerics on the ground, including Allied, neutral, and Japanese nationals. This chapter seeks to untangle the situation by clarifying the fault lines between what I call "Church realities" on the one hand and "Vatican diplomacy," on the other. Secondary sources are utilized together with (published) diplomatic correspondence of the HS about the occupation to contrast the occurrences in Manila with the Vatican's reactions. This research is limited by the sparsity of primary sources on HS diplomacy toward the Philippines, as the archival holdings of the Vatican could not be consulted. Still, the chapter provides a careful analysis of the published diplomatic correspondence in the "Actes et documents du Saint-Siège relatifs à la Seconde Guerre Mondiale" (ADSSGM). The contrast of those documents with the events in the Philippines helps to gain an approximate understanding of the difference between Church realities and Vatican diplomacy.

BACKGROUND: CATHOLICISM AND NATIONALISM IN THE PHILIPPINES

It is hard to overstate the impact of the four hundred years of Catholic doctrine on Filipino society. Historian David J. Steinberg went as far as to argue that the "ecclesiastical power of the Church rather than the temporal power of the Spanish crown was the great Westernizing force in the Philippines."[18] At the same time, however, the secularization of the state structure began relatively early, manifested most prominently in article 5 of the Malolos Constitution, the founding document of the short-lived First Philippine Republic (1898–1901). Article 5 mandated freedom of religion and the separation of church and state—a highly controversial proposal—which passed with a majority of only one vote in the revolutionary congress and thereby predated even the French concept of Laïcité by six years. It was inspired by similar concepts in other former European colonies, most notably in the US, albeit before the US became the Philippines' colonial power.[19] Hand in hand with this development went the first Church schism in East Asia, when the nationalist faction of Catholics split from Madrid and Rome, incorporating what became the Philippine Independent Church in 1902 (a.k.a. the "Aglipayan Church"). Most of these developments were caused by grievances about the discrimination of local Filipino clergy by the Catholic Church of Spain. In fact, the wide-spread indignation of indigenous elites over the execution of three Filipino priests in 1872 was a major driver of the entire movement that came to include secular nationalists, most famously the poet José Rizal, whose execution, in 1896, only further fanned the flames of the independence movement. In short, Catholicism and Nationalism in the Philippines are two inseparable parts of the same story. Crucially, the Filipinization of the Catholic Church was a long-standing issue for nationalists, which, outside of the Aglipayan Church, was not achieved.

The Spanish–American War of 1898, and the immediately adjacent Philippine–American War (1899–1902) that destroyed the First Republic, diminished Catholicism's role in state affairs. Not only did the new US administration implement the separation of church and state, but it strong-armed the Catholic Church into appointing American—or at least non-Spanish—clerics as heads of Catholic institutions, including four American bishops. Furthermore, it encouraged the arrival of protestant missionaries as a counterweight to the Catholics. However, slightly paradoxical, that period also provided far more possibilities for the Vatican's direct influence on the Philippines, because the withdrawal of the Spanish dissolved the *Patronato Real*, which gave the Spanish monarchs the sole right to exercise power over state *and* church affairs. It became possible for the Vatican for the first time, in 1901, to appoint an apostolic delegate who arrived in Manila a year later.[20]

Considering these developments around the turn of the century, it comes as no surprise that when the Japanese entered Manila forty years later, they found a Catholic Church that was still disproportionately dominated by white clergy. According to Japanese military sources, out of 3,901 clerics (ordained and secular), 39 percent were non-Filipino.[21] Eighteen of the highest offices of the Church were held by foreign-born men.²² Also, the distribution of power in the dioceses was characteristic. Although seven out of the ten archdioceses were headed by Filipino archbishops, the two most significant positions (the archbishop of Manila and the apostolic delegate) were held by an Irishman and an Italian.²³

CHURCH REALITIES: THE RELIGIOUS SECTION

The Philippines was drawn into the tempest of the Second World War immediately after Japan's attack on Pearl Harbor. It became a target like Hong Kong, Singapore, and the Dutch East Indies, after Japan had declared war on their colonial powers on December 8, 1941. Catholic clergy in the Philippines had expected belligerency to break out for a while, but the speed with which the Japanese advanced and overpowered the American forces was a shock to many.²⁴ There was no intense fight for the capital, as the US military declared it an "Open City"—that is, undefended, to spare the lively metropolis from destruction. Unopposed, Japanese troops entered Manila on January 2, 1942, establishing the Japanese Military Administration (JMA) of the Philippines. Although battles with US troops would not cease until May, and guerilla warfare would continue throughout the occupation period, the JMA became the most powerful administrative body on the archipelago for three years.

Naturally, preparations for the occupation had begun earlier, including considerations for the Catholic Church. The Japanese were well aware of the centrality of faith in pacifying the local population and ruling the islands through the collaboration of the Catholic elite. To that end, the army general staff formed the "Religious Section" (*shukyo-han*) as part of the Fourteenth Philippine Expeditionary Army. Its members were Japanese clergy and laypeople, tasked to spread JMA propaganda, framed as "explaining Japan's real intentions" in this "war of liberation." The section was active from January 1942 until late 1943.²⁵

For the historical evaluation of Church activities in the Philippines, the recruitment and the activities of the section is a particularly delicate affair because it involved high ranking members of Catholic officialdom with ties to the Vatican, including the archbishop of Tokyo, Doi Tatsuo, Bishop Taguchi, of Osaka, and the Apostolic Delegate in Japan, Paolo Marella.²⁶ The timing of events, the reactions of the actors involved, and the information that was shared with them are all important factors to consider. Also, a critical appreciation of the sources is essential, especially since the only information we have about the events in the Japanese Church stems from eyewitness reports. One comes from Shimura Tatsuya, a direct aide to Archbishop Doi, and the other one is the documentation (in Japanese) of the Religious Section, drafted by Taguchi. Historian Terada Takefumi has already evaluated both sources, but they still merit a closer look. Especially Shimura's claims are problematic because he wrote them down only in 1971—thirty years after they occurred—from memory, and he himself says that his account "is not a history book" but written to attest to the occurrences rather than the details.[27]

Shimura wrote that already on August 10, 1941—four months before Pearl Harbor—the Army requested a meeting with Doi and Taguchi. Only Taguchi from Osaka headed the call while Archbishop Doi sent Shimura in his stead. Shimura then reports that he had been worried that the Army, whom he had been afraid of, was about to communicate their opposition to the Catholic Church in Japan. But, to his surprise, they requested the Church's help in the planned occupation of the Philippines since a war with the US and Britain was (in their view) inevitable. The army asked them to supply fifty priests and one hundred fifty lay people to join the occupation forces in the Religious Section. Importantly, Shimura also states that the army commanders made him and Taguchi promise absolute secrecy and that he felt threatened that they might get killed if they shared the secret. Shimura explains that the next day he and Taguchi held a meeting with Doi and Marella in which they informed their superiors of the army's request. It was decided that although the request could not be heeded as an official Church policy, refusing it could mean great danger to the Japanese Church and that, as a compromise, Doi would send out Taguchi to recruit clerics who would want to join the army voluntarily. By November, Shimura had enlisted only three priests, five seminarians, and five lay people who were then mobilized by the army, becoming civilian employees of the military for a one-year term. Before the end of November, the volunteers were sent to Taiwan, where they waited for the looming invasion. Due to this readiness, they arrived in Manila only two days after the main occupation force, on January 4, 1942.[28]

Shimura's account is probably accurate on the timing and the overall developments of the Church deciding to search for volunteers, but it is questionable if he and Taguchi, in fact, shared the information about the planned invasion of the Philippines with Doi and Marella. If this information was accurate, it would mean that a Vatican diplomat, Marella, possessed definitive proof of Japanese plans for an attack on the United States, but for that, we lack an independent verification from the side of the HS. Considering the gravity of the situation—the proof that Japan was preparing an attack and the request for direct Church involvement—it is unlikely that Marella would not have sought to communicate the request to the HS. After all, Marella had been worried about a US–Japanese war for at least a year. Also, he had been reporting the

Japanese Foreign Ministry's positions to the HS and complained about the Army continually trying to use Japanese clergy for their purposes in China.[29]

Although it cannot be ruled out that Marella was informed about the war plans against the Philippines and kept it a secret or that he did inform the HS and that proof of this remains to be found, the available communication between Marella and the State Secretariat does not indicate that he was aware of the preparations. On November 29, for instance, Marella sent a report to the HS about an audience with the new Japanese foreign minister, Togo Shigenori, in which he reported, unquestioningly and as a matter-of-fact, that Togo had assured him of the pacifist intentions of Japan concerning the US.[30] Marella did not record doubts or disbelief about these assurances. Although Marella was known to hold rather Japanophile opinions, had he indeed known of the preparations for an invasion of the Philippines, that would throw new light on the apostolic delegate's role.[31] It is more likely that the details about the impending attack were not shared with him but that he was only informed about the army's request for Catholic support in occupied territories, which at this point included large parts of China.[32] It is not unlikely that Shimura and Taguchi would have kept the war plans of the army secret from their superiors, or at least from Marella.

Within days of their arrival, the Religious Section went to work on gaining the trust and cooperation of the local Catholic population, through visits of Catholic leaders, including Archbishop O'Doherty and Apostolic Delegate Piani, by holding masses and goodwill events, and—not unimportantly—by intervening toward the JMA and freeing Catholic enemy national clergy from the prisoner of war (POW) camps.[33] They were to be put under house arrest and furnished with documentation that would allow them to continue their spiritual work in the communities they served. The section would further ensure that Japanese troops did not enter or appropriate catholic premises, especially churches, and try to keep local clergy from harm.[34] Eyewitnesses from some of the religious orders confirmed years after the liberation of the Philippines that the Japanese were visibly keen on gaining the support from local Catholics in the attempt to win over the Filipino population for their cause of the Co-Prosperity Sphere and that, hence, the occupation forces remained overall benign to Catholic clergy at the beginning of the occupation.[35] However, moderation was only possible in places where the Religious Section was present. Torture and the murdering of clerics repeatedly happened outside Manila, including the murder of a German-born naturalized Filipino bishop, William Finnemann.[36]

All in all, trust was difficult to gain. For his part, Archbishop O'Doherty refused to lend his office to the propaganda efforts. In a meeting with the JMA on January 7, 1942, O'Doherty drew a clear line between the spiritual work of the Philippine Catholic Church and the temporal matters of politics on which it had nothing to say. According to the meeting minutes, the archbishop held that "the people and country were accustomed to the separation of church and state and that while the clergy exercised authority in things spiritual, it had always been the policy to refrain from taking part in matters purely political as enjoined by canon law; ... that he and his clergy would be glad to take part in anything which was for the good of the people, provided it was not contrary to canon law."[37] It borders on irony that the archbishop used the argument of the separation of church and state to defend his resistance to closer collaboration with the Japanese—it was the Catholic Church that had resisted the secularization of the Philippines for the longest time.[38] But in this context, it came in handy, and the archbishop did not grow tired of using it. At another meeting ten days later, he reinvigorated his point that he was, for institutional reasons, unable to help: "The Holy Father has expressly and strictly forbidden us from engaging in any other profession or activity but the religious. We are a company apart. We are willing to leave civil and political matters to minds better fitted or at least more interested in the pursuits of the world."[39] His refusal to lend his office to the Japanese went as far as even rejecting the distribution of leaflets, arguing that "I'm afraid that the nature of our work. Which is purely spiritual and has nothing to do with political matters, makes impossible my acceding to your request. My commission from the Holy Father is to teach the Catholic Religion, and I am expressly forbidden by the Holy Father from interfering in civil matters."[40] There was little to gain from the archbishop of Manila, who was soon placed under house arrest.

In response, the Religious Section requested the help of Taguchi, who, in the meantime, had been ordained bishop of Osaka. He arrived in Manila in March 1942. Not only was he more successful in his communication with O'Doherty and Piani, but he also became the main intellectual behind the setting of strategic goals for the section by formulating concrete policy actions that should be taken toward the Church and the Holy See. The four areas he outlined in several documents can be summarized as (1) furthering religious instructions among the population and at schools, (2) the protection of Church personnel and property, (3) the "Filipinization" of the Catholic clergy, and (4) concluding a concordat or a similar instrument with the HS.

The last two points merit special attention, as they directly touch on the triangular relationship between Japan, the Philippines, and the Vatican. The "Filipinization" of the Church was not only a wish of the JMA, who became convinced that far more foreign priests than only O'Doherty needed to be replaced. Considering the century-old grievances of nationalist Filipinos, it comes as no surprise that numerous local clergymen supported these attempts. The most official push for this came in March 1944, when Laurel took to the matter, writing a second letter directly to Pius XII to demand the replacement of foreign clerics in the Philippines.[41] Also, this letter remained unanswered.

On the issue of an agreement with the Vatican, Bishop Taguchi was all too aware of the centrality of something resembling a concordat if either the Filipinization of the clergy or the harmonious coexistence of the Church and Japan's Co-Prosperity Sphere was to be achieved. Not just the issue of the recognition of the JMA or later the Philippine Republic were crucial, but the power to appoint bishops, draft curricula for pupils, or decide on the teaching of laypeople, were beyond the episcopal powers of O'Doherty or Piani and needed a formal agreement. Besides, to safeguard the rights and privileges of the Catholic Church in the Philippines, a concordat or at least a *modus vivendi* (a temporary agreement) would be a crucial instrument. Alas, despite Taguchi's best efforts, the concordat never left the planning stage. On the one hand, that was due to the red lines of the Vatican on negotiations with occupied territories or puppet regimes, but on the other hand, also the JMA was not interested in granting too much scope for external interference with their propaganda efforts. It was one thing to leave Catholic clergy—even those of enemy nationality—a relatively free hand in implementing religious activities. But it was a completely different matter to open an independent diplomatic channel in a territory that the Japanese military designated as a warzone. For the same reason, Piani was forbidden from communicating directly with the State Secretariat and had to relay his messages to the apostolic delegate in Tokyo. It is still noteworthy, however, that Taguchi, in fact, created a nineteen-article draft for a concordat.[42]

It would be wrong to allege that Bishop Taguchi was principally working for the interests of the Japanese occupation forces. The documents he drafted show that while he was working in support of the strategic goals of the JMA, he was concerned with the well-being of the Catholic Church in the Philippines. Assuming that he believed that Japan's presence in the Philippines and the Co-Prosperity Sphere would be a reality in Southeast Asia for decades to come, his proposals would have been the cornerstones for the continued existence of the Catholic Church under Japanese hegemony in the region. History, of course, would go another way. Taguchi left the Philippines shortly after the establishment of the Republic, the Religious Section was dissolved, and while some more Japanese clerics arrived to teach Japanese and to remain in contact with priests and nuns, the further the war turned against Japan, the rougher the JMA started treating the Philippines Church.

DIPLOMACY: ALL QUIET IN THE EASTERN FRONT

The outbreak of the Pacific War caused problems in the communication between the HS and its Apostolic Delegates. In Tokyo, Marella could still send telegrams, but his more extensive reports that were sent by postal mail got delayed significantly. One of the final reports before the beginning of hostilities was sent at the end of November and did not reach the HS until late March. Only relatively short and constrained messages through the telegraphic system remained viable. In Manila, the situation was even worse for Piani, whom the JMA forbid from sending any communication directly to the HS but required his letters to go through Marella in Tokyo and be written in Japanese. Communication was hence greatly constraint and delayed. The first message from the Philippines that reached the State Secretariat on June 5 was a letter that Piani wrote on March 3. Marella delivered the content of the message in Italian, quoting Piani, but obviously paraphrasing him:

> it seems they [JMA] are willing to respect the Church and regular religious affairs in a spirit of conciliation. . . . It is not unlikely that some form of an agreement has to be reached. I, therefore, believe it to be appropriate that the Apostolic Delegate in Tokyo asked for instructions from the Holy See for possible religious accommodation in the Philippines. There are, in fact, serious questions, such as ecclesiastical property, ecclesiastical circumscription, religious teaching, matrimonial matters, etc. The Holy See can be informed through the [Japanese] Minister residing at the Holy See about the directive principles which the Japanese government intends to apply to regulate the relations with the Philippine Church, and the Minister himself shall investigate if the above-mentioned government intends to stipulate some sort of special convention under the form of a concordat or a modus vivendi.
>
> I would also believe it appropriate that such affairs should preferably be dealt with by the Apostolic Delegate in Tokyo since he is in a position to easily communicate with the [Japanese] Government and the Vatican.[43]

When reading this document, it is necessary to consider its context. Although Piani drafted the original message, he did so, knowing that it would be redacted by the JMA. Later, it was paraphrased by Marella in Italian, and here his words are reproduced in English (translated by the author). Nevertheless, a few insights about the diplomatic side of the occupation can still be reconstructed. For one, Piani apparently thought it would be wise to communicate that institutional questions of the Philippine Church need settlement through the HS. Since he certainly was aware of the surveillance of his letters, we must assume that his communication with Marella was as much aimed for consumption by the JMA as it was intended for the Vatican. Therefore, the letter can be regarded as a strategy to establish the limits of his office and thereby the limits of what the JMA could expect to gain through the highest representatives of the Church in Manila. Similarly, the requests concerning Ambassador Harada and the handling of official agreements through Marella must be understood in the same context. Piani tactically disempowered his own standing with the HS to deflect pressure from the Religious Section and the JMA on his office.

Secondly, that Piani included the observations for the potential necessity of a concordat or a *modus vivendi* make it likely that he agreed with Taguchi that negotiations with Japan to settle religious matters in the Philippines should be considered. The timing of Piani's writing, March 3, two days after Taguchi's arrival in Manila, and the reference to a *modus vivendi* if a concordat was not possible, are ominous. It is precisely the formulation that Taguchi used in the internal documents he drafted for the Religious Section. Lastly, the lack of any indication that Japanese clerics were present in the Philippines by either Piani or Marella seems to indicate that Piani did not deem this information communicable and that also Marella was either unaware of it or he, too, thought it was better not to inform the HS of the matter.

Unfortunately, Cardinal Maglione's answer to Marella and Piani is not part of the ADSSGM.[44] However, we know that the HS replied immediately from another one of Marella's telegrams dated June 8, in which he informed Maglione that, "according to his wishes," he instructed Piani of the following: "it is up to him [Piani] to enlighten local civil and military authorities. I respectfully recommended him, as a brother [in faith], to use all his authority to give Philippine Churches unity . . . with unifying opinion, actions regarding Bishops, Clergy, Religious Orders, being a necessary condition for commanding the respect of the military authority."[45] In other words, Marella told Piani to do everything in his power for his Church but without any special sanctioning from the HS and only within the limits of his office. It is a clear sign that the HS tacitly approved of Piani's strategy to delegate diplomatic matters away from the Philippines and not to serve as an interlocutor with the occupation forces.

It remains to assess the Vatican's views on the Japanese Religious Section, of which only little was known to the HS at the time. In fact, the first indications of the State Secretariat learning about Bishop Taguchi's presence in Manila can only be found for September 1942, when a diplomat of the Panama Ggvernment who had resided in Manila returned home and informed the apostolic delegate in Washington about the fact.[46] Although it is not impossible that the HS had heard rumors before, the news from Washington coincide with efforts from the HS to reestablish direct communication with Piani. That included, on October 3, for the first time, a demarche toward

Ambassador Harada. The State Secretariat implored him to use his good office and standing with his government to bring about direct communication with Piani.[47] The efforts failed.[48] Nevertheless, they serve as an indication that the HS got increasingly worried about the situation in Manila.

It is ironic that at nearly the same time, on October 12, the inhabitants of Manila would read in *The Tribune*, a popular daily newspaper that became a notorious mouthpiece for the JMA, that the Vatican was "Glad over Church Affairs" in the Philippines.[49] The short article (mis)informed its readers that "Competent Vatican circles today declared their complete satisfaction with the way Japan was looking after the interests of the Catholic churches in the Philippines. . . . It was gratefully noted by these quarters that Monsignor Taguti, Japanese Catholic bishop of Osaka, had proceeded to the Philippines to ascertain information about the interests of the Catholic churches there."[50] In fact, the opposite was the case. The reports about the presence of a Japanese bishop in Manila were becoming a diplomatic liability for the Vatican. On October 27, the State Secretariat was forced to react to a memorandum from the US representative about a (false) rumor that Taguchi had been elevated to the rank of a bishop and sent to Manila for the purpose of replacing Archbishop O'Doherty.[51] In reply to US representative Tittmann, Maglione made it clear:

1. That Mgr. Taguchi was promoted to the episcopate before the outbreak of the war between the United States and Japan.
2. That the Holy See did not send Mgr. Taguchi to the Philippines; but having learned from Washington that he had gone there, we asked the apostolic delegate in Tokyo for the reason for this trip. The apostolic delegate replied that Mgr. Taguchi has been mobilized and sent to Manila by the military authorities and that, apparently, his service will last for the entirety of the current year. The apostolic delegate himself has already raced to intervene and to obtain the return of Mgr. Taguchi to his diocese.
3. That the Holy See has not thought about nor will it think about replacing the archbishop of Manila.[52]

This was a strong rebuttal of the fears that the Vatican might tacitly support Japanese actions in Southeast Asia and a clear reaffirmation of its principle that for the time of hostilities, no official changes of ecclesiastical stewardship of local churches was acceptable to suit the preferences of the belligerents. Delicately, Maglione also recorded that he had informed Tittmann in the same discussion "that by demanding the substitution of Monsignor Riberi (Jerusalem), Monsignor Testa (Mombasa), and Monsignor Nuti (Egypt), the UK has created an ugly precedent and a pretext for others to do the same!" The HS was unwilling to replace clerics in the Japanese-occupied territories, but neither was it ready to do so in territories controlled by the allies, and the HS worried obviously about both sides setting examples for each other.[53]

THE SECOND REPUBLIC: AT THE INTERSECTION OF DIPLOMACY AND REALITY

On October 14, 1943, a Japan-friendly regime under José P. Laurel declared the independence of the Philippines and signed a pact of alliance with Tokyo. But the JMA did not leave the Philippines. Only the Religious Section, including Taguchi, had already gone back to Japan. A group of nineteen Japanese nuns and laywomen remained for one more year, the "Catholic Women's Religious Corps," who engaged in goodwill activities toward influential Filipino societies and Japanese language instruction.[54] Overall, however, the moderating effect that the representatives of Japan's Catholic Church exerted on the JMA waned in the second half of 1943. In June, the army confiscated the campus of the Ateneo de Manila, a Jesuit university. Other properties were also appropriated, and incarcerations of Catholic clergy suspected of espionage or collaboration with the guerillas became frequent.[55] Clergymen and nuns of enemy nationality were now arrested, and most of them brought to the civilian internment camp of Los Baños, south of Manila. The news of this only reached the HS in summer 1944.[56]

The Laurel government had unsuccessfully tried to solicit the recognition of the Vatican. The State Secretariat would merely acknowledge receipt of the message to its delegate in Tokyo, but nothing more. Even after Ambassador Harada used his office to approach the HS about the matter, Cardinal Maglione would simply explain to him that the HS "does not give recognition to states and new governments emerging through and being the cause of the war."[57] However, a few days later, in the same message in which Maglione communicates these affairs to Marella in Tokyo, he also encloses instructions to be given to Piani about his role in this delicate situation. Marella should inform Piani

> on behalf of the Congregation of Bishops [*SC Concistoriale*], in order to protect Catholic religious interests [in the Philippines], as professed by the vast majority of the Filipino people, that bishops can deal with local authorities in ecclesiastical affairs and that he [Piani] himself, not having a diplomatic character, can, if necessary, take up the interests of purely ecclesiastical affairs with the authorities, unofficially and de facto.[58]

These directions were, without doubt, intentionally kept vague. On the one hand, the HS stated the obvious that Piani had no diplomatic powers to conclude agreements or make official ecclesiastical decisions. That is an explicit reminder that the apostolic delegate in Manila could not speak or act in the name of the HS. On the other hand, the second part still authorized him to deal with Church matters pragmatically at his own discretion. It was the same stance that the HS had been practicing for more than ten years already toward Manchukuo, China, and other occupied territories, like Burma. The State Secretariat and the Propaganda Congregation were both firmly adhering to that principle.[59] The discretionary power to deal with ecclesiastical affairs as needed (without the knowledge or consent of the HS) enabled Piani to react to the increasing pressure that was put on the Philippine Church. For instance, the number of interned clergy at Los Baños became so great that he made it into an *ad-hoc diocese*, naming the Dutch national, Constant Jurgens, its bishop.[60] The formation of a diocese would have been well beyond his powers had it not been for the tacit agreement of the Vatican.

For the last sixteen months of the war, the work of the Church, both from Japan and locally, was mostly concerned with humanitarian and spiritual work. Although the Vatican never became a protecting power for any of the belligerents, the various foreign ministries of the Allies did approach the HS repeatedly for its help in communicating and carrying for its civilian and military internees in the occupied territories, including the Philippines.[61] That had to do with the church's privileged position since it was physically able to access the JMA, something that the protecting powers often could not do. Although it was custom that the jurisdiction of protecting powers extended into areas under occupation by a belligerent, Japan did not extend that right to the neutrals who protected its enemies' interests. Japan recognized protecting powers only in Japan itself and in the colonies under its sway before the war. For instance, although Switzerland acted as protecting power for the US and Britain in Japan and could visit (to some extend) the civilian and military POWs of these countries, that did not apply to the Philippines since Japan simply declared it as a "warzone," and thereby excluded the protecting powers from acting there. Even after the nominal independence of the Laurel Republic, no amelioration was possible because, like the HS, Switzerland did not recognize the new regime and could therefore not establish diplomatic relations. The same problem stood in the way of the Red Cross visiting POWs. Only in late 1944, the Japanese side signaled their willingness to grant the Red Cross permission to visit internment camps in the Philippines, but only as a bargaining chip to demand the same from the US in the pacific islands it had recently captured.[62] In this situation, the Vatican was in a unique position to have clerics in the territory who could approach the JMA.

Although not much did come of the official efforts of the Vatican to serve as a humanitarian go-between for POWs, the HS itself and the clerics on the ground tried to extend a helping hand.[63]

In the end, however, also the Church in the Philippines could do little but evacuate its premises once the war situation became precarious. Piani left his residence in early 1945, seeking shelter in a Jesuit house outside of central Manila. That was a stroke of luck as his residence would burn to the ground during the battle for the city in February. Although the Japanese commander in chief, General Yamashita Tomoyuki, ordered his troops to withdraw to the mountains, insubordinate officers refused, which led to horrible bloodshed in the streets of Manila. During the month-long fight, the worst atrocities of the entire three years were committed by Japanese soldiers against the local and foreign population. More than one hundred thousand civilians lost their lives. Most of the city was destroyed, including countless churches, monasteries, and other religious facilities. The HS protested heavily toward Ambassador Harada once the official news reached Pius XII in July, but the tragedy had already concluded by that time.[64]

CONCLUSION

This chapter assessed the relationship between Church realities and Vatican diplomacy during Japan's occupation of the Philippines. It showed that the Holy See's relationship with the Philippines was more delicate and confusing than that with Japan proper, not only because of the warfare but because of the lack of direct communication between the HS and Manila. Furthermore, since the JMA demanded the support of the Japanese Catholic Church during the occupation, Japanese clergy, foremost Bishop Taguchi, played an essential role in the triangular relationship between Manila, Tokyo, and the Vatican. This study also shows that the archbishop of Manila, as well as the apostolic delegate, tried to deflect JMA pressure on their offices. O'Doherty by arguing that Vatican policy forbids him from engaging in temporal matters, and Piani by requesting that the delegate in Tokyo, Marella, oversee negotiations concerning the Philippines. Those, however, never took place since the Vatican refused to recognize political changes in Asia that came out of warfare. The situation left the Philippine Church mostly isolated, which the Vatican acknowledged and tried to remedy, in 1943, by empowering Piani to overstep his ecclesiastical powers for the sake of guiding the local church but without speaking in the name of the HS toward the Laurel regime. Overall, the Vatican did not support Japan's occupation and reacted strongly against the abuse of the Japanese Catholic Church for the war effort. Japan's Military received only limited collaboration from the side of Japan's Catholic clergy. The few ordained Japanese who did venture to the Philippines did so out of their own volition and not due to Church policies. Among Filipino clergy, collaboration was strongest on the issue of "Filipinization" of the Church, which is no surprise since that had been an issue in the country for more than seventy years already. Overall, the Vatican adopted a wait-and-see strategy toward the occupation. The JMA, on the other hand, tried to actively abuse the image of the Catholic faith for its propaganda. In terms of Vatican neutrality, the Philippine case shows that in East Asia, the Vatican tried first and foremost to protect the interest of its churches and the Catholic flock and that the non-recognition principle was the primary tool through which it implemented its duty of neutrality in temporal affairs, as based on the Lateran Pacts.

NOTES

1. Assistant Professor at the Waseda Institute for Advanced Study, Tokyo. This chapter benefitted from the kind support of, Jesus Llanto, a researcher and writer based in the Philippines.

2. "Letter of President Quezon on the Death of Pope Pius XI," February 11, 1939. Government of the Philippines, *Official Gazette*. Retrieved January 22, 2021, last accessed on February 10, 2021 at www.officialgazette.gov.ph/1939/02/11/letter-of-president-quezon-on-the-death-of-pope-pius-xi.

3. Ibid.

4. Laurel wrote a letter to Pius XII on October 14, 1943, transmitted via Piani, of which Cardinal Maglione acknowledged receipt. He instructed Piani via Marella to convey the HS's thanks to Laurel, but without a letter and without indicating recognition; See ADSSGM, vol. 7, doc. 436, p. 671, "Le prsésident de Philippines Laurel au cardinal Maglione" (Manila, October 14, 1943) and doc. 446, p. 681, "Le cardinal Maglione au délégué apostolique à Tokyo Marella" (Vatican, October 25, 1943). In 1944, Maglione denied that the acknowledgment amounted to anything more but basic courtesy. See ADSSGM, vol. 10, doc. 8, p. 88, "Le délégué aposotolique a Londres Godfrey au cardinal Maglione" (January 10, 1944).

5. Takefumi Terada, "Christianity and the Japanese Occupation," in *Philippines-Japan Relations*, edited by Setsuho Ikehata and Lydia Yu-Jose (Manila: Ateneo De Manila University Press, 2003), 215.

6. Compare this with the cases of Spain, Sweden, or Switzerland. See Pascal Lottaz, "Neutral States and Wartime Japan: The Diplomacy of Sweden, Spain, and Switzerland toward the Empire" (National Graduate Institute for Policy Studies, 2018).

7. See, for example, the actions of Bishop Guerrero as documented in Takefumi Terada, "The Religious Propaganda Program for Christian Churches," in *The Philippines under Japan: Occupation Policy and Reaction*, edited by Setsuho Ikehata and Ricardo Trota Jose (Manila: Ateneo De Manila University Press, 1999), 240–41; see

also the statements of Filippino Bishops in Alfredo G. Parpan, "The Japanese and the Philippine Church, 1942–1945," *Philippine Studies* 37, no. 4 (1989): 251–53.

8. Pascal Lottaz and Florentino Rodao, "The Vatican, WWII, and Asia: Lessons of Neutral Diplomacy," in *Notions of Neutralities*, edited by Pascal Lottaz and Herbert Reginbogin (Lanham: Lexington, 2019).

9. See chapter 4 in this volume, "Neutrality to the Test: The Vatican and the Fascist Wars of the Thirties," by Lucia Ceci.

10. ADSSGM, vol. 5, doc. 328, p. 514, "Notes de la Secrétairerie d'Etat" (Vatican, April 8, 1942).

11. ADSSGM, vol. 11, doc. 127, p. 240, "Le délégué aposotolique à Tokyo Marella à Mgr Ottaviani" (Tokyo, March 24, 1944).

12. Lottaz and Rodao, "The Vatican, WWII, and Asia."

13. ADSSGM, vol. 5, doc. 497, p. 735, "La Secrétairerie d'Etat à la Délégation spéciale du Japon" (Vatican, October 3, 1942), and vol. 7, doc. 446, p. 681.

14. In English see Setsuho Ikehata and Lydia Yu-Jose, *Philippines–Japan Relations* (Manila: Ateneo De Manila University Press, 2003); Setsuho Ikehata and Ricardo Trota Jose, *The Philippines under Japan: Occupation Policy and Reaction* (Manila: Ateneo De Manila University Press, 1999).

15. For example, James Carroll, "Sentenced to Death—Destined for Life: Catholic Religious and Japanese Occupation," *American Catholic Studies* 113, nos. 3/4 (2002); David Joel Steinberg, "Philippine Collaboration in World War II" (Manila: Solidaridad, 1967); A. V. H. Hartendorp, *The Japanese Occupation of the Philippines*, vol. 1 (Manila: Bookmark, 1967); Louis Morton, *The Fall of the Philippines* (Washington, DC: Center for Military History, 1953).

16. In English, see J. L. Vellut, "Foreign Relations of the Second Republic of the Philippines, 1943–1945," *Journal of Southeast Asian History* 5, no. 1 (1964); Lydia Yu-Jose, "Philippine, American, and Japanese Relations as Seen through the Issue of Neutralization, 900 to 1939," in *Philippines-Japan Relations*, edited by Setsuho Ikehata and Lydia Yu-Jose (Manila: Ateneo De Manila University Press, 2003); Parpan, "Philippine Church."

17. Ramón Aguilós, "Church Realities in the Philippines: 1900–1965," *Instituto de Historia de la Iglesia* 8 (1999); David J. Alvarez, "The Vatican and the War in the Far East, 1941–1943," *The Historian* 40, no. 3 (1978); Olivier Sibre, *La Saint-Siège et l'Extrême-Orient (Chine, Corée, Japon): De Léon XIII à Pie XII (1880–1952)* [The Holy See and the Far East (China, Korea, Japan): From Leo XIII to Pius XII (1880–1952)] (Roma: École Française de Rome, 2012); a good summary can also be found in the unpublished work of Aaron James R. Veloso, "The Apostolic Delegation in the Philippines during the Second World War," University of the Philippines, Working Paper.

18. Steinberg, "Philippine Collaboration in World War II," 6.

19. Filomeno V. Aguilar, "Church–State Relations in the 1899 Malolos Constitution: Filipinization and Visions of National Community," *Southeast Asian Studies* 4, no. 2 (2015): 280–81.

20. Aguilós, "Church Realities in the Philippines: 1900–1965," 207–8.

21. Terada, "Religious Propaganda," 227.

22. Parpan, "Philippine Church," 458.

23. Piani was the titular archbishop of Nicosia, residing in Manila. The two other foreign archbishops were from the US (James Paul McCloskey, bishop of Jaro) and the Netherlands (Constant Jurgens, Bishop of Tuguegarao). For details see the "Catholic Church in Philippines," in the database *Catholic Hierarchy*, last accessed on April 20, 2021, at www.catholic-hierarchy.org/country/ph.html.

24. Carroll, "Sentenced to Death," 64.

25. Terada, "Japanese Occupation," 217–19, 25–26.

26. Japanese names are given with family names preceding given names.

27. See the introduction of Tatsuya Shimura, *Kyokai Hiwa* [A Secret Story of the Church] (Tokyo: Chuo Shuppansha, 1971).

28. Terada, "Religious Propaganda," 217–18; Terada, "Japanese Occupation," 223–24.

29. ADSSGM, vol. 4, doc. 242, pp. 357–58, "Le délégué aposotolique à Tokyo Marella au cardinal Maglione" (Tokyo, January 20, 1941).

30. ADSSGM, vol. 5, doc. 154, p. 320, "Le délégué aposotolique au Japon Marella au cardinal Maglione" (Tokyo, November 29, 1941). This rapport did not reach the HS until March 24 the next year.

31. See, for example, discussion about Marella's attitude in Sibre, *La Saint-Siège*, 695–705.

32. Marella reported in early 1941 that he was used to the Japanese Military wanting to make use of Japanese clerics to approach missionaries in China. See, ADSSGM, vol. 4, doc. 242, p. 358.

33. Terada, "Japanese Occupation," 229–30.

34. Aaron James R. Veloso, "The Catholic Church in the Philippines in One Hundred Years: From the Spanish Colonial Period to the End of the Marcos Dictatorship 1886–1986" (University of the Philippines, 2012), 90–102; Terada, "Religious Propaganda," 219–22.

35. Carroll, "Sentenced to Death," 64–65.

36. Veloso, "The Catholic Church in the Philippines," 91–94.

37. Hartendorp, *Occupation of the Philippines*, 227.

38. David Buckley, *Faithful to Secularism: The Religious Politics of Democracy in Ireland, Senegal, and the Philippines* (Columbia: Columbia University Press, 2017), 133–35; 41.

39. Hartendorp, *Occupation of the Philippines*, 228.

40. Ibid., 229.

41. ADSSGM, vol. 11, doc. 92, p. 202, "Le president des Illes Philippines Laurel au pape Pie XII" (Rome, March 11, 1944).

42. Published in English in Terada, "Religious Propaganda," 244–46.

43. ADSSGM, vol. 5, doc. 386, p. 591, "Le délégué aposotolique au Japon Marella au cardinal Maglione" (Peking, June 4, 1942).

44. The answer is not contained in the ADSSGM. It should be in the Secret Archives of the Vatican which could not be consulted for this research.

45. ADSSGM, vol. 5, doc. 391, p. 596, "Le délégué aposotolique au Japon Marella au cardinal Maglione" (Peking, June 8, 1942).

46. ADSSGM, doc. 462, p. 670, "Le délégué apostolique à Washington Cicognani au cardinal Maglione" (Washington, September 7, 1942).

47. ADSSGM, doc. 497, p. 735.

48. The Japanese Government officially declined the request on November 4; See ADSSGM, vol. 7, doc. 2, p. 74, "La Délégation du Japon à la Secrétairerie d'Etat" (Rome, November 4, 1942).

49. On the role of the Tribune see Ricardo Trota Jose, "The Tribune during the Japanese Occupation," *Philippine Studies* 38, no. 1 (1990); Ricardo Trota Jose, "The Tribune as a Tool of Japanese Propaganda, 1942–1945," *Philippine Studies* 38, no. 2 (1990).

50. *The Tribune*, "Vatican Glad Over Church Affairs Here," October 12, 1942. The difference in Taguchi's name stems from a different transcription of the Japanese characters.

51. Annex of ADSSGM, vol. 5, doc. 508, p. 750, "Notes du cardinal Maglione" (Vatican, October 27, 1942).

52. Ibid.

53. Maglione expressed the same fear that Japan could use this as an example for the treatment of Catholic clerics in Southeast Asia in ADSSGM, doc. 407, p. 608, "Notes du Cardinal Maglione" (Vatican, July 4, 1942); see also Sibre, *La Saint-Siège*, 673–74.

54. Takefumi Terada, "The Japanese Catholic Women's Religious Corps and Its Activities in the Philippines during World War II," *Senri Ethnological Reports* 31 (2002).

55. Veloso, "The Catholic Church in the Philippines," 90–102.

56. ADSSGM, vol. 11, doc. 186, p. 446, "Le délégué apostolique à Tokyo Marella au cardinal Malgione" (Tokyo, July 8, 1944).

57. ADSSGM, vol. 7, doc. 443, p. 679, "Notes du cardinal Maglione" (Vatican, October 22, 1943).

58. ADSSGM, vol. 7, doc. 446, p. 681.

59. Sibre, *La Saint-Siège*, 679–80.

60. Veloso, "The Catholic Church in the Philippines," 102. Jurgens had been bishop of Tuguegarao since 1928.

61. ADSSGM, vol. 9, doc. 6, p. 69, "Le délégué aposotolique a Londres Godfrey au cardinal Maglione" (London, January 5, 1943), doc. 133, p. 231, "Le cardinal Maglione au délégué apostolique à Tokyo Marella" (Vatican, Paril 5, 1943), and doc. 179, p. 281, "Le délégué apostolique a Londres Godfrey au cardinal Maglione" (London, May 9, 1943).

62. Sarah Kovner, "A War of Words: Allied Captivity and Swiss Neutrality in the Pacific, 1941–1945," *Diplomatic History* 41, no. 4 (2017): 741.

63. ADSSGM, vol. 8, doc. 564, p. 743–44, "Le délégué apostolique au Japon Marella au cardinal Maglione" (Tokyo, December 10, 1942).

64. ADSSGM, vol. 10, doc. 488, p. 577–78, "La Secrétairerie d? Etat à la Délégation special du Japon" (Vatican, July 18, 1945).

PUBLISHED PRIMARY SOURCES

Actes et Documents du Saint-Siège relatifs à la Seconde Guerre Mondiale (ADSSGM), vol. 4 (doc. 242, p. 357; doc. 497, p. 735), vol. 5 (doc. 154, p. 320; doc. 328, p. 514; doc. 407, p. 608; doc. 386, p. 591; doc. 391, p. 596; doc. 462, p. 670; doc. 497, p. 735; doc. 508, p. 750), vol. 7 (doc. 2, p. 74; doc. 436, p. 671; doc. 443, p. 679; doc. 446, p. 681), vol. 8 (doc. 564, p. 743), vol. 9 (doc. 6, p. 69; doc. 133, p. 231; doc. 179, p. 281), vol. 10 (doc. 488, p. 577), vol. 11 (doc. 8, p. 88; doc. 92, p. 202; doc. 127, p. 240; doc. 186, p. 4469).

SELECTED SECONDARY SOURCES

Alvarez, David J. "The Vatican and the War in the Far East, 1941–1943." *The Historian* 40, no. 3 (1978): 508.
Ikehata, Setsuho, and Lydia Yu-Jose. *Philippines–Japan Relations*. Manila: Ateneo De Manila University Press, 2003.
Ikehata, Setsuho, and Ricardo Trota Jose. *The Philippines under Japan: Occupation Policy and Reaction*. Manila: Ateneo De Manila University Press, 1999.
Lottaz, Pascal, and Florentino Rodao. "The Vatican, WWII, and Asia: Lessons of Neutral Diplomacy." In *Notions of Neutralities*, edited by Pascal Lottaz and Herbert Reginbogin. Lanham: Lexington, 2019.
Parpan, Alfredo G. "The Japanese and the Philippine Church, 1942–1945." *Philippine Studies* 37, no. 4 (1989): 451–66.
Shimura, Tatsuya. *Kyokai Hiwa* [A Secret Story of the Church]. Tokyo: Chuo Shuppansha, 1971.
Sibre, Olivier. *La Saint-Siège et l'Extrême-Orient (Chine, Corée, Japon): De Léon XIII à Pie XII (1880–1952)* [The Holy See and the Far East (China, Korea, Japan): From Leo XIII to Pius XII (1880–1952)]. Roma: École Française de Rome, 2012.
Terada, Takefumi. "The Religious Propaganda Program for Christian Churches." In *The Philippines under Japan: Occupation Policy and Reaction*, edited by Setsuho Ikehata and Ricardo Trota Jose. Manila: Ateneo De Manila University Press, 1999.
———. "The Japanese Catholic Women's Religious Corps and Its Activities in the Philippines during World War II." *Senri Ethnological Reports* 31 (2002): 293–308.
———. "Christianity and the Japanese Occupation." In *Philippines-Japan Relations*, edited by Setsuho Ikehata and Lydia Yu-Jose, 223–60. Manila: Ateneo De Manila University Press, 2003.
Vellut, J. L. "Foreign Relations of the Second Republic of the Philippines, 1943–1945." *Journal of Southeast Asian History* 5, no. 1 (1964): 126–42.
Veloso, Aaron James R. "The Catholic Church in the Philippines in One Hundred Years: From the Spanish Colonial Period to the End of the Marcos Dictatorship 1886–1986." University of the Philippines, 2012.
———. "The Apostolic Delegation in the Philippines during the Second World War." *University of the Philippines, Working Paper* (n.d.).

Yu-Jose, Lydia. "Philippine, American, and Japanese Relations as Seen through the Issue of Neutralization, 900 to 1939." In *Philippines-Japan Relations*, edited by Setsuho Ikehata and Lydia Yu-Jose, 47–80. Manila: Ateneo De Manila University Press, 2003.

Chapter Six

Pope Pius XII, Vatican Neutrality, and the Holocaust

Case Studies from the Newly Opened Vatican Archives

Suzanne Brown-Fleming

In the encyclical[1] *Humani Generis Unitas* (*Unity of the Human Race*),[2] drafted in 1938 but never issued, the authors made the following statement admonishing faithful Roman Catholics not to "remain silent" in the face of racism: "the struggle for racial purity ends by being uniquely the struggle against the Jews."[3] By 1945, this premonition of the ultimate consequences of racism and Jew-hatred—the murder of approximately six million Jews in the Shoah—had come to pass. The shelving of this draft encyclical by Eugenio Pacelli (Pope Pius XII, 1939–1958) and the pope's decision to remain neutral and impartial during World War II was the subject of vigorous debate both then and now.

Pope Pius XII followed "an official policy of impartiality" during World War II. In doing so, he followed the footsteps of his predecessors. As Dennis Castillo notes in his recent book, Vatican impartiality had roots in the Napoleonic wars, when Pius VII (1800–1823) "resisted pressure to align the Papal States with Napoleonic France" in the interest of championing peace, as opposed to siding with any particular power. A "peaceful policy" should extend "even toward those from whom evil may be expected," emphasized Pius VII.[4] One hundred years later, Cardinal Secretary of State Pietro Gasparri (1914–1930) championed "a diplomacy of accommodation and conciliation."[5] Pope Benedict XV (1914–1922), under the advice of Gasparri and then-Secretary of the Department of Extraordinary Ecclesiastical Affairs Pacelli, sought to play a role as a mediator during World War I and thus declared himself "impartial without preconception or judgment." While he hoped such an approach would earn him "the trust of both sides," instead, it "provoked suspicion" due to his "continual refusal to cite specific abuses and name the perpetrators."[6]

During the World War II period, scholars of the Catholic Church experienced a sense of déjà vu when reading about papal diplomacy in the century since the Napoleonic wars. Contemporary critics argued that Pope Benedict XV's alleged "papal silence" during the First World War regarding alleged atrocities "compromised the church and weakened the faith."[7] For scholars of the Catholic Church under Mussolini, Hitler, and World War II, the charge is a familiar one, made by Catholics themselves in real-time during the 1920s, 1930s, and 1940s.[8]

Article 24 of the Lateran Accords creating the Vatican City State (1929) was very specific with regard to the territory's international role. It provides us with a definition of neutrality as understood by the Vatican's Secretariat of State on the dawn of Hitler's election to power in January 1933. It read: "The Holy See declares that it desires to take, and shall take, no part in any temporal rivalries between other states, nor in any international congresses called to settle such matters, *save and except in the event of such parties making a mutual appeal to the pacific mission of the Holy See, the latter reserving in any event the right of exercising its moral and spiritual power*" (emphasis added).[9]

Put another way, well before the rise of Mussolini, Hitler, and the crimes of World War II and the Holocaust, the Vatican sought a path of remaining neutral in foreign politics and conflicts and negotiated with any government—regardless of its nature—to protect and promote Church interests, narrow and broad. For example, protection of church properties, schools, associations, and the ability of the Church to provide the sacraments, but also to promote Catholic values, especially with regimes deemed unfriendly to these values. This was the path to survival during the turbulent nineteenth century when the Church lost temporal power in Europe. From the perspective of the popes and their chief advisors, surviving meant brokering individual treaties called concordats, country by country and government by government, to protect the Church and Catholic life and practice. To that end, during the 1920s and early 1930s, "the Vatican concluded concordats with "authoritarian, democratic, socialist and fascist regimes" alike.[10] The list of the Vatican's concordats following World War I is dizzying: Austria (1934), Baden (1932), Bavaria (1924), Czechoslovakia (1928), Italy (1929), Latvia (1925), Lithuania (1927), Poland (1925), Portugal (1928), Prussia (1929), and Romania (1927).

We are left with a historical record that explains Pope Pius XII's stance during World War II. But what of the reference in the Lateran Accords to the Church's "reserving in any event the right of exercising its moral and spiritual power?" What did this mean in the face of the Holocaust and the unprecedented murder of millions of others, including Catholics? One answer comes from the contemporary observer and Carmelite nun Saint Edith Stein.

In April 1933, she wrote an impassioned letter to Pope Pius XI (1922–1939). In a lengthy letter analyzed elsewhere, she wrote, "For weeks, not only Jews, but also thousands of faithful Catholics in Germany—and I think all over the world—wait and hope for the Church of Christ to raise her voice and put a stop to this misuse of the name of Christ. Is not this deification of race and state, hammered into the masses via radio every day, an open heresy? Is not the war of annihilation against Jewish blood an abuse of our Most Holy Savior, the Most Holy Mother Mary, and our apostles? Does not all this stand in furthest opposition to the position of our Lord and Savior, who even on the cross prayed for his persecutors?"[11]

To explore the contradictions between neutrality and "the right of [the Church in] exercising its moral and spiritual power," the remainder of this chapter will focus on case studies from a new source: the recently opened Vatican Archives. On March 2, 2020, the multiple archives relating to Pius XII's pontificate opened to researchers. Important but incomplete documentation has been available since 1965 as part of the published series *Acts and Documents of the Holy See Relative to the Second World War*.[12] Also long available are archives from Pius XI's pontificate (since 2006) and those of the Vatican Office of Information for Prisoners of War, 1939–1947 (since 2004).[13] Announced by Pope Francis on March 4, 2019, the opening of these archives provides fresh material from which to consider Pope Pius XII, Vatican neutrality, and the Holocaust.

NEUTRALITY AS A MORAL FAILURE?

In 1945, Vatican officials received an undated, anonymous letter. Today, the letter rests in the Vatican Apostolic Archive, contained in a red folder labeled "Offenses against the Holy Father and against the Church." The year "1945" appears on the folder in red pencil. The enclosed entreaty bears the title "The attitude of the Catholic Church toward Adolf Hitler and the resulting responsibility."[14] To best appreciate its remarkable nature, it must be transcribed in full (see Appendix for full German):

> Before Adolf Hitler came to power, the German Catholic bishops and clergy were hostile to Hitler. They denied absolution to German Catholics who wanted to join the SA or the party; that is, they excluded them from the church community if there was no change in their attitude and political sympathies. Many Catholics were deterred from joining the SA or the party as a result.
>
> The attitude and actions of the bishops and clergy were probably in accordance with the attitude and instructions of Rome. The motives that led to this attitude, to the refusal of absolution, could only be religious and moral ones. It

was feared that Hitler's policies would be unchristian, even anti-Christian, and this apprehension was amply provoked by Hitler's book *Mein Kampf* and his speeches. We need only think of his unchristian antisemitism and his unchristian race theory.

After the "seizure of power" [1933], the pope was one of the first sovereigns to conclude a concordat with Hitler. With the help of Mr. [Franz] von Papen, the Concordat [*Reichskonkordat*] came into being, in which the pope recognized Hitler's government as legitimate and received assurances from Hitler of the recognition, respect, and protection of the Catholic Church and its rights (not least the payment of the salaries of the bishops and clergy) in Germany. By recognizing Hitler's government, the pope set an example. We might assume that this example acted as a stimulus for other countries. In any case, other states soon recognized Hitler also.

The German Catholic bishops and clergy abandoned their hostile stance after the conclusion of the Concordat. German Catholics were allowed to join the SA and the party without hindrance. The Catholic clergy assisted at baptisms, weddings, and funerals of SA members and party members. From their houses and from the churches, the swastika flag flew.

Hitler had assured the Catholic Church of respect and protection. And antisemitism? And racial policies? The burning of the Reichstag [parliament], the rigging of elections, the Röhm Affair [Night of the Long Knives], and many other things? Well, people probably thought that National Socialism was operating so savagely only during the struggle for power and amid the initial exuberance. It could be tempered and refined, [and] people believed this could best be achieved by Catholics joining its ranks and exerting their influence there. Let us assume that this was a sincere, good-faith belief. However, it might more easily be thought that the pope, with his political acumen and well informed by diplomatic representatives to the Vatican from almost every country, had seen through the nature and true intentions of Adolf Hitler and his helpers from the outset, but had set this better perception aside in the interest of expediency.

In any event: Soon after the seizure of power, the Berlin communists were put behind barbed wire without any legal justification. Concentration camps were set up, and, over the years, thousands of Germans and foreigners were imprisoned, tortured, and murdered. The inmates of mental institutions and psychiatric hospitals and other "unproductive elements [*Volksgenossen*]" were killed. In Warthegau, a real persecution and oppression of Catholics took place, and the churches there were closed. Catholics were disenfranchised, and many Catholic clergymen were imprisoned in concentration camps. Hitler gave a public speech announcing his intention to exterminate [Ausrottung] the Jewish race fundamentally; then, in 1938, the synagogues burned, and the Jewish atrocities began. Austria and Czechoslovakia were annexed by force. Poland was invaded and "defeated," and the extermination of the Poles began. Holland and Belgium, Denmark, and Norway were invaded, and a reign of violence and terror prevailed in these countries. When all this and a great deal more happened, it was no longer possible to apply the principle of good faith; no one could continue to believe that the direction of National Socialism could be changed, especially not the pope, who was better informed about everything than we others were. By then, the pope must have been convinced of the essential wickedness of Hitler and his helpers.

Shouldn't the pope have officially distanced himself from Hitler and terminated the Concordat with him? Hitler had undoubtedly given him justification for this cancellation by the frequent violation of the Concordat. Shouldn't the pope have broken off relations with Hitler and recalled his diplomatic representative from Germany? It was no longer necessary to weigh the consequences that such a decision could have. *For the Church, moral motives, not political ones, must come first* [Emphasis mine]. And I must never behave immorally, however adverse the consequences for me may be. Nor does the principle of choosing the lesser of two evils apply, for of two evils, both of which are immoral, I must choose neither, just as, faced with the choice between perjury and an ordinary lie, I must not choose the lie, the lesser evil.

If Jesus had possessed the political acumen of his successor, the pope, he would not have publicly reproached the leaders of the Jewish people, the scribes and Pharisees, for their immorality and denounced them as seducers of the people; rather, he would have engaged in diplomatic negotiations with them. Then they probably would not have crucified him.

I am well aware that German bishops protested in pastoral letters against many a thing done by Adolf Hitler. But these letters only went secretly from hand to hand and did not become public knowledge. I also know that many Catholic clergymen were sent to the concentration camps (in some cases because of out of step with the times' usage of expressions). None of these constituted official statements or pronouncements by Rome. Rome never officially declared itself against Adolf Hitler and his party, never distanced itself formally from Adolf Hitler, never broke off relations with him, never canceled the Concordat signed with him. The Vatican envoy was never recalled from Germany. To my knowledge, until 1941 (after that time, it was no longer possible for technical reasons), the nuncio, as the doyen of the diplomatic corps, expressed his (and thus the pope's) good wishes and those of the corps to Adolf Hitler on New Year's Day.

I said above that the pope, by concluding the Concordat with Hitler, had perhaps set an example that encouraged other states to do likewise. Certainly, he and the German bishops and clergy, by their conduct, largely influenced German Catholics and probably non-Catholics also in their attitude toward Hitler and his party. If the pope concluded a concordat with Hitler, if he maintained relations with Hitler until the end, if the German bishops and clergy, following Rome's instructions, declared it permissible to join the SA and the party, how could the ordinary man have seen any wrong in following Adolf Hitler, affirming his policies, or joining and remaining in the SA and the party? Could he not or should he not conclude from the pope and the clergy's view that the reports of evil deeds perpetrated by Hitler and the Nazis must surely be untrue or overstated, and that it probably was only a matter of slander and exaggeration by foreign propaganda?

Suppose the German party members, especially the Catholic ones, are now being prosecuted for their party affiliation and deprived of their positions, their assets, and their income. Are they not entitled to point to the pope's views and that of the German bishops and clergymen, which influenced their behavior in order to exonerate themselves? *Is not the pope, above all, partly responsible for their misfortunes? Should he not now declare this fact before the whole world in order to exonerate the persecuted party members?* [emphasis added]. The Pope is morally obliged to make this declaration, and he must do it before the arguments for the defense begin in Nuremberg, if only to exonerate the faithful son of the Catholic Church, Mr. [Franz] von Papen.[15] It is also believed that such a declaration by the pope is in preparation and will be made soon. Let us wait and see.

And the German Catholic bishops and clergy? They, who even under the former regime were treated tolerably well, by and large, who were not urged or even forced to join the SA or the party, who did not have their own economic livelihood and that of their wives and children at stake, as was the case with the German civil servants, are now seeking a new political line to secure their economic livelihood for the future. They are keeping themselves and their auxiliary officials, all the way down to messenger-level, free of all burdens, such as the heavy burdens of quartering [Allied] troops. For the rest, they are letting things take their course and remaining silent where they would have to confess.

Collective guilt, whose extent would be determined by national borders, does not exist. If there is collective guilt, then it exists only in the sense of Christianity, according to which the whole of mankind is responsible and liable for human sins. The historical examination also leads to this understanding.

In any case, we must give all Germans credit for what we ourselves did to escape doom, for they were much less able than we to recognize where Adolf Hitler's path would lead our people and the whole world. But what Christian peoples are doing today against their co-religionists of other nationalities must lead to the downfall of Christianity.

A fortnight ago, I heard a sermon by Pastor [Martin] Niemöller. He spoke of the collective German guilt, although he should have told us how it would have been possible for the individual private citizen to take a stand against Hitler. But mainly Niemöller was beating his own chest, emphasizing his own sin of omission and that of all Protestant clergy in Germany. (He does not mention the Catholic ones). He said that if the Protestant clergy in Germany (I think he mentioned the number 14,000) had stood united and unified against Hitler and National Socialism in time, then it might well have been possible that Hitler would have had them all dragged off to the concentration camps and killed. But then the eyes of the German population and the whole world would have opened in time, and it probably would not have come to the point of war.[16]

What Pastor Niemöller says about the Protestant clergy, fragmented into different confessions and lacking the unity of faith and the tight centralization of the Catholic clergy, applies even more to the latter! Rome's clear advice and guidance would have been sufficient to mold the Catholic clergy into a united front against Adolf Hitler. And, certainly, it is possible that Adolf Hitler would have had all the Catholic clergy dragged to the concentration camps and killed. But then they would have saved their conscience. Then the saying about the grain of wheat that must die to bear fruit would have come true. And the other saying: "If they have persecuted me, they will persecute you also." But of this, I am convinced: such a sacrifice would have preserved peace.

The Church did not make the sacrifice and did not show itself worthy of its Lord and Master. And while the doctrine of the Church tells us that Jesus took upon himself the sins of the whole world, others must atone for these sins of the Church.

It is highly likely that the author of this incredible letter was a German Catholic woman who had suffered at the hands of the Nazi regime herself. Her name was Maria Sevenich, a former communist who became a devout Catholic in the late 1930s.[17] The Gestapo arrested Sevenich multiple times, and she spent the last two years of the war in prison. She almost lost her life when prison guards massacred most inmates at Hirzenheim prison in the days before American troops arrived.[18] After the war, she became a politician in postwar Germany's Christian Conservative Party.[19] The parallels between this 1945 letter and Saint Edith Stein's 1933 letter are fascinating. Like Stein, Sevenich holds the Church accountable in a scathing account of the Church's utter failure, in her view, to exercise the moral and spiritual power called for in the Lateran Accords.

These two remarkable and deeply devout converts to Catholicism understood the core of the Church's duty to teach reciprocity, or love of neighbor. Sevenich took to task the pope himself and his German prelates. Let us turn to the messages German Catholics were hearing from Pope Pius XII in 1945 and test them against the definition of neutrality as defined in the Lateran Accords.

PAPAL BLESSINGS FOR NAZI OVERLORDS

In the fall of 1945, Pope Pius XII did not see himself as Sevenich did. He never made the declaration that Sevenich called for. Like Sevenich, he rejected German "collective guilt." Yet, Sevenich saw the pope and the German bishops as responsible and as needing to "atone." She spoke frankly about Catholics who collaborated with the Nazi movement, eagerly joining its ranks once the ban on party membership was lifted in March 1933.

On the other hand, the pope preferred remaining in the abstract when it came to who participated and who should be held responsible. He called National Socialism a "satanic ghost" in June 1945. Ghosts, after all, cannot be held to real-world consequences for their decisions. Best, rather, to move on. Instead, he called for "peace" and "brotherly understanding,"[20] in alignment with the 1929 Lateran Accords' language.

It remains puzzling that the Vatican chose to eschew neutrality and impartiality in the profoundly political issue of clemency for Germans indicted and convicted for war crimes by Allied courts in occupied Germany. I have written about this topic elsewhere, though some details are worth recapturing here. These efforts involved American-born cardinal Aloisius Muench, the most powerful American Catholic figure and influential Vatican representative in occupied Germany and subsequent West Germany between 1946 and 1959. Cardinal Muench held the diplomatic positions of the apostolic visitor, then regent, and finally Pope Pius XII's nuncio, or papal diplomat to Germany.

During the first weeks of December 1948, Muench met with Vatican nuncio to the United States Amleto Cicognani in Washington, DC, to discuss Germans indicted and convicted for war crimes by Allied courts in occupied Germany and now incarcerated in Landsberg and Spandau prisons. Monsignor Giovanni Battista Montini, undersecretary of state, future Saint Pope Paul VI (1963–1978), and one of Pope Pius XII's closest confidants, had requested that Cicognani approach Washington officials on behalf of convicted German war criminals sentenced to imprisonment or death. Cicognani, in turn, requested a meeting with Muench, who was visiting the United States on furlough from his post as a relief officer for the Vatican mission in Kronberg and liaison representative between American occupation officials and the German Catholic Church.[21]

After a discussion with Cicognani on December 6, Muench "wrote a memorandum on the Landsberg cases" for the nuncio, dated December 7. On December 14, Cicognani submitted the following petition to all occupation authorities (Allied and Soviet): "The Holy See . . . presents . . . a plea for mercy on behalf of German nationals condemned to death as war criminals by the military tribunals in Germany. Without any violation of justice, it is hoped that [occupation authorities will] commute the existing death sentences into other penalties, at least in those cases where there is even a slight doubt of guilt or where mitigating circumstances may be found."[22]

In the early fall of 1949, Pope Pius XII instructed Muench to write a letter supporting clemency for convicted German war criminals to General Thomas Handy, United States European Command (EUCOM) commander. Now papal regent (since October 1949), Muench could openly speak as a representative of the pope. "In the spirit of centuries-old traditions, the Church seeks to have justice tempered with mercy. In accord with the time-honored prerogative of the Church to intercede for even the worst of criminals, Pope Pius XII respectfully requests that clemency be shown," Muench wrote to General Handy on February 27, 1950.[23]

The motivations of Pope Pius XII and his advisors in clemency efforts for convicted German war criminals, most especially Catholic ones, can now be fully researched. The Vatican Apostolic Archive contains correspondence about several high-visibility cases, including that of Oswald Pohl. Pohl joined the Nazi party in 1926 and the SS in 1929. The SS, or Schutzstaffel, was an elite quasi-military unit of the Nazi party that served as Hitler's personal guard and as a special security force in Germany and the occupied countries. Pohl became chief of administration at SS headquarters in February 1934, responsible for the SS units and the concentration camps. Ultimately, he headed a sprawling organization responsible for recruiting millions of concentration camp inmates for forced labor units and responsible for selling Jewish possessions—jewelry, gold fillings, hair, and clothing—to provide funds to Nazi Germany.

On November 3, 1947, in the "US versus Oswald Pohl et al.," the US Army sentenced Pohl to death. During the three-year confinement in Landsberg prison that followed the trial, Pohl converted to Catholicism. This did not prevent his execution by hanging on June 8, 1951.[24] Muench exchanged multiple letters on the Pohl case with Montini. On April 2, Muench wrote to Montini, "I consider it my duty to remit to Your Excellency . . . newspaper articles which report news of the Holy Father sending a Papal Blessing[25] to Mr. Oswald Pohl, former General of the SS, sentenced to death in Landsberg."[26] Muench's second memorandum to Montini confirmed that, indeed, Pohl had received a Papal Blessing via telegram. The Christian News Service in Munich issued a clarification that, according to Landsberg prison chaplain Carl Morgenschweis, the telegram conferring the Papal Blessing was "purely private, and not a diplomatic step or a Vatican stance."[27] Specifically, a Father "Costantino Pohlmann" sent an urgent request to Pius XII with a request that a Papal Blessing be sent to Pohl on the eve of his death, in keeping with Catholic practice, and the pope did so. In Muench's view, this was "not at all a matter of a telegram from the Vatican, much less a position taken by the Pope on the Pohl case."[28]

In the third and final memo from Muench to Montini on the matter, Muench took the time to send to Montini—second only to the pope in terms of power and position—a copy of an essay Pohl had written while imprisoned. The essay was titled "My Way to God." Muench ensured Montini that the essay had come from the heart. Father Morgenschweis "closely followed the radical change of Pohl" and wrote the preface, confirming that in Father Morgenschweis's eyes, Pohl converted "only for the beneficial influence of God's grace" and marked "the sincere return to the Lord of a misguided soul."[29]

American authorities did not see things quite this way. John J. McCloy, who had not included Pohl in the controversial January 1951 Landsberg Report affirming clemency for ten of fifteen Landsberg prisoners sentenced to death, certainly did not.[30] Several weeks before issuing the January 31 clemency decision and report, McCloy found himself answering yet another plea from auxiliary bishop of Munich Johannes Neuhäusler.[31] "My dear Bishop Dr. Neuhäusler," McCloy wrote,

> I wish to reply to your letter of December 20, 1950, urging revocation of the death sentences passed upon German war criminals who are now confined in Landsberg prison. . . . Insofar as your petition for reduction of the death sentences passed on German war criminals applies to the cases of those persons convicted by the Nürnberg Military Tribunals, I would like to point out that the crimes for which these defendants were tried rank in some instances among the most atrocious known in history. They include mass murder and, in many instances, the undisputed testimony of reliable witnesses, as well as their own statements, establishing that these defendants were guilty of the torture and death of hundreds and, in many cases, thousands of helpless human beings.[32]

Within the Vatican, reminders of the Landsberg prisoners' actual crimes, "some of whom were up to their elbows in blood," as Muench noted, fell on deaf ears.

Two weeks after McCloy's January 31 decision, Cicognani wrote to Montini: "Since 1948, this Apostolic Delegation [in Washington], in obedience to the instructions received from the Secretary of State [in Rome], has been taking steps with [Allied officials] and has not omitted anything that would be of benefit to the cause of clemency." Cicognani continued, "As reported on December 13, 1948, January 4, 1949, and March 22, 1949, revisions of trials, suspensions of executions, and even communions of death sentences to prison were obtained. After Your Excellency's report of February 14, 1950, I resumed my interest in the fate of these condemned prisoners." But when pushed, American authorities returned time and again to the point McCloy had raised with Bishop Neuhäusler. When approached by the Holy See, Cicognani wrote to Montini, American leaders asked: "if the Holy See knew and could suggest some reason to grant clemency, because at this point, unfortunately, there is none." Further, the American Government did not know how "to answer the protests that are made . . . by governments, by Jews, by people of Polish origin and by relatives and friends of the countless victims mercilessly suppressed."[33]

To conclude, these brief case studies are by no means definitive. Rather, they are a beginning in what will be many years of careful research into the issue of papal neutrality and impartiality during and after the Holocaust. The inherent tensions within article 24 of the Lateran Accords echo even today. Because of the incongruity between the roles of a neutral city-state and that of the pope's role as God's representative on earth, as Sevenich put it so well, "the Catholic clergy assisted at baptisms, weddings, and funerals of SA members and party members. From their houses and from the churches, the swastika flag flew."

As we have seen, large parts of the Church hierarchy opted for a policy of urging indiscriminate mercy. They also seem to have adopted a policy of indiscriminate rescue by their participation in the so-called Ratline, the organized evacuation of Nazi criminals from Europe. Why did parts of the Church participate in the Ratline and plead so consistently and vociferously for convicted Nazi war criminals after 1945, when the pope needed no longer fear Nazi reprisals? One hypothesis, further articulated in chapters two and four of *The Holocaust and Catholic Conscience*, is that the Church identified itself as a church of "mercy" rather than a Church of "vengeance," a Church of love rather than a Church of reprisal. On its face value, these are noble sentiments, but a deeper look at the documentation exposes the hypocrisy of such a self-understanding. Notions of "mercy" and "forgiveness" had their opposite in "Old Testament" notions of "revenge." Church officials in this era overlooked the suffering of the Jewish people at the hands of the Nazis and their Axis partners, hoping to move on swiftly to forgive, forget, and battle atheistic Communism. Indeed, the broad participation of Christians, and Catholics specifically, in Nazi and Axis crimes made the desire to "forgive and forget" all the more attractive.

NOTES

1. The views as expressed are the author's alone and no not necessarily represent those of the United States Holocaust Memorial Museum or any other organization.

2. The story of this never-issued draft encyclical is prominently featured in the recent Public Broadcasting System (PBS) documentary *Holy Silence*, by Steven J. Pressman (2019). See https://www.pbs.org/show/holy-silence/, accessed February 14, 2021. It has also been the subject of several books, including Peter Eisner, *The Pope's Last Crusade: How an American Jesuit helped Pope Pius XI's Campaign to Stop Hitler* (New York: William Morrow, An Imprint of Harper Collins Publishers, 2013); Georges Passelecq and Bernard Suchecky, *The Hidden Encyclical of Pius XI*, translated from the French by Steven Rendall (New York: Harcourt Brace, 1997), among others.

3. Frank J. Coppa, *The Papacy, the Jews, and the Holocaust*. Washington, DC: The Catholic University of America Press, 2006, 169.

4. Dennis A. Castillo, *Papal Diplomacy from 1914 to 1989: The Seventy-Five Years War* (Lanham, MD: Lexington Books, 2020), 126.

5. Frank J. Coppa, *The Policies and Politics of Pope Pius XII: Between Diplomacy and Morality* (New York: Peter Lang, 2011), 57.

6. Ibid, 60.

7. Ibid, 62.

8. For example, see the 1933 letter from Edith Stein to Pope Pius XI, in Suzanne Brown-Fleming, "May Your Holiness Act in the Interest of Protecting Those who Remain Morally Thinking People:" Vatican Responses to Antisemitism, 1933. Search and Research Lectures and Papers, International Institute for Holocaust Research, Yad Vashem: The World Holocaust Remembrance Center, 2017.

9. Castillo, *Papal Diplomacy from 1914 to 1989*, 81.

10. Coppa, *The Policies and Politics of Pope Pius XII*, 66.

11. Raised in an Orthodox Jewish family, Edith Stein studied philosophy in Breslau, Göttingen, and Freiburg, Germany. Stein converted to Catholicism in 1922. In 1933, Stein lost her post at the Pedagogical Academy in Münster because of the April 7 law for the Restoration of the Professional Civil Service. She became a Carmelite nun in Cologne, taking the name Teresia Benedicta of the Cross. After the Kristallnacht pogrom of November 9 and 10, 1938, Stein left Germany for the Netherlands. In retaliation for a pastoral letter issued by Dutch bishops criticizing the Third Reich, in January 1942, the Nazi regime murdered Stein in Auschwitz. In 1998, Pope John Paul II canonized her as a saint of the Roman Catholic Church. See Brown-Fleming, "May Your Holiness Act in the Interest of Protecting Those who Remain Morally Thinking People," 19–23.

12. *Actes et documents du Saint-Sìege relatifs à la seconde guerre mondiale*, 12 vols., edited by Pierre Blet, Robert A. Graham, Angelo Martini, and Burkhardt Schneider(Vatican City: Libreria Vaticana, 1965–1981).

13. Archivo vaticano, *Inter arma caritas: l'Ufficio informazioni vaticano per i prigionieri di guerra istituito da Pio XII, 1939–1947*, 2 vols, Città del Vaticano : Archivio segreto vaticano, 2004.

14. Vatican Apostolic Archive (Archivio Apostolico Vaticano, hereafter AAV), Arch. Nunzio Berlino, buste 103, fasc. 10, "Offese contro il Santo Padre e contro la Chiesa. 1945."

15. On October 18, 1945, the chief prosecutors of the International Military Tribunal (IMT) held in Nuremberg, Germany, brought charges against twenty-four leading German officials, among them Franz von Papen. This places the document as having been written in October 1945.

16. This is likely a reference to the so-called Stuttgart declaration. At an ecumenical gathering in Stuttgart of Protestant leaders from the United States, Britain, France, Holland, Norway, and Sweden on October 17 through 19, 1945, Pastor Niemöller made his now famous statements atoning for German crimes on behalf of German Protestants. See Matthhew D. Hockenos, *Then They Came for Me: Martin Niemöller, the Pastor Who Defied the Nazis* (New York, NY: Basic Books, 2018), 176–78.

17. Evidence in a different archive points to Maria Sevenich as the author. Copies are also held at the Archive of the Archdiocese of Munich and Freising in the Johannes Neuhäusler papers (N266). One copy of the letter has the name "Maria Sevenich" written on it. See Mark Edward Ruff, "Katholische Kirche und Entnazifizierung," in *Die Katholische Kirche im Dritten Reich. Eine Einführung*, second edition, edited by Christoph Kösters and Mark Edward Ruff 142–53 (Freiburg im Breisgau: Herder, 2018). Ruff references the document briefly in his essay on page 147. I am deeply grateful to Professor Ruff for checking his research notes for these details.

18. Letter from F. Przyluski, Chief, Tracing Section, PCIRO, International Tracing Service, US Zone, to Maria Meyer-Sevenich, Kolenfeld, June 4, 1948, 6.3.3.2/90790833/ITS Digital Archive, USHMM.

19. See https://www.kas.de/en/web/geschichte-der-cdu/biogram-detail/-/content/maria-meyer-sevenich, accessed February 15, 2021.

20. Mark Edward Ruff, *The Battle for the Catholic Past in Germany, 1945–1980* (Cambridge University Press, 2017), 16.

21. Suzanne Brown-Fleming, *The Holocaust and Catholic Conscience: Cardinal Aloisus Muench and the Guilt Question in Germany, 1946–1959* (South Bend: University of Notre Dame in association with the United States Holocaust Memorial Museum, 2006), 80.

22. Ibid., 81.

23. Ibid.

24. Ibid., 82–86.

25. The Apostolic Blessing or Pardon at the Hour of Death is part of the Last Rites in the Catholic tradition.

26. AAV, Archiv. Nuncio Berlin, Buste 159/Fasc. 42 (II-A-c-15 Kriegsgefangene 1950–1959), 81–83. Prot. No. 4176/51/II B (hand-written): Letter from Cardinal Aloisuis Muench, Kronberg, to Monsignor Giovanni Battista Montini, Rome, April 2, 1951. The subject heading is "Oswald Pohl case."

27. Ibid., Prot. N. 4182/51/II B, Muench to Montini, April 3, 1951.

28. Ibid.

29. Ibid., Prot. N. 4182/51 and Prot. N. 4250/51/II B, Muench to Montini, April 25, 1951.

30. Brown-Fleming, *The Holocaust and Catholic Conscience*, 86.

31. For more on Neuhäusler's experience incarcerated in Dachau, see Suzanne Brown-Fleming, "Johann Baptist Neuhäusler and Torture in Dachau," in *Losing Trust in the World: Holocaust Scholars Confront Torture*, edited by John K. Roth and Lenny Grob, 67–82 (Seattle: University of Washington Press, 2016).

32. AAV, Archiv. Nuncio Berlin, Buste 159/Fasc. 42 (II-A-c-15 Kriegsgefangene 1950-1959), p. 55. Letter from John J. McCloy, Frankfurt am Main, to Auxiliary Bishop Johannes Neuhäusler, Munich, January 16, 1951.

33. Ibid., p. 73. N. 199/51: Cigognani, Apostolic Delegation United States of America, Washington, to Montini, Rome, February 14, 1951.

SELECTED BIBLIOGRAPHY

Blet, Pierre, Robert A. Graham, Angelo Martini, and Burkhardt Schneider, eds. *Actes et documents du Saint-Siège relatifs à la seconde guerre mondiale*. 12 volumes. Vatican City: Libreria Vaticana, 1965–1981.

Brown-Fleming, Suzanne. "May Your Holiness Act in the Interest of Protecting Those who Remain Morally Thinking People:" Vatican Responses to Antisemitism, 1933. Search and Research Lectures and Papers, International Institute for Holocaust Research, Yad Vashem: The World Holocaust Remembrance Center, 2017.

———. *The Holocaust and Catholic Conscience: Cardinal Aloisius Muench and the Guilt Question in Germany, 1946–1959*. South Bend: The University of Notre Dame in association with the United States Holocaust Memorial Museum, 2006.

Castillo, Dennis A. *Papal Diplomacy from 1914 to 1989: The Seventy-Five Years War*. Lanham, MD: Lexington Books, 2020.

Coppa, Frank J. *The Papacy, the Jews, and the Holocaust*. Washington, DC: The Catholic University of America Press, 2006.

———. *The Policies and Politics of Pope Pius XII: Between Diplomacy and Morality*. New York: Peter Lang, 2011.

Eisner, Peter. *The Pope's Last Crusade: How an American Jesuit helped Pope Pius XI's Campaign to Stop Hitler*. New York, NY: William Morrow, An Imprint of Harper Collins Publishers, 2013.

Passelecq, Georges, and Bernard Suchecky. *The Hidden Encyclical of Pius XI*. Translated from the French by Steven Rendall. New York: Harcourt Brace, 1997.

Ruff, Mark Edward. *The Battle for the Catholic Past in Germany, 1945–1980*. Cambridge: Cambridge University Press, 2017.

Steinacher, Gerald. *Nazis on the Run: How Hitler's Henchmen Fled Justice*. Translated from the German by Shaun Whiteside. Oxford: Oxford University Press, 2012.

Part III

INTO THE COLD: 1950–1990

Chapter Seven

No Neutrality in Ideology
The Holy See and the Cold War
Piotr H. Kosicki

"How many divisions does the pope have?"—Joseph Stalin's October 1944 quip to Winston Churchill has taken on legendary status in the annals of European history.[1] Yet, remarkably little attention has been paid to the concepts implicit in Stalin's dismissal of the Catholic Church as an international actor. Key among these was the permanent neutrality of the Holy See. In Stalin's eyes, this legal neutrality, agreed within article 24 of the 1929 Lateran Accords, amounted to a complete defanging of the modern Roman Catholic Church in the international arena.

By taking a synoptic view of the Cold War, this chapter shows that Stalin got it wrong. Indeed, the nature and intensity of the Holy See's engagement in secular political affairs ebbed and flowed with the twentieth century's passage. But the Holy See could, and did, exert profound ideological influence on the twentieth-century international system, all while respecting the formal confines of permanent neutrality.

Too often in scholarship on the twentieth-century Catholic Church, these lines have blurred, with the result that ideological entanglement has been presumed to negate legal neutrality. Scholars have been especially fond of conceptualizing in these terms the pontifical transition between Pius XII and John XXIII following the former's death in 1958. What historian Peter C. Kent has called the "lonely Cold War of Pope Pius XII" did indeed give way to a "Vatican *Ostpolitik*," a *détente* struck between the Holy See and some of the communist governments of Central and Eastern Europe.[2] Yet normalization, whether achieved or merely pursued, did not negate neutrality. As Giuliana Chamedes has rightly underscored, even where it overlapped with interstate diplomacy, Vatican anti-communism remained first and foremost "an ambitious cultural crusade."[3] Even with the election in 1978 of Pope John Paul II, who followed the example of Pope Pius XII in inserting the Holy See into global anti-communism and its attendant public diplomacy, permanent neutrality was fundamentally upheld.

It is crucial to distinguish from the outset here between ideological and legal neutrality.[4] An absence of ideological neutrality did not equate with the renunciation of neutrality under international law. Indeed, the shifting priorities of different twentieth-century pontiffs point to the rich and complex interplay between the Catholic Church's ideological Cold War against communism and the Holy See's comprehensive commitment to permanent neutrality. This chapter reconstructs this empirical story while also spelling out its implications for the longer view of the Holy See as a permanently neutral actor in the secular realm. Its leadership nonetheless entailed firm ideological commitments, most notably concerning communism. The fact of the matter is that, whether a given pontiff chose ideological Cold War or diplomatic normalization with communist regimes (or both), neither of these directly impinged upon permanent neutrality.

MAGISTERIUM VERSUS INTERNATIONAL LAW

Stalin's dismissive wartime attitude toward the Holy See of Pope Pius XII offers a useful entry point into key questions about the Universal Church's modern history. The Soviet leader raised a very practical matter in his October 1944 conversation with Churchill—that of the terms for peace and diplomacy in the wake of the Second World War, as dictated by a *Realpolitik* approach to international law. There was a specific context to this exchange: one month earlier, the Red Army had stood by and watched idly from across the Vistula River as German occupying forces subdued the massive Warsaw Uprising. Yet even with the Polish underground army reeling and Soviet-backed communists claiming sovereign right to lead Poland, Winston Churchill exhorted Stalin at the Moscow Conference of 1944 not to trample the Poles' religious freedoms.[5] In this context, Joseph Stalin saw peace as something to be dictated according to fait accompli. To his mind, the pope had no business in a conversation about the future of the international order. But the Soviet leader was wrong: the implication that the Catholic Church was irrelevant to the pursuit of peace is a grave error in terms.

A helpful corrective can be found in works by Herbert Reginbogin and Pascal Lottaz, who have distinguished between "moral neutrality" and "legal neutrality." Lottaz, for example, challenges claims that the Holy See's international position during World War II was not neutral but partisan in favor of the Axis Powers. The question is not empirical but definitional: Lottaz, therefore, challenges claims of the papacy's abandonment of neutrality as being founded on "ill-defined moral conceptions" of neutrality rather than actual legal or diplomatic categories.[6] This is about more than Pius XII's clearly and repeatedly expressed preference for fascism over liberalism.[7] The Holy See's twentieth-century leaders assumed clear ideological stances—in some cases, even incorporating that ideology into Church magisterium—but the Holy See's legal standing did not change as a result. In this respect, long-abandoned were early-twentieth-century dreams of a "Catholic capture of international law," whereby the Holy See, and not the ill-fated League of Nations, would have emerged from the Great War as arbiter and exemplar for the enforcement of legal norms in the international system.[8]

Scholars differ in their assessments of the exact "year zero" for the Cold War, variously citing 1944, 1945, 1946, or 1947—but in fact, the clock can instead be started in the 1930s, if not indeed in 1917.[9] If scholars of the Cold War abandon the outmoded, all too restrictive picture of the Cold War as a strictly bipolar conflict between the United States and Soviet Russia, the resulting plural meanings of the Cold War—or, as Lorenz Lüthi has recently put it, of the Cold Wars—make for slippery terrain within the broader study of permanent legal neutrality.[10] Since it both was, and was not, formally a conflict under international law, the Cold War presented the Holy See with a diverse array of options for involvement or non-involvement within the international system or of a hybrid approach that in fact became the Holy See's approach of choice.

How, then, can we distinguish the legal category of permanent neutrality from the ideological commitments that rendered the Catholic Church a prominent actor at various points in the Cold War? After all, moral commitments translated remarkably quickly to social and political commitments, and for the scholar, it can therefore be quite difficult to make a precise determination. If we take one particularly telling example—the election of the first non-Italian pope since the sixteenth century, Pope John Paul II from Poland, in 1978—the question becomes even more complicated. After all, at the moment he was elected to head the Holy See, Cardinal Karol Wojtyła was actually a citizen of the Polish People's Republic, one of the key communist states implicated within the ideological struggles of the Cold War.

This chapter draws a sharp distinction between negotiations over diplomatic recognition—whether in concordat diplomacy or merely in attempts at normalization—and social teaching or political ideology. Epistemically, the Cold War challenged the global perception of the Holy See's 1929 permanent neutrality commitment by blurring the lines between the social and the legal.[11] Yet documents about diplomatic normalization (or abrogation thereof) operated on an entirely different register from papal encyclicals and Holy Office decrees. Church magisterium may have been binding upon individual

Catholics by canon law, but the Holy See's protocols for sovereign engagement remained remarkably constant within the international system. Even though certain Roman pontiffs—notably, Pius XI, Pius XII, and John Paul II—left behind a trail of virulently anti-communist declarations and prohibitions, it was not the Holy See that had abrogated concordats with communist countries in the 1940s and 1950s. In fact, at the turn of the 1960s and 1970s, the Holy See became the driving force behind a series of normalizations with communist Eastern Europe.

Historian Giuliana Chamedes has made the case that Eastern Europe is the place where twentieth-century papal diplomacy was born: a frontier region where the Holy See's "concordat revolution" could unite religious conservatives and secular strongmen in common cause against both communism and liberalism.[12] Reflecting on the canonical images of Lenin resting in his mausoleum or Stalin smirking at Yalta, we may be tempted to assume that the origins of papal diplomacy in a region that was overrun in the 1940s by Moscow-backed forces necessarily canceled out a chance that the Holy See could hold fast to permanent neutrality throughout the Cold War. Particularly telling is the fate of the interwar Polish Republic, whose self-styled political leadership nominally survived as a "government-in-exile" in London, not just through World War II,[13] but indeed until 1990. In that year, the presidential insignia of the long-defunct Second Polish Republic were transferred with great pomp and circumstance back from London to Warsaw following the democratic election of Lech Wałęsa, the former Solidarity trade union leader and Nobel Peace Prize Laureate, as president of Poland.[14] By continuing to recognize the diplomats of interwar Poland for nearly three decades after the war's end—and, by extension, refusing to acknowledge the postwar communist diplomats—the Holy See could be understood to be taking sides. Poland's case speaks to the complexity that Eastern Europe has spelled for scholars seeking to make sense of the Holy See's international entanglements. Indeed, the origins of concordat diplomacy in a region where sovereignty and recognized political authority were so profoundly contested throughout the Cold War necessitates a more fine-grained approach than the historiography has to offer to determine if and when the Holy See continued to respect its permanent neutrality commitments.[15]

In the Lateran Accords of 1929 concluded with the government of Benito Mussolini, the Holy See committed to perpetual neutrality (permanent neutrality) in the international system unless otherwise called upon by conflicting parties seeking peace with the help of the Holy See to be a neutral arbitrator in temporal matters. Article 24 of the Lateran Accords states clearly: "In regard to the sovereignty appertaining to it also in international matters, the Holy See declares that it desires to take, and shall take, no part in any temporal rivalries between other States, nor in any international congresses called to settle such matters, save and except in the event of such parties making a mutual appeal to the pacific mission of the Holy See." At the same time, the Lateran text explicitly precluded moral or ideological neutrality, with the Holy See "reserving, in any event, the right of exercising its moral and spiritual power."[16]

So, where exactly does "neutrality" begin and end? Given the Cold War's profoundly destabilizing influence on international law, there is a high degree of historical contingency to this question. Neutrality, as the Hague Convention of 1907 intended, implied a willingness to lend diplomatic services ("good offices") to any of the warring parties in a conflict in the interest of limiting suffering.[17] And yet, as Pascal Lottaz and Herbert Reginbogin have noted, "The Cold War, too, was not a war in the classic sense, but an international system, mentally framed to justify war-like measures against the 'enemy.'"[18] Understood not merely as an event but indeed as an epistemic framework, the Cold War has thus profoundly challenged the entire field of international law.

The Cold War's transformative impact on neutrality as a discursive field necessarily limits the historian's ability to adjudicate the Holy See's place in the conflict within simple binary terms of partiality or impartiality. If the whole point of neutrality is, in fact, to resist or constrain war through moderation, then the Cold War—in introducing the notion that a war could be further distinguished as "cold" or as "hot"—re-wrote altogether the vocabularies of alignment, neutrality, and rights. Lottaz and Reginbogin observe, "Suddenly, the well-defined notions of 'impartiality,' or 'rights and duties of neutrals,' were set aside or replaced by considerations for 'non-alignment' and 'ideology.'"[19] And yet the Holy See's legal position throughout the Cold War remained one of continuity, despite the ebb and flow of diplomatic and ideological engagement.

Although he died in 1939, seven months shy of the Second World War and almost a decade before the Cold War, Pope Pius XI succeeded in overhauling the Universal Church to see in Soviet Russia its primary ideological antagonist. His was a Cold War *avant la lettre*, and it is, therefore, instructive to look back to the classic statement of the Church's anti-communist turn, Pius XI's 1937 encyclical *Divini Redemptoris*.[20] "Bolshevistic and atheistic communism" was the subtitle of this encyclical, which insisted that communism "strips man of his liberty, robs human personality of all its dignity, and removes all the moral restraints that check the eruptions of blind impulse."[21]

The key question was: at what point would the Holy See be crossing a line, transgressing a certain boundary, in its capacity as a sovereign actor in the international arena? *Divini Redemptoris* sought to carve out a field of autonomous action for the Universal Church that would complement, rather than complicate, the permanent neutrality declaration contained within the Lateran Accords. The interwar pontiff maintained, for the times, a remarkably restrained approach to Church involvement in secular affairs, while nonetheless mincing no words that "the State must allow the Church full liberty to fulfill her divine and spiritual mission, and this in itself will be an effectual contribution to the rescue of nations from the dread torment of the present hour."[22]

Permanent legal neutrality for the Holy See in the 1930s implied not only a robust notion of church-state separation but also a clear moral imperative for making non-neutral ideological declarations. For Pius XI, the matter was simple enough: communism was evil, and "the evil we must combat is at its origin primarily an evil of the spiritual order."[23] By emphasizing the idea of a "spiritual order," the interwar pontiff attempted to keep the Holy See formally on the sidelines of any interstate conflict, all while diagnosing a certain malaise and mobilizing the Church as an international community bound by conviction and piety. After all, one of the most prominent public faces of the "cold war" waged by the Holy See in the 1920s and 1930s came in the form of concordat diplomacy—intending to shore up anti-communist governments across Europe with mutually recognized guarantees of the Church's standing within national societies. A decade or two later, among the first signal points of the Holy See being dragged into the geopolitical Cold War that began amidst the ashes of World War II were the successive abrogations of interwar concordats that had been concluded in Central and Eastern Europe: Poland (concluded 1925, abrogated 1945), Romania (concluded 1927, abrogated 1948), Czechoslovakia (concluded 1927, abrogated 1950), and Yugoslavia (concluded 1935, abrogated 1952). The concordats with Latvia and Lithuania were rendered irrelevant by the fact of those countries' incorporation into the Soviet Union in 1940.[24]

Dating the Cold War from the end of World War II through the peaceful disintegration of communist regimes in Europe's east in 1989–1991 entails an examination of four pontiffs: Pius XII (1939–1958), John XXIII (1958–1963), Paul VI (1963–78), and, of course, John Paul II (1978–2005). However, the real focus lies in the era of Stalinism's rise and fall in Central and Eastern Europe, contained entirely within the pontificate of Pius XII. To the extent that historians of the Cold War are at all aware of the Holy See's actions and priorities, these historians might typically pose the question: at what point did Pope Pius XII shift the Universal Church away from anti-modernism into a reluctant alliance with political liberalism in the service of what the pontiff described in his 1944 Christmas message as "true democracy"?[25]

THE MYTH OF THE "CHURCH OF SILENCE"

Seven years after that famed radio address, Pope Pius XII intoned, "Hands tied, lips sealed, the Church of Silence responds to our invitation. She shows with her gaze the still fresh graves of her martyrs, the chains of her confessors . . . her silent holocaust."[26] What separated the two Christmas messages was the end of the Second World War and the establishment of Moscow-backed (except for Albania and Yugoslavia) communist regimes across Central and Eastern Europe. With varying degrees of rapidity and intensity, the new governments launched frontal assaults on the national episcopal leaderships. Between 1946 and 1953, the primates of Czechoslovakia, Hungary, Poland, and Yugoslavia were all taken into custody. Except for Poland, all faced public show trials.[27]

Perhaps the most famous case was that of József Cardinal Mindszenty, archbishop of Esztergom and primate of the Hungarian Church. Arrested, tortured, and paraded through a show trial, Mindszenty became the *cause célèbre* for religious martyrdom in the newly communist European east. Pope Pius XII developed a deep personal attachment to Mindszenty's case, denouncing and excommunicating his prosecutors and jailers and circulating pastoral letters calling out Hungary's new government as having betrayed the rule of law and violated the sanctity of religious freedom. At the conclusion of Mindszenty's show trial, Pius XII personally addressed the following words to the cardinal's episcopal colleagues in Hungary: "a grievous crime has been committed against your illustrious college, the Roman Catholic Church, and all defenders of the freedom and dignity of man. We have learned that Our dear son, cardinal of the Holy Roman Church, József Mindszenty, archbishop of Esztergom, has been wantonly thrown into prison."[28]

At first blush, it may seem difficult to square Rome's harsh reaction in defense of the Hungarian primate with an ongoing commitment to permanent neutrality. After all, Mindszenty's became the paradigmatic case of a Church "silenced" by Central and Eastern Europe's new rulers. And yet, the pontiff's own words make clear that he felt that there was little that the Holy See could do to intervene. Excommunicating Hungary's communist rulers was a pastoral action visited upon individuals, not a bellicose declaration of one state (the Holy See) against another (the Hungarian People's Republic).

The individualized nature of these condemnations—or, more commonly, threats of condemnation—becomes apparent when examining one of the most telling documents produced by the Holy See of Pope Pius XII: the 1949 Holy Office decree on communism. In the wake of World War II, the Holy Office played an outsized role in determining the ideological entanglements of the Church within the international system, all while entangling the Church far less than one might expect. The Holy Office issued one of the more famous documents of the early Cold War era about the spiritual perils facing party-affiliated communists and their declared allies. On 1 July 1949, the Holy Office issued a decree laying out the following questions:

1. Is it licit to join or show favor to Communist parties?
2. Is it licit to publish, distribute, or read publications that support Communist doctrine or activity, or to write for them?
3. May Christians who knowingly and freely commit the acts in parts 1 and 2 be given the sacraments?
4. Do Christians who profess, defend or promote materialistic Communist doctrine incur the penalty of excommunication as apostates from the Christian faith, with the penalty reserved so that it may only be lifted by the Holy See?[29]

Each of the first three questions was answered negatively, with the fourth and final question resoundingly affirmed under penalty of ex-communication. But one question remained unresolved: could communist ideals, or even simply being a loyal citizen of a communist regime, result in canon law sanction?

For this reason, crucial though the "Church of Silence" trope is for understanding the ideological commitments of Pius XII's Holy See, an excessive focus on this trope can blind us to more profound continuities within the international position of the Holy See.[30] If we think of a "Church of Silence," after all—featuring a response to the martyrdom of Catholic faithful and the cooptation of Church structures behind the emerging Iron Curtain—the pontiff's options were limited: just ex-communication or containment. The Holy See of Pope Pius XII ultimately pursued a policy analogous to that of the US State Department as inspired by then-Policy Planning staff director George Kennan: focus on France, Italy, Austria, and Belgium, to keep out communist influence. In the United States, the pope relied heavily on New York's Francis Cardinal Spellman to inveigh publicly on behalf of ideological anti-communism; Spellman even took the controversial step of endorsing Joseph McCarthy, a move that the cardinal never subsequently retracted.[31] Spellman's decision provoked intense division among American bishops, contributing to what Patrick McNamara has described as a "Catholic cold war" *within* American Catholicism. In the end, perhaps Pius XII's ideological commitment to anti-communism resonated far more clearly than any American Catholic stance. Historian Peter C. Kent has even claimed that the early Cold War pontiff saw US foreign policy on the whole as insufficiently anti-communist, to the end of pursuing his own "lonely Cold War." But this "war" was driven by propaganda and pressure applied at the national or sub-national levels, not as a matter of international law.[32]

To be clear, the Holy See *did* insert itself into the domestic political decision-making of sovereign countries, especially in Western Europe—and nowhere more so than in Italy. By calling upon national-level politicians and the social structures of Catholic Action to aid the anti-communist camp in the April 1948 Italian parliamentary election campaign, the Holy See became one of the decisive agents in Italian national politics. The Universal Church thereby became a player, an agent, and an actor in Cold War debates, but by the same token, was not going to "dirty" its hands directly in engineering national policy—and therefore remained apart from sovereign decision-making. Instead, the Holy See looked to statesmen belonging to the political family known as Christian Democracy. Scholars have amply documented how aggressively Pius XII lobbied Italian prime minister Alcide De Gasperi, French prime minister/foreign minister Robert Schuman, and other European Christian Democratic leaders throughout the first decade following the conclusion of World War II.[33] Rather than a question of neutrality between two actors in the international arena, this became a matter of limiting attempts by the papacy to dictate programmatic issues to individual Catholic politicians—and even the most loyal of Christian Democrats pushed back quite successfully, as Andrea Riccardi has demonstrated in the case of the leader of Italian Christian Democracy.[34] Therefore, ecclesiastical attempts to exploit national politics in the early Cold War era did not explicitly challenge the principle of the Holy See's permanent neutrality within the international system. In his 1951 Christmas message, Pius XII was quite clear about this, declaring that "there can be no question of the Church renouncing her political neutrality for the simple reason that she cannot serve purely political interests."[35]

Acknowledgment of the unique role played by Christian Democracy in Western Europe—this was, after all, the political family that launched (West) European integration in the wake of the Marshall Plan—aids us in the task of disentangling ideology from the law in the first years of the Cold War. As James Chappel has pointed out, Christian Democracy was at the heart of a fundamental ideological re-orientation among (West) European Catholics when it came to the international—read: anti-communist—obligations of Catholics living in a secular state: "In the 1930s, mainstream Catholics had called on strong states, and often authoritarian ones, to stave off Communism and 'Defend the West,' by military means if necessary. In the long 1950s, this grim imaginary melted away . . . with Christian Democrats leading the way, economic growth became a key litmus test of political legitimacy."[36] In other words, rather than cast anti-communism principally as a doctrine of spiritual salvation, Christian Democrats in Belgium, Italy, and West Germany pivoted toward an economic logic predicated on the notion that Christian families needed unfettered access to markets to flourish and thereby expand the world population of Christians. Ordoliberalism became the West German Christian Democratic Union's byword, with rational choice theory outpacing dogmatic claims in defense of a "Church of Silence."[37]

Simply put, the Christian Democrats drifted toward common ground with liberalism. As a consequence, Christian Democratic statesmen became even less likely to look to the Holy See to intervene actively in the international system. The Holy See's continued permanent neutrality helped to assure Christian Democrats a free hand in the conduct of secular political affairs.

To the east of the Iron Curtain, too, Catholics were seeking to ensure that the Holy See would not overstep the lines of sovereignty. For all the manifold tragedies—torture, imprisonment, assassination—visited upon clergy and laity alike in the years of Stalinism, pastoral life went on in the countries of the emerging Soviet Bloc. As I have written elsewhere, "Central and Eastern Europe in the 1950s constituted neither a pastoral vacuum nor a graveyard of martyrs for the Roman Catholic Church."[38]

Belief in the Holy See's permanent neutrality's inviolability even encouraged East European counterparts to pursue "progressive" equivalents to Christian Democracy in secular politics. This meant recasting Thomas Aquinas as a progenitor of secular "revolution" and cherry-picking from Catholic social teaching to assert its common ground with Marxism. The pursuit of self-styled Catholic socialism in communist-dominated Central and Eastern Europe involved a commitment, not just to a flagrantly non-neutral ideology, but indeed to a project devoted to the very unmaking of permanent neutrality. The Catholic Church, in other words, was to be brought into line with a Soviet vision of international law that sought to criminalize war itself.[39] Most Catholic socialists aspired to eventual positions of secular political leadership that would presumably allow them to apply direct diplomatic pressure on the Holy See. In the short term, the idea was to preserve formal Catholic neutrality—especially to drive a wedge between the Holy See and Western states—while playing in the long run at an ultimate embrace of communist governments by the Holy See.

This, of course, was sheer fantasy, especially in the face of Pius XII's preference for seeing behind the Iron Curtain only a martyred "Church of Silence." And yet Catholic advocates of "revolution"—clergy as well as laity—thereby carved out for themselves a space for action, especially in overwhelmingly Catholic (even if communist-dominated) Poland.[40]

The starting assumption was that canon law exempted citizens of communist-run countries from obedience to the July 1949 Holy Office decree. After all, the biblical (Matthew 22:21) division between the things of Caesar and the things of God precluded the Church from mandating treason to secular government, which in turn would mean that Catholics could not be forced to choose their faith over their citizenship. Therefore, the July 1, 1949 decree on communism stopped well short of committing the Holy See to anything even resembling an abandonment of permanent neutrality. The decree contained an explicit declaration of ideological commitment, yet it was only really enforced in very rare instances. Typically, a challenge needed to be brought forth in a public forum west of the Iron Curtain.[41]

Noteworthy is the Polish example of the organization called PAX, which insisted on allowing communists to complete their self-styled "revolution" first, on the assumption that Catholics could bide their time before swooping in to "Christianize" the revolution from within. In the summer of 1955, however, *L'Osservatore Romano* published a Holy Office decision that placed key PAX publications on the Index of Banned Books. The Roman decision railed against Catholic socialism as "an indescribable attempt to pass off the communist regimes as respecting the liberty of the Catholic Church."[42] In the eyes of the Roman bureaucracy, self-styled Catholic socialism in no way resembled the parliamentary socialism that the Church had grudgingly come to accept in the West after World War II; rather, it was little more than a fig leaf hiding communist commitments. Even in the case of PAX, however, the Holy See kept itself far removed from any kind of pronouncement on the legal standing of communist regimes and their citizenries.

NEUTRALITY VERSUS NORMALIZATION

Understanding the place of a concept like permanent neutrality within a conflict as complex as the Cold War also requires a host of meaningful distinctions between what preceded and what followed the death of Pope Pius XII. These must include the significant shifts in progress by the end of the 1950s within the Catholic Church's involvement in secular debates about the global political economy: de-Stalinization behind the Iron Curtain, decolonization of Europe's overseas empires, and the transition to a different phase of the global Cold War marked above all by conflict in Indochina.[43] In parallel, of course, the Universal Church leadership found itself divided on the eve of its own internal revolution, the Second Vatican Council.

Scholarly accounts of the Holy See during the Cold War typically treat Pius XII's death in 1958 as a pivot point in Rome's shift from mourning a "Church of Silence" to pursuing negotiation and normalization at the highest levels with the communist parties of Central and Eastern Europe. Described as a "Vatican *Ostpolitik*," this turn to diplomacy played out in parallel with the *aggiornamento* initiated by John XXIII and continued by Paul VI.[44] The lesson is not that John XXIII renounced all of his predecessor's commitments, but rather that John XXIII and Paul VI sought engagement and normalization where Pius XII had emphasized the bearing of witness in the face of persecution—and in fact, *both* of these approaches were consonant with the Holy See's permanent legal neutrality.

Thus, it was that three decades after the conclusion of the Lateran Accords, Pope John XXIII served on the eve of the Cuban Missile Crisis as an intermediary between the two key state actors in the Cold War: the United States and the Soviet Union.[45] Especially noteworthy are the audiences that John XXIII held in the early 1960s with various prominent political figures from behind the Iron Curtain, including, most famously, his March 1963 meeting with Nikita Khrushchev's son-in-law Alexei Adzhubei. The shuttle diplomacy of John XXIII yielded not only the first explicit discussion within Church magisterium of the threat of nuclear annihilation—in the 1963 encyclical *Pacem in Terris*—but also tangible achievements on behalf of religious freedom, notably in the release of long-imprisoned Ukrainian Greek Catholic prelate Josyf Slipyj.[46]

With the Second Vatican Council as backdrop, the Holy See of the 1960s sought negotiation and normalization. "Vatican *Ostpolitik*" is something of a misnomer: borrowed from scholarship on late-Cold War dialogues between East and West Germany, the Church's "Eastern" negotiations actually began almost a decade before Willy Brandt's ascension to the chancellorship of the Bundesrepublik. Long-time West German press correspondent Hansjakob Stehle succinctly defined the Vatican's *Ostpolitik* as "defense of one's own interests through confrontation where coexistence is impossible, through compromises where they seem to be tolerable, through cooperation where there are partners for it."[47] Although Pope John XXIII set the tone, his death from cancer in 1963 left the fine-grained, long-term work to Pope Paul VI, assisted by key Holy See prelates such as Agostino Casaroli, Luigi Poggi, and Antonio Samorè.

In the 1940s and 1950s, the future Paul VI had been a high-ranking prelate and confidant of Pope Pius XII. Therefore, it is essential to see in his papacy an attempt to combine the respective goals of Pius XII and John XXIII. For the Holy See of Paul VI, the purpose of Vatican *Ostpolitik* was partial or complete normalization of diplomatic relations with the Soviet Bloc: not as a gesture to the communist regimes, but as a way of restoring the diplomatic relations built in the 1920s and 1930s by, among others, the future Pius XII himself in the diplomatic service of his predecessor. Therefore, the goal was to come as close as possible to the restitution of the concordats abrogated unilaterally by communist regimes in the late 1940s or early 1950s. The Holy See prioritized Hungary (which Cardinal Mindszenty, for example, interpreted as a betrayal), which led to partial normalization in 1964, and Yugoslavia, which gained full normalization in 1970.[48]

The Vatican's pursuit of *Ostpolitik* preceded and served as a model for *détente* and compromise on mutual sovereignty guarantees between communist and non-communist state entities—in other words, across the epistemic lines demarcated by Marxism-Leninism. The Holy See's signature achievement as a Cold War mediator—in the spirit of the 1907 Hague language of "good offices"—came with Pope Paul VI's dispatching of Archbishop Agostino Casaroli to represent the Holy See at the Helsinki Conference on Security and Cooperation in Europe. Among others, Casaroli played a decisive role in the final formulation of the 1975 Helsinki Final Act's text on human rights and fundamental freedoms. As Lorenz Lüthi notes, "Casaroli deemed involvement a suitable tool to firm up those concessions that the Vatican had received in bilateral talks from individual socialist states, and more generally a key Vatican contribution to world peace."[49] In the end, the Helsinki Act's recognition of the "inherent dignity of the human person" reflected the position of Catholic social teaching that human rights required respect for human personhood following a long tradition dating back to Thomas Aquinas. Casaroli's work on Vatican *Ostpolitik* and on the Helsinki Final Act ultimately led Pope John Paul II to appoint him Secretary of State for the Holy See.[50]

Even though Poland, as the Soviet Bloc's most Catholic country, was arguably the top priority for Church diplomats in the 1960s, the Polish case took a back seat to Hungary and Yugoslavia insofar as it proved especially complicated due to territory disputed between German and Polish pastoral care. We see the same phenomenon discussed in Kurt Martens's chapter in this volume, in other words, the long-term deferral by the Holy See of normalization of apostolic administration when the facts on the ground had been changed. As an example, in 1945, Joseph Stalin adjusted Poland's borders, thereby incorporating into sovereign Polish territory dioceses and archdioceses long administered by Germans. Only in 1972 would the conversation move beyond temporary apostolic administration to full recognition of Polish pastoral care over Pomerania and Silesia following Paul VI's Bull *Episcoporum Poloniae coetus*.[51]

The tipping point came with the death of one uniquely positioned Polish diplomat, Kazimierz Papée, the long-lived former ambassador of the Polish government-in-exile to the Holy See. In the 1930s, Papée began his diplomatic career as Polish-language administrator of the Free City of Gdańsk/Danzig, whose neutrality guarantees originated with the League of Nations. Having been appointed the Second Polish Republic's ambassador to the Holy See in 1939, Papée would outlive that Republic. After Stalin convinced the Allies to shift their recognition to the communist government of Poland created in 1944, Papée spent three decades as a living link between the Holy

See and a government-in-exile that existed only on paper and in banquet halls in London.

By the sixth year of his posting at the Vatican, Papée had effectively become a man without a country, representing the large Polish political exile community scattered across Western Europe and the Americas, and yet in practice losing legitimacy with each passing year, as the London-based government-in-exile split into successive factions and lost the diplomatic recognition of all major powers. Interwar Poland's ambassador to the Holy See nonetheless continued to be recognized until the end of Pius XII's pontificate as Poland's legitimate ambassador in the Vatican (communist Poland transmitted messages to the Vatican through its ambassador to Rome). As soon as John XXIII replaced Pius XII, Papée lost his accreditation, yet even then, the prewar diplomat retained a vague status as plenipotentiary, thereby complicating any attempt at normalization with the Polish People's Republic.

The complexity of the Polish case highlights the grey area entwining neutrality and normalization in the Cold War history of the Holy See. The transfer of recognition from Poland's government-in-exile to its postwar Moscow-backed government arguably could have been seen as a violation of permanent neutrality—especially since Papée continued to reside in Rome until he died in 1979. Yet Paul VI's master diplomat Agostino Casaroli seized on the momentum of Willy Brandt's German *Ostpolitik* to advance the promise of Roman recognition of Polish sovereignty over formerly German lands. The bizarre coexistence of having an exiled ambassador at the Holy See and a communist ambassador in Rome ended finally and fully in the 1970s.[52]

In the midst of the Vatican *Ostpolitik* campaign, Pope Paul VI issued the 1964 encyclical *Ecclesiam Suam*. To what extent could the Holy See interface and interact formally with not just Catholics from behind the Iron Curtain but actual representatives and agents of the communist regimes? During the third and fourth sessions of the Second Vatican Council, Council fathers debated the extent to which *Ecclesiam Suam* might be read as categorically precluding the Holy See's recognition of sovereign governance by communist regimes; Polish primate Stefan Cardinal Wyszyński notably interpreted the encyclical in this way. Yet the text makes clear that the rejection of communist ideology in no way impinged upon neutrality commitments, nor should it prevent the kind of diplomatic engagement that made subsequent normalization possible: "We have today no preconceived intention of cutting ourselves off from the adherents of these systems and these regimes. For the lover of truth, discussion is always possible."[53]

THE POPE FROM BEHIND THE IRON CURTAIN

When Karol Cardinal Wojtyła was elected to the throne of St. Peter in October 1978, a range of unique legal questions presented themselves concerning the new pontiff's standing with respect to the Holy See's permanent neutrality. Unlike his Italian-born predecessors, the first non-Italian elected to the papacy since 1523 held a passport issued by communist Poland. Although he would travel on a Vatican passport as Pope John Paul II, Wojtyła's Polish citizenship was never revoked.

If anything, John Paul II's legal standing with one foot on either side of the Iron Curtain worked to the Catholic Church's distinct advantage—and, arguably, the cause of anti-communism in Poland—by putting the leadership of communist Poland in an impossible situation. Eight months after his election, in June 1979, Pope John Paul II made his first trip back to Poland, as the first of three "pilgrimages" that he would make to his homeland before the fall of the Iron Curtain. When Wojtyła returned to Poland in 1979 as head of state of the Holy See, he laid the groundwork for giving real political and legal teeth to the Holy See's involvement in 1970s debates about human rights.[54]

By energizing and attracting millions of Poles to his outdoor public sermons, John Paul II demonstrated that a challenge to communist sovereignty was possible. The seeds were thus sown for the pursuit of state-level commitments to workers' justice, challenging Polish workers to seize justice for themselves in a way that exploded the parameters of Catholic socialism. One year later, the *Solidarność* (Solidarity) trade union movement was born. John Paul II's pilgrimages to Poland were the apogee of the Holy See's Cold War moral non-neutrality. Yet the Holy See took great care—especially in its collaboration with Ronald Reagan's and Margaret Thatcher's governments—to preserve permanent legal neutrality.[55]

At the core of the Holy See's overall trajectory through the Cold War, then, was a balancing act between ideological and moral non-neutrality and permanent legal neutrality concerning sovereign commitments within the international system. Herbert Reginbogin and Pascal Lottaz have rightly underscored that neutrality must constrain war and focus on the pursuit of peace. John Paul II gave voice to a similar understanding in his landmark 1991 encyclical *Centesimus Annus*. Issued in the final months of the Cold War, a mere seven months before the collapse of the Soviet Union, this document commemorating the centennial of Leo XIII's launching of Catholic social teaching (*Rerum Novarum*, 1891) recast the collapse of communist regimes in Central and Eastern Europe as a story of peace achieved by grace, but without force. The Polish-born pope thereby tethered the (secular) judgment of history to the judgment of God.[56] The outcome was a story highlighting peace as the endpoint of the Universal Church's engagement in the temporal international order by explaining the revolutions of 1989 that dismantled communist regimes across Eastern Europe by peaceful means (except for Romania) as a product of Divine Grace. John Paul II contended, "Undoubtedly, the struggle which led to the changes of 1989 called for clarity, moderation, suffering, and sacrifice. In a certain sense, it was a struggle born of prayer, and it would have been unthinkable without immense trust in God, the Lord of history, who carries the human heart in his hands. It is by uniting his own sufferings for the sake of truth and freedom to the sufferings of Christ on the Cross that man is able to accomplish the miracle of peace."[57]

Centesimus Annus suggests that the Holy See came full circle back to commitments made in 1929, yet the fact of the matter is that those commitments were never abandoned. John Paul II's goal was to position the Church as having waged and won an ideological and spiritual victory over communism without compromising its own neutrality. Along the way, the Holy See shifted its public message about communist Central and Eastern Europe from distress at unilaterally abrogated concordats and concern over the persecution of Iron Curtain Catholics in the Stalinist years to the aggressive pursuit of diplomatic normalization with communist regimes in the 1960s and 1970s. In the final analysis, it becomes clear that moral or ideological neutrality was antithetical to the Holy See's aims throughout the Cold War. By the same token, however, the Holy See remained remarkably consistent in its legal and political commitments to permanent neutrality, even as the Cold War shook the epistemic foundations of that order.

NOTES

1. Quoted in Hiroaki Kuromiya, *Stalin: Profiles in Power* (New York: Pearson, 2005), 160.

2. Peter C. Kent, *The Lonely Cold War of Pope Pius XII: The Roman Catholic Church and the Division of Europe, 1943–1950* (Montreal: McGill-Queen's University Press, 2002). The concept "Vatican *Ostpolitik*" entered mainstream historiography via Hansjakob Stehle, *Eastern Politics of the Vatican 1917–1979*, trans. Sandra Smith (Athens, OH: Ohio University Press, 1981).

3. Giuliana Chamedes, *A Twentieth-Century Crusade: The Vatican's Battle to Remake Christian Europe* (Cambridge, MA: Harvard University Press, 2019), 5.

4. I follow here especially the important typologies of "neutrality" laid out in Pascal Lottaz and Herbert R. Reginbogin, eds, *Notions of Neutralities* (Lanham, MD: Lexington Books, 2019).

5. Piotr H. Kosicki, *Catholics on the Barricades: Poland, France, and "Revolution," 1891–1956* (New Haven, CT: Yale University Press, 2018), 1–2.

6. Pascal Lottaz and Florentino Rodao, "The Vatican, World War II, and Asia: Lessons of Neutral Diplomacy," in Lottaz and Reginbogin, *Notions of Neutralities*, 215–38, at 215.

7. The scholarly debate continues to rage between Pius XII's defenders and his prosecutors—and indeed is likely to reignite once scholars begin publishing in earnest on the vast materials from his pontificate declassified in 2020 by order of Pope Francis. It is important to distinguish between the pontiff's well-documented and clear preference for anti-liberal strongman rulers and his reputed support for the Third Reich, which remains a matter of polemic. For the most important and nuanced recent work, see, for example, Chamedes, *A Twentieth-Century Crusade*, 207–37; Robert A. Ventresca, *Soldier of Christ: The Life of Pope Pius XII* (Cambridge, MA: Belknap Press of Harvard University Press, 2013), 169–218; Hubert Wolf, *Pope and Devil: The Vatican's Archives and the Third Reich*, trans. Kenneth Kronenberg (Cambridge, MA: Belknap Press of Harvard University Press, 2010).

8. Chamedes, *A Twentieth-Century Crusade*, 26.

9. For key critical reflections on these debates, see, for example, Odd Arne Westad, "The Cold War and the International History of the Twentieth Century," in Melvyn P. Leffler and Odd Arne Westad, eds, *The Cambridge History of the Cold War* (Cambridge: Cambridge University Press, 2010), volume 1: *Origins*, 1–19; David C. Engerman, "Ideology and the Origins of the Cold War," in Leffler and Westad, *Cambridge History of the Cold War*, 1: 20–43.

10. Lorenz M. Lüthi, *Cold Wars: Asia, The Middle East, Europe* (Cambridge: Cambridge University Press, 2020).

11. See, for example, Matthew Craven, Sundhya Pahuja, Gerry Simpson, with Anna Saunders, eds., *International Law and the Cold War* (Cambridge: Cambridge University Press, 2020).

12. Chamedes, *A Twentieth-Century Crusade*, 14.

13. See, for example, Martin Conway and José Gotovitch, eds., *Europe in Exile: European Exile Communities in Britain 1940–1945* (New York: Berghahn, 2001).

14. See, for example, Piotr Wandycz, "The Polish Political Emigration and the Origins of the Cold War," *Polish Review* 47, no. 2 (2002): 317–24.

15. On the challenges of squaring national and legal boundaries at the end of the Cold War, see especially Timothy Snyder, "The Normative Nation-State (1989–1991)," in *The Reconstruction of Nations: Poland, Ukraine, Lithuania, Belarus, 1569–1999* (New Haven, CT: Yale University Press, 2003), 232–55.

16. "Conciliation Treaty" [1929], in *Vatican City Foreign Policy and Government Guide* (Washington, DC, and Vatican City: International Business Publications, 2013), volume 1: *Strategic Information and Developments*: 83–84. More generally on the Lateran Accords, see, for example, David I. Kertzer, *The Pope and Mussolini: The Secret History of Pius XI and the Rise of Fascism in Europe* (New York: Random House, 2014), 98–116; John F. Pollard, *The Papacy in the Age of Totalitarianism, 1914–1958* (Oxford: Oxford University Press, 2014), 122–59; Peter C. Kent, *The Pope and the Duce: The International Impact of the Lateran Agreements* (New York: St. Martin's Press, 1981).

17. See especially Part II ("Good Offices and Mediation") of the Hague Convention of October 18, 1907, available at https://www.loc.gov/law/help/us-treaties/bevans/m-ust000001-0577.pdf; Herbert Reginbogin, "Neutrality: Past Lessons and Visions: Providing Peace, Security, and Justice in the Twenty-First Century," in Lottaz and Reginbogin, *Notions of Neutralities*, 185–212, at 189.

18. Pascal Lottaz and Herbert R. Reginbogin, "Introduction," in Lottaz and Reginbogin, *Notions of Neutralities*, ix–xviii, at xiv.

19. Lottaz and Reginbogin, "Introduction," xiii.

20. On Pius XI's Cold War *avant la lettre*, see, for example, Kosicki, *Catholics on the Barricades*, 21–61; Chamedes, *A Twentieth-Century Crusade*, 121–66; Kent, *Lonely Cold War of Pope Pius XII*, 13–18.

21. Pius XI, *Divini Redemptoris*, March 19, 1937, available at https://w2.vatican.va/content/pius-xi/en/encyclicals/documents/hf_p-xi_enc_19370319_divini-redemptoris.html.

22. Pius XI, *Divini Redemptoris*.

23. Pius XI, *Divini Redemptoris*.

24. See, for example, Piotr H. Kosicki, "Introduction," in Piotr H. Kosicki, ed., *Vatican II behind the Iron Curtain* (Washington, DC: Catholic University of America Press, 2016), 1–26, at 12. The broader role of concordat diplomacy is one of the core themes of Chamedes, *A Twentieth-Century Crusade*.

25. Pius XII, Radiomessaggio di Sua Santità Pio XII ai Popoli del Mondo intero," December 24, 1944, available at https://www.vatican.va/content/pius-xii/it/speeches/1944/documents/hf_p-xii_spe_19441224_natale.html. On what Pius XII meant by "true democracy," see, for example, Kent, *Lonely Cold War of Pope Pius XII*, 81.

26. Quoted at Jonathan Luxmoore and Jolanta Babiuch, *The Vatican and the Red Flag: The Struggle for the Soul of Eastern Europe* (New York: Geoffrey Chapman, 1999), 103.

27. Piotr H. Kosicki, "The Catholic Church and the Cold War," in Artemy M. Kalinovsky and Craig Daigle, eds., *The Routledge Handbook of the Cold War* (London: Routledge, 2014), 259–71, at 263; Piotr H. Kosicki, "Vatican II and Poland," in Kosicki, *Vatican II behind the Iron Curtain*, 132–33.

28. Pius XII, Pronouncement, February 14, 1949, reproduced at József Mindszenty, *Memoirs of József, Cardinal Mindszenty*, trans. Richard Winston and Clara Winston (London: Weidenfeld and Nicolson, 1974), 327–28, at 327. On Mindszenty, see also chapter 8 in this volume, "The Holy See's Efforts to Secure the Departure of Cardinal Mindszenty: Diplomacy in a Cold War Context," by Arpad von Klimo and Margit Balogh.

29. The Latin-language original appears at *Acta Apostolicae Sedis* 41 (1949): 334. The "official" commentary appeared in English translation at "The Decree of the Holy Office against Communism: Some Implications," *The Tablet*, August 6, 1949.

30. I make this case at greater length in Kosicki, "Introduction."

31. See, for example, Patrick McNamara, *A Catholic Cold War: Edmund A. Walsh, S.J., and the Politics of American Anticommunism* (New York: Fordham University Press, 2005), 169.

32. See, for example, Kent, *Lonely Cold War of Pope Pius XII*, 5.
33. See, for example, Philippe Chenaux, *Une Europe Vaticane? Entre le Plan Marshall et les Traités de Rome* (Brussels: Éditions Ciaco, 1990), 31–43; Kent, *Lonely Cold War of Pope Pius XII*, 217–236; Ventresca, *Soldier of Christ*, 241–48.
34. Andrea Riccardi, *Pio XII e Alcide De Gasperi: Una storia segreta* (Rome: Laterza, 2003).
35. Quoted at Ventresca, *Soldier of Christ*, 250.
36. James Chappel, *Catholic Modern: The Challenge of Totalitarianism and the Remaking of the Church* (Cambridge, MA: Harvard University Press, 2018), 214.
37. See, for example, Georg Milbradt, "The Prospects of Christian Democracy in Contemporary Europe: Experiences from Germany," in Piotr H. Kosicki and Sławomir Łukasiewicz, eds., *Christian Democracy across the Iron Curtain: Europe Redefined* (London: Palgrave Macmillan, 2018), 439–48, at 439–41.
38. Kosicki, "Introduction," 15.
39. See the profoundly important overview of the Soviet vision of international law in Francine Hirsch, *Soviet Judgment at Nuremberg: A New History of the International Military Tribunal after World War II* (Oxford: Oxford University Press, 2020).
40. Kosicki, *Catholics on the Barricades*, especially 218–302.
41. Kosicki, *Catholics on the Barricades*, 158–63, 272–74.
42. "La necessità di due condanne," *L'Osservatore Romano*, June 29, 1955. On the condemnation of PAX, see Mikołaj Stanisław Kunicki, *Between the Brown and the Red: Nationalism, Catholicism, and Communism in 20th-Century Poland—The Politics of Bolesław Piasecki* (Athens, OH: Ohio University Press, 2012), 107–10.
43. See, for example, Elizabeth Foster, *African Catholic: Decolonization and the Transformation of the Church* (Cambridge, MA: Harvard University Press, 2019); Piotr H. Kosicki, "The Catholic 1968: Poland, Social Justice, and the Global Cold War," *Slavic Review* 77, no. 3 (2018): 638–60; Lüthi, *Cold Wars*, 462–86.
44. See, for example, the essays collected in Kosicki, *Vatican II behind the Iron Curtain*; also, Stehle, *Eastern Politics of the Vatican*; András Fejérdy, ed., *The Vatican "Ostpolitik" 1958–1978: Responsibility and Witness during John XXIII and Paul VI* (Rome: Viella, 2015); Roland Cerny-Werner, *Vatikanische Ostpolitik und die DDR* (Göttingen: V & R Unipress, 2011).
45. Gerald P. Fogarty, "Vatican II and the Cold War," in Kosicki, *Vatican II behind the Iron Curtain*, 27–49, at 35–46.
46. Andrea Riccardi, *Il Vaticano e Mosca, 1940–1990* (Rome: Laterza, 1993), 242–45.
47. Stehle, *Eastern Politics of the Vatican*, 5.
48. Arpad von Klimo, "Vatican II and Hungary," in Kosicki, *Vatican II behind the Iron Curtain*, 50–74; Ivo Banac, "Vatican II and Yugoslavia," in Kosicki, *Vatican II behind the Iron Curtain*, 75–98.
49. Lüthi, *Cold Wars*, 484.
50. See, for example, Gianni La Bella, "Paolo VI, la diplomazia e l'impegno per la pace," *Revue d'Histoire Ecclésiastique* 110, nos. 3–4 (2015): 846–71; Roberto Morozzo della Rocca, *Tra Est e Ovest: Agostino Casaroli diplomatico vaticano* (Cinisello Balsamo: San Paolo, 2014); Cerny-Werner, *Vatikanische Ostpolitik und die DDR*.

51. See, for example, Wojciech Kucharski, *Komuniści i Watykan: Polityka komunistycznej Polski wobec Stolicy Apostolskiej 1945–1974* (Warsaw: IPN-KŚZpNP, 2019); Wojciech Kucharski, "Stabilizacja polskiego Kościoła na Ziemiach Zachodnich i Północnych w świetle raportów polskich dyplomatów w Rzymie z lat 1945–1972," in Wojciech Kucharski, ed., *Droga do stabilizacji polskiej administracji kościelnej na Ziemiach Zachodnich i Północnych po II wojnie światowej: W 40. Rocznicę wydania konstytucji apostolskiej Pawła VI "Episcoporum Poloniae coetus"* (Wrocław: Ośrodek "Pamięć i Przyszłość," 2013), 121–36.

52. See, for example, Jan Żaryn, *Kościół w Polsce w latach przełomu (1953–1958): Relacje Ambasadora RP przy Stolicy Apostolskiej* (Warsaw: Neriton/IH PAN, 2000); Antoni Dudek, "Problem normalizacji stosunków między PRL a Stolicą Apostolską w latach 1971–1977," *Mazowieckie Studia Historyczne*, no. 2 (1999): 63–75.

53. Paul VI, *Ecclesiam suam*, August 6, 1964, available at http://www.vatican.va/content/paul-vi/en/encyclicals/documents/hf_p-vi_enc_06081964_ecclesiam.html; Kosicki, "Introduction," 20–22.

54. James Ramon Felak, *The Pope in Poland: The Pilgrimages of John Paul II, 1979–1991* (Pittsburgh: University of Pittsburgh Press, 2020), 21–68. Felak's chapter on the 1979 pilgrimage is entitled "Catalyst."

55. Marie Gayté, "The Vatican and the Reagan Administration: A Cold War Alliance?" *Catholic Historical Review* 97, no. 4 (2011): 713–36.

56. For an important critical reading of the concept, see Joan Wallach Scott, *On the Judgment of History* (New York: Columbia University Press, 2020).

57. John Paul II, *Centesimus Annus*, May 1, 1991, available at http://www.vatican.va/content/john-paul-ii/en/encyclicals/documents/hf_jp-ii_enc_01051991_centesimus-annus.html.

SELECTED BIBLIOGRAPHY

Chamedes, Giuliana. *A Twentieth-Century Crusade: The Vatican's Battle to Remake Christian Europe*. Cambridge, MA: Harvard University Press, 2019.

Fejérdy, András, ed. *The Vatican "Ostpolitik" 1958–1978: Responsibility and Witness during John XXIII and Paul VI*. Rome: Viella, 2015.

Felak, James Ramon. *The Pope in Poland: The Pilgrimages of John Paul II, 1979–1991*. Pittsburgh: University of Pittsburgh Press, 2020.

Fogarty, Gerald P. "Vatican II and the Cold War." In *Vatican II behind the Iron Curtain*, edited by Piotr H. Kosicki, 27–49. Washington, DC: Catholic University of America Press, 2016.

Kent, Peter C. *The Lonely Cold War of Pope Pius XII: The Roman Catholic Church and the Division of Europe, 1943–1950*. Montreal: McGill-Queen's University Press, 2002.

Kosicki, Piotr H. "The Catholic Church and the Cold War." In *The Routledge Handbook of the Cold War*, edited by Artemy M. Kalinovsky and Craig Daigle, 259–71. London: Routledge, 2014.

———. *Catholics on the Barricades: Poland, France, and "Revolution," 1891–1956*. New Haven, CT: Yale University Press, 2018.

———. "Vatican II and Poland." In *Vatican II behind the Iron Curtain*, edited by Piotr H. Kosicki, 127–98. Washington, DC: Catholic University of America Press, 2016.

Pollard, John F. *The Papacy in the Age of Totalitarianism, 1914–1958*. Oxford: Oxford University Press, 2014.

Stehle, Hansjakob. *Eastern Politics of the Vatican 1917–1979*. Translated by Sandra Smith. Athens, OH: Ohio University Press, 1981.

Chapter Eight

The Holy See's Efforts to Secure the Departure of Cardinal Mindszenty

Diplomacy in a Cold War Context

Arpad von Klimo and Margit Balogh

On September 29, 1971, the Hungarian Cardinal József Mindszenty concelebrated mass in St. Peter's, on the side of Pope Paul VI. The day before, the cardinal had boarded an airplane in Vienna, after having arrived from Budapest. A dramatic story that had begun on November 4, 1956, fifteen years earlier, had come to an end. On that day, a massive phalanx of one thousand Soviet tanks had rolled into the Hungarian capital, and Mindszenty had asked the United States Legation (since 1967, Embassy) for refuge.[1]

From this day on, the Hungarian primate's case had become a complicated challenge for international diplomacy, which had engaged not only the United States, Communist Hungary, and the Vatican governments, but also the Soviet Union. A long and complicated diplomatic situation unfolded, until Cardinal Mindszenty would leave the US Embassy and his home country. The media used the case for Cold War propaganda and speculated about secret backdoor negotiations involving various diplomats and others from both sides of the Iron Curtain. What were the Holy See's attempts to enable a solution to the crisis in a very complex situation that involved three parties that did not have diplomatic relations: Communist Hungary, the United States, and the Holy See? To move forward, the Holy See had to adapt and use approaches that likely would have been anathema to Mindszenty himself, who vehemently rejected negotiations with a Communist government. It took fifteen years, three popes, and four US presidents, as well as evolution in the Cold War and the relations between the Holy See and the Soviet-dominated World, to find a solution for Cardinal Mindszenty. In detailing these events, the Holy See used neutrality to resolve a complicated Cold War situation.[2] The meaning of "neutrality" here included contacts with both sides and the willingness to meet and negotiate with all sides equally. In contrast to Cardinal Mindszenty,

Vatican diplomats were open for negotiations with the Communist leadership of Hungary and were in close contact with US diplomats as well.

MINDSZENTY AND HIS REFUGE IN THE US LEGATION UNTIL 1963

In the center of the case stood Cardinal József Mindszenty (1892–1975). The cardinal has been mostly forgotten today, except in Hungary.[3] However, in the early phase of the Cold War and again during the 1970s and 1980s, he was known and remembered as a fierce, legendary fighter against Communism in the United States and other Western countries. His reputation in the Soviet Bloc was, correspondingly, rather negative. Mindszenty was born in 1892 in a small town in Western Hungary, not far from the Austrian border, to a family of small landowners, with the German name Pehm. As a priest, Mindszenty was a very good organizer and a voice that could not easily be missed.

Already in 1918, after the fall of the Habsburg monarchy, his loud critique of the new government brought him into conflict with state authorities and ultimately jail. Throughout the authoritarian Horthy regime, he supported the legitimist opposition. Until 1964, he would still use the title "Prince Primate of Hungary," in letters to US presidents, which expressed his opinion that the unwritten constitution of the old Hungarian Kingdom—theoretically in place until the proclamation of the Republic in 1946—was still valid which included a number of royal privileges to the archbishop of Esztergom who was the primate of Hungary.[4] In 1947, the Hungarian Republic abolished all feudal ranks and titles (law IV, 1947), and four years later, Pope Pius XII had outlawed such titles under canon law.[5] As long as he could, Mindszenty would publicly demonstrate his loyalty to the cause of the monarchy.

In 1941, he changed his name to Mindszenty—that was the place of his birth (Csehimindszent), and it sounded like nobility (von Mindszent). However, it was also interpreted as a protest against growing German influence in Hungary since 1938, when Austria was integrated into Hitler's "Greater Germany." In the same year, Mindszenty was nominated bishop of Veszprém. During the war, he protested against the pro-Nazi government under Szálasi. He was imprisoned again. This gained him "anti-fascist" credibility, although he had not protested the Holocaust, but rather the war and its devastating impact on Western Hungary. In 1945, Pope Pius XII named him Archbishop of Esztergom and Primate of Hungary, not least because of many expected conflicts with the new government and the Soviet occupation army. Very soon, Mindszenty clashed with the new regime on the question of land reform. After the Communist Party lost the elections of November 1945, they began to destroy the other political parties, piece by piece, using what was called "salami tactics" and in 1948 erected a Stalinist dictatorship. By that time, Mindszenty had become the sole leader of the anti-Communist opposition, mobilizing hundreds of thousands of believers during the 1947–1948 year dedicated to the Virgin Mary, Patroness of Hungary. His arrest on Christmas 1948 and the show trial against him was almost a logical outcome of this successful anti-Communist campaign. Among international protests—most prominently by Pope Pius XII—from Australia to Western Europe and North America, Mindszenty became a symbol of anti-Communism and the struggle for religious freedom. During the 1956 revolution against the Stalinist regime in Hungary, the cardinal was liberated for a few weeks, addressed the Hungarian nation in a radio broadcast, and fled to the United States legation. The Austrian Ambassador to the Holy See reported that some in the Vatican had somewhat expected Mindszenty to "stay with his flock."[6] Indeed, the new Pope, St John XXIII, who was elected two years later, said that "the Primate of Hungary, having been required to choose in the early hours of November 4, 1956, should have chosen the prisons of the regime rather than American asylum."[7]

Most of the main differences between the Vatican and Mindszenty were based on the understanding of his role: Was he, primarily, a priest, a pastor for his flock, or was he the representative of the Hungarian nation? He tended more and more toward the latter, perhaps because he considered the Communist regime to be illegitimate (similar to the Hungarian constitution or "Fundamental Law" introduced in 2010) and therefore held on to the older title of "Prince Primate" that also described high rank in the royal hierarchy just under the monarch.[8] Mindszenty believed he was not only a Christian martyr but also the representative of a "martyr-nation" that the victors of World War had victimized, which had "mutilated" the former Hungarian Kingdom through the 1920 Treaty of Trianon.[9] It seemed as if he saw his role as primate of Hungary mainly in this context and less in his service to the Universal Church. In 1958, when the situation in Hungary worsened and the regime escalated its repression of the opposition, the Holy See was concerned about Mindszenty's safety and asked him to consider leaving the legation. According to the US *chargé d'affaires*, Ackerson, the cardinal, was afraid that the Sacred College did not understand his position as the "last remaining representative of 'legitimate' government in Hungary."[10] Soon after, the plan was leaked, and the Hungarian government refused to let Mindszenty leave. Instead, the Communists staged "protest demonstrations" in front of the US legation.

Until 1963, the cardinal was not allowed to exchange letters with anyone except the US government. Since then, his letters to the Vatican were forwarded. This had to do with the fact that by 1963, the US administration had changed their attitude toward the cardinal, now wishing him to leave the legation voluntarily. Until then, during the first seven years of his sojourn in the legation, the relations between the superpowers were considerably strained, and Mindszenty's refuge symbolized the conflict. The Soviet and Hungarian Communist government behaviors and views during this time extended to the brutal suppression of any opposition, the executions of a number of leaders of the 1956 revolution, and the incarceration of thousands which further hardened the positions of both sides. In 1957, the Hungarian government, led by János Kádár (who would rule until 1989), even threatened to arrest Mindszenty should he leave the legation. The regime stated that Mindszenty "could no longer perform an ecclesiastical function,"[11] and the execution of any of his decrees would count as a criminal offense against the laws of the state.[12] In reality, the Communist regime was content that Mindszenty stayed in the US legation and that they did not have to deal with the thorny question of putting him on trial again and increasing his reputation as a martyr.

FROM EISENHOWER TO NIXON: THE CHANGING ATTITUDE OF THE US ADMINISTRATION

For the various United States administrations between 1956 and 1971, from Eisenhower to Nixon, Mindszenty was first a useful propaganda tool in the Cold War. But when the Cold War entered a different stage in the early to mid-1960s, the situation changed, and Mindszenty became increasingly a diplomatic burden.

President Eisenhower, just re-elected, officially welcomed Mindszenty to stay as a "guest" in the US legation, thus presenting the cardinal as proof to the claim that the United States protected religious freedom and human rights, threatened by the Soviet Union and its allies.[13] Mindszenty supported this view in a note, published a few days later by the US administration, in which he declared that the United States, serves the highest ambitions of mankind: "God, charity, wisdom, and human happiness." However, Eisenhower did not like that the cardinal asked him as the president of the United States to "liberate" his country.

President Eisenhower's successors (Kennedy, Johnson, Nixon) also allowed Mindszenty to stay in the US representation, but political circumstances changed remarkably during these fifteen years. However, the US administration made it clear that it had to be Mindszenty's decision only if he would leave the embassy. Meanwhile, the relations between the United States, Hungary, and the Soviet Union began slowly to improve.

In the early 1960s, the conflict about the Hungarian revolution of 1956, which had been openly fought out in the United Nations' halls, was ended through compromise.[14] This was also made possible by decolonization because the independent African nations that had entered the United Nations during that time did not show much interest in the "Hungarian question."[15] More important was the outcome of the Cuban Missile Crisis and Pope John XXIII's role in easing tensions between the superpowers. In December 1962, the Kádár regime had agreed in secret talks that Hungary would declare an amnesty and release most political prisoners while the United States influenced the United Nations to take the "Hungarian Question" off its agenda.[16] Since then, Washington mainly was interested in improving relations with Budapest and extending trade between the two countries. Mindszenty's presence in the United States legation—which was raised to an embassy's status in 1967—was increasingly regarded as an obstacle to these initiatives. Even for the Vatican.

VATICAN *OSTPOLITIK*, 1963–1969: THE SECOND VATICAN COUNCIL, THE AGREEMENT WITH THE KÁDÁR REGIME, AND THE SITUATION OF THE CHURCH IN HUNGARY

In 1958, Pope Pius XII had excommunicated three representatives of the state-sponsored "peace priest" movement in Hungary.[17] During the few days he was in freedom during the 1956 revolution, Mindszenty had even abolished the entire "movement." These excommunications were just one of the thorny issues that overshadowed Rome's relationship with Budapest's Communist regime. Pope John XXIII's convocation of a universal council in the Vatican, which began in 1962, facilitated new diplomatic initiatives that resulted in a partial agreement with the Hungarian government in 1964.[18] This document has to be understood in the context of *"Vatican Ostpolitik,"* a term used by journalists and scholars since the 1970s to describe the policy of détente of West Germany toward the Soviet Union, Poland, and other Eastern European countries. In the Catholic Church context, it referred to a new, more conciliatory approach the Vatican applied in its relationship with Communist countries.[19]

This change in the direction of the Holy See's foreign policy resulted from the fears of nuclear annihilation, grown because of the Cuban missile crisis, which brought the world close to an apocalyptic disaster. However, it also has to be understood in the context of Vatican anxieties about the church's situation in Communist Hungary. Before the establishment of the Communist dictatorship in Hungary, at the end of the Second World War, the Catholic

Church was still a potent and influential social institution, owning much of the land, overseeing thousands of schools, dozens of publishing houses and newspapers, and supported by organizations and associations of Catholic laypeople counting hundreds of thousands of members. But now, only a decade later, the church represented but a small, marginalized minority. The Communist state, in the words of Hungarian theologian András Máté-Tóth, "strictly controlled and limited the movements and public communication of the Hungarian Church in a number of ways."[20] An inimical state surrounded the Catholic Church in Communist Hungary. The ties between the Hungarian hierarchy and Rome were almost completely cut off. Since the last nuncio had left the country in 1945, Hungary and the Vatican have had no diplomatic relations. Concerns inside the Vatican about the churches behind the "Iron Curtain" grew, and the priorities shifted toward ways to ensure the church's very existence and ability to offer the sacraments to their believers.

One of the most complex problems was the right to nominate Hungarian bishops, which the Hungarian government had granted to the Pope alone in the *Intesa Semplice* of 1927, a right that the Communists did not acknowledge.[21] To be prepared for this struggle, the Vatican planned to install a secret "catacomb" or "underground" hierarchy. At the same time, Rome was increasingly interested in gathering first-hand information on the situation on the ground. The Polish Primate, Cardinal Wyszyński, had advised John XXIII to meet representatives from the 'silenced church' in the Communist countries of Europe. Therefore, Roncalli invited the bishops from Communist countries to meet him personally in Venice, but the Hungarian bishops were not allowed to leave the country for this purpose.

Meanwhile, in 1962, the Soviet, East German, Hungarian, and Czechoslovak Communist leadership began to see the Council as an opportunity to gather more and better information about the "bulwark of imperialism" in Rome, and, at the same time, to gain more influence on opinions inside the Catholic camp.[22]

A handful of representatives of the Hungarian Church were allowed to participate in the sessions of the Second Vatican Council in Rome. However, they left virtually no visible trace.[23] Most of them were also reporting to the Hungarian Secret Police, although in some cases, they might have been double-agents who also provided confidential information from Hungary to the Vatican. Anyway, the Vatican's new interest for priests in the areas of Soviet domination led to first contacts and negotiations to get them out of there. These new contacts between the different sides of the Cold War could later be used to solve the problems around the Mindszenty case.

A very prominent case was that of the head of the Ukrainian Greek Catholic Church, Ukrainian Archbishop of Lviv (Lemberg), Josyf Slipyj

(1892–1984), who had been languishing in Soviet Labor camps since 1945. The release of Slipyj was related to the mediation by Pope John XXIII in the Cuban Missile Crisis.[24] The Vatican price was silence about the terrible conditions of the Ukrainian Catholics in the Soviet Union. Slipyj pledged to remain silent, for which the Italian government and the Vatican authorities vouched.[25] Mindszenty would not have agreed to that. But the release of the Ukrainian Archbishop signaled a willingness of both the Vatican and the Communist governments to try out the way of negotiations. The time for *Ostpolitik* and Cardinal Agostino Casaroli (1914–1998) as special envoy for the Soviet Bloc had come. Already before Slipyj's release in 1962, Casaroli began negotiations with Hungary, Czechoslovakia, and other Communist governments. Asked about the possibility of a release of Mindszenty, the Hungarian government asked for a number of concessions by the Holy See, among others, acknowledging the traditional *ius supremi patronatus*, which gave them the right to get involved in the appointment of bishops. The Hungarian Communists also asked for guarantees that Mindszenty would not engage in "activities against the People's Republic of Hungary," and finally, that the cardinal had to plead to be pardoned regarding his prison sentence. Mindszenty was not included in the 1963 amnesty because, as party leader Kádár explained, his actions in 1956 had made him a "repeat offender."[26] It is clear that this last condition would never be accepted by Mindszenty, who regarded the Hungarian government, its laws, and the judiciary system as illegal.

But now that the ice had slowly started to melt, the Vatican wanted to ascertain what Cardinal Mindszenty's conditions were. For this, they sent the archbishop of Vienna, Cardinal Franz König as personal representative of the pope to Budapest to gather information about Mindszenty.[27] The Viennese cardinal also understood his role as a mediator with a special responsibility for the Catholics in the Soviet sphere.[28] He also headed the Secretariat for the Dialogue with the Non-Believers in the Vatican, based on the Encyclical *Ecclesiam Suam*. König would visit Mindszenty eleven times until 1971.

During his first visit to Budapest, König first spoke with the Hungarian Bishops Conference secretary, who told him that the State Office of Churches had no objection to the visit. The Viennese cardinal arrived in the car of the Austrian envoy signaling the arrival of a neighboring neutral country to Hungary.[29] In the conversation with the Viennese archbishop, Mindszenty clarified that he would not ask to be pardoned by Kádár. In a letter to König, Mindszenty laid out his far-reaching conditions, which would have annulled a part of the repressive Communist measures against the Catholic Church in Hungary and therefore had no chance of being even considered by Kádár.[30] A month later, in May 1963, Casaroli met Bishop Endre Hamvas (1890–1970), the Hungarian bishops' conference secretary, before he began his negotiations with the government in Budapest. His talks with the Hungarian government were the first direct contacts between the two sides since 1945 and indirectly recognized the Vatican's competence in religious matters. In the course of the negotiations, it came out that the Hungarian regime was more interested in solving the question of Mindszenty than the Holy See, which was more concerned about the situation of the Catholic Church in the country and wanted to have direct communication between the Hungarian hierarchy and the Vatican.

After John XXIII passed away, the new pope restarted the talks with the Hungarian regime. In the next sessions of the Second Vatican Council, Pope Paul VI met with Bishop Hamvas and others from the Hungarian delegation. At this moment, the Holy See, the United States administration, and the Hungarian Communist leadership were all interested in improving their relations. Mindszenty was upset about these developments, emphasizing to a counselor in the US legation that he was not "only a spiritual leader of Hungary" but also "a political leader."[31]

In the meantime, the Hungarian Communists showed their willingness to solve issues of church-state relations. They hoped that an agreement with the Vatican would improve their international reputation and make way for a rapprochement with the United States. A year later, on September 15, 1964, a "partial agreement" between the Holy See and Hungary was signed. It was a major diplomatic success for the regime of János Kádár. The document included a compromise regarding the nomination of bishops. Now, both parties had to agree on the candidates, although the Hungarian State still had the last word. On the same day, Rome appointed five new bishops to vacant Hungarian sees. While the Vatican accepted the nomination of new bishops favored by the Communist government, the Hungarian regime agreed to install a few bishops and priests it had previously prevented. The four new bishops and two of the formerly banned bishops took part in the new Hungarian delegation to the Second Vatican Council, now consisting of fourteen members. The two other issues that the partial agreement attempted to resolve were the oath that Catholic priests and bishops had to swear to the Hungarian Constitution of 1949. As a compromise, the oath now included the words "inasmuch as it befits a bishop or priest."[32] Finally, the Hungarian Pontifical Ecclesiastical Institute in Rome, which hitherto had been controlled by exiled priests, was handed over to the Hungarian bishops' conference as a place to offer comprehensive education to Hungarian priests. However, it also became a central hub for Hungarian intelligence gatherings inside the Vatican, as recent research has shown.[33]

In the context of the agreement, both parties stated that they kept their different positions on the *causa* Mindszenty.[34] The partial agreement did not resolve other contested issues, such as the freedom of bishops and priests' administration of their affairs or religious education in schools, etc.

The agreement was a major success for Kádár and Hungarian Communist diplomacy, while the Vatican was harshly criticized for not gaining significant improvements for the Church's situation in the country.[35] The Hungarian government even introduced new restrictions on priests' work and made a few arrests of priests engaged with youth groups, which were considered an "illegal activity."[36] And the "partial agreement" did not lead to the restoration of diplomatic relations between the Holy See and Hungary.

When Pope Paul VI met President Johnson a year later, a discussion of the status of Mindszenty in the US legation in Budapest was dropped from the agenda, obviously because the issue did not have priority.[37] This was even the case when in 1967, Hungary and the US restored full diplomatic relations, and the legation was elevated to the status of an embassy. The background of these events improved the ties between both countries and the United States' growing interest in expanding trade. Cardinal Mindszenty was not happy about this development. He thought that any concession toward Communists in Hungary or elsewhere was naïve.

After 1968, the Hungarian regime eased its suppression of religious activities in the aftermath of the Prague Spring because it was anxious about growing tensions within society. However, this did not prevent Hungarian authorities from starting another major campaign against Catholic youth groups in 1970, leading to a few arrests. Still, this was in no way comparable to the bloody persecution during the establishment of the Stalinist dictatorship in the early 1950s.

THE FINAL YEARS, 1969–1971

While the Holy See and the Hungarian Communists did not see Mindszenty's situation as an urgent issue at that time, both did not have an interest in the cardinal being outside and free to express his opinions. For US diplomats inside the embassy, the case was more pressing. Not only did Mindszenty take up some space in a relatively small building, but US ambassadors were also increasingly concerned about the health of the almost eighty-year-old prelate and possible complications in case he would need medical support. Alfred Puhan (1913–2005), the new US ambassador to Hungary since May 1969, was eager to solve the problem.[38] According to Hungarian sources, he told representatives of the regime that Mindszenty was a "stubborn and inflexible old man who is impossible to deal with."[39] Puhan had the idea to involve all three parties, the Kádár regime, the State Department, and the Holy See, to make concessions in order to make Mindszenty's departure possible.

One problem for Mindszenty to agree to his departure was his legacy. What would happen if he would leave the embassy and the country? A partial solution to this problem opened up when Paul VI issued his encyclical *Pastoralis migratorum cura* in 1969, in which the Pope emphasized that diasporas should be supported so that they could keep their faith, language, and culture. This could be a field in which Mindszenty could be helping his nation. The encyclical offered Mindszenty a way to leave the embassy without the feeling that he was "abandoning" his flock. He could maintain his dignity as the shepherd of the Hungarian diaspora all over the world. Finally, he would not give the impression that the Communists had "defeated" him.

One of the main concessions the Communist government awaited from the Holy See was the annulment of the excommunication, by papal decree in 1957, of three priests who had shown their loyalty to the regime by being very active in their support of the government and the so-called peace priest movement.[40] In exchange, the Holy See had significant concerns in resolving major problems of improving the Catholic Church in Hungary, more influence on the nomination of bishops, and better communication with the Hungarian hierarchy. Finally, in October 1970, Vatican state secretary, Jean Villot, agreed that the ex-communications of the "peace priests" would be lifted. Half a year later, Pope Paul VI welcomed the Hungarian foreign minister, János Péter, a former Calvinist bishop, in Rome. During the audience, the pope expressed his wish to solve the case of Cardinal Mindszenty.

While the three diplomatic parties seemed to come closer to an agreement, the Holy See brought in a new figure that would help to convince Mindszenty to agree to his departure: The Hungarian exiled priest, Monsignor József Zágon, canon of the Basilica of St. Maria Maggiore in Rome, and a leading representative of the Hungarian diaspora and exiled clergy since 1949, became a new key player in the negotiations.[41] In June 1971, Paul VI prompted Cardinal König to travel back to Budapest. This time, two representatives from the Holy See met him: Cardinal Giovanni Cheli, a Vatican diplomat, and Monsignor József Zágon. This group's presence—the Austrian cardinal König, the high-ranking diplomat from Rome, Cardinal Cheli, and the representative of the Hungarian diaspora and exiled priests, Monsignor Zágon, emphasized the increased commitment of the Holy See to find a solution which translated into heightened pressure on Mindszenty. Cardinal König had informed Mindszenty that the United States wanted him to leave the embassy.[42] Before the meetings, Mindszenty insisted that he would like to stay there until his death. Then, Monsignor Zágon met with the Cardinal three times, between June 25 and 27. Zágon managed to convince Mindszenty that he himself would make the final decision to leave the embassy and the country. According to documents from the US Embassy, Zágon told the cardinal: "The world is apt to forget, and it can only with difficulty judge the sojourn in the Embassy as a necessary sacrifice for the Church. The Holy Father, on the other hand, is considering such a solution which would place Your Eminence's sacrifice in a new light and which would raise it all the more, in its moral significance, in world public opinion, would in no way detract from its merits, and would serve as an example for the entire Church." [43]

Cardinal Mindszenty then asked under which conditions the Hungarian regime would allow him to leave the country. There were four: Mindszenty would keep his titles as Archbishop of Esztergom and Primate of Hungary but would lose all rights related to these titles. The second condition was that an apostolic administrator would take over these rights. Mindszenty agreed to this, but not in writing, and he also demanded that the Pazmaneum in Vienna, a seminary that was still controlled by the Vatican and Hungarian exiled priests and not by the Communist State, should remain under his jurisdiction. According to Cardinal Cheli, Mindszenty also gave his word that he would "maintain silence on [the] Hungarian political situation."[44] Mindszenty later denied that he had agreed to that condition. The final condition concerned Mindszenty's Memoirs. He would not be allowed to publish them but to hand them over to the Vatican. Mindszenty probably did not agree to this point because one of the reasons why he did finally leave the embassy was his hope that he could safeguard his memoirs and publish them in the West, which he did in 1974, a year before his death. The cardinal himself presented them at the Frankfurt Book Fair of that year, and they came out simultaneously in English and several other languages.[45] Mindszenty seemed to have agreed on the first three conditions, although he declined to sign a document. He also refused to give a date of his departure when Zágon asked him to do this.[46] Finally, Cardinal József Mindszenty signed a form in which he agreed that he would leave the US Embassy. He was obviously not completely content with this because he wrote a letter to President Nixon on the same day (June 27, 1971), complaining that the Vatican wanted him to leave.[47] In the letter, he asked the president whether he should really go, arguing that his departure could undermine the hope instilled in the many Hungarian émigrés and "slaves" (the Hungarian population).[48] The cardinal was probably hoping that Nixon would encourage him to stay. The next day, Mindszenty wrote to the pope about his decision to depart from the country, calling this the "heaviest cross" of his life.[49] Paul VI answered two weeks later, approving of Mindszenty's decision and looking forward to his arrival in Rome.

In the meantime, Nixon had replied to Mindszenty's letter, making sure that the United States had no interest in him staying. Nixon wrote: "Your decisions about the future are, of course, ones between yourself and the Vatican. I know that in reaching them you and His Holiness will be guided by your faith, by the interests of the Church, and by your concern for its ministry to the people of Hungary. I fully understand the difficulties involved in making your decision."[50]

Until 1963, both the United States and the Holy See did not engage in solving the problem of Mindszenty's situation in the US legation. Instead, the United States used him as a propaganda tool while the Holy See had no channels of communication to the Hungarian Communist regime until the exchange of letters concerning the invitations of Hungarian bishops to the Second Vatican Council. However, after 1963, both had a growing interest in Mindszenty leaving the embassy. In the end, Cardinal József Mindszenty left the US Embassy and Hungary on September 29, 1971.

NOTES

1. "1956: Soviet troops overrun Hungary," November 4. *On This Day 1950–2005*, BBC last accessed on February 18, 2021 at http://news.bbc.co.uk/onthisday/hi/dates/stories/november/4/newsid_2739000/2739039.stm.

2. Margit Balogh's detailed description of the years between 1956 and 1971 can be found in her monumental, two-volume biography of Cardinal Mindszenty. See, Margit Balogh, *Mindszenty Jóysef (1892–1975)* (Budapest: Bölcsészettudományi Kutatóközpont, 2015), volume 2, chapter 9: "A Vendég (the Guest)," 1049–1280.

3. Cf. Arpad von Klimo, "Catholic Identity in Hungary—The Mindszenty Case," *Hungarian Studies* 24, no. 2 (2010): 189–213 [törölhető].

4. For Mindszenty's use of the title "Prince Primate" until 1964, see József Puciłowski, "The Last Prince-Primate of Hungary," *New Eastern Europe* 9, no. 4 (2013): 201–4. The "Law regarding the abolishment of certain titles and ranks" of 1947 (1947. évi IV. Törvény egyes címek és rangok megszüntetéséről) is published online at https://net.jogtar.hu/jogszabaly?docid=94700004.TV.

5. Decree of May 12, 1951 of the *Sacra Congregatio Consistorialis* (Sacred Consistorial Congregation). See "Decretum de vetito civilium nobiliarium titulorum usu in Episcoporum inscriptionibus et armis," *Acta Apostolico Sedis* 43 (1951): 480.

6. Austrian State Archive (Österreichisches Staatsarchiv, ÖStA), A, AdR, BMfAA, Sektion II-pol. Zl. 63–Pol/56. Report of Joseph Kripp, Austrian ambassador to the Holy See, November 21, 1956.

7. Archives du Ministère des Affaires étrangères (AMAE), AD Série: Europe, 1956–1960, sous-série: Hongrie, dossier 103, Questions religieuses, juillet 1958–décembre 1960, fol. 86. Report no. 631/EU of Jean Paul-Boncour, the French legate in Budapest, on information supplied by the Italian legate concerning the Vatican's position. Budapest, December 9, 1958.

8. See also Arpad von Klimo, "Anticommunism and Détente. Mindszenty, the Catholic Church, and Hungarian émigrés in West Germany, 1972," *Central European History* 54, no. 3 (2021): 466–90, for the declaration of the Communist era being "illegal" in the 2010 Fundamental Law, cf. Katalin Miklóssy and Heino Nyyssönen. "Defining the New Polity: Constitutional Memory in Hungary and Beyond," *Journal of Contemporary European Studies* 26, no. 3 (2018): 322–33.

9. For Mindszenty's references to Trianon, cf. Klimo, "Anticommunism and Détente," Regarding the general cult around Trianon: Anna Menyhért, "The Image of the 'Maimed Hungary' in Twentieth Century Cultural Memory and the Twenty-First Century Consequences of an Unresolved Collective Trauma: The Impact of the Treaty of Trianon," *Environment, Space, Place* 8, no. 2 (2016): 69–97.

10. NARA RG 84, Records of the Foreign Service Posts of the Department of State, Hungary, Records Relating to Cardinal Mindszenty 1956–1972, Mindszenty classified 1958. Telegrams nos. 133 and 7 from Acting Chargé d'Affaires G. G. Ackerson to the State Department and to the US Embassy in Rome, October 15, 1958.

11. Hungarian National Archives (Magyar Nemzeti Levéltára, MNL), OL XIX–A–21–d–0013/1957, and MNL OL XIX–A–21–e–107/1957/Eln. 2.

12. Ibid.

13. *New York Times*, November 13, 1956, 21.

14. Cf. Georg Kastner, *Ungarn 1956 vor der UNO* (Innsbruck: StudienVerlag, 2010).

15. Kastner, *Ungarn 1956*, 272.

16. Arpad von Klimo, *Hungary Since 1945* (London and New York: Routledge, 2018), 71.

17. The movement of "peace priests" was an organization, controlled by the Communist secret police, of Catholic priests who were engaged in official "peace" propaganda of the regime. Cf. József Pál, *Békepapok* [*Peace priests*] (Budapest: Egyházfórum, 1995).

18. Arpad von Klimo, "Hungary and Vatican II. The Catholic Church between Communist Control and New Religious Movements," in *Vatican II Behind the Iron Curtain*, edited by Piotr Kosicki (Washington, DC: CUA Press, 2016), 50–74; see also András Fejérdy, *Pressed by a Double Loyalty: Hungarian Attendance at the Second Vatican Council 1959–1965* (Budapest, New York: Central European University Press, 2016).

19. One early use of the term was Dennis Dunn, "The Kremlin and the Vatican: Ostpolitik," *Religion in Communist Lands* 4 (1976): n. 4. The standard book was Hans-Jakob Stehle, Die Ostpolitik des Vatikans (Hamburg: Piper, 1975), translated *The Eastern Politics of the Vatican, 1917–1979* (Athens: Ohio University Press, 1981); with regard to most recent research, cf. Karl-Joseph Hummel, ed., *Vatikanische Ostpolitik unter Johannes XXIII und Paul VI, 1958–1978* (Paderborn: Schöningh, 1999); Roland Cerny-Werner, *Vatikanische Ostpolitik und die DDR* (Göttingen: V & R unipress, 2011).

20. András Máté-Tóth, "A II. Vatikáni Zsinat és a magyar elhárítás". (The II Vatican Council and the Hungarian observation), last accessed January 8, 2021 at http://arts.u-szeged.hu/download.php?docID=26196.

21. András Fejerdy, "Szentszéki stratégiák a magyarországi püspöki székek betöltése érdekében 1945–1964 között" [Strategies of the Holy See Regarding the Filling of Vacant Bishoprics between 1945 and 1964], *Történelmi Szemle* LV (2013) 2: 291–305.

22. Csaba Szabó, *A Szentszék és a Magyar Népköztársaság kapcsolatai a hatvanas években* [The relations between the Holy See and the Hungarian People's Republic in the 1960s] (Budapest: Szent István Társulat/Magyar Országos Levéltár, 2005). On the spy web around and inside the Vatican: Tamás Majsai, "'Ismereteimet soha, senkinek nem fedhetem fel.' Papi ügynökök a Vatikán előszobáiban" ["'What I know I will never reveal to anyone.' Priests as Spies in the Vatican Antechamber"]—I. Rész, *Beszélő folyóirat* 12 (2007): n12, last accessed on February 18, 2021 at http://beszelo.c3.hu/cikkek/%E2%80%9Eismereteimet-soha-senkinek-nem-fedhetem-fel%E2%80%9D.

23. For more details, see Klimo, "Hungary and Vatican II."

24. Gerald P. Fogarty, SJ, "Vatican II and the Cold War," in *Vatican II behind the Iron Curtain*, 27–49.

25. Stehle, *Geheimdiplomatie im Vatikan*, 291.

26. Quoted in the document collection *Mindszenty és a hatalom*, edited by Zoltán Ólmosi (Budapest: Lex, 1991), 96.

27. Mária Pallagi, "Ein unerwünschter Gast—Kardinal Mindszenty in der Amerikanischen Botschaft und die Besuche von Kardinal König (1956–1971)—Die Ostpolitik des Vatikans gegenüber Ungarn und der Fall Mindszenty," in *Österreich und Ungarn im Kalten Krieg*, edited by István Majoros, Zoltán Maruzsa, and Oliver Rathkolb (Budapest and Vienna: ELTE BTK and Universität Wien, 2010), 373–405.

28. Annemarie Fenzl, Kardinal König, and Kardinal Mindszenty, "Die Ostpolitik des Vatikan," in *József Kardinal Mindszenty in Wien (1971–1975)*, edited by Csaba Szabó (Wien: Collegium Hungaricum, 2012), 59–80, at 61.

29. For more details, see Ádám Somorjai, ed., Sancta Sedes Apostolica et Cardinalis Ioseph Mindszenty II: Documenta 1956–1963 (Budapest: METEM, 2009), 67–69, 151.

30. See Somorjai, Sancta Sedes, 136–37.

31. NARA RG 59, GR of the Department of State, Bureau of European Affairs, Office of Eastern European Affairs, Records relating to Hungary 1941–1977, Box 11, June 19, 1963–Dec 4, 1963. Letter of Turner B. Shelton, Counselor of the US Legation, to Robert McKisson, September 10, 1963.

32. For the text of the agreement, see Margit Balogh, András Fejérdy and Csaba Szabó, "Az 1964-es magyar–szentszéki részleges megállapodás," *ArchívNet* 18, no. 6 (2018), last accessed on February 18, 2021, at http://www.archivnet.hu/az-1964-es-magyar-szentszeki-reszleges-megallapodas.

33. Stefano Bottoni, "A Special Relationship. Hungarian Intelligence and the Vatican, 1961–1978," in *NKVD/KGB Activities and its Cooperation with other Secret Services in Central and Eastern Europe 1945–1989* (Bratislava: Anthology of the international and interdisciplinary conference, 2008), last accessed on February18, 2021, atwww.upn.gov.sk/publikacie_web/zbornik-nkvd-EN.pdf.

34. MNL OL XIX–A–21–e–0022–20/a/1964. Minutes, September 15, 1964.

35. Cf. Open Society Archive. (OSA) Radio Free Europe (FRE), Report, Hungary, September 18, 1964, last accessed on February 18, 2021, at https://catalog.osaarchivum.org/catalog/osa:4c728ca2-b27a-46fa-b636-c831371dd0b1.

36. Arpad von Klimo, "Katholische Jugendgruppen in Ungarn in der zweiten Hälfte der sechziger Jahre. Die Gruppen um Regnum Marianum—ein religiöses Netzwerk?" in *Improvisationen. Gesellschaftliche Subsysteme in Ostmitteleuropa und in der DDR*, edited by Annette Schuhmann (Köln, Weimar, and Wien: Böhlau, 2008), 121–37.

37. László Borhi, *Magyar-amerikai kapcsolatok, 1945–1989: Források* [*Hungarian-American Relations, 1945–1989: Sources*] (Budapest: MTA Történettudományi Intézet, 2009), 449.

38. The French Ambassador reported about Puhan's determination to solve the problem. Cf. AMAE AD Série: Europe 1961–1970, Saint-Siège, dossier 77, "Cardinal Mindszenty 1966 a 1970." Report no. 485/EU of Raymond Gastambide, French Ambassador in Budapest, July 10, 1969, last accessed on February 18, 2021, at https://history.state.gov/departmenthistory/people/puhan-alfred.

39. Zoltán Szatucsek, "Makacs öregúr vagy nemzetmentő vátesz? Diplomáciai egyeztetések Mindszenty sorsáról 1970–1971-ben" (Stubborn Old Man or Saviour of the Nation? Diplomatic Exchanges about Mindszenty's Fate in 1970–1971"), in Közel-Múlt: Húsz történet a 20. századból (*Near Past: 20 Stories from the Twentieth Century*), edited by György Majtényi and Orsolya Ring (Budapest: Magyar Országos Levéltár, 2002), 20–35.

40. Csaba Szabó, "Kardinal Mindszenty verläßt Ungarn im Jahre 1971," in *Kardinal Mindszenty in Wien*, 29–46, at 37.

41. Mária Pallagi, "Der Mann, den seine Zeit ins Exil schickte" (Kardinal Mindszenty, Kardinal König und die Vatikanische Ostpolitik), *Öt Kontinens (ELTE BTK)* 2 (2013): 337–70.

42. Fenzl, *Kardinal König*, 75.

43. NARA RG 84, Records of the Foreign Service Posts of the Department of State, Hungary, Subject Files Relating to Cardinal Mindszenty 1956–1972, Box 5, Cardinal Mindszenty July–December 1971. Pro memoria. Subject: Visit with Jozsef Cardinal Mindszenty, Primate of Hungary and Archbishop of Esztergom, at the American Embassy in Budapest, June 25–27, 1971.

44. Ádám Somorjai and Tibor Zinner, "Washingtonból jelentjük: A budapesti amerikai nagykövetség Mindszenty bíboros tevékenységére vonatkozó, 1971-ben keletkezett iratai" ("Report from Washington: Documents from the US Embassy in Budapest in relation to Cardinal Mindszenty in 1971."), Századok 144, no. 1 (2010): 153–54.

45. Cf., last accessed on February 18, 2021, at https://www.worldcat.org/search?qt=worldcat_org_all&q=Mindszenty+Memoirs.

46. NARA RG 84, Records of the Foreign Service Posts of the Department of State, Hungary, Subject Files Relating to Cardinal Mindszenty 1956–1972, Box 5, Cardinal Mindszenty July–December 1971. Pro memoria, June 25–26–27, 1971.

47. Presidential Advisor Henry Kissinger noted that "the actual text is rather difficult to understand, since the Cardinal wrote in English," which sometimes gave

rise to problems of interpretation. Nixon Library, NSC Files, Box 828, Name Files, Mindszenty, Cardinal (April 1970–May 1974). Memorandum for the President from Henry A. Kissinger, July 12, 1971.
48. The letter is published in "Do Not Forget This Small Honest Nation." Cardinal Mindszenty to 4 US Presidents and State Secretaries 1956–1971 as Conserved in American Archives and Commented by American Diplomats. A Documentary Overview, edited by Ádám Somorjai, OSB., and Tibor Zinner (Bloomington, IN: Xlibris, 2013), 372.
49. A detailed contemporary account is given in L'Osservatore Romano, September 29, 1971.
50. "Do Not Forget This Small Honest Nation," 373.

SELECTED BIBLIOGRAPHY

Balogh, Margit. *Mindszenty József (1892–1975)*. Budapest: Bölcsészettudományi Kutatóközpont, 2015.
Borhi, László. *Magyar-amerikai kapcsolatok, 1945–1989: Források (Hungarian-American Relations, 1945–1989: Sources)*. Budapest: MTA Történettudományi Intézet, 2009.
"Do Not Forget This Small Honest Nation." Cardinal Mindszenty to 4 US Presidents and State Secretaries 1956–1971 as Conserved in American Archives and Commented by American Diplomats. A Documentary Overview. Edited by Ádám Somorjai, OSB, and Tibor Zinner. Bloomington, IN: Xlibris, 2013.
Fejérdy, András. *Pressed by a Double Loyalty. Hungarian attendance at the Second Vatican Council 1959–1965*. Budapest and New York: Central European University Press, 2016.
Klimó (a kiadvány címlapján ékezetekkel szerepel a név, ezért javítottam), von. "Anticommunism and Détente. Mindszenty, the Catholic Church, and Hungarian Émigrés in West Germany, 1972." *Central European History* 54, no. 3 (2021): 1–25. DOI:10.1017/S0008938920001089
Kosicki, Piotr, ed. *Vatican II behind the Iron Curtain*. Washington, DC: Catholic University of America Press, 2016.
Pallagi, Mária. "Der Mann, den seine Zeit ins Exil schickte." *Kardinal Mindszenty, Kardinal König und die Vatikanische Ostpolitik*. Öt Kontinens (ELTE BTK) 2 (2013): 337–70.
Sancta Sedes Apostolica et Cardinalis Ioseph Mindszenty II. Documenta 1956–1963. Edited by Ádám Somorjai. Budapest: METEM, 2009.
Somorjai, Ádám, and Zinner, Tibor, eds. "Washingtonból jelentjük: A budapesti amerikai nagykövetség Mindszenty bíboros tevékenységére vonatkozó, 1971-ben keletkezett iratai" (Report from Washington: Documents from the US Embassy in Budapest in relation to Cardinal Mindszenty in 1971)). *Századok* 144, no. 1 (2010): 153–54.
Szabó, Csaba, ed. *József Kardinal Mindszenty in Wien (1971–1975)*. Wien: Collegium Hungaricum, 2012.

Part IV

POST-COLD WAR: 1990–2020

Chapter Nine

Pope Francis and Vatican Sovereignty

Massimo Faggioli

PAPAL DIPLOMACY DURING FRANCIS: AREAS AND CRISES

In February 2019, the Vatican secretary of state, Cardinal Pietro Parolin, addressed a study day at the University LUMSA (Libera Università degli Studi Maria SS Assunta di Roma) in Rome to mark the ninetieth anniversary of the signing of the Lateran Pacts. Cardinal Parolin stated that through its use of "positive neutrality," "the Holy See does not limit itself to simply looking out the window but contributes to building a dialogue between the parties involved."[1] Being in this kind of perpetual "dialogue" with states, he continued, is intended to "assure humanity a worthy future."[2] For example, the Vatican's stance on Venezuela was shaped by this concept. Cardinal Parolin described the Vatican's position on the Venezuelan crisis as one of "positive neutrality . . . not an attitude of someone sitting in front of a window and observing indifferently; it is an attitude of being with the parts in order to overcome the conflict."[3]

This is part of a bigger picture of the role of the papacy in Francis's pontificate. Francis has interpreted the neutrality and sovereignty of the Vatican in new ways, in the context of what can be called "the liminal papacy" of Francis: the emphasis on the peripheries also means a redefinition of boundaries and borders in this age of new walls.[4]

There is a long history of the active engagement of the Vatican in international affairs. The fact that the Holy See accepts the existing division of states and their sovereignty is part of the post-Vatican II Era of the papacy and its international diplomatic posture. The Holy See is a firm supporter of international law and international institutions; it has great respect for the United Nations, which it sees as mirroring the theology of the unity of the human family. This reflects an acceleration in the degree of involvement with the secular world, especially after World War II and during the Cold War.[5]

Under Pope Francis's pontificate, there is a continuation in terms of this approach to world affairs. In the first seven years of Francis's pontificate, among his trips outside Italy (2013–2020, until the COVID-19 travel hiatus), less than one-third of his visits were to European countries, with the vast majority of journeys taking place in Asia, followed by a similar percentage of trips to Latin American countries—together with Africa this is the demographic future of the Church. But he did not limit himself to his flock. Only roughly half of the nations he visited have a Catholic majority, while the other half comprises countries with a Muslim majority, an Eastern Orthodox majority, or a Buddhist majority. Eight of the European nations he visited were historically non-Catholic (Albania, Bosnia and Herzegovina, Greece, Sweden, Romania, Bulgaria, and Macedonia). The recent apostolic trip to Iraq, undertaken in March 2021, fits this pattern.

This teaching of the pope as a pilgrim with his apostolic trips has not been isolated from a new engagement of the Holy See, active in many international crises that mark the crisis of the international order: the confidential role of mediation for the end of the embargo of the United States against Cuba in 2014 and the constitutional crisis in Venezuela since 2016; the public pressure made on the situation in Myanmar, Central African Republic, Syria, Ukraine, and Crimea, between North and South Korea; the moral suasion between Israel and Palestine especially during his trip of May 2014; the support given to the European Union multiple times, especially between 2014 and 2017.

A specific kind of diplomatic engagement (which had already started with John Paul II) produced the landmark agreement of September 2018 with the People's Republic of China on the issue of bishops' appointments, renewed in October 2020.[6] In April 2019, in the Vatican, Pope Francis got on his hands and knees before South Sudan's government's leaders and its opposition, kissing their feet and imploring them to maintain peace.[7] In September 2020, Francis called for a day of prayer and fasting on Friday for Lebanon.[8]

The Holy See has used the pope's voice, and its network of papal diplomats accredited as observers to international organizations to advocate for migrants, for nuclear disarmament, for a joint effort in the care for creation, against human trafficking, and modern-day slavery. The pope himself also reaffirmed the political and juridical nature of the Holy See symbolically, such as when Francis rescued twelve Muslim refugees from a detention camp in Lesbos in April 2016 and took them to Rome on the papal flight, an extraordinary privilege available to the pope as the sovereign of the Vatican City State.[9]

ROME AND THE PAPACY: FROM THE DUALISM WITH THE EMPIRE TO THE GLOBAL PERSPECTIVE

The diplomatic engagement of the papacy in international affairs must be seen in the Church's long history of international diplomacy. The dualism between papacy and empire in the early second millennium led to a rare occasion by creating one of the longest-living legal institutions to regulate the relations between church and political entities: the Concordat of Worms 1122.[10] It inaugurated a particular form of relationship between the church and political authorities. The concordat defined the spaces of autonomy and freedom of the Church in a context shaped by a growing contestation of the "absolute" nature of ecclesiastical power. The concordat policy was a key instrument of the Holy See's foreign policy until the second half of the nineteenth century, when it seemed to halt due to the growing mistrust—not only from the Church's part—in this instrument's effectiveness. But in the aftermath of the end of the First World War, in a situation marked on the one hand by the defeat and disappearance of some traditional interlocutors—the empires (the Russian, the German, the Austro-Hungarian, and the Ottoman Empires)—and on the other by the emergence of many new protagonists cobbled together from these empires on the international scene, new nation-states.[11] It was Pius XI who would pave the way for a new intense phase in the creation of concordats, which would soon lead to define the twentieth century as the "Age of Concordats." In this context, the particular role played the 1929 Lateran Treaties—a completely unique kind of concordat, not comparable with others, given the implications for the Vatican's territorial sovereignty. The Lateran Pacts consisted of a treaty, which defined the mutual relations between the Italian State and the Holy See on the level of international law, and a concordat, concerning the discipline of ties between the state and the Catholic confession; the treaty also had internal provisions typical of a concordat and not only provisions of international law. With the Lateran Treaties, the Catholic Church recognized the existence of an Italian State and definitively set aside any legal claim on Rome's territory.

The legal and political solution given, at the international level, to the "Roman Question" came to fruition, in a new way, after World War II and with the first pope elected after the end of the war, John XXIII.[12] There is parallelism here between John XXIII (known previously as Angelo Giuseppe Roncalli) and Pope Francis. John XXIII inherited a church that was supposed to be firmly on the side of NATO and the anti-Communist alliance at the height of the Cold War. However, his last encyclical, *Pacem in Terris* (April 11, 1963), liberated the church from this geopolitical and ideological alignment, a shift already somewhat implicit in Vatican II. Roncalli saw that shift with particular clarity, and the diplomatic circles in the West received it with great concern.[13]

Fifty-five years later, Pope Francis inherited a post-9/11 Catholicism in which the neoconservative narrative (especially in the Anglosphere) sees the church as part of an ideological and political anti-Muslim alliance. Francis has disavowed that ideological narrative of Catholicism. In this context, the political pushback against John XXIII's encyclicals *Mater et Magistra* (1961) and *Pacem in Terris* (1963) are analogous to the ideological criticism of the exhortation *Evangelii Gaudium* (2013), of the encyclical *Laudato Si'* (2015), and more recently of the *Document on Human Fraternity for World Peace and Living Together* (2019, also known as the Abu Dhabi document, signed with the Grand Imam of Al-Azhar in Cairo, Ahmad Al-Tayyeb), and of the encyclical *Fratelli Tutti* "on fraternity and social friendship."[14]

This global re-alignment by Pope Francis is based on a few critical intellectual foundations. The first theme draws on the concept of positive neutrality—a work in progress so associated with Pope Francis. It has to do with the shift from a dualistic understanding of the relations between the Church and the world to an understanding of the Church in the world consistent with the ecclesiology of the pastoral constitution *Gaudium et Spes*, the last of the final documents approved by Vatican II, on December 7, 1965.[15]

Second, there is an interpretation of global history. Francis embodies a post-European Catholic sense of the Church's universality, with a clear understanding of the meaning of the "irruption of America" (in the sense of Latin America) in history. The irruption of America in history signified by the Latin America of Pope Francis means not only the end of the Spanish colonial empire but also a rearranging of historical narratives concerning the other European empire, namely, the British, whose role in the history of global Christianity between the eighteenth century and the twentieth century is crucial. This irruption of America in history means a new protagonist of the *pueblo*. Nevertheless, the relationship between the *ad intra* and *ad extra* in contemporary Catholicism has both a geopolitical and a geo-cultural dimension. Also typical of Francis's pontificate is the intimate connection between Catholic ecclesiology and an internationalist view of globalization that refuses to shrink Catholicism to an identity-driven religious community with a geopolitical center housed in the West.[16]

Francis's global perspective entails relativizing Catholicism's historical traumas in the West, Europe, and that incredibly intricate relationship between papal history and modern Italian history. It became visible in his speech of February 3, 2020, for the 150th anniversary of Rome as the capital of Italy:

Remembering the event of Rome Capital, on the eve of the Second Vatican Council, Cardinal Montini said: "It seemed like a collapse; and for the pontifical territorial dominion it was. . . . But Providence, as we now see well, had arranged things differently, almost dramatically playing in the events." The proclamation of Rome as Capital was a providential event, which at the time caused controversy and problems. But Rome, Italy and the Church itself changed: a new history began. . . . I would like to recall, secondly, the years of Vatican Council II, from 1962 to 1965, when the city welcomed the Council Fathers, ecumenical observers, and many others. Rome shone as a universal, Catholic, ecumenical space. It became a universal city of ecumenical and interreligious dialogue, of peace. One saw how much the city meant for the Church and for the whole world. . . . Rome will have a future if we share the vision of a fraternal, inclusive city, open to the world. On the international scene, full of conflict, Rome could be a city of encounter."[17]

Francis's interpretation of Rome's role in the global world follows Paul VI's and is an integral part of his vision of the papacy and the Catholic Church's role. In 1870 the Italian troops entered Rome, where the court and government of the new kingdom of Italy were transferred the following year. For more than one thousand years, the pope had been the temporal ruler of the Papal States. The definitive loss of the Papal States (after a first interruption by Napoleon between 1796 and 1815) and the end of the temporal power of the pope was interpreted in a providential manner by Paul VI one century later, in 1970: the pope talked about the end of the Papal States as the liberation of the papacy from the burden of having to govern, as a king, a state. This has liberated spiritual and moral energies that have become even more necessary for the global Catholic Church's papacy. This entails a re-interpretation of the role of the city of Rome for the whole world: with Francis, there is a further step compared to the acknowledgment of that fact of history given by Paul VI fifty years before.

As a pope from Argentina, for Francis, it is a matter of history but also geography. The spiritual geography of the new pope became an integral part of the pontificate from the first few moments: a pope almost from "the end of the world" from Rome—as he said in his first address to the people in St. Peter's Square immediately after his election in the evening of March 13, 2013.[18] The fact that Francis's background from Argentina is peripheral in the historical geography of Catholicism, compared to his predecessors on the throne of Peter, had an impact, from the beginning of the pontificate, on his way of dealing with the transition from the archbishop of Buenos Aires to the bishop of Rome and pope of the Catholic Church: for instance, the decision not to live in the papal apartment should not be understood only as a sign of humility, but also as a symbolic re-inculturation of the papacy, beginning with the physical and geographical spaces it occupies. Moreover, this re-inculturation is especially significant and visible in a city like Rome, which re-signified itself many times, but in the early modern period, it was especially built to be a court, a theater, and a stage for the papacy and the Church.

Elected in 2013, Pope Francis (known until then as Jorge Mario Bergoglio) was never part of that Roman court and stage, in stark departure from his predecessors. Indeed, as Jorge Mario Bergoglio, he had even spent some time in a sort of internal exile from his Church and his religious order, the Jesuits, in Cordoba, Argentina.[19] Later, as archbishop, a deep-seated experience for Bergoglio was to get out and go to the peripheries of his diocese: this enabled him to develop "a 'theology of the city,' which is something quite rare in today's Catholicism."[20] His role as an outsider was part of his Argentinian life, as it is for his Roman life: he is a real outsider in Rome; a stranger to its particular ecclesial, clerical, and curial sociability, with no Roman circle or milieu in his pre-papal life because he was never a student or professor at a Roman university nor had he worked in Rome as a Curia official.

Francis's favorite places to meet people and spend time are not the same as those of his predecessors, even the immediate predecessors on Peter's throne. As bishop of Rome, he has drawn a new map, one that is vastly different from the traditional plan of papal power in the "holy city" created and solidified between the Renaissance and the Baroque period—this was when the image of Rome was rebuilt after the end of the Great Western Schism. During the first half of the fifteenth century, the papal court was reconstituted, a crucial transitional period for the city's rebirth.

In the recent history of Rome, the label of "holy city" had often been used for political-ecclesiastical operations that were very far from Francis's view of politics—from the "conciliation" between the Holy See and the Fascist regime in 1929 to the maneuvering to elect a far-right mayor for Rome in 1952. Francis has discarded the vestiges of the imperial and political papacy (such as the red shoes and the summer residence of Castel Gandolfo) and is bringing Rome much closer to becoming a truly "holy city" that brings the bishop of Rome closer to the immigrants and refugees, to prison inmates, and the marginalized. The geography of Francis's action is much more focused on prisons, hospitals, slums, and refugee camps than it is on pontifical universities and academies and the halls of the ecclesiastical and political power of the city capital of Italy and the central government of Roman Catholicism. Contrary to his predecessors until Benedict XVI, Francis never used the papal palace of Castel Gandolfo (sixteen miles from Rome), acquired by the papacy in 1596; in 2016, Francis decided to turn that summer residence into a museum.

The decentralization of the Church with the pope's election from Argentina coincided with Italy's decentralization from the international scene in a geopolitical shift of power toward other European countries (especially Germany) and other areas of the world (especially Asia). Francis came to Rome when it was very evident that the city was transitioning from being one of the world's capitals to one of the many peripheries of politics and religion. At the same time, Francis is faithful to Rome's special genius related to the Italian peninsula's geography and the city's contradictory identities: sacred yet profane, religious yet anticlerical, glamorous yet surrounded by poverty, admired yet reviled. It is not only the city of Rome, whose relationship with the papacy has historically fluctuated significantly—from a warm embrace to threats against the people's physical safety. It is also the Italian peninsula. Francis is a pope whose map of Italy is significantly different from that of his predecessors. From his first trip outside Rome in July 2013 to Lampedusa's island, Francis is a pope who prefers to visit peripheral but symbolically essential places rather than big cities. For example, he traveled to the small cemeteries of Bozzolo and Barbiana in Northern and Central Italy on June 20, 2017, where two important Italian priests for twentieth-century Italian Catholicism, Father Primo Mazzolari and Father Lorenzo Milani, were buried. Despite their hierarchical obedience to authorities, their teaching and witness, especially in favor of a culture of peace and their radical critique of a hypocritical, "law and order," bourgeois Catholicism created tensions with the institutional Church. It ultimately led to a marginalization also in the memory of the Catholic community. Francis was the first pope and the first prelate to publicly acknowledge these two priests' contributions.

The new spiritual geography of the papacy could also be seen in the town of Nomadelfia in Tuscany, where on May 10, 2018, Francis visited the community of families started there in 1947 by Father Zeno Saltini—one of the many priests inspired by "holy madness" and ministering in the peripheries of twentieth-century Italian Catholicism.

Francis's distance from the traditional stages of papal power signal the desire to be physically close to the forgotten locations of human drama in the geography of today's world. The peripheries of Italy have offered opportunities to convey his message early on in his pontificate. As he said in his homily in Lampedusa in July 2013, as the first bishop in Italy to visit that tragic transit point for refugees between the South and the North of the world, between Europe, Africa, and the Middle East: "So I felt that I had to come here today, to pray and to offer a sign of my closeness, but also to challenge our consciences lest this tragedy be repeated."[21]

LIMINALITY AND MARGINALITY

A powerful second theme necessary to understand Francis's view of the papacy's role is the geographical and existential marginality in the globalized world impacted by the chronological liminality of this moment in history.

For a long time, Francis's pontificate has been viewed almost as if it were hanging in the vacuum between the sudden end of the previous pontificate and the beginning of his pontificate. It is about the unfinished transition from one pontificate to another because Pope Benedict XVI decided to resign, to become "emeritus" (a title that did not exist before and is theologically and canonically questionable), and to live in the Vatican as "emeritus" in conditions not dramatically different than when he was pope.

However, there is a deeper liminality at the heart of this pontificate. The first liminal character of Francis's papacy has to do with the way Jorge Mario Bergoglio became pope, inaugurating a pontificate while his predecessor was not entirely over in the eyes of the global Church: Francis on the threshold between the old and the new.[22] There is a liminality of Pope Francis that begins with his very election in the conclave, but that symbolizes the entire pontificate and its meaning for global Catholicism: a critical junction in the history of the Catholic Church between an "already" and a "not yet" which can be understood only with the effort to look at this pontificate from a multilayered historical perspective.

Simultaneously, when writing about a pope, one must remember that Christianity is both history *and* geography. This is particularly true for Francis's pontificate. The liminality of Francis is, at the same time, historical and geographical. His emphasis on the margin and the peripheries also entails a redefinition of boundaries and borders. Francis is a pope from the margins, visibly challenging the revival of the borders in our political discourse. In Francis's imagination, the border is more a *limen* (in Latin, "threshold") than a *limes* (in Latin, "rigid frontier"). The liminality concept is key to understanding Francis's pontificate because of his reinterpretation of the borders in this age of new walls. It is a border that relates and connects "the other" more than excludes. This is at the heart of Francis's project in which liminality is a central aspect of the *pontifex*, etymologically the "bridge-builder": both *geographically*—a new map of the global world in the disruption of globalization—and *historically*—the effort to reconnect the Church and tradition in a non-traditionalist way.

Francis's liminality, his being on the border (*limes*) between the old and the new, is a fact determined by his Latin American background, his coming from a family of Italian migrants to South America, and the moment that his pontificate represents in the history of the papacy. Francis did not take distance or neutralize from this aspect of his biography for fear of destabilizing the papal office. On the contrary, Francis has turned this into a particular attention to the peripheries and the marginalized in a complex articulation of an "explicit and implicit topology," a particular mapping and naming of the sources of his doing theology: explicit in his drawing from popular piety of Catholics on the margins, and implicit in his drawing from forms of believing and thinking of the people of God.[23]

Francis has used the concept of "peripheries" from the beginning of his pontificate as a metaphor of social marginality having to do with the political and economic system than with the ecclesial. The encounter with "the marginalized" calls more the responsibility of the Christian community. Francis encourages Christians not to marginalize the sick, the poor, the outcast social sinners. A significant moment in Francis's opposition was when, during the in-flight press conference back from the trip to Brazil on July 28, 2013, the pope talked about gays as marginalized.[24] For Francis, marginalization is a spiritual and ecclesial temptation and, therefore, also a theological issue. He talked about this in his homily during the Mass with new cardinals created at the consistory, on February 15, 2015, when he spoke about Jesus's Gospel as "reinstatement" of the marginalized: "*Compassion* leads Jesus to concrete action: *he reinstates the marginalized!* These are the three key concepts that the Church proposes in today's liturgy of the word: the *compassion* of Jesus in the face of *marginalization* and his desire to *reinstate*."[25]

Francis's turn to the peripheries and the marginalized therefore started early in his pontificate. His major documents can and must be read through this lens of a decentering of the pope and the magisterium toward new outposts of the Church.[26] This compassion as attention to the marginalized can be seen from the new pastoral approach on LGBT persons in the Church as well as the reordering Catholic moral and theological priorities in a departure from the slogans of the American "culture wars."

His is the church of his namesake Francis of Assisi, who taught that one should preach the gospel with as few words as possible.

This liminal and peripheral turn of the Church also means a repositioning in Francis's imagination and language about other actors in the world of this time: Church, state, and society are not seen in a Christendom-like scenario of the subjection of state and society to the Church, but squarely in a Vatican II and post-Vatican II worldview, where the "marginal Jew," Jesus Christ,[27] and his relationship with the social and geographical peripheries of his time have become more paradigmatic than before for the Roman papacy.

ACTIVISM, PEACE, AND NEUTRALITY

There is a third theme that emerges from Pope Francis's new understanding of Vatican neutrality's role for the mission of the Catholic Church: the activity and activism for building a culture of peace. Francis has addressed the relationship between neutrality and peace many times.

In the Angelus of Sunday August 18, 2013, commenting on the reading in the New Testament of Luke 12:51 ("Do you think that I have come to give peace on earth? No, I tell you, but rather division"), Francis made clear his vision of neutrality:

> Jesus does not bring neutrality; this peace is not a compromise at all costs. Following Jesus entails giving up evil and selfishness and choosing good, truth and justice, even when this demands sacrifice and the renunciation of our own interests. And this indeed divides; as we know, it even cuts the closest ties. However, be careful: it is not Jesus who creates division! He establishes the criterion: whether to live for ourselves or to live for God and for others; to be served or to serve; to obey one's own ego or to obey God.[28]

Francis continued after the Angelus: "Following Jesus is not neutral; following Jesus means being involved because faith is not a superficial decoration; it is a strength of the soul!"[29]

Francis had no qualms in showing his embrace of one of the significant shifts in modern Catholic magisterial tradition since Vatican II: from a church concerned with the task of granting the label of "just war" to the rulers of the Christian West to a global church actively engaged for peace. One of the most dramatic moments when the pope's authority was on display on the world scene on September 7, 2013, when the pope presided at the vigil for peace for Syria. He did not make the legal claim of the superior moral authority of the Church over the nations. Nevertheless, his appeal (which had followed the Angelus of September 1) was not vague in its intentions, in the context of those days when many expected American military strikes in Syria:

> I ask the Lord that we Christians, and our brothers and sisters of other religions, and every man and woman of goodwill, cry out forcefully: violence and war are never the way to peace! Let everyone be moved to look into the depths of his or her conscience and listen to that word which says: Leave behind the self-interest that hardens your heart, overcome the indifference that makes your heart insensitive towards others, conquer your deadly reasoning, and open yourself to dialogue and reconciliation.[30]

In the homily delivered on January 1, 2016, in the Vatican Basilica, during the jubilee of mercy, Francis opposed mercy and neutrality:

> All of us are called to immerse ourselves in this ocean [of mercy], to let ourselves be reborn, to overcome the indifference which blocks solidarity, and to leave behind the false neutrality which prevents sharing. The grace of Christ, which brings our hope of salvation to fulfillment, leads us to cooperate with him in building an ever more just and fraternal world, a world in which every

person and every creature can dwell in peace, in the harmony of God's original creation.[31]

In an important speech delivered in Bologna in October 2017, Francis invited to reflect on the role of the church and the war:

> A hundred years ago, the cry of Benedict XV, who had been Bishop of Bologna, was raised, who defined the war as a "useless massacre" (*Letter to the leaders of the belligerent peoples*, August 1, 1917). To dissociate in everything from the so-called "reasons for the war" seemed to many almost an affront. But history teaches that war is always and only a useless massacre. Let us help ourselves, as the Italian Constitution states, to "repudiate war" (art. 11), to undertake paths of nonviolence and paths of justice, which foster peace. Because in the face of peace we cannot be indifferent or neutral. Cardinal Lercaro here said: "The Church cannot be neutral in the face of evil, wherever it comes from: her life is not neutrality, but prophecy" (Homily, January 1, 1968). Not neutral, but stand up for peace![32]

That speech was important not only for the reference to his predecessor Benedict XV but also to the cardinal archbishop of Bologna, Giacomo Lercaro, who was abruptly "resigned" by Paul VI in 1968 a few weeks after (and probably also because of) the homily he had delivered in Bologna on January 1, 1968, against the US bombings in Vietnam.[33]

In a speech delivered on October 18, 2017, to a delegation called "Religions for Peace," Francis highlighted the task of religions:

> The religions, with their spiritual and moral resources, have a specific and unique role to play in building peace. They cannot be neutral, much less ambiguous, where peace is concerned. Those who engage in acts of violence or try to justify them in the name of religion gravely offend God, who is peace and the source of peace, and has left in human beings a reflection of his wisdom, power and beauty.[34]

Pope Francis's activism can also be seen on social issues and his familiarity with social change movements, like the "World Meeting of Popular Movements," which he met several times during his pontificate.[35] In his October 28, 2014, address to the participants in one of these meetings, Francis connected his view of the movements with his strong emphasis on social justice:

> Here we are in this Old Synod Hall (now there is a new one), and synod means precisely "to walk together." May this be a symbol of the process that you have begun and are carrying forward. Grassroots movements express the urgent need to revitalize our democracies, so often hijacked by innumerable factors. It is impossible to imagine a future for society without the active participation

of great majorities as protagonists, and such proactive participation overflows the logical procedures of formal democracy. Moving towards a world of lasting peace and justice calls us to go beyond paternalistic forms of assistance; it calls us to create new forms of participation that include popular movements and invigorates local, national, and international governing structures with that torrent of moral energy that springs from including the excluded in the building of a common destiny. And all this with a constructive spirit, without resentment, with love.[36]

CONCLUSION

Pope Francis has reinterpreted Vatican neutrality as a "positive neutrality" for a new engagement in social and political issues, including at the international level. It is a unique engagement that is ineluctably at tension with traditional diplomatic practice. This diverse nature—religious and diplomatic—of the activity of the Vatican is true in the twenty-first century as it was true in the twentieth when for example, there was a close collaboration between the Vatican and the US administrations aimed at avoiding potential conflicts between Rome and Washington (over, for example, the war in Vietnam, nuclear tests, and NATO or the language used to describe *détente*).[37]

In the new global situation in which Pope Francis was elected, "positive neutrality" has been part of the latest phase in the discovery of the global dimension of the world by the papacy: the turn to a self-understanding more aware of the non-European and non-American Catholic Churches and the richness and complexity of the one human family. This has been manifested in his apostolic trips' destinations since the very beginning, like the July 2013 trip to Lampedusa and the homily on the "globalization of indifference." The encyclical *Laudato Si'* "On care for our common home" does not address the Holy See's international position but rejects the concept of neutrality of science and technology. The encyclical *Fratelli Tutti* does not use the word "neutrality" but affirms a decisive role for the papacy in concert with other religious traditions to build a social friendship. It is yet one more example of Francis's papacy's view of the necessity to avoid a misguided sense of neutrality. In *Fratelli Tutti,* there is the affirmation of necessity for the state and politics to avoid both false technocratic neutrality and theocratic temptations.[38]

However, another element that determines the possibilities for a "positive neutrality" is the shift from a geopolitical alignment between the Vatican and the West to a different set of alignments that avoid an identification between Catholicism and the Occident. This has opened new possibilities and exposed more than before the limits to what the Holy See can do and say in a twenty-first-century world. It remains to be seen, for example, what will be the meaning of the Vatican's "positive neutrality" regarding the situation in China: the persecution of the Uighurs and Hong Kong where, after the Vatican's agreement with China on the appointment of bishops in September 2018, the predicament of Catholics and human rights generally has worsened under the tighter grip of Beijing on the former British colony. Thus far, the Holy See has not made its voice heard in public, but only through supposedly back-channel diplomacy to address these human rights issues. Archbishop Paul Gallagher, the Vatican's secretary for relations with states, stated in an interview in March 2021: "I don't think that 'grandstanding' statements can be terribly effective. . . . I think you have to ask what effect [a statement] is going to have? Is it going to produce a positive change, or does it make the situation more complicated for the local church and for relations with the Holy See? At the moment, we feel that's the right approach."[39]

In the case of China, the Holy See has understandably chosen a different course of action compared not only to the case of Venezuela but also of Myanmar (which the pope visited in November 2017 and referred to multiple times after the coup of February 2021)[40] and Iraq (which the pope visited in March 2021),[41] in both cases with a direct plea by the pope to the authorities to respect human rights.

Pope Francis has sent unequivocal signals about his intention to remain silently neutral on political issues involving his own native Argentina and—what is more unusual for the pope—also for Italy. On the other hand, the language of positive neutrality has become part of the local Catholic Church's patrimony dealing with political and social turmoil. For example, in his August 2020 memorandum "Lebanon and Active Neutrality," Cardinal Bechara Rai, patriarch of Antioch of the Maronites (Lebanon), made direct reference to the concept of active neutrality as the guarantee of the country's unity and its historical role in the international context.[42] Simultaneously, the concept of neutrality of the Catholic Church found quite different interpretations if one looks, for example, at the very different ways Pope Francis and the US bishops have dealt, just in the last decade, with the Obama, Trump, and Biden administrations.[43]

Italian historian Alberto Melloni called the choice of Pope Francis to call a great diplomat, Pietro Parolin, from his Venezuela post back to Rome and to appoint him secretary of state "a restoration" (meant in a positive way) of the diplomatic tradition of the Holy See shaped by Cardinal Agostino Casaroli (secretary of state, 1979–1990) and by Angelo Tardini before him (from Sostituto of the Secretariat of State, in 1935, to cardinal secretary of state, 1958–1961): "The papacy of Francis, therefore, marks a novelty that does not end in the fraternal and modest style that the bishop of Rome uses: it is a change of paradigm that will affect and has already affected the balance in international relations."[44]

The liberation of new energies of the papacy for more active neutrality has undoubtedly to do with Pope Francis's biography and background. Francis is a Catholic of European descent and knows Europe, but a Europe-centered focus does not dominate his worldview and understanding of history. The pivot toward Asia and the Middle East has meant for some traditional interlocutors of the Holy See a painful rearranging of the papacy's geopolitical priorities: less privileged attention to Europe and, in a particular way, a new parameter for the relationship with the United States. It is a change of era compared to necessity, during the Cold War, not to interfere with the US role in maintaining international security. This has enabled him and the Catholic Church to look at the world and interact with it in new ways and recognize the changing demographics of the Church.

NOTES

1. Cardinal Pietro Parolin, *Speech for the 90th Anniversary of the signing of the Lateran Pacts* (LUMSA University, Rome, February 8, 2019), reported in Vatican News accessed March 7, 2021, in https://www.vaticannews.va/en/vatican-city/news/2019-02/cardinal-pietro-parolin-holy-see-protecting-human-person.html.

2. Ibid.

3. Ibid.

4. Massimo Faggioli, *The Liminal Papacy of Pope Francis. Moving toward Global Catholicity* (Maryknoll NY: Orbis, 2020).

5. Francis Rooney, *The Global Vatican: An Inside Look at the Catholic Church, World Politics, and the Extraordinary Relationship Between the United States and the Holy See* (Lanham, MD: Rowman & Littlefield, 2013); see also Giuliana Chamedes, *A Twentieth-Century Crusade: The Vatican's Battle to Remake Christian Europe* (Cambridge MA: Harvard University Press, 2019).

6. *Communiqué concerning the signing of a Provisional Agreement between the Holy See and the People's Republic of China on the appointment of Bishops*, September 22, 2018, accessed March 7, 2021, in https://press.vatican.va/content/salastampa/it/bollettino/pubblico/2018/09/22/0673/01468.html#IN; *Communiqué on the extension of the Provisional Agreement between the Holy See and the People's Republic of China regarding the appointment of Bishops*, October 22, 2020, accessed March 7, 2021, in https://press.vatican.va/content/salastampa/it/bollettino/pubblico/2020/10/22/0542/01260.html#ing.

7. See Andrea Tornielli, "Il gesto del Servo dei servi di Dio," *Vatican News*, April 12, 2019, accessed March 7, 2021, in https://www.vaticannews.va/it/papa/news/2019-04/papa-francesco-bacia-piedi-leader-sud-sudan-ritiro-vaticano.html.

8. See Robin Gomes, "Pope Calls for Day of Prayer, Fasting in Solidarity with Lebanon," *Vatican News*, September 2, 2020, accessed March 7, 2021, in https://www.vaticannews.va/en/pope/news/2020-09/pope-audience-lebanon-appeal-day-prayer-fasting-sept4.html.

9. See Massimo Faggioli, *Catholicism and Citizenship: Political Cultures of the Church in the Twenty-First Century* (Collegeville MN: Liturgical Press, 2017), 67–93.

10. See Ernst Werner, *Zwischen Canossa und Worms: Staat und Kirche 1077–1122* (Berlin: Akademie-Verlag, 1973).

11. The European nation-states carved out of the four empires were Hungary, Czechoslovakia, Yugoslavia, Finland, Latvia, Lithuania, Estonia, and the Soviet Union.

12. The expression "Roman Question" refers to the conflict between the Holy See and the Italian national movement first, and between the Holy See and the new unitary state, for sovereignty over Rome after 1870 until 1929, see Saretta Marotta, "La questione romana," in *Cristiani d'Italia, Chiese, società, stato 1861–2011*, edited by Alberto Melloni (Roma: Istituto della Enciclopedia Italiana Treccani, 2011), vol. 1, 641–54.

13. See Andrew Preston, *Sword of the Spirit, Shield of the Faith: Religion in American War and Diplomacy* (New York: Knopf, 2012), 519.

14. Pope Francis, the Grand Imam of Al-Azhar Ahmad Al-Tayyeb, *Document on Human Fraternity for World Peace and Living Together*, February 4, 2019, accessed March 7, 2021, in http://www.vatican.va/content/francesco/en/travels/2019/outside/documents/papa-francesco_20190204_documento-fratellanza-umana.html.

15. Vatican II, pastoral constitution on the Church in the modern world, *Gaudium et Spes* (December 7, 1965), accessed March 7, 2021, https://www.vatican.va/archive/hist_councils/ii_vatican_council/documents/vat-ii_const_19651207_gaudium-et-spes_en.html.

16. See Massimo Borghesi, *Jorge Mario Bergoglio: Una biografia intellettuale. Dialettica e mistica* (Milano: Jaca Book, 2018), English translation: *The Mind of Pope Francis: Jorge Mario Bergoglio's Intellectual Journey*, translated by Barry Hudock (Collegeville MN: Liturgical Press, 2019), 56–57.

17. Francis, *Message on the occasion of the celebrations for the 150th anniversary of Rome as capital of Italy*, February 3, 2020, accessed March 7, 2021, http://www.vatican.va/content/francesco/en/messages/pont-messages/2020/documents/papa-francesco_20200203_messaggio-romacapitale.html.

18. See "Primo saluto del Santo Padre Francesco," March 13, 2013, accessed March 7, 2021, http://www.vatican.va/content/francesco/it/speeches/2013/march/documents/papa-francesco_20130313_benedizione-urbi-et-orbi.html.

19. See Paul Vallely, *Pope Francis: The Struggle for the Soul of Catholicism* (New York: Bloomsbury, 2015), 111–25.

20. Andrea Riccardi, *Periferie: Crisi e novità per la Chiesa* (Milano: Jaca Book, 2016), English translation: *To the Margins: Pope Francis and the Mission of the Church* (Maryknoll, NY: Orbis Books, 2018), 8.

21. Francis, *Homily during the Mass at Lampedusa*, July 8, 2013, accessed March 7, 2021, at https://w2.vatican.va/content/francesco/en/homilies/2013/documents/papa-francesco_20130708_omelia-lampedusa.html.

22. Faggioli, *The Liminal Papacy*, 2–3.

23. Michael Quisinsky, "Prolegomena einer Theologie als Lebenswissenschaft 'auf der Grenze': Papst Franziskus und die theologische Erkenntnislehre," *Theologie und Glaube* 107 (2017): 137–56, esp. 139–44.

24. Francis, *Text of the Press Conference of July 28, 2013*, accessed March 7, 2021, at http://w2.vatican.va/content/francesco/en/speeches/2013/july/documents/papa-francesco_20130728_gmg-conferenza-stampa.html.

25. Francis, *Homily at the Mass with New Cardinals*, February 15, 2015, accessed March 7, 2021, at http://w2.vatican.va/content/francesco/en/homilies/2015/documents/papa-francesco_20150215_omelia-nuovi-cardinali.html; emphasis in original.

26. Francis, *Homily at the Mass with New Cardinals*, February 15, 2015, accessed March 7, 2021, at http://w2.vatican.va/content/francesco/en/homilies/2015/documents/papa-francesco_20150215_omelia-nuovi-cardinali.html.

27. See John P. Meier, *A Marginal Jew: Rethinking the Historical Jesus*, 5 vols. (New Haven, CT: Yale University Press, 1991–2015).

28. Francis, *Text of the Angelus of August 18, 2013*, accessed March 7, 2021, at http://www.vatican.va/content/francesco/it/angelus/2013/documents/papa-francesco_angelus_20130818.html.

29. Francis, *Text of the Angelus of August 18, 2013*, accessed March 7, 2021, at http://www.vatican.va/content/francesco/it/angelus/2013/documents/papa-francesco_angelus_20130818.html.

30. Francis, *Words at the Vigil of Prayer for Peace*, September 7, 2013, accessed March 7, 2021, at http://www.vatican.va/content/francesco/en/homilies/2013/documents/papa-francesco_20130907_veglia-pace.html.

31. Francis, *Homily for the Solemnity of Mary, Most Holy Mother of God*, January 1, 2016, accessed March 7, 2021, at http://www.vatican.va/content/francesco/en/homilies/2016/documents/papa-francesco_20160101_omelia-giornata-mondiale-pace.html.

32. Francis, *Speech to Students and Academics*, Bologna, October 1, 2017, accessed March 7, 2021, at http://www.vatican.va/content/francesco/it/speeches/2017/october/documents/papa-francesco_20171001_visitapastorale-bologna-mondoaccademico.html (translation from Italian mine).

33. See Giuseppe Battelli, "Lercaro, Dossetti, la pace e il Vietnam," in *Araldo del Vangelo. Studi sull'episcopato e sull'archivio di Giacomo Lercaro a Bologna 1952–1968*, edited by Nicla Buonasorte (Bologna: Il Mulino, 2004), 185–304.

34. Francis, *Speech to a Delegation of "Religions for Peace,"* October 18, 2017, accessed March 7, 2021, at http://www.vatican.va/content/francesco/en/speeches/2017/october/documents/papa-francesco_20171018_delegati-religionsforpeace.html.

35. Pontificia Comisión para América Latina, *La irrupción de los Movimientos Populares: "Rerum novarum" de nuestro tiempo*, edited by Guzmán Carriquiry and Gianni La Bella (Città del Vaticano: Libreria Editrice Vaticana, 2019).

36. Francis, *Address to the Participants in the World Meeting of Popular Movements*, October 28, 2014, accessed March 7, 2021, at http://w2.vatican.va/content/francesco/en/speeches/2014/october/documents/papa-francesco_20141028_incontro-mondiale-movimenti-popolari.html.

37. P. Peter Sarros, *US-Vatican Relations, 1975–1980: A Diplomatic Study* (Notre Dame, IN: University of Notre Dame Press, 2020), esp. 225–29.

38. See Massimo Faggioli, "Pope Francis and the Nation-State: Fratelli Tutti as Critique of Radical Orthodoxy," in Berkley Forum (Berkley Center, Georgetown University), October 26, 2020, accessed March 7, 2021, at https://berkleycenter.georgetown.edu/responses/pope-francis-and-the-nation-state-fratelli-tutti-as-critique-of-radical-orthodoxy.

39. About the situation in Hong Kong, see the interview with Archbishop Paul Gallagher, the Vatican's secretary for relations with states, by Gerald O'Connell, published in the Jesuit magazine *America* in three installments in March 2021, https://www.americamagazine.org/politics-society/2021/03/23/pope-francis-oppression-myanmar-china-hong-kong-240302, accessed April 8, 2021.

40. See Francis, *Udienza generale* (March 17, 2021), accessed March 17, 2021, at https://press.vatican.va/content/salastampa/it/bollettino/pubblico/2021/03/17/0160/00338.html and https://www.vaticannews.va/en/pope/news/2021-03/pope-francis-myanmar-appeal-general-audience-wednesdsay.html.

41. See especially Francis, *Meeting with Authorities, Civil Society and the Diplomatic Corps* (Baghdad, March 5, 2021), accessed March 17, 2021, at http://www.vatican.va/content/francesco/en/speeches/2021/march/documents/papa-francesco_20210305_iraq-autorita.html.

42. The English translation from Arabic of Patriarch Béchara Boutros Raï's memorandum of August 7, 2020, "Lebanon and Active Neutrality," accessed March 7, 2021, at https://syriacpress.com/blog/2020/08/18/memorandum-on-lebanon-and-active-neutrality-syriac-maronite-patriarch-bechara-boutros-rai/.

43. For the contrast between the cordial relations between the Vatican and presidents Obama (2009–2017) and Biden (2021–) on one side and the tense relations of the US bishops with the same Democratic administrations on the other side, see Massimo Faggioli, *Joe Biden and Catholicism in the United States* (New London, CT: Bayard, 2021); Manlio Graziano, *In Rome We Trust: The Rise of Catholics in American Political Life* (Stanford, CA: Stanford University Press, 2017).

44. Alberto Melloni, "La politica estera del Vaticano e l'arrivo di Papa Francesco al pontificato," in *Atlante geopolico Treccani* (Roma: Treccani, 2014), accessed March 7, 2021, at https://www.treccani.it/enciclopedia/la-politica-estera-del-vaticano-e-l-arrivo-di-papa-francesco-al-pontificato_%28Atlante-Geopolitico%29/.

SELECTED BIBLIOGRAPHY

Borghesi, Massimo. *Jorge Mario Bergoglio: Una biografia intellettuale. Dialettica e mistica*. Milano: Jaca Book, 2018. (English translation: *The Mind of Pope Francis: Jorge Mario Bergoglio's Intellectual Journey*. Trans. Barry Hudock. Collegeville, MN: Liturgical Press, 2019.)

Faggioli, Massimo. *Catholicism and Citizenship: Political Cultures of the Church in the Twenty-First Century*. Collegeville, MN: Liturgical Press, 2017.

———. *The Liminal Papacy of Pope Francis: Moving toward Global Catholicity*. Maryknoll, NY: Orbis, 2020.

Riccardi, Andrea. *Periferie: Crisi e novità per la Chiesa*. Milano: Jaca Book, 2016. (English translation: *To the Margins: Pope Francis and the Mission of the Church*. Maryknoll, NY: Orbis Books, 2018.).

Vallely, Paul. *Pope Francis: The Struggle for the Soul of Catholicism*. New York: Bloomsbury, 2015.

Chapter Ten

Neutrality as an Aid to Holy See Diplomacy

Iraq and Syria, 1991–2011

Luke Cahill

When a pope appoints new cardinals, he places the red biretta on their head and, speaking in Latin, states: "libertate et diffusione Sanctae Romane Ecclesiae," translated as, "for the freedom and growth of the Holy Roman Church."[1] This chapter will argue that these two words, "freedom" and "growth," represent "possession" and "milieu" goals, respectively in Arnold Wolfer's typology.[2] Thus, freedom is a possession goal, and growth is a *milieu* goal.

Possession goals denominate ends that states seek to maximize their status or power, such as security or territory. In contrast, milieu goals describe ends that states seek to shape their international environment such as "growth."[3] This chapter argues that the Holy See demonstrates a combined traditional temporal and religious ontology, which is why it is difficult to make direct comparisons to other states. In essence, the Holy See's possession goals primarily protect Catholics and Christians in the Middle East.[4] Its milieu goals relate to promoting the common good, human rights, and ending war. In this context, Holy See neutrality serves as both a means and an end to realize both "freedom" and "growth." It is a means for political and theological reasons to guard the Holy See's independence while conducting diplomacy.

Nevertheless, neutrality is also an end. It helps it advance its milieu goals and sometimes facilitates mediation or improves communication. Rather than restricting Holy See diplomacy, neutrality is central to its stance. Being independent allowed the Holy See to avoid being caught between making its opposition to the war a matter of Catholic doctrine on the one hand while maintaining its legal neutrality on the other. Independence means the Holy See can keep to its theology by not being overtly dogmatic on one hand while maintaining its legal obligation to neutrality on the other. The advantages of Holy See neutrality will be illustrated by the 1991 and 2003 Iraq Wars and the 2011 Syrian conflict.

Neutrality has a long history, and its central tenets have various understandings, but for brevity, this chapter defines permanent neutrality as impartiality in war and long-term non-alignment in peacetime.[5] Where neutrality is mandated by international agreement, it affects the role a state plays in future conflicts, forbids the provision of military assistance, demands warring parties be treated equally, and disbars membership in military and economic alliances.[6] Outside of these obligations, it can conduct its diplomacy as it sees fit and join nonmilitary international organizations. Perhaps most importantly, it "has no duty of ideological neutrality."[7]

The Holy See is unique because it has a widely recognized international sovereignty that does not depend on possessing substantial territory. Sovereignty concerns a state's ability to act independently.[8] Since the 1933 Montevideo Convention, states have been defined as having: a permanent population, a defined territory, a government, and the capacity to enter into relations with other states.[9] While the Holy See could be recognized as a state by this measure,[10] it does not consider itself a state compared to others—its sovereignty is not based on having territory. This was evident between 1870 and 1929. During this time, the Papal States ceased to exist, and the Vatican City State "with the incumbent of the Holy See as its Head"[11] had not yet come into existence. Despite this, the Holy See was still able to conduct diplomacy and establish diplomatic relations.[12] Therefore, the basis of its sovereignty is spiritual.[13] It stems from its religious mission.[14] This is referred to as a "sui generis" entity.[15]

The Holy See's twofold nature is explicit when Cedric Ryngaert, professor of public international law at Utrecht University, argues that its sovereignty forms its "international competence in spiritual and value-laden matters."[16] Accordingly, its global mission is only partially similar to that of states.[17] This, in turn, shapes the secular and religious reasons behind its permanent neutrality. The political reasons are based on the 1929 Lateran Pacts,[18] which bind both the Holy See and Vatican City to permanent neutrality.[19] The international law scholar, Lassa Oppenheim, raises the issue that the sovereign statehood of the Holy See and the Vatican City is not always distinguishable in the field of international law. Others maintain that the Holy See and the Vatican City have two separate international personalities.[20] Regardless of the interpretation, both the Holy See and Vatican City are bound by the Lateran Treaty in renouncing interest in temporal affairs, excluding any mutual appeal for mediation, and in this capacity reserves the right to "use its spiritual and moral powers."[21] Religious reasons for this neutrality are grounded in the Holy See's intimate links with the Church and its theology and its priests acting as diplomats. The Church understands that many political and social questions cannot be answered clearly. Thus, varying interpretations occur.[22] Accordingly, Catholics can legitimately disagree on these political and social questions.[23]

Diplomacy is "the art of restraining the exercise of power."[24] This is seen repeatedly as the Holy See seeks to restrain those who use power in Iraq and Syria. Given the mixing of religion and politics, Holy See diplomacy combines them. One illustration is the Holy See diplomatic corps, who, as Jodok Troy, assistant professor at the University of Innsbruck, has argued are both "ordinary and ordained."[25] That is, they are ordinary individuals who work as diplomats. At the same time, all heads of mission are ordained Catholic priests. They are bound to follow the religious aspects of Catholic Social Teaching (CST), compiled in the *Compendium of the Social Doctrine of the Church*. At its core are the theological ideas of humankind's unity, the common good, and the dignity of the human person.[26] All these are Holy See milieu goals as they seek to shape the international environment in which states operate. Given CST's flexibility, this allows it to press its milieu and possession goals without compromising its neutrality.

Neutrality is vital for Holy See diplomats to ensure a central tenet of its diplomacy can occur, dialogue.[27] At times, this has enabled mediation to emerge.[28] Papal ambassadors are formally called apostolic nuncios. The Latin word "nuntius," meaning messenger, is the origin of the word "nuncio."[29] The similarity between these goals and international organizations such as the United Nations (UN), as both have milieu goals, has led scholars to view the two as having close links.[30] These links illustrate the Holy See's religious nature and the aspect of its diplomacy. However, the traditional or political character of the Holy See's diplomacy should not be overlooked.[31] Some have claimed it is capable of *Realpolitik*.[32] However, this might be more accurately described as a kind of religious *Machtpolitik* (the politics of force).[33] Consequently, Holy See diplomacy seeks to restrain the use of power by different actors.

While the Holy See opposed the wars in Syria and Iraq, this opposition was not equivalent to secular opposition but was linked to its spiritual role. It opposed the wars on religious grounds that killing is against the Commandments. It also opposed them due to its spiritual ontology that allowed the Holy See to voice its opposition and thus protect Christians in the region. Hence, the Holy See's resistance was a combined politico-theological effort. Moreover, although it opposed the wars, the Holy See never framed its opposition in terms of Catholic doctrine. Consequently, it maintained its neutrality.

1991 IRAQ WAR

Iraq invaded Kuwait in August 1990 after the Iran-Iraq War ended in a stalemate and low oil prices. The Holy See opposed US efforts to remove Iraq from Kuwait by force. Holy See's neutrality proved vital to its diplomacy as it was the mechanism through which it could protect its theology, advocate for its twofold goals, allow for dialogue, and protect its diplomatic independence.

The Holy See opposed the war for both theological and geopolitical reasons. These broadly reflect Holy See's milieu and possession goals, respectively, and how its neutrality is embedded in its framing and pursuit of these twin goals. Firstly, and most obviously, the Holy See opposes war through the Commandment, "Thou shalt not kill."

Stemming from this, the Holy See's contemporary reading of just war theory has a presumption against war.[34] The just-war theory is deemed so significant that it is mentioned in the Church's central theological teachings, the *Catechism*. However, the Church's reading (and Holy See's implementation) has shifted. While just war is not rejected in principle, the church in recent practice has concluded that today's conflicts do not meet the just war criterion—war should be a last resort, there should be a probability of success, and there should be proportionality.[35] Illustrating the shift Todd Whitmore, associate professor at Notre Dame University, argues that Pope Pius XII rejected conscientious objection.[36] The Second Vatican Council, in contrast, issued documents that praised, among other things, conscientious objection.[37]

An illustration of the Church's modern thinking is *Gaudium et Spes* (Joy and Hope), with a section entitled "Avoidance of War." It states how "the horror and perversity of war is immensely magnified by the addition of scientific weapons. For acts of war involving these weapons can inflict massive and indiscriminate destruction, thus going far beyond the bounds of legitimate defence."[38] Despite this, the Church never rejected the just war theory. While there were increasing doubts about any war's justifiability, it also knew that it could not condemn war as an article of faith or dogma. This can be seen in papal statements, where they opposed the Iraq wars and the Syrian conflict but made every effort not to condemn "war" outright.

Consequently, this (theologically based) neutrality allowed the Holy See to communicate with all parties involved and potentially mediate freely between them. In theory, there is no need for neutrality to be able to speak freely between adversaries. However, this overlooks the Holy See's unique ontology with its mixing of theology and politics. Without neutrality, the Holy See would not have been independently able to press for its own possession goals.

The Holy See also opposed the Iraq War. Its milieu's goals were to avoid conflict and halt the use of modern weaponry. Its possession goals were to protect Christians in Iraq by clearly opposing the forceable removal of Iraq from Kuwait. In doing this, the pope was advancing Holy See possession goals. He sought to delineate the differences between those states joining the UN-backed coalition and the Holy See stance, thereby demonstrating the importance of neutrality for its diplomacy.

Due to Iraq's diverse makeup, the Holy See was concerned about a clash of civilizations.[39] There was a concern that a regional backlash against Christians by Arabs might conflate indigenous Christians with Western states.[40] Protecting Iraq's indigenous Christians was the Holy See's principal possession goal throughout all three conflicts—Iraq 1991, 2003, and Syria 2011.

A review of the speeches and letters of Pope John Paul II makes this clear. The Holy See could not oppose the war as a matter of Catholic doctrine as it was a political issue where Catholics could disagree. At the same time, it was bound to legal neutrality from the Lateran Pacts. Thus, it had to balance not making its opposition a doctrinal position and violating its political neutrality by outright condemning the war. This also demonstrates how the Holy See believes it can raise its voice in the international sphere. Therefore, neutrality is an aid as it allows it to engage with the state system on its terms while protecting its ontology and diplomatic independence.

Initial reaction condemned Iraqi actions. The editorial in *L'Osservatore Romano* of August 9, 1990, asked what had happened to "the dignity and sovereignty of an independent State."[41] Interestingly, these comments were couched in political and legal language rather than theological or moral language. They viewed Kuwait as the injured party and implied that Iraq robbed the emirate of its "dignity." It is unclear if this was part of the Holy See strategy. For instance, there is a sharp contrast between this and the Pope's first comments on the Iraqi invasion.

The Pope's first mention of the war was during his Sunday Angelus on August 26. He noted the "grave violation of international law" and asked the assembled crowd to pray that "equitable solutions" to problems may be found.[42] These have been described as "framework-setting."[43] There was no explicit mention of Iraq or Kuwait. Terms like dignity or sovereignty disappeared. Concurrently, the pope mentioned equality. This may have been a reference to Kuwait or Iraq. Crucially, it is open to interpretation. However, these statements were balanced by the admission that Iraq invaded Kuwait. This phrasing was essential as it allowed the Holy See to remain open to dialogue with the Iraqi regime, not accepting the Iraqi invasion while pursuing its possession goals. Thus, showing how neutrality aids Holy See diplomacy by ensuring its independence.

On Christmas Day 1990, the pope used his traditional *Urbi et Orbi* blessing ("To the City and the World") to appeal for peace. He hoped that through "respect for the inalienable rights of people and nations, it is possible to identify and travel the paths of understanding and peace."[44] On the one hand, this statement expressed support for Kuwait and against the Iraqi invasion. However, at the same time, it also threaded a fine line between neither agreeing with nor dismissing Iraqi grievances.[45] It can be read as if accepting Saddam

Hussein's claims that his peace plan was sincere.[46] At the same time, it integrates a united humanity into the statement. This approach illustrates the Holy See's particular neutrality in balancing Iraqi and Kuwaiti needs, and Holy See's milieu goals of promoting peace, avoiding war, respect for human rights, and international law would have been harder to voice without neutrality.

In his 1991 New Year address to diplomats accredited to the Holy See, the pope spoke of two interrelated themes. The first was that Iraq broke international law but was not mentioned by name. The second theme was the equality of nations, with the weak not being dominated by the strong. Such ideas of state equality underpin Holy See diplomacy. During the speech, the pontiff spoke of how "now more than ever is the time for dialogue, for negotiation, and for affirming the primacy of international law."[47] This demonstrates the importance the Holy See places on dialogue and its milieu goals. Such goals are possible without neutrality, but Holy See neutrality is both a means and an end. It is a means because it facilitates the Holy See's conduct of diplomacy as well as an end in that it can help advance its milieu goals.

In a January 4, 1991, letter, John Paul II sought to independently advance both the Holy See milieu and possession goals by advocating peaceful resolution and warning of the dangers of modern weapons.[48] His message was addressed to Jacques Poos, president of the European foreign ministers at that time. He wrote of his concerns that international order was being enforced through weapons, with "disastrous consequences."[49] This is a possession goal as Christian lives would be lost with their use.

In advocating for milieu goals, the pontiff wrote there was no desire to renounce "international law," a reference to the Iraqi invasion. However, he also made clear that "the principle of equity demands that peaceful means such as dialogue and negotiation prevail."[50] This statement reflected the benefits of Holy See neutrality in pressing its milieu and possession goals and showing its independence from secular states. The Holy See's stance put distance between it and the "Western" coalition. Critically, its neutrality both forced and allowed the Holy See to take this independent stance. Its neutrality enabled it to protect its theology and possession goals but speak against the war. Therefore, its neutral stance was not just essential for its diplomacy but was vital to enable it to pursue its possession and milieu goals at the same time.

On January 15, 1991, hours before the deadline for Iraq to withdraw, the Pope published two letters to Iraq and the United States presidents.[51] Neutrality's benefits are seen as enabling the pope to advocate independently for the Holy See's goals to both leaders. To Saddam Hussein, the pope wrote how war does not solve problems and, referencing possession goals, how a conflict would kill "thousands of your fellow-citizens."[52] Referring to modern weaponry, the pope's letter to George H. W. Bush expressed how war has "tragic consequences."⁵³ He wrote how temporary injustices "might be momentarily met,"⁵⁴ but the effects would be far worse. He again called for dialogue so that "sovereignty may be restored to the people of Kuwait."⁵⁵ Neither letter simply accepted the position of the respective president but still advanced Holy See's goals. The letters sent to both heads of state show the seriousness with which the Holy See interprets its obligations to remain neutral. The Holy See's neutrality aided its diplomatic efforts to avert war. The letters demonstrated to Iraqis and those Arabs in the broader region that the Holy See opposed the war. Accordingly, those Christians living in Iraq could not be so easily conflated with the US-led coalition's Western powers. On the other hand, the pope's letter to George Bush accepted the need to restore Kuwaiti sovereignty.

These mapped onto its milieu and possession goals exploring the common theological and geopolitical reasons for Holy See neutral opposition. It allowed the Holy See to work within the narrow window of not making its opposition to the war part of Catholic doctrine and not violating its obligations to legal neutrality. Neutrality was also an end because it advanced its goals and allowed for communication and independence.

2003 IRAQ WAR

After the 9/11 attacks in 2001, both Afghanistan and Iraq were blamed for the bombings on the World Trade Centre. The Holy See's stance on Afghanistan was twofold. It urged adherence to the *jus in Bello* by arguing for aid to Afghans.⁵⁶ Simultaneously, it accepted the US stance for war by calling it an "armed reaction."⁵⁷ Implicit in this was that the war was a just reaction to the events in September. When US attention turned to Iraq, it shifted its stance. Holy See possession goals were to protect Christians by breaking the Muslim conflation between Christianity and the West. Its milieu goals were to support international law and protect the just war tradition. Through its neutrality, the Holy See vigorously protested the war facilitating the advancement of its goals. For the Iraq War, the Holy See's neutral stance or its reasons behind this remained unchanged.

Neutrality was an indispensable mechanism for the Holy See's independent opposition to the war and helped advance its goals within its theological and legal strictures. Other reasons were its perceived unilateralism and a desire to protect the just war tradition from preventive war while seeking enhanced disarmament and nonproliferation.⁵⁸ It also feared regional spill-over.⁵⁹ Finally, the Holy See's opposition to the war was based on a lack of a UN Security Council mandate.⁶⁰

The US Embassy explained the Holy See's view in diplomatic cables. One cable to Washington suggested the Holy See was aware of the nature of the Iraqi regime. The cable suggested that it might yet support a war notwithstanding the Vatican's approach toward neutrality. However, this was only after taking the consequences for Iraqis and "global stability" into account, and "only" with the consent of the UN.[61] This "global stability" reveals how the Holy See's milieu and possession goals were linked to UN opposition. The former was represented because it was based on international law, and the latter because the UN helped protect Middle Eastern Christians. This illustrates how its neutrality was a means to defend its independence. The Holy See may have been setting the conditions for its support so high as to be impossible for US acceptance. Crucially, Robert Shelledy's doctoral dissertation contended, "although the Vatican recognizes the moral ambiguity of neutrality, it appears to be more concerned with the dangers of a moral sanction of war than criticisms of neutrality."[62]

Like the 1991 war, the Holy See had both milieu and possession goals. In many respects, the goals were similar. Holy See's milieu goals were based on bolstering international law in general, and the UN. Neutrality was an aid to its diplomacy as it was a license to oppose the war independently of the UN system.[63] As with the 1991 War, Holy See possession goals were rooted in fear, real or not, of a clash of civilizations[64] and its impact on Iraqi Chaldean Catholics.

In December 2002, Archbishop Jean-Louis Tauran, then-secretary for relations with states, raised his concerns about Christians' safety in the region. He warned how war could be used to stoke anti-Christian ideas and violence: "we need to think about the consequences for the civilian population. . . . A type of anti-Christian, anti-Western crusade could be incited because some ignorant masses mix everything together."[65] This is a clear indication of the Holy See's possession goals in Iraq, linked to its milieu goals sought to bolster international law to restrain states. The Holy See would not have been able to take the position it did without its unique mix of politico-legal and theological neutrality; otherwise, it would have been pressured to choose to support or oppose the war. Both, as mentioned before, compromise the Holy See's diplomacy.

In his annual address to the diplomatic corps accredited to the Holy See, in January 2003, the pope warned of the dangers of war and the need for dialogue to resolve the issues while pursuing Holy See possession goals.[66] Neutrality helped this because it facilitated the pope's dialogue with ambassadors, where he could expound the Holy See's independent opposition and press its twofold goals. The pope's objections to war were clear, though Iraq is only mentioned explicitly twice. He noted, "the unresolved problem of the

Middle East, with the Holy Land and Iraq."[67] This could be interpreted as a reference to the Israeli-Palestinian dispute and the status of Christians in the region. These issues were reflective of its possession goals. He returned to emphasizing international law and its previous stress on milieu goals and community.

Consequently, the Holy See used the UN to bolster its milieu and possession goals, seek peace, and protect Middle Eastern Christians, respectively. In apocalyptic language, the pope asserted, *"choices need to be made so that humanity can still have a future."*[68] Both the UN and Holy See promote peace and human rights.[69] However, how they seek to implement this is based on profound philosophical differences. Accordingly, this leads them to disagree on matters of war and peace and their conception of the individual.[70] Therefore, the Holy See seeks to protect its possession goals or interests. Thus, its language may illustrate Holy See possession goals to make the Iraqi regime aware of its opposition to the war. When the pontiff explicitly mentioned the war, he said it could be resolved through the methods of "international law, honest dialogue, solidarity between States."[71] He mentioned the problems of the Middle East, the Israel-Palestine dispute, and only then Iraq described as "the land of the Prophets."[72] The pope did not mention Iraqi human rights abuses. US diplomatic cables state the pope "made a strong appeal against war," adding that "he did not close the door on war as a last option."[73] The embassy may have framed the Pope's speech in this way to please the Bush administration. This framing does not discount the Holy See's neutral stance. US Ambassador Nicholson stressed how the speech "avoided direct criticism of the US."[74]

In January 2003, Cardinal Walter Kasper, then-president of the Pontifical Council for Promoting Christian Unity, doubted the war's justness. In addition, he added that "often Muslims make an identification ... between Christianity and the West. I think this war could become a very heavy problem and destabilize the entire region."[75] Cardinal Kasper's statement shows not only the links the Holy See draws between Christians and Muslims but how concerned it is for Christians in the region. Such comments underline the Holy See's possession goals. Moreover, these goals are not merely to protect Christians but are connected to milieu goals about the region's diversity, blurring the distinction between them. It sought to advance its milieu goals by supporting the UN and was also a possession goal as it was a means to protect these Christians. So, the UN sought to promote general peace. The Holy See was more concerned with advancing its possession goals, even if these clashed with the UN stance. As they converged on this occasion, the Holy See used the UN to bolster its antiwar position. Accordingly, neutrality is the means whereby the Holy See can advocate for these and protect its ontology. Notably, senior prelates stated their desire to maintain a Christian presence in the region.[76]

In February and March 2003, the Holy See sent special envoys to transmit papal letters to the presidents of Iraq and the United States. In February, Cardinal Etchegaray was dispatched to Iraq.[77] He delivered a letter from John Paul II that called for greater Iraqi co-operation with the UN.[78] Interviewed afterward, Etchegaray claimed that Saddam Hussein speaking to him was a sign of the "moral authority of the Pope."[79] Part of the reason for Etchegaray's meeting was Holy See neutrality. Naturally, this leaves aside the theological and legal benefits of neutrality that have been mentioned previously. Asked about the Iraqi Christians, Etchegaray replied, "Christians are Iraqis above all."[80] Following theology, it would have been more typical to stress the unity of all Catholics (or Christians). Instead, Cardinal Etchegaray seemed to emphasize Catholics' loyalty to Iraq, highlighting its possession goals. He may have wished to highlight Iraq's non-Christian population that Iraqi Chaldeans are not allied to any Western state. His framing of Iraqi Christians as Iraqis was a way to bolster their safety.

Cardinal Etchegaray's mission was complemented by special envoy Cardinal Laghi's to the United States in March 2003. Neutrality allowed the Holy See to distinguish its position from George W. Bush's. Laghi delivered a letter to President Bush from John Paul II.[81] His mission was complicated as a tiny number of US bishops voiced support for the war in narrow terms.[82]

McAndrews underlines the unique nature and significance of Cardinal Laghi's visit: "no representative of the Catholic power structure had personally told the president what he had only heard and read. So Cardinal Laghi's visit assumed a special niche in the Catholic campaign to dissuade the Methodist commander in chief from attacking the Muslim nation."[83]

Further, Allen recounts Laghi's statement. In it, Laghi stressed how force must account for the consequences of "the suffering people of Iraq and those involved in the military operation, a further instability in the region and a new gulf between Islam and Christianity."[84] Laghi was advocating for Holy See milieu goals and encouraging Iraq and the US to use the UN. His statement also demonstrated Holy See possession goals, how his mission had "precious little to do with changing minds in the White House" but instead was speaking to "Cairo and Tehran, Khartoum and Peshawar, and Jakarta and Abuja. Laghi's very presence in Washington speaks a message to the Islamic street: This is not our war."[85] In meeting President Bush, Cardinal Laghi was illustrating the Holy See's opposition.

In his usual Sunday Angelus, the day before hostilities started, John Paul II urged Iraq to comply with the US to avoid war. The pope's statement advanced both milieu and possession goals because it served the Holy See's narrow possession goals of protecting Christians and milieu goals because it would mean working with the UN. This highlights the difficulty in separating them from each other. During the same speech, he urged the UN Security Council to use force only "after having exhausted every other peaceful solution."[86] The pope ended, advocating talks, though Saddam Hussein's deadline to leave Iraq for exile was hours away. This may have been an attempt to balance what may have been perceived as the Holy See's focus on the US stance. Contemporary reports indicated how US diplomats discouraged the pope from sending Cardinal Laghi to the White House, "saying that the dispute is not between Hussein and Bush but between Hussein and the United Nations."[87]

This section had demonstrated that before the 2003 Iraq War, Holy See neutrality aided its diplomacy in pursuit of its milieu and possession goals. Neutrality allowed it to oppose the war without breaking its theological requirements independently. Concurrently, neutrality was essential as it facilitated communication, such as the envoys sent to Baghdad and Washington, DC. Furthermore, neutrality meant it could advocate for its possession goals. Correspondingly, the Holy See sought to weaken the Arab conflation between Christianity and the West. It consistently connected its milieu and possession goals, illustrating the difficulties in separating one from the other. Neutrality, far from constraining the Holy See, was essential for it to pursue these goals.

SYRIAN CONFLICT: 2011–2016

The Syrian conflict began with protests as part of the 2011 Arab uprisings. Like Iraq, Syria was a multi-faith state with a sizeable Christian minority. Before 2011, approximately 10 percent of Syrians were Christians, around two million people. Roughly 500,000 belonged to the Syriac Orthodox Church and 125,000 to the Armenian Apostolic Church. Various Eastern Catholics were thought to make up approximately 400,000.[88] Most Syrians—70 percent—are Sunni Muslims, with about 12 percent Alawites.[89] There is a historical precedent for this, with the Holy See seeking to protect Catholics in Syria during the Ottoman Empire.[90] This shows that the long-term possession goals of the Holy See have remained stable. Neutrality is an essential component of this.

Again, neutrality enabled the Holy See to advance both its milieu and possession goals. Its milieu goals consisted of ending the war and promoting human rights. Like in Iraq, its possession goals were to protect and sustain Christians living in Syria.

The pope first referred to Syria was in June 2011 when the new Syrian ambassador to the Holy See was accredited.[91] With the conflict becoming more violent, the Holy See continued maintaining its strict neutrality to press for human rights and (Christian) Syrians' rights. None of the pope's comments were specific and only referenced general principles. Benedict stressed that unity could "only" be based on the dignity of each individual. This highlights the Church's conception of human rights and how peace is both a milieu and possession goal. Benedict also spoke of how "listening, dialogue, and collaboration must be recognized as the means through which the various members of society may compare their points of view and thus achieve a consensus."[92] By saying this, Benedict was advancing Holy See's milieu goals. Evidently, these relate to its "narrower" possession goals about retaining Christians in the region. He hinted that only through tolerance, respect for the individual, and dialogue could the war end. He did not elaborate on who was to take these steps or how they were to be implemented. No mention was made of the protester's actions, and no blame was assigned. Neutrality forced him from these steps. Nevertheless, it enabled the Holy See to press its milieu and possession goals in its own unique way in line with its special status.

Similarly, instead of condemning the Syrian regime for what it was doing to its own people, Benedict XVI went on to speak ambiguously about "the events that have occurred in recent months"[93] in the region and how these showed a wish for improvements in "the areas of economy, justice, freedom, and participation in public life."[94] In many ways, the pope's words align with Vatican II documents affirming democracy.[95] His comments on "participation in public life" could be interpreted as cautious support for Syria's greater representation. However, he did not say that Assad was blocking this. Nor did he endorse a particular form of participation. Thus, Holy See's neutrality, political and theological aspects were maintained while aiding its diplomacy. Not surprisingly, the pope explicitly mentioned Christians in Syria and how Christians, "as citizens," benefit Syria. This reiterates what Cardinal Etchegaray said in 2003 in Iraq, seeing Iraqis not as Christians or Catholics but as citizens. Rather than single out the Syrian conflict, Benedict made the general point about global suffering and the need to negotiate a solution. Overall, Benedict's speech illustrated how essential neutrality is to the Holy See. It allowed the pope to press the Holy See's milieu goals of dialogue and respect for human rights and retain diplomatic links with Syria and press for its possession goals, reminding the ambassador of the benefits they give to Syria, not as Christians or Catholics but as "citizens."

The next crucial reference was August 7, which illustrated the freedom neutrality gives and to Holy See's unique diplomacy. After prayers, Pope Benedict mentioned the "escalating episodes of violence."[96] He added how he restated his "appeal" to the Syrian government *and* people that "coexistence may be re-established as soon as possible and an adequate response be made to the legitimate aspirations of the citizens, with respect to their dignity, to promote stability throughout the region."[97] Notably, his appeal against violence went to both people and the government. Instead, its neutral stance allowed it to raise the issue in line with its religious mission but not be overly prescriptive in keeping with its theology and legal obligations. Accordingly, it was the best of both worlds. Neutrality gave it the freedom to speak to its twofold goals (within the confines of its theology) against the violence and yet remain open to communicating with the Syrian government.

During Pope Benedict's 2012 address to the diplomatic corps, Syria was next mentioned, where he connected the war in Syria to the Arab Spring and called for human dignity to be respected.[98] Neutrality assisted in this because it meant the Holy See could speak without breaking its theological or legal obligations. There was only one explicit reference to Syria in the context of the Arab Spring. The pope framed this with young people suffering from "poverty and unemployment and are fearful of an uncertain future."[99] He went on to describe how to move forward. The ideal choice is "through the recognition of the inalienable dignity of each human person."[100] By restating the core CST principle of human dignity, Benedict was pressing milieu goals to the assembled diplomats.

Holy See neutrality allowed it to avoid choosing between its milieu (theology) and its possession goals. Neutrality meant it could raise its (constrained) voice without breaching any theological or legal obligations. More pointedly, Pope Benedict went on to note how respect for the person should end violence and that "social solidarity [not] turn into [a] mere means for maintaining or seizing power."[101] This may have been an indirect reference to those who misuse calls for solidarity, such as pro-Assad groups who marched on "Friday for National Unity."[102] He went on to mention Syria explicitly, expressing his concern about the violence. He did not pass judgment on the merits of one side or the other. Nor did he place any interpretation on the violence. Pope Benedict simply stated how he prayed for an end to the violence and dialogue, "encouraged by the presence of independent observers."[103] The Holy See may have hoped that it could leverage its spiritual mission to mediate by affirming general principles of human dignity.[104] Benedict's reference to independent observers may have been an offer of Holy See mediation. This was agreed[105] but was unable to occur.[106] Neutrality allowed the pope to urge an end to violence without breaking its neutrality's legal or theological elements. Thus, it could pursue its milieu goals, and thence, its possession goals without being encumbered by having to "choose a side," with all the complications that come with making a choice.

The next significant mention of Syria was in September 2012. On his way to Lebanon, a reporter asked the pope about Syria and what the Church was doing to keep Christians in Syria and the region. Benedict replied that there must be an end to the war and prayer in order "to demonstrate the possibilities for dialogue" and the end of weapons importation.[107] All of these link to the Holy See's milieu goals and peace and respect for human dignity. Additionally, at the end of the answer, Pope Benedict said that "we should find ways of accepting each person in his otherness . . . the respect that religions have for one another."[108] Further evidence of this could be seen when the pope said that "it is time for Muslims and Christians to come together to put an end to violence and war."[109] Given the statements by Cardinal Kasper and Archbishop Tauran before the 2003 war, this could be a reference to how some Muslims equate Christianity with the West. Given Holy See possession goals in the region, if Muslims were better able to accept Christians, he may be implying that life would be more comfortable for them. Pope Benedict's reply also illustrates the interlinking between the milieu and possession goals—how one cannot be separated from the other.

Attending the Geneva II conference in 2014, Archbishop Silvano Tomasi proposed ways to end the conflict.[110] Neutrality permitted it to suggest its own peace plan and advocate for its twofold goals. These comprised: talks that had the purpose of an immediate, unconditional ceasefire; more generous humanitarian aid and reconstruction; aid to Syria from other states; community rebuilding and reconciliation where "all religious faiths . . . reach a deeper mutual knowledge," and lastly, continuing dialogue to resolve regional issues.[111] Other proposals did not emphasize religious dialogue and connected the Syrian crisis to the region's broader issues, as John Paul II did in 1990.[112] Holy See neutrality allowed it to propose its own peace plan and advance its milieu and possession goals through the proposal.

Consistent with Holy See diplomacy in 1991 and 2003, Pope Francis sent a letter to Bashar al-Assad in December 2016.[113] Of course, non-neutral states can send letters to other countries. Holy See neutrality meant it might have been received with less bias, making dialogue possible, enabling its unique goals. The letter urged Assad to end the war and ensure civilians were protected and aid was delivered unimpeded.[114] The newly created cardinal-apostolic nuncio, Cardinal Zenari, delivered the message, which was unusual as Francis said Zenari was to "remain as apostolic nuncio in the beloved and troubled Syria."[115] The letter showed how essential such communication is to the Holy See.[116] In a sign that Assad was willing to communicate with the Holy See, he responded to Francis's letter.[117] Had the Holy See not been neutral, this may have been, if not impossible, far less likely.

This section has argued that Holy See neutrality aided its diplomacy in Syria for four reasons: it allowed the Holy See to protect its theology by not becoming too specific; adhere to its legal obligations of neutrality, thereby maintain its independence; raise issues and allow communication between the Holy See and the Syrian government. Neutrality enabled it to advance both its milieu and possession goals.

CONCLUSION

This chapter has argued that neutrality, far from being a constraint, benefited Holy See diplomacy for four reasons: it allowed it to protect its theology, advance its milieu and possession goals, and allow for communication and autonomy. Neutrality was a means and end. It was a means because it was the vehicle through which the Holy See conducted its diplomacy; it was also an end, as it aided in pursuing its milieu goals.

Given its ontology, its neutrality stems from the combination of theological and politico-legal factors. On the one hand, its theology forbids concrete solutions to social and political questions where Catholics can legitimately disagree on the best course of action. Thus, it cannot pronounce specific actions by governments as more or less legitimate than others. Since 1929, the Lateran Pacts mandate the Holy See and the Vatican City State to permanent neutrality.[118] Consequently, it opposed all conflicts but could maintain its neutral status. This opposition was not that of a secular state. Instead, the Holy See opposition did not oppose one side and support the other but sought to chart an impartial and neutral course between the warring parties.

The Holy See opposed the 1991 Iraq War. Its neutral status meant it could oppose the war for not meeting the just war criteria, which has become stricter over time. Concurrently, it could advance its milieu and possession goals. These were to avoid war and halt the use of modern weaponry. Its possession goals were to protect Iraqi Chaldean Catholics and Christians in the region through its vocal opposition. The Holy See feared that Arabs conflate Christians with "the West," and there could be reprisals. Neutrality allowed the Holy See to press for its twofold goals independently without choosing sides while guarding its theology against becoming overly specific.

The 2003 war was like the 1991 war. The Holy See used its neutrality to support the UN's remit in opposing the war. Simultaneously, it used phrases like "global stability" to allow room for manoeuvre should the Security Council have supported the US-led coalition. Its possession goals remained the same in 2003 as they were in 1991, to vocally oppose the war to ensure minimal harm comes to Christians in the region. As in 1991, neutrality allowed Holy See diplomacy to carve an independent path between the pro and antiwar camps and advance its own goals.

The Syrian conflict that began in 2011 saw a state with a more extensive and more diverse Christian community enter the Holy See's neutral diplomacy. As the conflict worsened, the Holy See urged the Syrian ambassador and people to respect human dignity and resolve the crisis. Its possession goals remained stable and protected Christians. Like Iraq, the Holy See stressed Syrian Christians as Syrians first. At no point did the Holy See express a view that one side has greater legitimate rights or was more to blame than the other. As with the wars in Iraq, the Holy See sought to protect Catholics and Christians in Syria. The need for Christians and Muslims to "come together" was stressed repeatedly. Far from constricting Holy See diplomacy, neutrality allowed it to protect its theology, advance its twofold goals, and do so without alienating any side. Equally, it was a method to enable the Holy See to communicate directly with Bashar al-Assad. Neutrality allowed a greater efficacy for advocating milieu and possession goals.

NOTES

1. *Ad laudem omnipotentis Dei, et Apostolicae Sedis ornamentum, accipite biretum rubrum, Cardinalatus dignitatis insigne, per quod significatur usque ad sanguinis effusionem pro incremento christianae fidei, pace et quiete populi Dei, libertate et diffusione Sanctae Romanae Ecclesiae vos ipsos intrepidos exhibere debere* (To the glory of Almighty God and the honour of the Apostolic See receive the red biretta, as a sign of the dignity of the cardinalate, signifying your readiness to act with courage, even to the shedding of your blood, for the increase of the Christian faith, for the peace and tranquillity of the people of God and for the freedom and growth of Holy Roman Church), Benedict XVI, "Ordinary Public Consistory for the Creation of New Cardinals for the Imposition of the Biretta and the Assigning of the Ring and Title or Deaconry" Vatican, last accessed August 12, 2020, at https://www.vatican.va/news_services/liturgy/libretti/2012/20120218.pdf.

2. Arnold Wolfers, *Discord and Collaboration: Essays on International Politics* (Baltimore: Johns Hopkins Press, 1962), 67–81.

3. Wolfers, *Discord and Collaboration: Essays on International Politics*.

4. The Catholic Church is made up of twenty-four Churches. The Roman Catholic, being the most populous of these, makes up the Latin/Roman Rite. The Chaldean Catholic Church originating in what is now Iraq, is one of twenty-two other Eastern Catholic Churches. Their origins are mostly in the Middle East and Asia. All recognize, and are in full communion with, the pope.

5. Leos Müller, *Neutrality in World History* (London: Routledge, 2019), 3.

6. Hanspeter Neuhold, "Permanent Neutrality in Contemporary International Relations: A Comparative Perspective," *Irish Studies in International Affairs* 1, no. 3 (1982): 13–26.

7. Josef L. Kunz, "Austria's Permanent Neutrality," *The American Journal of International Law* 50, no. 2 (1956): 418–25.

8. Gaetano Arangio-Ruiz, "On the Nature of the International Personality of the Holy See," *Revue belge de droit international* 29 (1996): 354–69.

9. Montevideo Convention on the Rights and Duties of States, article 1, December 26, 1933, last accessed July 3, 2020, at https://www.jus.uio.no/english/services/library/treaties/01/1-02/rights-duties-states.xml.

10. H. Lauterpacht, "Recognition of States in International Law," *The Yale Law Journal* 53, no. 3 (June 1944.)

11. Robert Jennings and Arthur Watts, eds., *Oppenheim's International Law: Volume 1, Peace*, ninth edition (Oxford: Oxford University Press, 1992), 328.

12. "Diplomatic Relations of the Holy See," Permanent Observer of the Holy See to the United Nations, last accessed July 3, 2020, at https://holyseemission.org/contents/mission/diplomatic-relations-of-the-holy-see.php.

13. Robert A. Graham, *Vatican Diplomacy: A Study of the Church and State on the International Plane* (Princeton, NJ: Princeton University Press, 1959), 15.

14. Cedric Ryngaert, "The Legal Status of the Holy See," *Goettingen Journal of International Law* 3, no. 3 (2011): 829–59.

15. Ibid.

16. Ibid.

17. Luke Cahill, "Special and Not Special: The Holy See, The 1991 Iraq War, and the United Nations Conferences of 1994 and 1995," *Diplomacy and Statecraft* 31, no. 3 (September 2020): 509–33.

18. Lateran Pacts, Conciliation Treaty, article 24, February 11, 1929, last accessed August 24, 2020, at http://www.uniset.ca/nold/lateran.htm.

19. Ryngaert, "The Legal Status of the Holy See."

20. Jennings and Watts, *Oppenheim's International Law*

21. Lateran Pacts, Conciliation Treaty, article 24, February 11, 1929, last accessed July 3, 2020, at http://www.uniset.ca/nold/lateran.htm.

22. Robert P. George, "Some Thoughts on Natural Law and International Order," in *International Society: Diverse Ethical Perspectives*, edited by David Mapel and Terry Nardin (Princeton: Princeton University Press, 1998), 56.

23. Timothy Backous and William C. Graham, eds., *Common Good, Uncommon Questions: Topics in Moral Theology* (Mahwah, NJ: Paulist Press, 2014).

24. Henry Kissinger, *A World Restored: Metternich, Castlereagh and the Problems of Peace, 1812–1822* (Boston: Houghton Mifflin, 1957), 2.

25. Jodok Troy, "'The Pope's Own Hand Outstretched': Holy See Diplomacy as a Hybrid Mode of Diplomatic Agency," *The British Journal of Politics and International Journal Relations* 20, no. 3 (2018): 521–39.

26. "Compendium of the Social Doctrine of the Church, Pontifical Council for Justice and Peace," Vatican, 2006, last accessed July 6, 2020, at https://www.vatican.va/roman_curia/pontifical_councils/justpeace/documents/rc_pc_just_peace_doc_20060526_compendio-dott-soc_en.html.

27. Drew Christiansen, "Holy See Policy Towards Iraq," in *Iraq: Threat and Response*, edited by Gerhard Beestermöller and David Little (Hamburg: LIT Verlag Munster, 2003), 89; Bernadito Auza, "Security Council Open Debate on Mediation and Settlement of Disputes. Statement of HE Archbishop Bernadito Auza Apostolic

Nuncio and Permanent Observer of the Holy See to the United Nations," Holy See Permanent Observer to the UN, August 29, 2018, last accessed July 6, 2020, at https://holyseemission.org/contents/statements/5b8713a6d8281.php.

28. James L. Garrett, "The Beagle Channel Dispute: Confrontation and Negotiation in the Southern Cone," *Journal of Interamerican Studies and World Affairs* 27, no. 3 (Autumn 1985): 81–109.

29. Nathalie Rivère de Carles (ed.), *Early Modern Diplomacy, Theatre and Soft Power: The Making of Peace* (London: Palgrave Macmillan, 2016).

30. Alan Chong and Jodok Troy, "A Universal Sacred Mission and the Universal Secular Organization: The Holy See and the United Nations," *Politics, Religion, and Ideology* 12, no. 3 (2011): 335–54; Jodok Troy, "Two 'Popes' to Speak for the World: The Pope and the United Nations Secretary-General in World Politics," *The Review of Faith and International Affairs* 15, no. 3 (2017): 67–78; Silvano Maria Tomasi, *The Vatican in the Family of Nations: Diplomatic Actions of the Holy See at the UN and Other International Organizations in Geneva* (Cambridge: Cambridge University Press, 2017).

31. Cahill, "Special and Not Special."

32. John L. Allen, *All the Pope's Men: The Inside Story of How the Vatican Really Thinks* (New York: Doubleday, 2004), 43.

33. John Bew, *Realpolitik: A History* (Oxford: Oxford University Press, 2016).

34. "The Challenge of Peace: God's Promise and Our Response a Pastoral Letter on War and Peace," *National Conference of Catholic Bishops*, May 3, 1983, last accessed July 13, 2020, at http://www.usccb.org/upload/challenge-peace-gods-promise-our-response-1983.pdf; see, Christian Nikolaus Braun, "The Catholic Presumption against War Revisited," *International Relations* 34, no. 4 (December 2020): 583–602.

35. Ronald Patrick Stake, "The Holy See and the Middle East: The Public Diplomacy of Pope John Paul II" (MA Thesis, Naval Postgraduate School, 2006), 67.

36. Todd D. Whitmore, "The Reception Approaches to War and Peace in the United States," in *Modern Catholic Social Teaching: Commentaries and Interpretations*, edited by Kenneth R. Himes, Lisa Sowle Cahill, Charles E. Curran, David Hollenbach, and Thomas A. Shannon (Washington, DC: Georgetown University Press, 2005), 499.

37. John Dear, *The God of Peace: Toward A Theology of Nonviolence* (Eugene, OR: Wipf and Stock, 2005), 115.

38. Paul VI, "The Fostering of Peace and Promotion of a Community of Nations," Section I, The Avoidance of War, no. 80, in *Gaudium et spes: Pastoral Constitution on the Church in the Modern World*, December 7, 1965, last accessed July 13, 2020, at http://www.vatican.va/archive/hist_councils/ii_vatican_council/documents/vat-ii_const_19651207_gaudium-et-spes_en.html.

39. Stake, "The Holy See and the Middle East," 66.

40. Allen, *All the Pope's Men*, 325.

41. Robert Shelledy, *Legions Not Always Visible on Parade: The Vatican and International Relations* (PhD diss., University of Madison-Wisconsin, 2003), 189–90.

42. John Paul II, "Angelus," Vatican, August 26, 1990, last accessed July 14, 2020, at http://w2.vatican.va/content/john-paul-ii/it/angelus/1990/documents/hf_jp-ii_ang_19900826.html.

43. George Weigel, *Witness to Hope: The Biography of Pope John Paul II 1920–2005* (New York: HarperCollins, 1999), 619.

44. Clyde Haberman, "Pope, in Christmas Message, Warns on a Gulf War," *New York Times*, December 26, 1990, last accessed July 14, 2020, at http://www.nytimes.com/1990/12/26/world/pope-in-christmas-message-warns-on-a-gulf-war.html.

45. Robert Dodaro, "The Gulf War and the Just-War Theory: View from the Vatican," *New Blackfriars* 73, no. 859 (1992): 200–209.

46. Freedman and Karsh, *The Gulf Conflict*, 101–2.

47. John Paul II, "Address of His Holiness John Paul II to the Diplomatic Corps accredited to the Holy See," Vatican, January 12, 1991, last accessed July 14, 2020 at http://w2.vatican.va/content/john-paul-ii/en/speeches/1991/january/documents/hf_jp-ii_spe_19910112_corpo-diplomatico.html.

48. John Paul II, "Message of John Paul II to Jacques Poos, President of the Council of Ministers of Foreign Affairs of the European Community," Vatican, January 4, 1991, last accessed July 14, 2020, at https://w2.vatican.va/content/john-paul-ii/en/letters/1991/documents/hf_jp-ii_let_19910104_jacques-poos.html.

49. Ibid.

50. Ibid.

51. John Paul II, "Messages of John Paul II to His Excellency Saddam Hussein, President of Iraq, and to His Excellency George Bush, President of the United States of America," Vatican, January 15, 1991, last accessed July 15, 2020, at http://w2.vatican.va/content/john-paul-ii/en/speeches/1991/january/documents/hf_jp-ii_spe_19910115_saddam-hussein-bush.html.

52. Ibid.

53. Ibid.

54. Ibid.

55. Ibid.

56. John Paul II, "Angelus," Vatican, October 28, 2001, last accessed July 16, 2020, at http://www.vatican.va/content/john-paul-ii/en/angelus/2001/documents/hf_jp-ii_ang_20011028.html.

57. John Paul II, "Address of John Paul II to the Members of the Curia, of the Papal Household and of the Vicariate of Rome," Vatican, December 22, 2001, last accessed February 9, 2021, at http://www.vatican.va/content/john-paul-ii/en/speeches/2001/december/documents/hf_jp-ii_spe_20011222_roman-curia.html.

58. Christiansen, "Holy See Policy towards Iraq," 92.

59. D. Brent Hardt, "Holy See and the Roadmap for Iraq Public Diplomacy," Wikileaks Public Library of US Diplomacy, September 13, 2002, last accessed July 16, 2020, at https://wikileaks.org/plusd/cables/02VATICAN4444_a.html.

60. Matthew A. Shadle, *The Origins of War: A Catholic Perspective* (Washington, DC: Georgetown University Press, 2011), 202.

61. Hardt, "Holy See and the Roadmap for Iraq Public Diplomacy."

62. Shelledy, *Legions Not Always Visible on Parade*, 185.

63. Cahill, "Special and Not Special."
64. Samuel P. Huntington, *The Clash of Civilizations and the Remaking of World Order* (London: Simon & Schuster, 2002).
65. Allen, *All the Pope's Men*, 325.
66. John Paul II, "Address of His Holiness Pope John Paul II to the Diplomatic Corps Accredited to the Holy See," Vatican, January 13, 2003, last accessed July 21, 2020, at http://w2.vatican.va/content/john-paul-ii-en/speeches/2003/january/documents/hf_jp-ii_spe_20030113_diplomatic-corps.html.
67. Ibid.
68. Ibid. (emphasis in original).
69. Troy, "Two 'Popes' to Speak for the World."
70. Cahill, "Special and Not Special."
71. John Paul II, "Address of His Holiness" January 13, 2003.
72. Ibid.
73. Jim Nicholson, "Pope's Message to Diplomatic Corps Focuses on War, Peace and Solidarity Among Nations," Wikileaks Public Library of US Diplomacy, January 14, 2003, last accessed July 21, 2020, at https://wikileaks.org/plusd/cables/03vatican135_a.html.
74. Ibid.
75. Allen, *All the Pope's Men*, 331.
76. John L. Allen, "Preventing a 'Spiritual Disneyland' in the Holy Land," *National Catholic Reporter*, July 21, 2011, last accessed July 21, 2020, at https://www.ncronline.org/blogs/all-things-catholic/preventing-spiritual-disneyland-holy-land.
77. "Iraqi President Meets Papal Envoy Etchegaray," *The Irish Times*, February 15, 2003, last accessed July 21, 2020, at http://irishtimes.com/news/iraqi-president-meets-papal-envoy-etchegaray-1.461842.
78. "Pope Enters Iraq Fray," BBC, February 10, 2003, last accessed July 21, 2020, at http://news.bbc.co.uk/1/hi/world/middle_east/2743987.stm.
79. Jim Cosgrove, "Saddam Has the Will to Avoid War, Cardinal Etchegaray Says," *National Catholic Register*, March 2, 2003, last accessed July 21, 2020, at http://www.ncregister.com/site/article/saddam_has_the_will_to_avoid_war_cardinal_etchegaray_says/.
80. Ibid.
81. Allen, *All the Pope's Men*, 354.
82. Art Laffin, "Bishops Called to Speak out Against Iraq War," *National Catholic Reporter*, December 24, 2004, last accessed April 11, 2021, at http://natcath.org/NCR_Online/archives2/2004d/122404/122404r.htm.
83. Lawrence J. McAndrews, *What They Wished For: American Catholics and American Presidents, 1960–2004* (Athens, GA: University of Georgia Press, 2014), 338.
84. Allen, *All the Pope's Men*, 354.
85. John L. Allen, "Mission to White House sends message to Islam," *National Catholic Reporter*, March 14, 2003, last accessed July 21, 2020, at http://www.natcath.org/NCR_Online/archives/031403/031403e.htm.

86. John Paul II, "Angelus," Vatican, March 16, 2003, last accessed July 21, 2020, at http://w2.vatican.va/content/john-paul-ii/en/angelus/2003/documents/hf_jp-ii_ang_20030316.html.

87. Allen, "Mission to White House."

88. "Syria: Cradle of the Christian Faith," Catholic Near East Welfare Association, 2010, last accessed July 22, 2020, at https://cnewa.org/magazine/syria-33485/?highlight=syria.

89. "Syria's beleaguered Christians," BBC, February 25, 2015, last accessed July 21, 2020, at https://www.bbc.co.uk/news/world-middle-east-22270455.

90. Agnes De Dreuzy, *The Vatican and the Emergence of the Modern Middle East* (Washington, DC: Catholic University of America, 2016).

91. Benedict XVI, "Address of His Holiness Benedict XVI to HE Mr Hussan Edin Aala New Ambassador of the Syrian Arab Republic to the Holy See," Vatican, June 9, 2011, last accessed July 23, 2020, at http://www.vatican.va/content/benedict-xvi/en/speeches/2011/june/documents/hf_ben-xvi_spe_20110609_ambassador-syrie.html.

92. Ibid.

93. Ibid.

94. Ibid.

95. Daniel Philpott, "Christianity and Democracy: The Catholic Wave," *Journal of Democracy* 15, no. 2 (April 2004): 32–46.

96. Benedict XVI, "Angelus," Vatican, August 7, 2011, last accessed July 23, 2020, at http://www.vatican.va/content/benedict-xvi/en/angelus/2011/documents/hf_ben-xvi_ang_20110807.html.

97. Ibid.

98. Benedict XVI, "Address of His Holiness Pope Benedict XVI to the Members of the Diplomatic Corps Accredited to the Holy See," Vatican, January 9, 2012, last accessed July 24, 2020, at http://www.vatican.va/content/benedict-xvi/en/speeches/2012/january/documents/hf_ben-xvi_spe_20120109_diplomatic-corps.html.

99. Ibid.

100. Ibid.

101. Ibid.

102. "Syria: Pro-Government Protesters Mark 'Friday of National Unity,'" *Daily Telegraph*, July 1, 2011, last accessed July 25, 2020, at https://www.telegraph.co.uk/news/worldnews/middleeast/syria/8611205/Syria-pro-government-protesters-mark-Friday-of-National-Unity.html.d.

103. Benedict XVI, "Members of the Diplomatic Corps, 2012."

104. Amanda McFarlane, "The Holy See's Diplomacy: An Analysis of Papal Mediation in the Middle East," *Florida Journal of International Law* 28, no. 167 (2016): 167–93.

105. "Pope Allies with Ayatollahs in Syria Mediation Effort," *Al-Monitor*, October 19, 2012, last accessed July 29, 2020, at https://www.al-monitor.com/pulse/ru/politics/2012/10/pope-benedict-ayatollah-sistani-to-mediate-syria-crisis.html.

106. Benedict XVI, "General Audience," Vatican, November 7, 2012, last accessed August 2, 2020, at http://www.vatican.va/content/benedict-xvi/en/audiences/2012/documents/hf_ben-xvi_aud_20121107.html.

107. Benedict XVI, "Interview of the Holy Father Benedict XVI with Journalists during the Flight to Lebanon," Vatican, September 14, 2012, last accessed August 3, 2020, at http://www.vatican.va/content/benedict-xvi/en/speeches/2012/september/documents/hf_ben-xvi_spe_20120914_incontro-giornalisti.html.

108. Ibid.

109. Ibid.

110. Silvano Tomasi, "Intervention by Archbishop Silvano M. Tomasi Head of the Holy See Delegation," Vatican, January 22, 2014, last accessed August 5, 2020, at http://www.vatican.va/roman_curia/secretariat_state/2014/documents/rc-seg-st-20140122_tomasi-pace-in-siria_en.html.

111. Ibid.

112. Dodaro, "The Gulf War and the Just-War Theory."

113. Cindy Wooden, "Pope writes to Syrian president, pleading for peace and aid corridors," *Catholic News Service*, December 13, 2016, last accessed August 6, 2020, at https://www.catholicnews.com/services/englishnews/2016/pope-writes-to-syrian-president-pleading-for-peace-and-aid-corridors.cfm.

114. Ibid.

115. "19 November: consistory for the creation of new cardinals, 09.10.2016," Press Office of the Holy See, October 9, 2016, last accessed August 11, 2020, at https://press.vatican.va/content/salastampa/en/bollettino/pubblico/2016/10/09/161009c.html.

116. Dominique Mamberti, "Archbishop Mamberti on the Church's Diplomacy," *Zenit*, November 12, 2013, last accessed August 12, 2020, at https://zenit.org/2013/11/12/archbishop-mamberti-on-the-church-s-diplomacy/.

117. Crux Staff, "Syria's Assad Says Pope Francis Has 'Incomplete' Picture of the War," *Crux*, December 10, 2019, last accessed August 17, 2020, at https://cruxnow.com/church-in-the-middle-east/2019/12/syrias-assad-says-pope-francis-has-incomplete-picture-of-the-war/.

118. Lateran Pacts, Conciliation Treaty, article 24, February 11, 1929, last accessed August 24, 2020, at http://www.uniset.ca/nold/lateran.htm.

SELECTED BIBLIOGRAPHY

Allen, John L. *All the Pope's Men: The Inside Story of How the Vatican Really Thinks*. New York: Doubleday, 2004.

———. "Mission to White House sends message to Islam." *National Catholic Reporter*, March 14, 2003.

Bew, John. *Realpolitik: A History*. Oxford: Oxford University Press, 2016.

Braun, Christian Nikolaus. "The Catholic Presumption against War Revisited." *International Relations* 34, no. 4 (December 2020): 583–602.

Cahill, Luke. "Special and Not Special: The Holy See, The 1991 Iraq War and the United Nations Conferences of 1994 and 1995." *Diplomacy and Statecraft* 31, no. 3 (September 2020): 509–33.

Dodaro, Robert. "The Gulf War and the Just-War Theory: View from the Vatican." *New Blackfriars* 73, no. 859 (1992): 200–209.

Kissinger, Henry. *A World Restored: Metternich, Castlereagh and the Problems of Peace, 1812–1822*. Boston: Houghton Mifflin, 1957.

McFarlane, Amanda. "The Holy See's Diplomacy: An Analysis of Papal Mediation in the Middle East." *Florida Journal of International Law* 28, no.167 (2016): 167–93.

Ryngaert, Cedric. "The Legal Status of the Holy See." *Goettingen Journal of International Law* 3, no. 3 (2011): 829–59.

Chapter Eleven

The Church and the Bomb
Holy See Diplomacy and Nuclear Weapons
Maryann Cusimano Love

Pope Francis and the Catholic Church have doubled down on their opposition to nuclear weapons.[1] For the Holy See, neutrality does *not* mean the Catholic Church is neutral on issues such as nuclear disarmament. As Massimo Faggioli notes in this volume and his book *The Liminal Papacy of Pope Francis*, the Holy See strives for a role of "positive neutrality."[2] This is not a "bystander" neutrality, but one committed to bringing marginalized voices from the periphery to participate in dialogue, mainly through the United Nations and multilateral institutions, which reflects Catholic theology of the unity of God's diverse human family, mirroring the unity of a Trinitarian God. Pope Francis and Holy See diplomats have played a critically essential role in raising voices from the periphery, bringing atomic and nuclear weapons survivors to testify at the United Nations and multilateral fora, such as Archbishop Joseph Mitsuaki Takami of Nagasaki. Putting a human face on nuclear disarmament issues has raised awareness of the danger and humanitarian impact of nuclear weapons, achieving the long-sought treaty banning nuclear weapons, and renewing commitment to deeper nuclear disarmament at a time when nuclear arms control and disarmament are threatened. The Catholic Church has long worked for nuclear disarmament and a nuclear weapons ban, using its dual positions as an ancient prestate actor[3] with more than 1.3 billion followers in every country, and as a sovereign actor with the oldest diplomatic corps on the planet. The Church is working simultaneously to change both nuclear weapons policy as well as the normative framework by which we judge nuclear weapons, so as to strengthen the nuclear taboo at a time when it is being undermined.[4]

Seventy-five years ago, the first atomic bombings in Hiroshima and Nagasaki killed more than 150,000 people and decimated the Catholic Church in Japan and Asia.[5] Holy See diplomacy thus brings a unique perspective to nuclear disarmament, both the voice of the Hibakusha, the witnesses and survivors of the atomic bombings, and the voice of nonnuclear and neutral states.[6]

As Pope Francis noted in his visit to Hiroshima on November 24, 2019, "The use of atomic energy for purposes of war is immoral, just as the possessing of nuclear weapons is immoral, as I already said two years ago. We will be judged on this. Future generations will rise to condemn our failure if we spoke of peace but did not act to bring it about among the peoples of the earth. How can we speak of peace even as we build terrifying new weapons of war? How can we speak about peace even as we justify illegitimate actions by speeches filled with discrimination and hate?"[7] These positions were included in the papal encyclical *Fratelli Tutti*, released on the feast of St. Francis Assissi in October 2020.[8]

Holy See diplomacy marked a long-sought victory on January 22, 2021, when the Treaty for the Prohibition of Nuclear Weapons (TPNW) entered into force. The Holy See helped sponsor several Humanitarian Impact of Nuclear Weapons conferences prior to negotiations of the TPNW, raising awareness of the horrific effect of nuclear weapons. When official talks began for the ban treaty, Holy See diplomats worked closely with other neutral countries. I assisted the Holy See Mission at the United Nations in these efforts. The Holy See was the first state to sign and ratify the treaty. Pope Francis's urgent statements about the immorality of nuclear weapons, including his trips to Hiroshima and Nagasaki, drew attention to the issue, helping the TPNW reach the fifty state parties needed for the treaty to enter into force. The Nobel Peace Prize was awarded to this effort to ban nuclear weapons, an effort supported by Holy See diplomacy since the beginning of the nuclear age. Although no nuclear states have agreed to the TPNW, Holy See diplomats see the TPNW as a way to change the moral and policy framework, working with and through international law and institutions, consistent with and working to fulfill the commitments of the Nuclear Nonproliferation Treaty.

This chapter will examine Holy See diplomacy on nuclear weapons from the 1940s to the present, including the Holy See's backdoor diplomacy to de-escalate the Cuban Missile Crisis to advance nonproliferation and TPNW. To understand Holy See's diplomacy on nuclear weapons, one must appreciate three elements: first, the Catholic Church's relationship to sovereignty; second, that the Catholic Church is not a national church; and third, that the Holy See is not neutral regarding nuclear weapons. Because of the demographics of the Catholic Church, spread across all countries and nations, and growing in the Global South, nuclear disarmament and nuclear nonproliferation is necessary to preserve peace and also to preserve the Church, internally and externally. This chapter will explore these themes while analyzing the Holy See's diplomacy on nuclear weapons policies.

THE CATHOLIC CHURCH AND SOVEREIGNTY

The Catholic Church (and most other major religious actors) are not nonstate actors; they are *prestate* actors.[9] Thousands of years before the concept of sovereign countries was ever invented, religious organizations created institutions and performed (and still perform) functions that are today associated with sovereign states. Religious organizations had laws, courts, schools, universities, hospitals, media, humanitarian aid departments, diplomatic emissaries, and so on, and registered births, marriages, and deaths, millennia before sovereign states ever created such institutions or engaged in these activities. The Catholic Church trained its diplomats long before other countries began the practice of professional training of a diplomatic corp. Only a very small number of today's 193 sovereign states have been around since 1648. Most sovereign states are very new, only created after the Second World War, after the demise of European colonialism, or even more recently, after the end of the Soviet Empire in 1991.[10]

The sovereign state is a newcomer around the world today, often with limited response capabilities to global issues such as nuclear nonproliferation and nuclear disarmament. In contrast, transnational religious networks are well-established, including in areas where the capacity and legitimacy of the sovereign state are limited. Religious transnational networks that were created for one purpose, such as education or charitable work, have expanded to address other issues, including nuclear disarmament issues and working to free the world of nuclear weapons.

The Catholic Church has a long-term and nuanced view of sovereignty, impacting its approach to nuclear weapons policy. Because it preceded the sovereign state system by sixteen centuries, the Catholic Church has long experience working with and within political units that were not sovereign states, from tribes to empires.

But unlike other neutral states, the Holy See operates both within and outside the sovereign state system, with a foot in both camps, able to readily work with and negotiate with sovereign states on nuclear disarmament while maintaining extensive operations and transnational networks, which collaborate with global civil society networks, operating across and within sovereign state borders in all countries.

This insider/outsider position of the Holy See gives the Catholic Church a distinct stance toward sovereignty and more opportunities to press on nuclear disarmament issues because of its distinct stance toward sovereignty. The Catholic Church believes the sovereign state exists to serve humans and human communities, not the other way around. For many of the world's most vulnerable people, sovereign control is either absent or predatory. Nearly one-third of the world's population, more than two billion people, live in failed or failing states, absent the conditions of law and order, *tranquilitas ordinas*, which make human development possible.[11] According to Freedom House, more than 36 percent of the world's people live in forty-three countries where the state deprives them of fundamental human rights and freedoms.[12] Like Sudan or Rwanda in 1994, the worst of these states are predatory, killing their own people in genocides. The Catholic Church does not stand on the sidelines where sovereign states are unable or unwilling to protect human life and dignity, and the common good. As Massimo Faggioli points out, the Church practices "positive neutrality," walking with vulnerable people from the peripheries.[13] However, unlike traditional NGOs, the Catholic Church is not an "outside actor" coming into a country to aid people in need. The Catholic Church is already in all countries around the world, and thus is both an internal and an external actor, which provides creative opportunities for diplomacy and advocacy on nuclear disarmament.

THE CATHOLIC CHURCH IS NOT A NATIONAL CHURCH

Holy See diplomacy on nuclear weapons is distinct because the Holy See does not align with a single nation or state. It is not coincidental that the Holy See practices neutrality among political alliances and that Catholic teaching on peace and war emphasizes just peace principles and practices prized by neutral states: the centrality of building social cohesion and equity across ethnic, racial, national, and religious lines. These principles have their roots in practice honed within the Church and external relations.[14]

Holy See diplomacy on nuclear weapons is distinct because the Catholic Church is not a national church. Its 1.3 billion followers live in every country globally and are members of diverse cultures, ethnicities, nations, and races. A nation is a group of people with a shared cultural, linguistic, ethnic, racial, or religious identity—such as the Sioux nation of the US plains or the Kurds in Iraq, Turkey, Iran, Armenia, and Syria. There are eight thousand nations (in a low estimate). In contrast, a sovereign state or country is an internationally recognized unit of political authority over a given territory, such as the United States of America or Iraq. There are 193 sovereign states. National boundaries—where various ethnic or linguistic groups are located—are elastic and often do not coincide with sovereign state boundaries. For example, the Basques live on either side of the border between Spain and France.[15] From its inception, the Catholic Church has included people of diverse national backgrounds and thus has built skills and traditions for engagement with people of various national backgrounds.

Today, Catholics live in nuclear and nonnuclear weapons states and hail from diverse national identities. As I note in my book *Global Issues*, data show that geographically, most of the major religions never left the cradle where they were born. Most Hindus live in India, and most Buddhists live in Asia, and so on. The exception is Christianity having the largest single sect in the world. In particular, Catholicism is most threatened in its "cradle," but is more evenly dispersed across geographic regions.[16] Immediately, Jesus and his first followers spread the faith beyond Jews in his home region to Romans, Samaritans, Greeks, Africans, and Asians. Because Catholicism is not a national church, Catholic believers and institutions have had to hone skills of national neutrality and inclusion, of encounter, dialogue, deep listening, and working with others, as Pope Francis describes in *Fratelli Tutti*.[17] As James Joyce described it succinctly, Catholic means "Here Comes Everybody."[18]

These skill sets and orientations of encounter, dialogue, neutrality, and openness to people from different nations are necessary for the Church's very survival, amidst internal and external cultural pressures. A century ago, most Catholics lived in the Global North, North America and Europe, including many in the original nuclear weapons states. Today most Catholics live in the Global South, in Latin America, Africa, and increasingly in Asia, in countries that have created formal Nuclear Weapons Free Zones.[19] Pope Francis may be the first pope of the modern era to hail from the Global South's nuclear-weapons-free zones, but he will not be the last.

As Pope Francis reminded us in Nagasaki, "The Catholic Church is irrevocably committed to promoting peace between peoples and nations. This is a duty to which the Church feels bound before God and every man and woman in our world."[20]

HOLY SEE DIPLOMACY AND NUCLEAR WEAPONS

"Vatican neutrality" does not mean the Holy See is neutral regarding nuclear weapons.

Pope Francis and Holy See diplomats play a critically essential role in raising awareness of the danger of nuclear weapons, renewing commitment to deeper nuclear disarmament, multilateralism, and respect for international law when nuclear arms control and disarmament are threatened.[21] Today nuclear weapons states are building new nuclear weapons and have threatened to use nuclear weapons in response to nonnuclear attacks, including cyberattacks, further eroding the nuclear taboo.[22] Historic nuclear arms treaties and their associated verification regimes have been destroyed. Former President Trump ended the Intermediate Nuclear Forces (INF) Treaty, signed by US President Ronald Reagan and Soviet Premier Mikhail Gorbachev, which heralded the end of the Cold War. The INF Treaty stopped the development and positioning of destabilizing weapons which shortened the time decision-makers had to respond, increasing the likelihood of a nuclear accident and nuclear weapons use. The Open Skies Treaty, a longstanding transparency and verification treaty, was likewise ended by Trump. With only two days left before it was set to expire in February 2021, the US and Russia extended the New START (strategic arms reduction treaty) for another five years. New START limits the overall numbers of US and Russian strategic arms, and is the last remaining arms control treaty between the US and Russia, who together command more than 90 percent of the world's nuclear arms. These provocative nuclear weapons developments are viewed negatively by nonnuclear weapons states as violations of the 1968 Nuclear Nonproliferation Treaty, in which nuclear weapons states agreed to work toward nuclear disarmament, not nuclear weapons expansion. The Holy See has decried the deterioration of the nuclear disarmament regimes and has called for a return to diplomatic agreements to reduce the world's nuclear weapons.

Against this backdrop, Pietro Cardinal Parolin, secretary of state of the Holy See, addressed the United Nations, urging persistence in adverse times:

> One might be tempted to lose hope in face of the setbacks, the impasse or the very slow progress in the disarmament agenda, in particular in the area of nuclear disarmament. However, perseverance and determination should characterize our common efforts to move toward the elimination of nuclear weapons. We must make every effort to avoid dismantling the international architecture of arms control, especially in the field of weapons of mass destruction. . . . We must work tirelessly to restore any possibility of dialogue and to fight the trust-deficits, which unfortunately are characteriz[ing] the current situation of disarmament, as well as in the building of our common and collective security.[23]

For this purpose, Pope Francis traveled to Japan to raise awareness on the continued need for nuclear disarmament and support for dialogue and diplomacy on the seventy-fifth anniversary of the atomic bombings of Hiroshima and Nagasaki. Knowing international media attention would follow him, Pope Francis traveled to Japan to draw world attention to the epicenters of those atomic bomb blasts. He visited with the hibakusha, called on the world to ban nuclear weapons, and returned to support nuclear disarmament treaties. As Pope Francis urged in Nagasaki, despite recent setbacks in nuclear arms control and disarmament, "we must never grow weary of working to support the principal international legal instruments of nuclear disarmament and nonproliferation, including the Treaty on the Prohibition of Nuclear Weapons."[24]

In Hiroshima and Nagasaki, the pope reiterated the Church's long-standing position calling for deeper disarmament, nonproliferation, a ban against nuclear weapons and nuclear testing, and increased international law and cooperation to achieve this. As will be discussed shortly, Pope Francis's position is not new; it has been the consistent Catholic position since the dawn of the nuclear age. At memorial services at ground zero in Hiroshima and Nagasaki, he echoed his remarks to the United Nations in 2015, "An ethics and a law based on the threat of mutual destruction and possibly the destruction of all mankind are self-contradictory and an affront to the entire framework of the United Nations. There is an urgent need to work for a world free of nuclear weapons, in full application of the [nuclear] Nonproliferation Treaty [NPT], in letter and spirit, with the goal of a complete prohibition of these weapons."[25]

The Church's concern with these issues is not new. Before nuclear weapons were ever invented and used, the Holy See had warned against them multiple times. The world's first supranational science organization was founded in 1603 in Rome, with Galileo Galilei as an early member. Later renamed the Pontifical Academy of Sciences and moved within Vatican City, the group worked to further the dialogue between faith and reason and discuss nuclear science. The academy includes Nobel Prize winners and other top scientists of all faiths and none. During WWII, the body included Max Planck and other nuclear scientists, who apprised the Holy See on atomic research. Pope Pius XII worked to promote the sciences and the Pontifical Academy of Science, believing there was no conflict between science and faith as we all "read the Book of Nature."[26] He took a particular interest in promoting the Pontifical Academy of Sciences. As a result of these interactions, Pope Pius XII warned against the use of advancements in atomic science for bombs and war rather than peaceful purposes *before* the US created and used nuclear weapons. In 1941 he noted that advances in nuclear science posed a risky "double-edged sword," as the war-torn world repeatedly exploited scientific advancements for destructive ends. In 1943, at the suggestion of Max Planck, Pope Pius XII warned against the dangers of atomic war and urged world leaders to prevent the use of nuclear bombs. While noting the potential benefits of the peaceful use of atomic power, he warned, "it is, however, essential to prevent the process from taking place as an explosion because otherwise the consequence could be catastrophic not only in itself but for the whole Planet."[27] In 1944, Pope Pius reminded the world that war could not be a legitimate mechanism of resolving international disputes; the increasingly "monstrous means of hostility" that served to "destroy all that has been built up throughout the ages" made such justifications for war "out of date."[28]

These warnings were not heeded. The United States decimated the Catholic Church in Japan and Asia when it dropped atomic bombs on Hiroshima and Nagasaki seventy-five years ago, killing more than 150,000 people. The Catholic Church had survived centuries of persecution in Japan and had just celebrated rebuilding its cathedral in Nagasaki, the largest Catholic Church and community in Asia at the time when US atomic bombs destroyed the congregation at worship and 70 percent of Japanese Catholics. Japanese archbishop of Nagasaki Joseph Takami, himself a *hibakusha*, a survivor of the atomic bombing (in utero), told me of the generational impact of the bombings of Hiroshima and Nagasaki to this day.[29] Those who survived the nuclear blasts were discriminated against. People shunned them for marriage, jobs, and social interaction, fearful that they might transmit radiation sickness to others.

Many in Japanese society blamed Catholics for the attacks. Since Nagasaki was the center of Catholicism in Japan and Asia and one of the attack sites, some posited it was "holy retribution" for the abandonment of traditional Japanese religious practices. Some Catholics framed the event in sacrificial terms that they were the "sacrificial lamb" to pay for the war guilt of Japan's role in starting WWII. None of those views helped relations between Japanese Catholics and the rest of Japanese society.[30] During the visits to Hiroshima and Nagasaki of Pope John Paul II in 1981 and Pope Francis in 2019, both pontiffs reiterated that the atomic bombings had nothing to do with divine wrath but were the work of human hands.[31]

Pope Pius XII decried the atomic bombings, calling nuclear weapons "the most terrible weapons that the human mind has ever conceived," noting that "every act of war directed to the indiscriminate destruction of whole cities or vast inhabited areas is a crime against God and man." Pope Pius XII had an audience with US General Dwight Eisenhower (stationed in Germany at the time), General Mark Clark (in Austria), and Lieutenant General John Eisenhower (Dwight Eisenhower's son and aide) in the immediate aftermath of the dropping of the bombs on Hiroshima and Nagasaki. The pope warned the US generals against committing war crimes,[32] urged them to build a just, positive peace, and reminded them of their moral and legal duties toward defeated enemies and the needs of civilians harmed by war.

Holy See diplomats called for the complete elimination of nuclear weapons and international safeguards to control the spread of atomic weapons and knowledge, stop nuclear weapons testing, focus on the humanitarian effects of nuclear weapons and invest in human development rather than nuclear weapons. This remains the Holy See's position on nuclear weapons to this day. The Holy See supported the creation of the United Nations and the first piece of business taken up by the new body, eliminating nuclear weapons. Pope Pius XII urged that "every possible effort must be made to avert (atomic warfare) through international agreement."[33]

Influenced by the testimony of Catholic atomic bomb victims and the input of the Pontifical Academy of Sciences, Pope Pius XII was one of the earliest voices to note the terrible humanitarian impact of nuclear weapons precluded their use in testing and politics. Pope Pius and Albert Einstein were early protagonists against atomic testing. Eventually, this position prevailed, yielding both the partial ban against nuclear weapons testing and later the Comprehensive Test Ban Treaty. Thus, at the dawn of the atomic age, the Holy See clearly denounced as illicit "the whole nuclear weapons enterprise, deterrence included."[34]

Many Catholic countries allied with Holy See diplomats. Costa Rica proposed (in 1958) what would become the world's first nuclear weapons-free zone for Latin America. Also, in 1958, Ireland proposed the first resolution at the United Nations to prohibit the further dissemination of nuclear weapons. This proposal would eventually become the NPT, the Nuclear Nonproliferation Treaty.

US Catholic senator John F. Kennedy also favored a ban on nuclear weapons testing, since 1956. As president, he announced a moratorium on nuclear testing while negotiations were underway, but progress stalled over on-site verification of underground testing sites, and the talks were not revived until after the Cuban Missile Crisis.[35]

A high point for Holy See diplomacy on nuclear weapons came in October 1962, when Saint Pope John XXIII helped de-escalate the Cuban Missile Crisis. The two Johns, "Good Pope John," and the first Catholic US president, John F. Kennedy, had major crises on their hands in October 1962.

Pope John XXIII had just opened Vatican II on October 11, 1962. He had invited leaders of other religions, including Russian Orthodox, to the proceedings. Some hailed this historic move as a landmark in international and ecumenical relations. Others, particularly Christian Churches persecuted by the Soviet Union, decried the move. When a delegation of Russian Orthodox clergy arrived at Vatican II, the Ukrainian Greek Catholic Church leaders objected. The Catholic Church was anti-communist in aim, but there were debates about the means. The Soviet Union was persecuting religious, seizing and razing church property, outlawing religious practices, and killing and sending religious leaders to prison, including Ukrainian Greek Catholic Church leader Josyf Slipyj been imprisoned for seventeen years in a Siberian gulag. Pope John XXIII had served as a Holy See diplomat to Eastern Europe, spending a decade in Bulgaria before moving to other posts in Greece and Turkey, working with Eastern Orthodox communities. He used these contacts and relationships as Pope, engaging in dialogue and negotiations with people behind the Iron Curtin. But as Vatican II opened, the Ukrainian Greek Catholic delegation denounced the presence of the Russian Orthodox as

"Communist representatives" in Rome. At the same time, Archbishop Slipyj remained in Soviet prison while the Ukrainian Greek Catholic Church delegation threatened to derail the proceedings.[36]

Meanwhile, in the US, President John Kennedy was dealing with his own Soviet crisis. On October 16, US spy planes had discovered Soviet nuclear missiles being transferred to the Soviet ally, Cuba, ninety miles off the coast of Florida. The initial recommendation to President Kennedy by Air Force general Curtis "bombs away" LeMay was for US forces to respond with debilitating airstrikes on Cuba, followed up by a ground invasion, as the only means to ensure the destruction of the Soviet missiles. Other advisors and Kennedy, concerned that this would immediately lead to direct nuclear war between the US and Soviet Union, sought less escalatory responses. The US imposed a naval blockade, termed a "defensive quarantine," around the island of Cuba, seeking to turn back Soviet ships before the nuclear weapons in Cuba could become operational. In a televised speech on the evening of October 22, Kennedy announced the quarantine and told the world of the imminent threat of nuclear war. The US deployed more than 200 ships over a 500-mile radius north of Havana. With the news cameras rolling, diplomatic efforts deteriorated, as neither side wanted to appear to "back down" from the precipice.[37]

With the military forces of both countries on "hair trigger" alert, each hour provided numerous incidents in which the US and USSR nearly blundered into nuclear war by accident. For example, the US Navy dropped depth charges to force Soviet subs to surface or turn around, not knowing these Soviet subs were armed with fourteen-kiloton nuclear torpedoes and had the independent authority to detonate their nuclear weapons. Two of the three Soviet officers on board the submarine B-59 argued that the depth charges were a US attack, and since war had already broken out, they should discharge their nuclear weapons. If not for the opposition of Soviet officer Vasili Arkhipov, a nuclear attack might have been unleashed due to misperception. Kennedy bemoaned to an advisor, "do you realize that if I make a mistake in this crisis, 200 million people are going to get killed?"[38]

During those thirteen days in October of 1962, the United States and the Soviet Union almost blew the world to bits in a nuclear war. Participants thought the chance of nuclear war between the US and USSR was about even, 50/50. In those dark hours, Kennedy did what many Americans feared he might when they elected the first Roman Catholic president; Kennedy turned to the pope, suggesting the pontiff might be able to open a channel outside the US State Department to reach Khrushchev. It was not the only back door JFK knocked on. ABC newsman John Scali, journalist Norman Cousins, Columbia University president Andrew Cordier, the Brazilian government, even the president's brother Robert Kennedy also carried messages to Khrushchev, trying to de-escalate the situation.[39] Saint Pope John XXIII set aside the pressing business of Vatican II and stayed up late the night of October 24, walking back and forth between the chapel and his desk as he prayed about the lines he wrote, imploring Khrushchev and Kennedy to seek a diplomatic, not a military resolution. The next day he made his plea, carried on Vatican radio and Catholic media to the whole world. The pope used direct diplomacy via the radio so that his message would be heard immediately. There was no time to waste in a situation moving this quickly and no time for delays via diplomatic channels.

> We beg all governments not to remain deaf to this cry of humanity. That they do all that is in their power to save peace. They will thus spare the world from the horrors of a war whose terrifying consequences no one can predict. That they continue discussions, as this loyal and open behaviour has great value as a witness of everyone's conscience and before history. Promoting, favouring, accepting conversations, at all levels and in any time, is a rule of wisdom and prudence which attracts the blessings of heaven and earth. May they hear the anguished cry which rises to heaven from every corner of the earth, from innocent children to old men, from persons and communities: peace, peace![40]

Newspapers around the world carried the pope's message, including, unusually, in Russia. The official newspaper of the Soviet Communist Party, Pravda, carried the story with the headline of the unchanged, word-for-word first line of the pope's speech, "We beg all governments not to remain deaf to this cry of humanity."[41]

Russian Premier Khrushchev and President Kennedy received the message. Many factors led to the successful de-escalation of the Cuban missile crisis. Both Kennedy and Khrushchev negotiated a way back from the brink against pressures from "hawks" in their own countries. The Soviets agreed to remove their missiles from Cuba. The US agreed to eventually remove its (outdated) Jupiter missiles from Turkey, something Kennedy believed he had ordered before the crisis but had not been carried out.[42] Both sides agreed to put more safeguards in place. But Pope John XXIII's intervention did help to open space for dialogue and de-escalation, helping to create a face-saving way to back down. Khrushchev later thanked Pope John XXIII for his helpful intervention. Surprisingly, despite the USSR's atheism, Khrushchev even sent Pope John XXIII a handwritten Christmas card that December. Pope John XXIII received Khrushchev's daughter and son-in-law at the Vatican a few months later.

Help also flowed in the other direction. During the Cuban missile crisis, the papal outreach to Khrushchev also helped resolve the Soviet imprisonment of

Ukrainian Greek Catholic Church Archbishop Josyf Slipyj. The same backdoor channels that were activated in the Cuban missile crisis were also used to secure the release of Archbishop Slipyj in January 1963. As in the Cuban missile crisis, the Holy See used discretion to conduct its diplomacy in a face-saving manner. There was no international media or press conference. A travel route was plotted from Moscow to Rome that would draw minimal fanfare.[43]

This exchange illustrates the points raised earlier. Holy See neutrality and engagement across identity groups are necessary both for internal Church relations and external international affairs.

From those first words the Pope penned between Khrushchev and Kennedy in the wee hours of October 24, 1962, emerged the encyclical, *Pacem in Terris,* issued on Holy Thursday in April of 1963, just a few months before Pope John XXIII died. It remains a key framework for Holy See diplomacy. For the first time, a papal encyclical was addressed not just to Catholics, but to the whole world, to all people of goodwill. The language of the Pontiff's message was not only the specific language of Catholicism but was the common language of human rights.

Drawing on the recent experience of the Cuban Missile crisis, Pope John XXIII argued in *Pacem in Terris* that "Nuclear weapons must be banned. A general agreement must be reached on a suitable disarmament program, with an effective system of mutual control."[44] The encyclical also noted that "the fundamental principle on which our present peace depends must be replaced by another, which declares the true and solid peace of nations consists not in equality of arms but in mutual trust alone."[45] This echoed the Holy See diplomacy on nuclear weapons of his predecessor, Pope Pius XII. But St. Pope John XXIII elevated the position by its inclusion in a papal encyclical. An encyclical is not a mere speech or comment by the Pope; it is an authoritative teaching of the Catholic Church, the highest form of teaching, but for the constitution of the Catholic Church. The encyclical was read widely and debated publicly. It also had a political impact on nuclear weapons policy.

The Limited Test Ban Treaty was concluded four months later after President Kennedy de-linked the more controversial underground testing ban from the ban on atmospheric and ocean testing.

After *Pacem in Terris* and the Cuban Missile Crisis, Catholic countries renewed and intensified their efforts to create treaties banning nuclear weapons, nuclear proliferation, and nuclear testing. During the Cuban Missile Crisis, Brazil offered a UN draft resolution proposing a Latin American Nuclear Weapons Free Zone, but it stalled in the UN.

Days after the release of *Pacem in Terris*, Mexico took the initiative and announced on April 29, 1963, that it and other (Catholic) Latin American countries would sign a multilateral treaty banning nuclear weapons in Latin America to create the world's first nuclear-weapons-free zone. These negotiations yielded the Treaty of Tlatelolco in 1967.

The encyclical was a rebuke to those self-declared "realists" of the Cuban Missile Crisis who did not want to negotiate with the Soviets but argued instead for the US invasion of Cuba. *Pacem in Terris* clarifies that following Jesus the Prince of Peace is not an optional activity for Christians, or only the job of Holy See diplomats but must translate into action by all.

The encyclical was instantly controversial. Many around the world, including Khrushchev and other prior critics of the Catholic Church, hailed the document as ushering in a new moment of engagement and commitment to the common good. Others thought the pope too naive and optimistic about the complex realities of the Cold War and world affairs, too soft on communists, too relativistic to believe that non-Catholics could be partners. Many of these cultural fissures revealed in *Pacem in Terris* widened with Vatican II and remain today.

The encyclical was also mirrored by President Kennedy, who echoed many of the themes of *Pacem in Terris* in his famous commencement address at American University a few weeks later in June 1963. Kennedy announced closer relations with the Soviet Union, a moratorium on nuclear testing, renewed negotiations to end the nuclear arms race, and a renewed commitment to international law and organizations as means to a more positive, just, sustainable peace, all points of Holy See diplomacy raised in *Pacem in Terris*. In an unusual move, Kennedy's speech was broadcast and published in full in the Soviet Union.

Holy See nuclear diplomacy under Pope Paul VI continued the trajectory of *Pacem in Terris* and had new opportunities after the Holy See joined the United Nations in 1964 as a Permanent Observer, and Pope Paul VI was invited to address the United Nations in 1965. The pope delivered his famous "Never again war!" speech,[46] deriding nuclear arms as incapable of being the basis of true peace, but instead noting they are an obstacle to efforts to build peace and solidarity, and divert resources from the poor. The Second Vatican Council participants who were still convened in Rome continuing the meetings of Vatican II enthusiastically applauded Pope Paul VI upon his return and included these positions in the key Vatican II document, *Gaudium et Spes*, the constitution of the Church in the modern world. The nuclear arsenals of the US and Soviet Union had exploded. At the dawn of the nuclear age, the US had a handful of atomic weapons. At the height of the Cold War, the US and Soviets had a combined 66,000 nuclear weapons, many times more destructive than the bombs that decimated Hiroshima and Nagasaki. These massive investments in nuclear weapons were made simultaneously as global anti-poverty development needs were acute, as evidenced by the needs of newly decolonized countries and the inequities suffered by minority communities in the US, highlighted in the US civil rights movement. The rationale for these large nuclear arsenals and heavy expenditures in nuclear weapons offered by the US and the Soviet Union was deterrence that these large nuclear arsenals provided "peace of a sort." The Holy See notes the argument in *Gaudium et Spes* before criticizing deterrence as an untenable position morally, and an unstable basis of peace, thus returning to the Holy See's diplomatic position of calling for deeper disarmament leading to the eventual abolition of nuclear weapons.

> Whatever be the facts about this method of deterrence, men should be convinced that the arms race in which an already considerable number of countries are engaged is not a safe way to preserve a steady peace, nor is the so-called balance resulting from this race a sure and authentic peace. Rather than being eliminated thereby, the causes of war are in danger of being gradually aggravated. While extravagant sums are being spent for the furnishing of ever new weapons, an adequate remedy cannot be provided for the multiple miseries afflicting the whole modern world. . . . The arms race is an utterly treacherous trap for humanity, and one which ensnares the poor to an intolerable degree.[47]

Gaudium et Spes is not a robust endorsement of nuclear deterrence, but a call to move beyond it.

Pope Paul VI set the standard for the modern papacy, which Pope John Paul II would later follow. He was the first to travel outside Italy in more than 150 years, and with the accessibility of the airplane, he became the first pope to travel to Africa, the first pope to visit every continent, and the first pope to visit the Holy Land since Saint Peter. Personally engaging with people worldwide and witnessing the poverty of newly decolonized peoples reinforced Pope Paul VI's commitment to social justice and human development; nuclear weapons undermined both.

Nuclear disarmament remained a primary concern of Holy See diplomacy. The Nuclear Nonproliferation Treaty was the first international treaty signed by the Holy See since the 1815 Treaty of Vienna. To underline the Holy See's commitment to nuclear disarmament, the Holy See's secretary of state traveled to Moscow to show support for the treaty, a move unheard of at the time.

Much has been written about Polish Saint Pope John Paul II's rise to the papacy as being a factor in helping to end the Cold War. But the portrayal of John Paul II as a nuclear "hawk," as opposed to John XXIII and Pope Paul VI's "dovish" stance on nuclear weapons, is not accurate. Pope John Paul II repeatedly reiterated the traditional Catholic positions on nuclear weapons, decrying nuclear war and the nuclear arms race, and calling for disarmament.

He traveled to Hiroshima and Nagasaki, visited the *hibakusha* nuclear survivors, and advocated for a return to disarmament and away from the arms build-up and threats of nuclear war use of the Reagan years. Pope John Paul II's championing of the need for nuclear disarmament was deeply appreciated by Japanese Catholics, who erected a statue outside the rebuilt Urakami Cathedral in Nagasaki to commemorate this solidarity.

As millions of citizens, including Dorothy Day and Catholic nonviolent movements such as Pax Christi, protested in the streets around the world calling for a freeze on nuclear weapons and disarmament, the various regional Catholic bishops conferences disagreed about the morality of nuclear deterrence. The US Catholic bishops conference undertook a critical, extensive study and consultation on nuclear weapons policy. The resulting pastoral letter from the US bishops, "The Challenge of Peace," called for a renewed commitment to peacebuilding at every level, for nuclear disarmament, international laws, and institutions to reduce nuclear dangers, and money saved to be invested instead in development. In short, it was an affirmation of traditional Holy See diplomacy on nuclear weapons.

The US bishops' pastoral letter moved slightly, providing a more detailed analysis of deterrence and recognizing a *temporary* and *strictly limited* moral acceptance of some nuclear weapons possession for deterrence purposes only, as a step on the road to deeper disarmament. Previous Church statements had not gone this far in detail. But in practice, the nuclear powers had nuclear weapons arsenals, so Holy See diplomacy always held that the nuclear disarmament process would have to take place step-by-step, with verifiable agreements that would build trust for further disarmament. This meant that the Holy See acknowledged deterrence but did not recommend it. Each discussion of deterrence was coupled with a warning to move beyond it, as seen in *Pacem in Terris* and *Gaudium et Spes*. As the US bishops noted, "Deterrence is not an adequate strategy as a long-term basis for peace; it is a transitional strategy justifiable only in conjunction with resolute determination to pursue arms control and disarmament."[48] Holy See diplomacy sought to negotiate the different positions internal to the Church and to make the existing situation safer, through bans on nuclear testing and nuclear proliferation, at the same time as it sought to move toward a world free of nuclear weapons, moving beyond deterrence, as deterrence was not an adequate, just, or stable basis of peace.

Those who misrepresent Pope Saint John Paul II as an ardent supporter of nuclear deterrence are mistaken. In his 1982 speech to the United Nations, he urged deep support for disarmament twenty-one times. He only mentioned deterrence twice, once negatively as the "balance of terror," and once dismissing deterrence as immoral as a permanent position, "certainly not as an end in itself."⁴⁹ Also, as a matter of Church teaching, a papal speech to the United Nations, and a pastoral letter issued by one bishops' conference, do not have the same weight of Church teachings as papal encyclicals and of the Church constitution, which carry greater authority. The US bishops' pastoral letter was a laudatory and vital effort to engage in dialogue with the issues of the day. The process of inclusion and outreach that surrounded the pastoral was an important model. But it in no way "overruled" the Holy See's continued efforts to seek a world free of nuclear weapons.

The distance between Pope John Paul II's stance on nuclear weapons and his forebearers, as well as the current Pope Francis, should not be exaggerated. While it is true that Pope Francis has noted that the possession of nuclear weapons is impermissible as well as nuclear weapons use, this has been the Church's position since the dawn of the nuclear age. Holy See diplomats always warned that the continued possession of nuclear weapons would lead to a false sense of security, an abuse of resources, and risks of disaster, just as Pope Francis notes today. Additionally, the 1983 US Catholic bishops' position was actually a critique, not an endorsement of the Reagan era's nuclear arms race and nuclear use arguments. The "strictly conditioned" acceptance of nuclear deterrence "as a step on the path toward deeper disarmament" was a call to de-escalate the role of nuclear weapons and to return to disarmament negotiations. These positions were not an acceptance of the Cold War nuclear weapons policies of 1983, but a critique of them. The larger documents urged a more profound commitment to disarmament and peacebuilding. "The need to rethink the deterrence policy of our nation, to make the revisions necessary to reduce the possibility of nuclear war, and to move toward a more stable system of national and international security will demand a substantial intellectual, political, and moral effort."⁵⁰

They called for change.

> In the words of our Holy Father, we need a "moral about-face." The whole world must summon the moral courage and technical means to say "no" to nuclear conflict; "no" to weapons of mass destruction; "no" to an arms race which robs the poor and the vulnerable; and "no" to the moral danger of a nuclear age which places before humankind indefensible choices of constant terror or surrender. Peacemaking is not an optional commitment. It is a requirement of our faith. We are called to be peacemakers, not by some movement of the moment, but by our Lord Jesus. The content and context of our peacemaking is set, not by some political agenda or ideological program, but by the teaching of his Church.⁵¹

The bishops described the possibility of a moral form of deterrence that did not then exist in the US and USSR.; the world's two largest nuclear arsenals did not meet their strict conditions. As summarized later by the US bishops, "In 1983, we judged that nuclear deterrence may be morally acceptable as long as it is limited to deterring nuclear use by others; sufficiency, not nuclear superiority, is its goal; and it is used as a step on the way toward progressive disarmament. . . . The eventual elimination of nuclear weapons is more than a moral ideal; it should be a policy goal."[52]

Any attempt to recast the US bishops and Pope John Paul II as endorsing US and Soviet nuclear arsenals is incorrect at best. Their "acceptance" of nuclear deterrence was limited and tepid at best, and clearly criticized the existing arsenals. It specifically was not an endorsement of a permanent state of affairs.

Pope John Paul II said "certainly not" to nuclear deterrence as a permanent stance or an end in itself in 1982. Pope Francis is more plain-spoken in his "certainly not" today.[53] Pope Francis and Pope John Paul II are in complete agreement that a negative peace is not sustainable, while a positive "Peace is possible. And because it is possible, peace is our duty: our grave duty, our supreme responsibility."[54] There is greater continuity between these positions than some commentators claim. Consider the Holy See's statement that the world is now challenged "to adopt a post-nuclear form of security. That security lies in the abolition of nuclear weapons and the strengthening of international law."[55] This was the Holy See diplomatic position under Pope John Paul II, twenty-eight years ago.

Then, and now, deeper disarmament requires building deeper relationships and dialogue, and the Church understands this will take time. As Archbishop Tomasi, secretary of the Holy See's Dicastery on Integral Human Development, said to me at the Catholic University of America in Washington, DC, "There is no illusion that the number of weapons will disappear as if by magic or after moral and legal condemnation. Therefore, the Holy See is equally engaged in a step-by-step dialogue with nuclear-armed states whose commitment remains crucial to the achievement of any serious and realistic discussion of nuclear arms control."[56]

Holy See diplomacy on nuclear disarmament and nonproliferation has been remarkably consistent and successful over the long haul, especially for a non-aligned state with no military or economic power to leverage. Moral diplomacy is better positioned on an issue such as nuclear weapons that so clearly resonates with teleological and existential questions. The world has significantly reduced the number of nuclear arms and committed to a nuclear weapons ban. But breaking the habit of a sense of "legacy rights"[57] to nuclear weapons for the nuclear powers will take more time and effort. Fortunately, Holy See diplomacy takes the long view.

NOTES

1. This chapter is excerpted from Maryann Cusimano Love, *God and the Bomb* (forthcoming); see also, Maryann Cusimano Love, "The Papal Vision Beyond the Bomb," *Arms Control Today* (May 2020).

2. Massimo Faggioli, *The Liminal Papacy of Pope Francis: Moving Toward Global Catholicity* (Maryknoll, NY: Orbis, 2020).

3. Maryann Cusimano Love, *Global Issues Beyond Sovereignty* (Lanham, MD: Rowman & Littlefield, 2020), 141–81.

4. Love, "The Papal Vision Beyond the Bomb."

5. Love, *God and the Bomb*; see also, Cusimano Love, "The Papal Vision Beyond the Bomb."

6. For more on Japanese Catholic Hibakusha, see Takashi Nagai, *The Bells of Nagasaki* (New York: Kodansha Amer Inc, 1994); Gwyn McClelland, *Dangerous Memory in Nagasaki: Prayers, Protests, and Catholic Survivor Narratives* (London: Routledge, 2020); for more on the early experience of the *hibakusha*, see John Hersey *Hiroshima* (New York: Alfred A. Knopf, 1946).

7. Pope Francis, "Full Text of Pope's Message in Hiroshima," (November 24, 2019), accessed February 21, 2021, at http://www.vatican.va/content/francesco/en/messages/pont-messages/2019/documents/papa-francesco_20191124_messaggio-incontropace-hiroshima.pdf.

8. Pope Francis, *Fratelli Tutti* (October 3, 2020), accessed February 21, 2021, at http://www.vatican.va/content/francesco/en/encyclicals/documents/papa-francesco_20201003_enciclica-fratelli-tutti.html.

9. There are exceptions in new religious organizations, including the Mormon Church (Church of Jesus Christ of Latter-day Saints) founded in 1830, Soka Gakkai International (founded in 1930), the Church of Scientology (founded in 1953 by L. Ron Hubbard in California), and Unitarian Universalism (founded in 1961). Love, *Global Issues Beyond Sovereignty*, 141–81.

10. Ibid., 5–49.

11. Ibid., 20–25.

12. Freedom House, "Freedom in the World 2020," accessed February 21, 2021, at https://freedomhouse.org/report/freedom-world/2020/leaderless-struggle-democracy.

13. Faggioli, *The Liminal Papacy of Pope Francis*.

14. For more on Just Peace, see Maryann Cusimano Love, "Just Peace and Just War," *Expositions Interdisciplinary Journal of the Humanities* 12, no. 1 (2018): 60–71; Maryann Cusimano Love, "Christian Transnational Actors Respond to Persecution," in *Under Caesar's Sword*, edited by D. Philpott and T. Shah (Cambridge: Cambridge University Press, 2019), 456–91; Maryann Cusimano Love, "Just Peace and Just War," speech at the United Nations March 8, 2017, and the US Embassy in Rome March 16, 2017; Maryann Cusimano Love, "Catholic Women Peacebuilders Internationally: Invisibility, Ideas, Institutions," in *Women, Religion, and Peacebuilding: Illuminating the Unseen* (Preface by President Jimmy Carter), edited by K. Marshall and S. Hayward (Washington, DC: US Institute of Peace Press, 2016), chapter 2; Maryann Cusimano Love, "What Kind of Peace Do We Seek," in *Peacebuilding:*

Catholic Theology, Ethics, and Praxis, edited by R. Scott Appleby, Robert Schreiter, and Gerard F. Powers (Maryknoll, New York: Orbis, 2011), 56–91; for more on the dual nature of Holy See diplomacy, see J. Troy, "The Pope's Own Hand Outstretched: Holy See Diplomacy as a Hybrid Mode of Diplomatic Agency," *The British Journal of Politics and International Relations* 20, no. 3 (May 2018): 521–39.

15. Love, *Global Issues Beyond Sovereignty*, 5–10.

16. Ibid., 141–81.

17. Pope Francis, *Fratelli Tutti* (October 3, 2020), accessed February 21, 2021, at http://www.vatican.va/content/francesco/en/encyclicals/documents/papa-francesco_20201003_enciclica-fratelli-tutti.html.

18. James Joyce, *Finnegan's Wake* (London: Faber & Faber, 1939), chapter 1.

19. Love, *Global Issues Beyond Sovereignty*, 350–53.

20. Pope Francis, "Full Text of Pope's Message in Nagasaki" (November 24, 2019), accessed February 21, 2021, at https://www.japantimes.co.jp/news/2019/11/24/national/full-text-of-pope-francis-nagasaki/#.Xtq7bVVKjIU.

21. This chapter is excerpted from Love, *God and the Bomb*; see also, Cusimano Love, "The Papal Vision Beyond the Bomb."

22. Nina Tanenwald, "How Strong Is the Nuclear Taboo Today?" *The Washington Quarterly* 41, no. 3 (2018): 89–109; see also Nina Tanenwald, *The Nuclear Taboo* (Cambridge: Cambridge University Press, 2007).

23. Cardinal Parolin, Statement by His Eminence Cardinal Pietro Parolin, Secretary of State of the Holy See, Head of the Delegation of the Holy See to the Seventy-Fourth Session of the United Nations General Assembly High-Level Plenary Meeting to commemorate and promote the International Day for the Total Elimination of Nuclear Weapons (September 2019), accessed February 21, 2021, https://press.vatican.va/content/salastampa/en/bollettino/pubblico/2019/09/27/190927b.html.

24. Pope Francis, "Full Text of Pope's Message in Nagasaki" (November 24, 2019), accessed February 21, 2021, at https://www.japantimes.co.jp/news/2019/11/24/national/full-text-of-pope-francis-nagasaki/#.Xtq7bVVKjIU.

25. Pope Francis, "Message to the General Assembly of the United Nations" (September 25, 2015), accessed February 21, 2021, at http://www.vatican.va/content/francesco/en/speeches/2015/september/documents/papa-francesco_20150925_onu-visita.html.

26. Pontifical Academy of Sciences (2017), accessed February 21, 2021, at http://www.casinapioiv.va/content/accademia/en/magisterium/piusxii.html.

27. Pope Pius XII, "Address to the Pontifical Academy of Sciences" (February 21, 1943), accessed February 21, 2021, at http://www.academyofsciences.va/content/accademia/en/magisterium/piusxii/21february1943.

28. Pope Pius XII, "Radio Message for Christmas" (December 24, 1944), accessed February 21, 2021, in Italian language original available at https://w2.vatican.va/content/pius-xii/it/speeches/1944/documents/hf_p-xii_spe_19441224_natale.html.

29. Cusimano Love, *God and the Bomb*.

30. H. Miyazaki, "The Catholic Church, Peace, and Hope in Nagasaki: Bishop Aijiro Yamaguchi's War Experience," Nagasaki Shimbun (August 12, 2020), and remarks to the Catholic Peacebuilding Network event "Are Nuclear Weapons an

Absolute Evil?" (October 5, 2020), accessed March 31, 2021, at https://kroc.nd.edu/news-events/events/2020/10/05/are-nuclear-weapons-an-absolute-evil/.

31. Gwyn McClelland, *Dangerous Memory in Nagasaki: Prayers, Protests and Catholic Survivor Narratives* (London: Routledge, 2020).

32. Pope Pius XII, "Address Negli Ultimi Sei Anni Setting Forth the Principles Which Should Inspire Future International Agreements to Ensure Lasting Peace" (December 24, 1945), accessed February 21, 2021, in Italian language original available at https://w2.vatican.va/content/pius-xii/it/speeches/1945/documents/hf_p-xii_spe_19451224_negli-ultimi.html; P. C. Kent, *The Lonely Cold War of Pope Pius XII* (Montreal: McGill-Queens Press, 2002).

33. Pope Pius XII, Christmas Message (December 24, 1954), accessed May 26, 2021, at https://www.vatican.va/content/pius-xii/it/speeches/1954/documents/hf_p-xii_spe_19541224_ego-declinabo.html.

34. Christopher Hyrnkow, "'Nothing but a False Sense of Security': Mapping and Critically Assessing Papal Support for a World Free from Nuclear Weapons," *Humanitarian Consequences of Nuclear Use* (May 14, 2019), 51–81, accessed February 21, 2021, at https://doi.org/10.1080/25751654.2019.1610932.

35. Love, *God and the Bomb*.

36. Karim Schelkens, "Vatican Diplomacy After the Cuban Missile Crisis: New Light on the Release of Josyf Slipyj," *The Catholic Historical Review* 97, no. 4 (October 2011), Catholic University of America Press, accessed February 21, 2021, at https://www.jstor.org/stable/23053063.

37. G. Allison and P. Zelikow, *Essence of Decision: Explaining the Cuban Missile Crisis*, second edition (New York: Longman, 1999).

38. National Archives (2012), "Cuban Missile Crisis," accessed February 21, 2021, at https://www.archives.gov/publications/prologue/2012/fall/cuban-missiles.html.

39. Maryann Cusimano Love, "Pacem in Terris: Peace and Change," *Woodstock Report* 101, Georgetown University (October 2011).

40. Pope John XXIII, Radio Address, Vatican Radio (October 25, 1962).

41. Drew Christiansen, SJ, "*Pacem in Terris*," in *Modern Catholic Social Teaching*, edited by Kenneth Himes (Washington, DC: Georgetown University Press, 2005), 217–43, at 221; and Francis Rooney, *Inside the Vatican* (Lanham, MD: Rowman & Littlefield, 2015), 122.

42. G. Allison and P. Zelikow, *Essence of Decision: Explaining the Cuban Missile Crisis*, second edition (New York: Longman, 1999).

43. Unknown to the Soviets, however, the archbishop did manage to ordain a bishop clandestinely before he left, ensuring that the underground church would continue under Soviet rule. If the Soviets believed shipping off the archbishop would end the Church, they were mistaken.

44. Pope John XXIII, *Pacem in Terris* (April 11, 1963), 112, accessed February 21, 2021, at http://www.vatican.va/content/john-xxiii/en/encyclicals/documents/hf_j-xxiii_enc_11041963_pacem.html.

45. Ibid.

46. Pope Paul VI, "Address to the United Nations" (October 4, 1965), accessed February 21, 2021, at http://www.vatican.va/content/paul-vi/en/speeches/1965/documents/hf_p-vi_spe_19651004_united-nations.html.

47. *Gaudium et Spes*, "Pastoral Constitution on the Church in the Modern World," (December 7, 1965), 81.

48. US Catholic Bishops, *The Challenge of Peace* (May 3, 1983), Summary I.B.3.

49. Pope John Paul II, "Message to the General Assembly of the United Nations" (June 7, 1982), 8, accessed February 21, 2021, at http://www.vatican.va/content/john-paul-ii/en/messages/pont_messages/1982/documents/hf_jp-ii_mes_19820607_disarmo-onu.html.

50. USCCB, "The Challenge of Peace" (May 3, 1983), 196, accessed February 21, 2021, at https://www.usccb.org/upload/challenge-peace-gods-promise-our-response-1983.pdf.

51. USCCB, "The Challenge of Peace" (May 3, 1983), 333, accessed February 21, 2021, at https://www.usccb.org/upload/challenge-peace-gods-promise-our-response-1983.pdf.

52. USCCB, "The Harvest of Justice is Sown in Peace" (1993), no. 1, accessed February 21, 2021, at https://www.usccb.org/resources/harvest-justice-sown-peace.

53. Love, The Papal Vision Beyond the Bomb."

54. Pope John Paul II, "Message to the General Assembly of the United Nations" (June 7, 1982), 8, accessed February 21, 2021, at http://www.vatican.va/content/john-paul-ii/en/messages/pont_messages/1982/documents/hf_jp-ii_mes_19820607_disarmo-onu.html.

55. Archbishop Renato Martino, "Address to the United Nations Committee on Disarmament," *Origins*, 23 (November 4, 1993), 382.

56. Archbishop Silvano Tomasi, interview with the author, and also touched upon in the Q&A period after Archbishop Tomasi, Remarks at the Catholic University of America, Washington, DC (January 30, 2020).

57. Archbishop Paul Richard Gallagher, "On the International Day for the Total Elimination of Nuclear Weapons" (October 2, 2020), accessed on May 20, 2021, at https://holyseemission.org/contents//statements/5f694333bcf80.php.

SELECTED BIBLIOGRAPHY

Appleby, R. Scott, Robert Schreiter, and Gerard Powers. *Peacebuilding: Catholic Theology, Ethics, and Praxis*. New York: Orbis, 2010.

Faggioli, Massimo. *The Liminal Papacy of Pope Francis: Moving Toward Global Catholicity*. Maryknoll, NY: Orbis, 2020.

Himes, Kenneth. *Modern Catholic Social Teaching*. Washington, DC: Georgetown University Press, 2005.

Love, Maryann Cusimano. *Global Issues Beyond Sovereignty*. Lanham, MD: Rowman & Littlefield, 2020.

Tanenwald, Nina. *The Nuclear Taboo*. Cambridge: Cambridge University Press, 2007.

Chapter Twelve

Vatican's / Holy See's Approach to Nonproliferation

The United States and Japan

Saho Matsumoto

Just before ending the Second Vatican Council in December 1965, Pope Paul VI, who had recently succeeded John XXIII, declared that the Vatican would officially join the United Nations as a Permanent Observer. The move was timed to coincide with the first reconciliation with the Orthodox Church since the Great Schism of 1054. This was the historical moment when the Holy See's official diplomatic commitment to international organizations really began. It is also well known that this decision followed soon after Pope John XXIII's role in helping to mediate a solution to the Cuban missile crisis through his contact with Alexei A. Adzhubei, the son-in-law of Nikita Khrushchev, the Soviet leader, and the first Catholic US president, John F. Kennedy.[1] Thus, from the start, the Vatican's relations with international organizations were influenced by the issue of the threat of nuclear war. Accordingly, as a neutral power and as a Permanent Observer to the United Nations, the Vatican tried to play an important role in dealing with nuclear issues during the Cold War, which has continued in the post–Cold War period up to the present.

Following the Cuban Missile Crisis, nuclear issues encompassed in the Nonproliferation Treaty (NPT) became central to US–Soviet rivalry until the end of the Cold War. The NPT was negotiated by the Eighteen Nation Committee on Disarmament, a United Nations–sponsored organization based in Geneva, Switzerland, from 1965 to 1968. It opened for signature in 1968 and entered into force in 1970. The Holy See ratified the NPT in February 1972. The NPT consists of three principles: nonproliferation, disarmament, and the right to use and develop nuclear technology peacefully.

The Vatican's attitude toward the NPT and other nuclear issues has been dominated by the parallel moral, ethical, and theological debates on the meaning of "just war theory" in the present day and whether the Holy See should follow that theory or adopt a view akin to pacifism. On the one hand, the former led to the argument that nuclear deterrence could be justifiable under strict conditions and a step forward to eventual nuclear disarmament. On the other hand, pacifism pointed out the need to oppose nuclear weapons absolutely, as seen in the nuclear freeze movement. The division between these two stances has been evident even within the Catholic Church. In particular, the American Catholic Church was clearly divided into conservatives within the hierarchy, who upheld the idea of "just war," and the liberals/radicals parish priests.[2]

Since the time of St. Thomas Aquinas and the medieval School of Salamanca based on a Thomistic understanding of natural law, the Vatican had upheld the idea of "just war." This idea stated that war is one of the worst evils that humanity can suffer and that a diplomatic resolution is always preferable before war has started. However, the Salamanca School reasoned that war could be the last resort when necessary to prevent an even greater evil. There is also an argument that "just war" is possible in self-defense, but what degree of self-defense is justifiable is a matter of debate.[3] Because of the timing of the Cuban Missile Crisis and the beginning of US intervention in the Vietnam War, Pope John XXIII's 1963 encyclical *Pacem in Terris* (*Peace on Earth*) has been interpreted as an expression of a pacifism that denied this "just war" theory.

While *Pacem in Terris* appears to be a radical departure in Catholic social teaching on war and peace, it is questionable however if it really means total pacifism. According to Charles E. Curran, a mistake in translating from Latin to English was made, making it appear that the Pope was embracing pacifism. In reality, *Pacem in Terris* does not advocate pacifism but rather rejects war to restore violated rights while still holding that defensive wars might be legitimate.[4] This was in line with previous practice. Even during the Second World War, in his Christmas message in 1944, Pope Pius XII had opposed most types of warfare, apart from defensive wars aimed at repelling present injustices in line with "just war" theory.[5]

It is also important to note that in its final section, the encyclical argued for the need for improved relations between nations, including collective action to assist other states. As collective security is one of the UN's founding principles and article 51 of the UN Charter guarantees the right to collective security and self-defense, if *Pacem in Terris* shared the same norms, it should not be understood as adapting total pacifism.[6]

According to an article by David Corey, "*Pacem in Terris* and the Just War Tradition," the arguments in the encyclical can be seen as linked to the debate within the Catholic Church during the Cold War about whether nuclear deterrence was morally acceptable or not. Some figures within the Church argued against nuclear weapons because they involved a "threatening strategy" that is morally wrong; thus, possessing the nuclear weapon itself is immoral. Corey points out, however, that the conservative bishops rejected this argument, but at the same time, they also opposed the orthodox defenders of deterrence, who argued that it could be justified as a necessary evil. Following the lead of the Vatican, the bishops instead elaborated an "interim ethic" whereby nuclear deterrence could be morally acceptable if it met three criteria: sole use, meaning that its use is limited to deterring the use of nuclear weapons; sufficiency, meaning that it is not based on achieving nuclear superiority; and disarmament, meaning that it is used as a step toward disarmament.[7] From a US Catholic perspective, particularly that of the conservative bishops, it was important to show Catholic loyalty to the nation, particularly during wartime. Spellman, for example, was a vocal supporter of the US–Vietnam war.[8] On December 23, 1981, his successor, Cardinal Terence Cooke, applied the traditional "just war" theory to the idea that nuclear deterrence can be tolerated if a nation sincerely seeks to reduce arms.[9] He once stated that deterrence was not satisfactory or safe, but could be considered morally "tolerable."[10]

CASAROLI'S DIPLOMACY ON THE NPT

The theological and moral debates on "just war" and possessing nuclear armament were important, but it is equally significant about the Church's stance to note that during and after the Cold War, the deterrence argument radically shifted due to geopolitical changes and other elements. It might, for example, be the case that the NPT worked well during the Cold War, but it is no longer so useful in the post–Cold War period. The Vatican as a religious organization is regarded as expressing a moral voice for the Christian world and is expected to be consistent in principle. However, the Vatican as an actor in the international order, in reality, has a pragmatic approach toward diplomacy.

Indeed, the Vatican's pragmatic approach in the field of nuclear arms can be seen in its relations with the Eastern Bloc during and after the Cold War.

The literature on the Vatican's diplomatic negotiations with the Eastern Bloc during the Cold War on the NPT and other nuclear issues is not extensive. One reason for that is the lack of available historical documents in the Vatican Archives. Although the main part of the Vatican Secret Archive was finally opened up in March 2020, the documents are available only up to 1957, and any documents after the period are not yet open to the public. The same problem affects the records of the Vatican secretary of state, which contain documents on the Vatican's foreign affairs, such as the Nunzio files.

However, the papers of Cardinal Agostino Casaroli, which are kept in the historical archives of Piacenza, where he originally came from, cover the period up to the end of the Cold War and are therefore a valuable primary source regarding the Vatican's role. Digitalized copies of the Casaroli papers at the historical archives of Piacenza are available at the Archives for the Vatican Secretary of State.[11] All this material provides a significant source for understanding the Vatican's approach to *Ostpolitik* nuclear diplomacy.

Agostino Casaroli was one of the most important actors in Vatican diplomacy during the Cold War as its main negotiator with the Eastern Bloc. Even before becoming the secretary of state in 1979, Casaroli was important. Since 1961 he was undersecretary of the Sacred Congregation for Extraordinary Ecclesiastical Affairs, effectively deputy foreign minister. He was a signatory for the Vatican of the partial agreement between the Holy See and Hungary in Budapest on September 15, 1964. He then negotiated with the Communist Czechoslovak government over the appointment of František Tomášek as apostolic administrator of the Archdiocese of Prague in February 1965. He was appointed secretary of the Sacred Congregation for Extraordinary Ecclesiastical Affairs on June 29, 1967. During the period following Vatican II, Casaroli gained a reputation as a highly skilled diplomat who could negotiate with regimes hostile to the Catholic or even any Christian churches.[12]

Amongst the Casaroli papers, one can also find a copy of the NPT agreement, which the Vatican signed on February 25, 1971. The records contain a detailed account of where the Vatican stood in terms of the NPT. It states that, although the contents and conditions of NPT were supposed to be an inspiration for peace but were limited in terms of disarmament and détente, the treaty was still a significant step forward on the way of disarmament. The document continues:

> The Treaty is designed to stop the distribution of nuclear weapons . . . and thus is a way to reduce any danger for the destruction of human beings. It aims for nuclear arms to be completely under the control of the international organization and to promote the disarmament process.[13]

Thus, the Vatican's attitude was that it approved the NPT Agreement as a step forward to nuclear disarmament.

Despite its positive attitude to NPT, the Vatican was critical of the unequal position between the three nuclear weapon states (NWS), including the Soviet Union (1968), the United Kingdom (1968), and the United States (1968), and the non-nuclear-weapon states (NNWS). Although the treaty allowed the NNWS to have access to peaceful applications of nuclear technology, under article 3, the Treaty declared that the NNWS had to pledge to accept IAEA safeguards first in order to verify that their nuclear activities served only peaceful purposes. This rule, in fact, has led countries like India and Japan to describe the NPT as an "unequal treaty."[14]

Although aware of the problems facing the NPT, the Vatican's sincere wish was expressed in the NPT's Article VI: Each party "undertakes to pursue negotiations in good faith on effective measures relating to cessation of the nuclear arms race at an early date and nuclear disarmament, and on a treaty on general and complete disarmament under strict and effective international control."[15]

CASAROLI AND SILVESTRINI'S NEGOTIATIONS ON THE NPT WITH MOSCOW IN MARCH 1971

While expressing idealistic and optimistic views toward the NPT, Casaroli had to face up to *Realpolitik* when negotiating with the Soviet leaders about nuclear nonproliferation. Casaroli went to Moscow between February 24 and March 1, 1971, to negotiate with the Soviets directly on the NPT issue, alongside the question for Christians religious freedom within the Soviet Union.[16]

Casaroli, with Bishop Achille Silvestrini, who was the Holy See's delegate to the United Nations conference on the peaceful use of nuclear energy in Geneva in 1971, and Professor John Kwaku Nimo (a member of the "Consilium") came to Moscow to deliver the instrument of adhesion of the Holy See to the Treaty on the Nonproliferation of Nuclear Weapons in 1971.[17] The participants in the meeting from the Soviet government were: Deputy Minister Semen Kozvrev, who was the Soviet ambassador to Italy; Mr. Juri Dubinine, deputy director of the European office Mr. Povel Medvedovsky, deputy director of the first European Office Mr. Oleg Avramenko, counselor of the same office; Mr. Anver Starkov, third secretary of the same office, acting as an interpreter. The important meeting took place on February 25, 1971, and Andrei Kozyrev, Soviet ministry of foreign affairs, expressed that he was very pleased with the Holy See's adherence to the Treaty of Nonproliferation of Nuclear Weapons.[18]

The USSR considered the NPT to be an essential step on the path of complete nuclear disarmament, which it hoped would be pursued in the interests of all peoples. It noted with satisfaction that the Holy See also wanted to carry out this act in Moscow. Kozyrev said that he already knew about the Vatican's commitment to the NPT through the Soviet Ambassador to Rome, but it was even more pleasing to directly meet and talk with Casaroli and other Holy See's representatives.[19]

A long conversation took place between Casaroli and Kozyrev. The contents of the conversation include a mini-history of Soviet-Vatican relations since 1968 when the Holy See had already expressed its approval with the NPT Treaty. Casaroli stated: "The Holy See considers it of great interest to be able to speak, on a confidential and cordial level, with representatives of the USSR about problems of general interest for humanity. The Holy Father's talks with Mr. Podgorny (1967) and with Mr. Gromyko (1970), and other contacts through the staff of the Soviet Embassy in Rome have made it possible to establish an ongoing dialogue."[20]

This statement demonstrates that the Holy See and the Soviet Union had been in regular communications, including during the period of Soviet invasion to Prague in 1968, and the still-unsolved Berlin question.

Kozyrev, for his part, stated that the Holy See had great knowledge and information regarding the situation of the Soviet Union and the Eastern European countries, including the affairs of the Warsaw Pact, and as well as that of the Western European including NATO affairs. Therefore, he stated that the Vatican, with its multiple information channels, would be in a great position to assist with the forthcoming Helsinki Conference alongside Finnish President Kekkonen. To this, Casaroli responded by noting:

> The Holy See welcomes the idea not only of generic security initiatives in Europe, but concretely of a group conference proposed as a means to achieve it. In conjunction with the visit of the Finnish President Kekkonen to the Holy Father, a positive response was given to the proposal of that government in Helsinki for multilateral contacts for information purposes. In these days (February 23), the Holy See has given an answer, through the Belgian Government, to the NATO countries (it was made known confidentially to the Minister Counselor of the USSR Embassy in Rome).[21]

Therefore, the Holy See seems to have been happy to mediate between the Warsaw Pact and NATO through the Finnish channel. Although the Vatican and Finland were not particularly close, both were neutral.

This close communication between the Holy See and the Soviet Union helped to reduce tensions over nuclear arms. Indeed, it is worth noting that the Soviet Foreign Minister Andrei Gromyko, who played a central role in the establishment of détente with the United States by negotiating the ABM Treaty, the Partial Nuclear Test Ban Treaty, and the SALT I and II, among others, had four audiences with Pope Paul VI between 1970 and 1974.

The Casaroli papers cover not only his direct involvement with security issues but also the Vatican's interaction with European security organizations such as the Conference on Security and Co-operation in Europe (CSCE) and NATO. For example, on February 23, 1971, the council of public affairs of the Catholic Church received a copy of an official committee report of NATO through the ambassador of the Holy See to Belgium, demonstrating the Vatican's direct involvement in security issues such as NATO's negotiations with the Warsaw Pact. After a statement of approval of NATO, despite, of course, avoiding any military commitment, the document says, "The Holy See has also expressed its conviction that only a balance of power, even if it constitutes a mean which can appear sometimes almost the only one possibility to contain the outbreak of conflicts."[22] The statement ended with the Vatican's strong approval of the goals of the Helsinki conference (CSCE), which came of a Finnish proposal for greater security cooperation between the West and the East.

Casaroli's private papers and Pope Paul VI's official open letter to Casaroli demonstrate his close involvement and the Vatican's role in the final session of the Helsinki Accords in the July through August 1975 third phase of (CSCE) and afterward. After the Cold War, the CSCE (later OSCE) became the only multilateral organization in which the West and East, including the US and the Soviet Union, could talk directly about security issues. Casaroli indeed acted as the chairman of the final CSCE conference in Helsinki because he was regarded as an important and trusted meditator between the two hostile parties.

POPE JOHN PAUL II, HIS SECRETARY OF STATE, CASAROLI, AND REAGAN

Pope John Paul II was elected as the pope in October 1978. He came from the communist state, Poland, and it was only three months later, on January 24, 1979, when Gromyko, who was still the Soviet foreign minister, had an audience with him, speaking for one hour and 45 minutes in Russian. Five months later, on June 18, 1979, the SALT II agreement was signed in Vienna. However, subsequently, the US Senate chose not to ratify the treaty in response to the Soviet invasion of Afghanistan in December 1979. There was also the problem of the Soviet Union deploying intermediate-range nuclear forces (INF) in the form of the SS-20 missile in Eastern Europe in 1979.[23]

The new Pope ordained Casaroli as a cardinal on June 30, 1979, and then appointed him as the secretary of state on July 1, 1979. About one year and half years later, Reagan was elected as president of the United States in November 1980 and then inaugurated on January 20, 1981. In mid-December 1981, the Vatican announced that Casaroli was to visit Washington in a private capacity and that he would meet with President Reagan and Assistant Secretary of State William Clark in what became a "working lunch." In the US National Archives (NARA), there is a White House document dated December 15, 1981, about the detailed conversation between the president and Cardinal Casaroli, including the nuclear weapon issue.[24] It took place with another six people attending, including James Baker, James W. Nance, Allan Holmes, Dennis C. Blair, Archbishop Pio Laghi, and Monsignor Audrys Backies. Casaroli started talking about the martial law which had just been imposed in Poland two days before the meeting. The discussion between the two central figures went on to cover the broader political and religious situation in the Eastern Bloc. Then Casaroli cited the words of an American diplomat in Budapest whom he had met in 1963 that "the policy of the US was to avoid a nuclear confrontation with the Soviet but to work for small openings in the Iron Curtain, to plant the seeds of freedom."[25] This was how the talk turned to the main topic of conversation, the nuclear issue.

The background to this talk was that in October 1980, the Soviet and United States had begun negotiations, as the Preliminary Intermediate-Range Nuclear Forces Talks, in Geneva, Switzerland. Reagan's formal talks had subsequently begun on November 30, 1981 with the Soviet leader, Leonid Brezhnev. Reflecting on the current situation, Reagan duly related to Casaroli his view that: "currently the only way to deter nuclear war was to arm as strongly as the potential opponent. However, this was not good enough. There could be miscalculations and accidents. It was necessary to reduce the number of forces on both sides. The United States had made a start in Geneva, offering to dismantle one type of missile. It was hoped that his start could be turned into wider moves towards arms reduction."[26] Reagan, thus himself, pointed out the potential problem of nuclear deterrence and admitted the importance of arms reduction.

Cardinal Casaroli followed this question up in a talk with the US Secretary of State Alexander Haig and asked if it might not be better to accept an imbalance in nuclear forces so long as the US and NATO had a small but significant deterrent on their own. Rejecting such an approach, Haig explained that a significant imbalance created conditions for more aggressive diplomacy by the other side, and in addition, removed the incentive for further reductions in nuclear arms.[27]

The pope himself shared Casaroli's hopes regarding this matter. There are a number of letters between Reagan and Pope John Paul II at the Reagan Library. According to Paul Lettow's work, based on extensive work on the Reagan Library's primary sources, in spite of his hawkish image, Reagan's ultimate desire was the eventual reduction and then, in the longer term, the complete elimination of nuclear weapons.[28] Thus, both the pope and Reagan seemed to share a similar approach towards the nuclear disarmament process.

It is a well-known fact that Reagan and Pope John Paul II collaborated to support Solidarity in Poland. However, among the letters between the two, one can find that the president suggested that the US and Soviet arms control talks in Geneva, and the UN's Conference on Disarmament (CD), established in 1979, would be an important step towards removing the threat of nuclear warfare.[29] It is pretty surprising to find that the US Republican president, who was regarded as a military expansionist, including in the field of nuclear arms, and the charismatic religious leader who always sought peace shared the same ultimate goal of nuclear abolition.

As well as seeking to influence the US president, Pope John Paul II also made an important speech at the General Assembly of the United Nations in June 1982. He began by talking about his predecessor, Pope Paul VI's message in June 1978 at the First Special Session of the United Nations devoted to Disarmament, which had become political wisdom for the international community. He also cited the words of Pius XII on December 24, 1946, referring to the tragedy of Hiroshima as "the might of new instruments of destruction" which "brought the problems of disarmament into the center of international discussions under completely new aspects." He used language such as "reduction of armaments as well as greater safeguards against possible misuse of these weapons." And then described the current situation in which many people and groups were more and more frightened by the possibility of nuclear warfare in the case of "the irresponsible parties unleash some nuclear war."[30] He went on:

> In current conditions "deterrence" based on balance, certainly not as an end in itself, but as a step on the way toward a progressive disarmament, may still be judged morally acceptable. Nonetheless, in order to ensure peace, it is indispensable not to be satisfied with this minimum which is always susceptible to the real danger of explosion.
>
> What then can be done? In the absence of a supranational authority of the type Pope John XXIII sought in his encyclical *Pacem in Terries*, one which one would have hoped to find in the United Nations Organization, the only realistic response to the threat of war still is negotiation. Here I would like to remind you of an expression of Saint Augustine which I have already cited in another context: "Destroy war by the words of negotiations, but do not destroy men by the sword." Today once again, before you all, I reaffirm my confidence in the power of true negotiations to arrive at just and equitable solutions. Such negotiations demand patience and diligence and most notably lead to a reduction of armaments that is balanced, simultaneous and internationally controlled.[31]

This speech was controversial because John Paul II's reference to the word "deterrence" provoked debate about whether the Vatican approved a conditional nuclear deterrence or not. It seemed to show that the pope might have similar views with President Reagan on nuclear deterrence.

The pope's attitude towards nuclear deterrence naturally influenced the bishops of the Catholic Church in the United States. According to Jared

McBrady's article on the United States National Conference of Catholic Bishops' pastoral letter titled "The Challenge of Peace," there was at this time a division between the conservative bishops who believed in the nuclear deterrent and the others who believed in a more pacifist view of nuclear weapons. Indeed, the US Catholic bishops were divided almost in half. On one side were those such as Auxiliary Bishop Gumbleton, who was president of the US branch of Pax Christi, which helped to organize the nuclear freeze movement, and on the other side, figures such as Auxiliary Bishop John O'Connor of the Military Vicariate, who argued that the use of tactical nuclear weapons could perhaps be justified. There was also Archbishop Joseph Bernardin of Cincinnati, who was to be the head of the committee for the National Conference of Catholic Bishop's pastoral letter. He was known as a mediator and consensus builder between the two opposed groups and was also highly trusted by Pope John Paul II.[32] What is surprising is that this committee that drew up the pastoral letter on nuclear weapons included Reagan himself and members of Reagan's administration staff such as Haig, Clark, Allen, and William Casey. They were all Catholic, apart from the president himself.[33]

THE NPT IN THE POST–COLD WAR PERIOD AND POPE FRANCIS'S NEW APPROACH TO NUCLEAR DISBARMENT

It is clear that the nuclear ethical and strategic argument shifted after the Cold War and that the conditional approval of the nuclear deterrence that existed during the Cold War came to an end. Soon after the end of the Cold War during the 1990s, the arms reduction process made a degree of progress in talks between the United States and Russia, but new problems emerged elsewhere as North Korea left the NPT and India and Pakistan rejected ratification of the treaty.

The reason is that the disappearance of the communist and nuclear giant, the Soviet Union, brought about profound changes in the international order. In the new unstable climate possessing nuclear weapons was considered attractive by some powers that were concerned about their security. For these states, the NPT came to be seen as an unfair international agreement, as it restrained their freedom of action. This problem of the NPT, the unequal relationship between the nuclear-weapon states (NWS) and the nonnuclear-weapon states (NNWS), had already been pointed out by the Vatican as early as 1971.

Most notably, India argued that the NPT had created a club of "nuclear haves" and a larger group of "nuclear have-nots" by restricting the legal possession of nuclear weapons to those states that had tested them before 1967, but the treaty had never explained what ethical grounds there were for such discrimination. India's External Affairs Minister Pranab Mukherjee said during a visit to Tokyo in 2007: "If India did not sign the NPT, it is not because of its lack of commitment for NPT, but because we consider NPT as a flawed treaty and the need for universal and non-discriminatory verification."[34]

The crisis of the NPT for the post–Cold War period was thus not so much in the European region but in the Asian-Pacific region, such as Indian–Pakistan nuclear tension and then North Korea. For India, which had been in a border dispute with China since 1962, the fact that China could sign the NPT in 1996 and be allowed to join the ranks of the NWS, while India was still defined as a NNWS, was intolerable. It, therefore, made the US–India civil nuclear special deal in 2006. Moreover, the China–Pakistan nuclear deal was even more unforgivable for India. According to a report published by the US Department of Defense in 2001, China had provided Pakistan with nuclear materials and given critical technical assistance in constructing Pakistan's nuclear weapons development facilities. This was clearly in violation of the NPT, of which China was a signatory.

It could be said that after the end of the Cold War, Asia and even in Europe lost international confidence in the NPT. Recognizing this problem, the Organization for Security and Co-operation in Europe (OSCE), which emerged out of the CSCE, became a new driving force for disarmament and nonproliferation in Europe. Since Pope John Paul II recognized this, the Vatican has been an active supporter of the broader anti-nuclear agenda. In particular, it has lobbied to sign the Comprehensive Nuclear-Test-Ban Treaty (CTBT) and the Treaty on the Prohibition of Nuclear Weapons (TPNW).[35]

As the background, we can see that since the end of the Cold War, the Vatican and its representatives have brought into question even the strictly conditional moral acceptance of deterrence. For example, during a talk at Georgetown University in 2010, Archbishop Celestino Migliore, the Holy See's permanent observer to the United Nations, decried the "second nuclear age" (the first being the Cold War), when nuclear terrorism is a threat, nuclear weapons are proliferating, and these weapons "are no longer just for deterrence but have become entrenched in the military doctrines of the major powers." Migliore argued that "[i]t is evident that nuclear deterrence is preventing genuine nuclear disarmament. Consequently, the conditions that prevailed during the Cold War, which gave a basis for the church's limited toleration of nuclear deterrence, no longer apply."[36]

From the Vatican's point of view, the Cold War was a period of ideological warfare against Godless communism. Communism was a threat from not only the nuclear giant, the Soviet Union, and the other countries under its sphere of influence but also enemies within. In order to fight against visible and invisible enemies, nuclear deterrence could be a helpful method.

As Reagan once stated, "this new mode of representing nuclear weapons breached the deterrence convention, i.e., the purpose of nuclear weapons is to avoid war, not fight war."[37]

It could be said that the Vatican and Reagan aimed at much the same goal—to win against the Godless and the nuclear-armed Soviet Union. For that program, the Vatican's negotiations with the Soviet Union and its sphere of influence acted as a mediator between the United States and the West and the Soviet Union and the East over nuclear and security issues in general, as well as trying to guarantee religious freedom and worship within the communist countries. However, once the Cold War ended, the Soviet Union did not exist any longer. Although Russia is still a nuclear state, the threat from communism had ended. This, among other things, meant religious freedom for Christians in Russia and Eastern Europe. Thus, the Vatican's perspective changed.

Thus, even though after the Cold War, the United States still stuck with nuclear deterrence, from the Vatican's point of view, this policy was no longer an appropriate or acceptable strategy because nuclear deterrence actually prevents nuclear disarmament. The Vatican's stance is evident in Pope Francis's speech on December 7, 2014, as a message to the Vienna conference on the humanitarian impact of nuclear weapons. He stated: "I extend warm greetings to the Hibakusha, as well as other victims of nuclear weapons testing who are present at this meeting. I encourage them all to be prophetic voices, calling the human family to a deeper appreciation of beauty, love, cooperation, and fraternity, while reminding the world of the risks of nuclear weapons which have the potential to destroy us and civilization."[38] He used here a Japanese word, "Hibakusha," which refers to those who suffered from the attacks by nuclear bombs on Hiroshima and Nagasaki. He continues that "Nuclear deterrence and the threat of mutually assured destruction cannot be the basis for an ethics of fraternity and peaceful coexistence among peoples and states." This is a strong message to deny the morality of nuclear deterrence because possessing nuclear armament could bring more "Hibakusha" by warfare as well as through nuclear tests.

Following Pope Francis's firm rejection of the concept of nuclear deterrence, the 2015 Review Conference of the Parties to the Treaty on NPT was held at the United Nations in New York from April 27 to May 22, 2015. Despite intensive efforts, this conference could not reach an agreement on the substantive part of the draft Final Document. Pope Francis was not satisfied with this outcome. Accordingly, he became an even more active campaigner for nuclear disarmament through the CTBT and the TPNW rather than focusing on the NPT itself, because, as he said in 2015, the NPT has failed.[39]

On November 10 to 11, 2017, the Holy See hosted the first international gathering on nuclear disarmament since the approval of the TNPW, a legally binding instrument to prohibit nuclear weapons, which had been signed by 122 countries at the United Nations in New York on July 7, 2017 (sixty-nine states, including all those that possessed nuclear arms, did not vote). Eleven Nobel Peace Laureates attended the Vatican's "Perspectives for a World Free from Nuclear Weapons and For Integral Disarmament," including Beatrice Fihn of the International Campaign to Abolish Nuclear Weapons (ICAN), the recipient of this year's Nobel Peace Prize, Clementine Hall.[40] ICAN had led a worldwide campaign to win the approval of the TPNW, which led to its being awarded the Nobel Peace Prize.

Following this, Setsuko Thurlow, a survivor of the Hiroshima atomic bomb and a leading figure in ICAN, and Akira Kawasaki, a Japanese representative of ICAN, and other Japanese nuclear peace campaigners, encouraged Pope Francis to engage in an apostolic journey to Japan, particularly Hiroshima and Nagasaki. This took place between November 23 and 26, 2019. Setsuko Thurlow was a thirteen-year-old schoolgirl when the United States dropped an atomic bomb on Hiroshima on August 6, 1945. Today, she is a leading figure in ICAN. Her powerful speeches have inspired countless individuals around the world to take action for disarmament. She jointly received the Nobel Peace Prize on behalf of the campaign at the ceremony in Oslo in 2017.[41] Meanwhile, Kawasaki has been a core member of ICAN's leadership since 2010 and served as its co-chair from August 2012 to June 2014. Since 2008, Kawasaki has coordinated the "Global Voyage for a Nuclear-Free World: Peace Boat Hibakusha Project," in which atomic bomb survivors travel the world to share their stories and call for a nuclear-free world.[42]

During his visit to Japan, Pope Francis also met the Hibakusha of the Fukushima nuclear power disaster in March 2011, and then he started questioning even the peaceful use of nuclear power, although the Holy See has been an active member of IAEA. Pope Francis's visit to Japan greatly impacted Japanese Catholics and non-Catholic people regarding nuclear disarmament. However, Japan as a state has not yet signed the TPNW. ICAN members regard this as "a great disappointment." Japan is under the umbrella of the US's nuclear arms, which one might argue to be necessary to prevent the nuclear threat from North Korea (and China) due to geographical proximity. This is precisely the same as the nuclear deterrence policy of the Cold War age, although many Japanese people would prefer to follow Pope Francis's pacifism.

NORTH KOREA AND NONPROLIFERATION

North Korea is one of the most concerning countries in terms of the NPT, and in regard to the Vatican's commitment to the NPT in Asia, Pope Francis's ambition is to negotiate with Chairman Kim. During his visit to South Korea in August 2014, the pope appealed for peaceful reunification with the North. Then in October 2018, the South Korean President Moon, a Catholic, had an audience with the pope again in Rome with a message that Kim Jong Un had invited Pope Francis to meet him in Pyongyang.[43] About three months before this message, the Vatican secretary for relations with states, Bishop Paul Gallagher, visited the Joint Security Area on the Demilitarized Zone between North and South Korea on July 5, where he said, "it is a very historic period, a period of hope and the Holy Father is supporting that movement."[44] The Catholic bishops in South Korea have also been making a great effort for reunification with the North. President Moon met President Kim on September 21, 2018. And on October 7, 2018, US secretary of state Mike Pompeo met with Kim Jong Un in North Korea to discuss the details for a second summit between President Donald Trump and Chairman Kim to continue the negotiation of the denuclearization of the Korean peninsula, according to the State Department.[45]

However, the second meeting between Trump and Kim did not materialize, and the peace talks on the nuclear issue apparently failed. However, Pope Francis's efforts still continued, and in May 2021, Pope Francis appointed Lazzaro You Heung-sik, the bishop of the South Korean city of Daejon, as the new prefect of the Congregation for the Clergy with the title of archbishop. The first Korean appointed to a senior position in the Holy See was regarded as a great hope for "announcing his plans to arrange a groundbreaking papal visit to North Korea."[46] The papal effort for peace talks with North Korea demonstrates that dealing with all countries with nuclear arms capacity, such as North Korea, based on an impartial, fair, and neutral basis is the Holy See's governing principle.

CONCLUSION

To conclude, as have seen above, during the Cold War, Vatican diplomacy, mainly through the work of Casaroli, accepted the idea of a nuclear deterrent basing its stance on the "just war" theory, despite some moral and theological criticism. This approach was justified in part because the Vatican was fighting Godless communism alongside the United States. However, after the Cold War geopolitical politics ended, some of the NNWS and the non-members of NPT started ignoring the NPT rules, and thus the NPT does not work as well as during the Cold War period. Indeed, Pope Francis declared the NPT to be a failure in 2015.

It has become more difficult for the Vatican to make any moral argument for the nuclear deterrent if some of the NPT rules have been ignored. However, this has been due to shifts with the international order rather than any change in the moral argument. It also may have something to do with the change of pontiff from John Paul II to Francis, although the Vatican attempts to present a consistent moral voice. The Holy See is undoubtedly a neutral power as a permanent observant at the UN, but its policies toward nuclear issue have differed depending on which pope is in charge and even which secretary of state is in place. Vatican diplomacy has been a mixture of pragmatism and morality.

According to article 24 of the Lateran Treaty, the Vatican will take "no part in any temporal rivalries between other States, . . . except in the event of such parties making a mutual appeal to the pacific mission of the Holy See."[47] This is a detailed, accurate description of the essential neutrality of the Holy See and the Vatican is at present exercising that role in its attempt to work for the denuclearization of the Korean peninsula.

NOTES

1. Giovanni Barberini, *La Politica del Dialogo, le carte Casaroli sull'Ostpolitik Vaticano* (Bologna: il Mulino, 2008); Achille Silvestrini, "Prefazione del cardinale," 798. It is originally kept as AC b. 1 f., 2, 2 of Casaroli papers of the Archives of Piacenza and its digital copies are kept at the Secretary of State Archive of the Vatican. It includes the detailed exchange between the Pope and Nikita Khrushchev through his son-in-law Alexei A. Adzhubei.

2. Jared McBrady, "The Challenge of Peace: Ronald Reagan, John Paul II, and the American Bishops," *Journal of Cold War Studies* 17, no. 1 (2015): 129–52.

3. Richard Tuck, *The Rights of War and Peace, Political Thought and the International Order from Grotius to Kant* (Oxford: Oxford University Press, 1999), chapters 2 and 3.

4. Charles E. Curran, "The Teaching and Methodology of Pacem in Terris," *Journal of Catholic Social Thought* 1, no. 1 (2004): 17–34, at 30.

5. John Courtney Murray, *We Hold These Truths: Catholic Reflections on the American Proposition* (Kansas City, MO: Sheed and Ward, 1960), 254–65.

6. Article 51 of the Charter of the United Nations states, "Nothing in the present Charter shall impair the inherent right of individual or collective self-defence if an armed attack occurs against a Member of the United Nations, until the Security Council has taken measures necessary to maintain international peace and security. Measures taken by Members in the exercise of this right of self-defence shall be immediately reported to the Security Council and shall not in any way affect the authority and responsibility of the Security Council under the present Charter to take at any time such action as it deems necessary in order to maintain or restore

international peace and security" (i.e., July 2, 2021) https://legal.un.org/repertory/art51.shtml.

7. David D. Corey, "*Pacem in Terris* and the Just War Tradition," *Journal of Military Ethics* 12, no. 2 (July 2013): 142–61, accessed July 2, 2021, https://sites01.lsu.edu/faculty/voegelin/wp-content/uploads/sites/80/2015/09/David-Corey.pdf.

8. John Cooney, *The American Pope: The Life and Times of Francis Cardinal Spellman* (New York: Dell Pub Co., 1986).

9. Kenneth A. Briggs, "Catholics Reassess Beliefs on War in Nuclear Age," *New York Times*, December 23, 1981, accessed July 2, 2021, https://www.nytimes.com/1981/12/23/us/catholics-reassess-beliefs-on-war-in-nuclear-age.html.

10. "Battling the Bomb in Church," *TIME Magazine*, January 4, 1982.

11. Casaroli private papers (*Carta di Casaroli*) were originally kept at the Historical Archives of Piacenza where he came from and then are currently kept at Archivio Storico della Segreteria di Stato Sezione per i Rapporti con gli Stati (Refer as A.S.R.S), a part of Secretary of State, Vatican City State. I must thank Archbishop Paul Richard Gallagher, secretary for relations with states within the Holy See's Secretariat of State to allow my access to the Casaroli private papers.

12. There are a number of publications mainly in Italian such as Marco Lavopa, *La diplomazia dei "piccoli passi": L'Ostpolitik vaticana di Mons Agostino Casaroli* (Rome: GBE, 2013), however, none of them are directly about NPT.

13. A.S.R.S, Carta di Casaroli, AC b.2f. 4, 2 (n.1050/71) Dichiarazione addizionale alla strumento di adesione al Tratto di non-proliferazione delle armi nucleari, 25 Febrraio 1971.

14. Ryohei Murata, *Memoire of a Japanese Diplomat (Under-Secretary for Foreign Affairs)*, volume 1 (Kyoto: Minerva Publisher, 2008), 212.

15. NPT's Article VI, please see (i.e., July 2, 2021) https://www.un.org/disarmament/wmd/nuclear/npt/text/.

A.S.R.S, Carta di Casaroli, AC b.2f. 4, 2 (n.1050/71) Dichiarazione addizionale alla strumento di adesione al Tratto di non-proliferazione delle armi nucleari, 25 Febrraio 1971.

16. The letter dated March 1, 1971, is about the official meeting but it includes a detailed account of the talks between him and the Soviet foreign minister on February 25, 1971 on NPT, NATO, Middle East and Vietnam. The reference is A.S.R.S, Carta di Casaroli, AC b.2f. 4, 2 (n.1050/71) Dichiarazione addizionale alla strumento di adesione al Tratto di non-proliferazione delle armi nucleari, 25 Febrraio 1971, and the letter dated March 1, 1971 is enclosed with this document.

17. Cardinal Achille Silvestrini headed and to the conference on compliance with the Treaty on the Nonproliferation of Nuclear Weapons in the same city in 1975. He was appointed undersecretary of the Council for the Public Affairs of Church on July 28, 1973. https://press.vatican.va/content/salastampa/en/documentation/cardinali_biografie/cardinali_bio_silvestrini_a.html.

18. A.S.R.S, Carta di Casaroli, AC b.2f. 5, 1, Relazione sulla missione di Mons. Casaroli a Mosca, 24 Febbraio–1 Marzo 1971, Missione di Casaroli a Mosca il deposito dello strumento di adesione della Santa Sede al Tratto sulla non-proliferzione della armi nucleari.

19. A.S.R.S, Carta di Casaroli, AC b.2f. 5, 2, Allegato 1, Incontro al Ministero degli Affari Esteri, 25 Febbraio, 1971.

20. Ibid.

21. Ibid.

22. A.S.R.S, Carta di Casaroli, AC b.2f. 1, 5, Nota verbale del Consiglio per gli Affari Pubblici del Chiesa all'Ambasciatore del Belgio presso la Santa Sede, 23 Febbraio, 1971.

23. The conservatives took the view that the threat which Soviet (SS-18) missiles posed to ground-to-ground missiles (of the Minuteman type) had not been eliminated. NATO's Defense and Foreign Ministers viewed the deployment of SS-20 missiles as a threat to security. NATO needed to preserve the credibility of its graduated response strategy in the face of modernization and expansion of Soviet theatre nuclear forces (TNFs).

24. NARA, NLS, M06-015, December 15, 1981, President's Working Lunch with Agostino Cardinal Casaroli.

25. Ibid.

26. Ibid.

27. Ibid.

28. Paul Lettow, *Ronadl Reagan and His Quest to Abolish Nuclear Weapons* (New York: Random House, 2005).

29. Letter Regan to the Pope January 11, 1982, the Ronald Reagan Presidential Library, Reagan papers, the Vatican, Pope John Paul II Folder, box 41.

30. Message of His Holiness Pope John Paul II to the General Assembly of the United Nations on June 7, 1982, accessed July 2, 2021, https://www.vatican.va/content/john-paul-ii/en/messages/pont_messages/1982/documents/hf_jp-ii_mes_19820607_disarmo-onu.html.

31. Ibid.

32. McBrady, "The Challenge of Peace," 132.

33. Massimo Franco, *Parallel Empire, The Vatican and The United States, Two Centuries of Alliance and Conflict* (New York: Doubleday, 2008), 88–91.

34. "India Seeks Japan's Support, Calls NPT 'Flawed,'" *The Times of India*, March 23, 2007,

accessed July 2, 2021, https://timesofindia.indiatimes.com/world/rest-of-world/india-dismisses-npt-as-flawed-treaty/articleshow/1799434.cms.

35. CTBT is a multilateral treaty that bans all nuclear tests, for both civilian and military use, in all environments. It was adopted by the United Nations General Assembly on September 10, 1996, but has not entered into force, as eight specific nations have not ratified the treaty. TPNW, or the Nuclear Weapon Ban Treaty, is the first legally binding international agreement to comprehensively prohibit nuclear weapons with the ultimate goal being their total elimination. It was adopted on July 7, 2017, opened for signature on September 20, 2017, and entered into force on January 22, 2021.

36. Celestino Migliore, Speech Forum at Woodstock Theological Institute, Georgetown University, March 16, 2010. For a summary of the talk, see Thomas Reese, "Vatican Questions Nuclear Deterrence," Georgetown University, May 12, 2010, accessed July 2, 2021.

37. Hugh Mehan, Charles E. Nathanson, and James M. Skelly, "Nuclear Discourse in the 1980s: The Unravelling Conventions of the Cold War, *Discourse and Society* 1, no. 2 (1990): 133–65, at 133.

38. Message of his Holiness Pope Francis on the occasion of the Vienna Conference on the Humanitarian impact on Nuclear Weapons, December 7, 2014, accessed July 2, 2021, https://www.vatican.va/content/francesco/en/messages/pont-messages/2014/documents/papa-francesco_20141207_messaggio-conferenza-vienna-nucleare.html.

39. Daryl G. Kimball, "Pope Calls for Nuclear Weapons Ban," *Arms Control Association*, October 2015, accessed July 2, 2021, https://www.armscontrol.org/act/2015-09/news/pope-calls-nuclear-weapons-ban.

40. Philip Pullella, "Pope, in Change from Predecessors, Condemns Nuclear Arsenals for Deterrence," *Reuters News*, November 10, 2017, accessed July 2, 2021, https://www.reuters.com/article/us-vatican-nuclear-idUSKBN1DA161.

41. "A-Bomb Survivor Urges Nuke Abolition in Audience with Pope," *Kyodo News*, March 21, 2019, accessed July 2, 2021, https://english.kyodonews.net/news/2019/03/206254ab711b-a-bomb-survivor-urges-nuke-abolition-in-audience-with-pope.html.

42. Patrick Parr, "ICAN Champions Grass-Roots Efforts to Persuade Japan and Others to Support a Nuclear-Free World," *The Japan Times*, August 6, 2018, accessed July 2, 2021, https://www.japantimes.co.jp/news/2018/08/06/national/ican-champions-grass-roots-efforts-persuade-japan-others-support-nuclear-free-world/.

43. "S. Korean president to meet Pope with message from N. Korea," *Vatican News*, October 9, 2018, accessed July 5, 2021, https://www.vaticannews.va/en/pope/news/2018-10/south-korea-visit-pope-francis-message-north-korea.html.

44. Courtney Mares, "Kim Jong Un invites Pope Francis to meet in Pyongyang," *Catholic News Agency*, October 9, 2018, accessed July 5, 2021, https://www.catholicnewsagency.com/news/39590/kim-jong-un-invites-pope-francis-to-meet-in-pyongyang.

45. Choe Sang-Hun, "North Korea Agreed to Allow Inspectors into a Key Nuclear Testing Site," *New York Times*, October 8, 2018, accessed July 5, 2021, https://www.nytimes.com/2018/10/08/world/asia/mike-pompeo-kim-jong-un-north-korea.html.

46. "Can South Korea's Archbishop Help Pave the Way for a Papal Visit to North Korea?" *Deutsche Welle*, June 17, 2021, accessed July 5, 2021, https://www.dw.com/en/can-south-koreas-archbishop-help-pave-the-way-for-a-papal-visit-to-north-korea/a-57933879.

47. The Text of Lateran Pacts of 1929, accessed July 5, 2021, http://www.uniset.ca/nold/lateran.html.

SELECTED BIBLIOGRAPHY

Barberini, Giovanni. *La Politica del Dialogo: Le carte Casaroli sull'Ostpolitik Vaticano*. Bologna, Il Mulino, 2008.

Corey, David D. "*Pacem in Terris* and the Just War tradition." *Journal of Military Ethics* 12, no. 2 (July 2013): 142–61.

Curran, Charles E. "The Teaching and Methodology of *Pacem in Terris*." *Journal of Catholic Social Thought* 1, no. 1 (2004): 17–34.

Fejerdy, Andras. *The Vatican Ostpolitik, 1958–1978: Responsibility and Witness during John XXIII and Paul VI*. Rome: Viella Roma, 2015.

Lettow, Paul. *Ronald Reagan and His Quest to Abolish Nuclear Weapons*. New York: Random House, 2005.

McBrady, Jared. "The Challenge of Peace: Ronald Reagan, John Paul II, and the American Bishops." *Journal of Cold War Studies* 17, no. 1 (2015): 129–52.

Chapter Thirteen

Power and Spirituality

The Collision of Canon and International Law

Herbert Reginbogin

Popes have been entrusted as "the Vicar of Christ and the pastor of the Universal Church on earth,"[1] exercising universal power over the Catholic Church. They are at the forefront of securing humanitarian aid pursuing all necessary measures to alleviate the civilian population's suffering in conflict situations. The Holy See has helped mediate peaceful settlements of international disputes or cease-fires to end hostilities during two world wars, between Chile and Argentina in 1978 and the Iran hostage crisis in 1979 to 1981, or the official re-establishment of diplomatic relations between the US and Cuba in 2015.[2] Even when the pope was officially without sovereign territory between 1870 and 1929 and thus deprived of the traditional attributes as a sovereign,[3] he was called upon by States to mediate settlements of international conflicts.[4] Even before the Vatican became a permanently neutral state, as laid out in article 24 of the Lateran Treaty (1929),[5] the pope maintained an aura of neutrality. Narratives about popes illuminate and depict their lines of impartiality and involvement in humanitarian efforts. At the outbreak of World War I, Pontiff Benedict XV, with his secretary of state, Cardinal Pietro Gasparri, required the Holy See to maintain a "line of impartiality" by forbidding any preference for any side at war.[6] Furthermore, the pope helped alleviate the suffering the war caused through various humanitarian papal relief work comparable to that of the International Red Cross helping prisoners of war, including civilians. Specifically, these actions illustrate the Holy See's theological views about "humanity" and "dignity" for mankind,[7] for which the Church has chosen for itself the role of an "expert in humanity."[8] Saint John Paul II even holds the Universal Declaration of Human Rights as a "milestone on the long and difficult path of the human race" and as "one of the highest expressions of the human conscience"[9] that emanate from the historical natural rights law theory like the American Revolution's Declaration of Independence, but unlike the Constitution of the United States operating under legal positivism with the view that the US Constitution is alive and evolving as society changes.[10] As a Permanent Observer to the United Nations with General Assembly (GA) resolution 58/314 as of July 16, 2004, formalizing the participation of the Holy See in the work of the United Nations,[11] the Holy See "represents a universal idealist mission to pursue peace and work towards universal human rights within religious interpretations."[12] The Holy See, according to the Vatican secretary of state, Cardinal Parolin, in February 2019 delivered an important speech at Rome's Libera Universita Maria SS. Assunta on the occasion of the ninetieth anniversary of the Lateran Treaty. He said that Pope Francis pursues a policy referred to as "positive neutrality" affirmed through the "perpetual dialogue" between the Holy See and various nations in building dialogue and contributing "to ensuring humanity a worthy future."[13] Thus, "to discern the opportunities and the points of potential conflict."[14] Notwithstanding all this, troubling contemporary illustrations of clergy abuse, non-disclosure of vital historical records, financial scandals, and other cover-ups have left rank-and-file Catholics and world public opinion disillusioned not only of the priesthood but of the entire Church's credibility. The American journalist and educator Peter Steinfels writes that they all confirm "a festering sense that Church leaders too often said one thing in public, believed another in private and acted in ways not necessarily consistent with each other."[15] These events have endangered the reputation of the Holy See in the international world order.

The Church appears to have a Janus face with dual personalities. One preys on followers, while the other plays an enormous spiritual and humanitarian role in the international realm. What role did neutrality play as canon and international law locked horns when dealing with international affairs?

The nature of these two personalities is, in fact, grounded in international law, which, on the one hand, recognizes the Holy See as a religious and spiritual entity, while, on the other hand, its statehood rests on the concept of the Vatican City as a sovereign territory with the pope as its leader. While the Holy See always was the highest authority in Catholicism, the fight about its territory and the "Roman Question" regarding the pope's temporal power as rulers of a civil territory was only settled through the Lateran Treaty. The dual character of the Vatican and the Holy See also rivals the neutrality they wish to portray, along with the troubling narratives of the Church's failure to fulfill its compelling vision of humanity and human dignity in the religious and secular realm today. They are set on a collision course as the practices they employ are founded in canon and international law.

Still viewing the humanitarian history of the Holy See in the context of the diplomatic system, several contradictory narratives are generated about the Catholic Church's chosen vision of a progressive human rights narrative in the twentieth and twenty-first centuries. The scholarly literature questions the Church's self-portrayal of embracing the values of "humanity," "dignity," and "neutrality" through Church clerics and officials. Through the shifting international personalities' dual legal usage, a dilemma is exposed within the temporal and spiritual contradictory self-image of a permanently neutral Vatican and criticized for not upholding its responsibility as a state and church as illuminated by the issues raised in the following cases:

1. Centuries-long worldwide cruelties of sex abuse and molestation of children and adult victims with thousands of pedophilia cases within the Catholic Church.[16]
2. Financial corruption resulting from the combination of no legal oversight and amoral finances demonstrated by money laundering crimes and malfeasance.[17]
3. The Vatican's unwillingness to seek justice for historical wrongs of the past by rebuffing the 2001 International Catholic-Jewish Historical Commission efforts to access Vatican archives of the Pontificate of Pius XII to investigate the role of Pope Pius XII during the Holocaust.[18]

CENTURIES-LONG WORLDWIDE CHILD ABUSE

Triggered by the scale of the abuse of children by Catholic clergy over the years going back almost some two decades ago, appalling figures were disclosed when in 2002, the United States Conference of Catholic Bishops (USCCB) decided it should study the problem. It commissioned the John Jay College of Criminal Justice in New York City to conduct a study about the sexual abuse of minors by Catholic priests from 1950 through 2002. Published in 2004 as *The Nature and Scope of Sexual Abuse of Minors by Catholic Priests and Deacons in the United States 1950–2002*, found after auditing some three hundred American dioceses that 4 percent or 4019 clergymen of some one hundred thousand "Catholic priests and deacons in active ministry between 1950 and 2002 were accused of the sexual abuse of a youth under the age of eighteen."[19] The USCCB, in updating and republishing its Charter for the Protection of Children and Young People, continued to cite the 2004 John Jay Report as a basis for its continued action in the way it was attempting to protect children and young people.[20] So far in 2018, in the past fourteen years, "29 US Catholic dioceses and religious orders have filed for bankruptcy protection during the ongoing sexual abuse crisis in the Catholic church: 26 dioceses and three religious orders, the Oregon

Province of the Jesuits and the Congregation of the Christian Brothers, and the Crosier Fathers and Brothers. The latest filings were by the Dioceses of Rockville Centre NY and Camden NJ, announced on October 1, 2020." Reports circulate that since the mid-1980s, Catholic dioceses and religious orders have paid out nearly $3 billion in out-of-court settlements and court orders awards. In July 2007, the Los Angeles diocese alone paid out US$660 million to five hundred victims.[21] In 2003, US$16 million was paid to eighty-one victims at the Mount Cashel Orphanage in Canada, and over $4 million to the St. John of God Order in New Zealand involving fifty-six complainants of sexual abuse by brothers. The Dublin archdiocese of Ireland examined nineteen bishops' responses to more than four hundred children's sexual abuses by at least 152 priests in Dublin. In other countries like Austria, Australia, Canada, Chile, and England, bishops themselves were involved in child abuse cases.[22]

Church leaders protected criminals known to them having confessed their sins during communion by not turning them over to state authorities for child abuse. Instead, the Catholic Church often relocated them to other locations within the Church or allowed them to depart the Church to choose a secular life without any accountability.[23] Due to theological reasoning and practical politics, the Holy See provided instructions calculated to keep the scale of complaints about children abuse by Catholic priests from the purview of civil and criminal law enforcement by claiming immunity according to the renowned distinguished trial counsel and international judge Geoffrey Robertson. He accuses the Roman Catholic Church of culpability concerning the worldwide sexual abuse of minors. To the extent that the Vatican City or the Holy See has either internationally recognized statehood or status that in any way approaches statehood to sustain any of the privileges that go with statehood, then any "normal" criminal investigation is impeded.[24]

After reviewing the facts through August 2011, Geoffrey Robertson concluded that the claims by the Vatican to be:

> immune from accountability for these offenses in civil, criminal, and international law, a claim which is heavily dependent upon its demand to be treated as a state with its own Canon Law rather than as an international religious organization with no power other than to discipline its priests. Its immunity in respect to the legal actions over clerical child abuse turns on this issue as well as the extraordinary influence over international social policy under its unique position as a non-member state of the UN and hence enabled, unlike other religions and human rights organizations, to promote its dogmas at conferences and conventions in countries where they are alleged to encourage discrimination against women and homosexuals and to handicap the fight against HIV/AIDS.[25]

In their administrative and policy-making roles within Vatican City, the hierarchy is protected as a state by sovereign immunity from monetary judgments issued outside of Vatican City. While ordained priests usually have no diplomatic immunity protecting them from legal actions, unlike cardinals of the Catholic Church, the *Code of Canon Law* codified in 1917 and updated by recent amendments has protected priests from legal actions. The code specifically outlawed the abuse of children under sixteen (the age is now eighteen) as a sin, listing a series of crimes, including engaging in delict acts with a minor, adultery, and bestiality, among others, for which clergy members could be "suspended, declared infamous, and deprived of office."[26] Priests could be dismissed from the clerical state by bishops without a canonical trial and, in more severe cases, be deposed[27] Five years later, in 1922, Pope Pius XI issued an instruction on the canon law" titled *Crimen Sollicitationis (Crimen)* containing procedures and penalties for such offenses. It was amended in 1962 but contained the same directive: "to be kept carefully in the secret archive of the Curia for internal use. Not to be published or augmented with commentaries."[28] The code also codified the Secret of the Holy Office, which was a vow of permanent silence that, if breached, led to automatic excommunication from the Church.[29] Knowledge of any crime involving sexual misconduct obtained through the Church's internal inquiries and trials was made subject to the Secret of the Holy Office.[30] "Canon 243, Section 2, established that all those belonging to the Roman Curia were obliged to observe secrecy regarding matters they knew by virtue of their role as a cleric" because, according to the aim of the Secret of the Holy Office, "containing 'scandal' within the walls of the Church meant that civil authorities would not be privy to any sexual misconduct occurring within the Church"[31] and sexual misconduct was to be delt with through the ecclesiastical courts.

In the case of Cardinal Bernard Francis Law's sexual abuse of children in the Roman Catholic Archdiocese of Boston, by knowingly not halting such abuse and consequently aiding and abetting illegal activities by a predator on children, he was compelled to resign as archbishop of Boston on April 11, 2002, and continued to live at the Vatican until he died December 20, 2017. He admitted that he had been reassigning pedophiliac priests to new parishes despite knowing how wrong this was, thus aiding and abetting such child abuse knowing that it could occur again. However, Pope St. John Paul II decided to take no punitive action and even appointed Law, still a cardinal, to the position of archpriest of the Basilica of St. Mary Major, one of Rome's most prominent churches. In that capacity, Law was named to lead Pope John Paul II's papal memorial services. The Vatican was viewed as having not grasped the scale of the problem and the trauma it caused its victims. The moral credibility of the universal Church was at stake as the scale of cover-ups continued in many dioceses and countries of child abuse. Consequently, much of the Church's moral credibility was lost as a result.[32] The State Attorney General's Office concluded that Cardinal Law had not broken any laws because the law requiring reporting abuse was not expanded to include priests until 2002.[33]

Already in 1996, the Irish bishops approached the Holy See with a proposal to allow mandatory reporting of all allegations of child sex abuse by priests. The Holy See rejected it, saying that it conflicted with canon law, and it did because mandatory reporting of child abuse would cause potential scandals in conflict with canon law that is built around the concept of "avoiding scandal." In 1996, the Australian bishops in *Towards Healing* required compliance with civil reporting laws, despite the potential conflict with canon law. The British bishops sought mandatory reporting in 2001 but to no avail. Also, the Americans asked for it in 2002, but in this case, the Holy See agreed to revise canon law to grant limited dispensation to the United States whereby reporting was allowed but only where the domestic law required it. There was a grave risk of bishops going to jail for breaching reporting laws in some American States. The dispensation was extended to the whole world in 2010.[34]

Because of this political/spiritual differentiation, complaints about clerics could also undoubtedly fall within the purview of spiritual matters, which would mean that the Holy See as the government of the Roman Catholic Church is responsible and should therefore not be covered by state immunity. However, US judges have not differentiated between the two international personalities based on the political/spiritual criterion. However, they have accorded the Holy See a status analogous to but not identical with a state awarding the privileges of state immunity from trial. In comparison, the Holy See's reporting to the Convention on the Rights of the Child Committee illustrates that it assumes no obligations under the Convention on the Rights of the Child as a state but portrays them as moral obligations drawing on its personality as the government of the Catholic Church.[35]

In January 2014, the United Nations Committee for the Rights of the Child required changes to canon law by abolishing the pontifical secret over child sex abuse allegations and imposing mandatory reporting. In September 2014, Pope Francis said no, that mandatory reporting would interfere with the sovereignty of independent states.[36]

In turn, the review process of the Holy See by the United Nations (UN) Committee on the Rights of the Child shows that the Holy See does not assume its obligations under the Convention on the Rights of the Child as a state but instead portrays them as moral obligations, drawing on its personality as the leader of the Catholic Church.[37] The committee writes that it is:

aware of the dual nature of the Holy See's ratification of the Convention as the Government of the Vatican City State, and also as a sovereign subject of international law having an original, non-derived legal personality independent of any territorial authority or jurisdiction. While being fully conscious that bishops and major superiors of religious institutes do not act as representatives or delegates of the Roman Pontiff, the Committee nevertheless notes that subordinates in Catholic religious orders are bound by obedience to the Pope in accordance with Canons 331[38] and 590.[39] The Committee, therefore, reminds the Holy See that by ratifying the Convention, it has committed itself to implementing the Convention not only on the territory of the Vatican City State but also as the supreme power of the Catholic Church through individuals and institutions placed under its authority.[40]

In response, the Holy See on September 24, 2014, reminded the committee that the Holy See only exercises full territorial sovereignty in the territory of the Vatican City State and that the Holy See "does not have the capacity or legal obligation to impose the above-mentioned principles upon the local Catholic churches and institutions present on the territory of other States and whose activities abide with national laws."[41] However, Pope Francis elected not to address the issue of the Pontifical Secret's rules related to the prevention of clergy sexual abuse and protection of children in 2014. However, by September 2018, Francis summoned a global bishop conference to address these issues, specifically February 21 through 24 in Vatican City. The summit, however, did not reach any final solutions. The following year the US bishops' conference in June of 2019 assembled, and it appears that an informal agreement was reached that bishops and cardinals who abuse or cover up abuse must be held accountable and that formal protocols must be established for handling such situations.[42]

As Pope Francis has so often declared zero tolerance for clergy who sexually abuse children, he turned his words into actions. On Tuesday, June 1, 2021, Pope Francis addressed a long-awaited change to the criminal section of the *Code of Canon Law*. The changes he made to Church law explicitly criminalize the sex abuse of children and include the sexual abuse of adults by priests who misuse their authority. Furthermore, laypeople in church offices are accountable via sanctions for similar sex crimes.[43] Almost two months later, former Cardinal Theodore McCarrick, whom the Vatican defrocked in 2019, became the first US cardinal to be criminally charged with a sexual crime against a minor, while Cardinal George Pell's conviction was overturned 2020 in Australia, the first-ever, "sitting" cardinal to face criminal charges for sex abuse.[44]

FINANCIAL CORRUPTION

When it also comes to avoiding criminal and civil lawsuits involving money laundering through the Institute for the Works of Religion (IOR), nowadays commonly known as the "Vatican Bank," or publicly acknowledging allegedly helping Croatia's pro-Nazi wartime government steal the assets of the Holocaust victims, judicial maneuverings between international and canon law related to the Vatican/Holy See complexity of statehood or international personality are applied and argued in courts and international relations.[45] The Vatican's image has long been stained by the Vatican Bank's glaring impunity associated with numerous scandals and stories tying mafia and mobsters to the high-ranking Italian Christian-Democratic Party in the 1990s and Vatican officials the likes of "if the Roman Catholic Church is but one of many faith-based international movements, and since the eclipse of the papal state nearly one-and-a-half centuries ago, the status in international law of its temporal headquarters in Rome should not be privileged."[46]

In 1983, the Italian authorities requested legal assistance to acquire records relating to Vatican Bank accounts in Switzerland's Banque du Gothard. Swiss courts allowed the seizure of records and upheld the decision on appeal. The Banque du Gothard subsequently entered an administrative law appeal before the Swiss Federal Tribunal, arguing that the Vatican Bank administrators enjoyed diplomatic immunity subject to the exclusive jurisdiction of the pope. Thus, Vatican Bank assets should be granted immunity from execution. It concluded that Vatican Bank officials in Switzerland had no diplomatic status, and the Swiss authorities must grant the request for mutual assistance. The Federal Tribunal recognized the status of the Holy See-Vatican as *sui generis* enjoying the rights akin to a state due to its historical religious legitimacy, unlike other religious organizations. However, the Federal Tribunal underscored that the Holy See's unique status to enjoy a state's rights also required it to accept the obligations of a state.[47]

In contrast, the attorneys for the Holy See ably blocked litigation by applying the dual personality related to restitution claims in the US class-action lawsuit *Alperin v. Vatican Bank* filed in 1999.[48] It dealt with the alleged role by the Vatican in recycling loot stolen by the pro-Nazi Ustaša regime in Croatia during World War II, having together with the Franciscan religious order enriched themselves from the Ustašan gold. In this case, surviving victims and their heirs Serbian, Sinti-Romani, Gypsy, and Jewish populations who were mercilessly robbed, murdered, or deported by the Ustaša Government in control of the Independent State of Croatia, a World War II–era puppet state of Nazi Germany and Fascist Italy[49] sought compensation from the Vatican Bank for accepting and money laundering stolen gold, currencies, and other valuables making up part of the Ustaša treasury estimated as much as $80 million (close to $800 million in late 1990s currency value). Some of the loot appears to have been transferred to Switzerland in the last year of the war, and some of the stolen assets helped fund a sanctuary at the pontifical college of San Girolamo in Rome, which was run by the Bosnian Croat Roman Catholic Father Dragonivic, a functionary in the fascist puppet Ustaša Government. This college was most likely funded, at least in part, according to US Undersecretary of State Stuart Eizenstat by the remnants of the Ustaša treasury with at least tacit acquiescence of some Vatican officials. It helped fugitive Croatian war criminals, including Ante Pavelić, the founder and head of the fascist ultranationalist organization Ustaša, with the pontifical college cooperation, by using the "ratline" to escape to South America in the early postwar years.[50]

The US courts showcase the legal challenges posed by the dual personality scenario and the inadequacy of the political/spiritual criteria distinguishing between the two personae in which the Vatican City State and the Holy See have routinely been held under the Foreign Sovereign Immunities Act (FSIA) as a foreign sovereign state in United States courts. While no differentiation is made about the capacity in which the Holy See acted, it has been challenging to assert jurisdiction over the Holy See as a defendant or codefendant in priesthood sexual abuse lawsuits. At least three cases have attempted to haul the Holy See into court under exceptions to the FSIA. They are civil cases over the restitution claims by Holocaust survivors and their heirs, as in the case *Alperin v. Vatican Bank and the Catholic Church*'s handling of clerics accused of child sexual abuse as in the cases *Doe v. Holy See*[51] and *O'Bryan v. Holy See*.[52] These cases highlight the various ways in which the Holy See has escaped prosecution within the US justice system.[53]

As previously mentioned, Pope Francis took steps on June 1, 2021, to deal with criminalizing child abuse within the Church. He also took action regarding financial corruption within the Vatican on December 28, 2020. Pope Francis issued a new law, reorganizing Vatican finances. All assets previously administered by the Vatican's Secretariat of State were to be transferred by January 1, 2021, to the Administration of the Patrimony of the Apostolic See (APSA), which functions as the Holy See's treasury and sovereign wealth manager. The APSA has total responsibility subject to unannounced checks by the Vatican's Secretariat for the Economy, which oversees the financial activities of the Holy See and Vatican City State. The Secretariat for the Economy also serves as the Papal Secretariat for Economic and Financial Matters. All liquid assets held in current accounts at the Vatican Bank and foreign banks were to be transferred by February 4, 2021, to the APSA. In the future, consolidated financial statements will be generated, providing greatly improved transparency to be operated solely at the pope's discretion.[54] Also, the former president of the Vatican bank for twenty years until 2009, Angelo Caloia, has been sentenced close to nine years in prison for money laundering and aggravated embezzlement as of early 2021, signaling that justice is being served.[55]

THE VATICAN SEEKS JUSTICE FOR HISTORICAL WRONGS OF THE PAST

Lastly, Pope Francis, by embracing the role the Holy See plays as a neutral, impartial mediator in settling disputes, has allowed scholars to do the same through opening the archives related to Pope Pius XII, the Curia, and the pontifical representations, ranging from 1939 to 1958. Many of the questions raised by the 2001 International Catholic-Jewish Historical Commission and allegations highlighted in the class-action lawsuit *Alperin v. the Vatican Bank* may be answered. Only time will tell as leading scholars begin to examine over more than two million documents about the Church's role during World War II.[56]

Pope Francis cleared the way for justice to be pursued in these three areas by reforming canon law in complementarity with international law to prosecute accused pedophiles more readily. In addition, he reorganized the fiduciary responsibilities of the Holy See to reflect greater transparency for financial transactions, rebuilding trust for those making donations to the Church, and attempting to restore credibility for seeking the truth even about the Vatican-Holy See's own role in the temporal world as the spiritual leader attempts to pursue peace in the international world order.

AN HISTORICAL DIMENSION OF THE CHURCH'S CHALLENGES FACING INTERNATIONAL AND CANON LAW: THE END OF THE PAPAL STATES AND THE RISE OF AN INTERNATIONAL PERSONALITY

Turning to the second half of the nineteenth century, the popes faced a world imbued with a cascade of multiple challenging threats. When French troops protecting the papal territory against the military threat of an Italian invasion were needed elsewhere due to the outbreak of the Franco-Prussian War, it left Rome and the Papal State militarily vulnerable for an invasion by the Kingdom of Italy on September 20, 1870. It culminated in the annexation of Rome, extinguishing the papacy's territorial sovereignty.

The world back then was in the grip of rising forces supportive of rationalism, liberalism, and materialism, transforming social and economic life in an ever-larger part of the continent perpetuated by the spread of the Industrial Revolution. These challenges to the Church were perceived by changing social classes to presage a brighter future while the old elite saw these movements as bearers of disaster attempting to dismantle religion and religious authority from public life.

When Pope Gregory the XVI died in 1846, his successor Pius IX who was barely on the papal throne, was confronted with uprisings across Italy due to a surging tide of Italian nationalism threatening the church's control of the Papal States. At the time, the Papal States was squeezed like a sandwich, from the north by the Austrian Habsburg's and from the south by the French as well threatened by a loosely organized group of insurgents who aspired to expel the colonial powers and establish a unified Italian republic with Rome as its capital. Pius viewed them with disdain and a threat. Determined to counteract these aspirations and not lose control of the church's empire and income, Pius attempted to loosen the repressive forms of government by loosening censorship and alluding to a more democratic form of government by creating a Consultative Assembly composed of lay representatives.[57] Nevertheless, these efforts were not able to delay the rebellious, revolutionary spirit of 1848 throughout Europe. The nationalists drove the Austrians from Milan, and Pius dispatched thousands of troops to protect Church's properties from possible Austrian retaliation. However, he soon reversed that decision declaring that the Church should not be at war with another devoutly Catholic nation such as Austria. Popular sentiment was at first enthralled with enthusiasm in fighting foreign powers on Italian soil but turned sour when Pius decided to discontinue the fight against Austria, claiming him a reactionary posing as a reformer.[58] On November 15, 1848, a mob of insurrectionists surged throughout Rome, causing the Pope to flee and not return until France's Louis Napoleon (later Napoleon III) sent thousands of troops to reclaim Rome for Pope Pius IX safe return to Rome nine months later. Pius would henceforth never consider any reforms or compromises, convinced that modern thought caused the disorder. Worries about the chaos in Rome were soon replaced by concerns over the church's dire financial situation, which led to major loans to the Church by the Rothschild family in Paris.

At the same time, the Jews continued to be notoriously discriminated against by him leading to the widely publicized incident in 1858 where the Bologna papal police (Inquisition) kidnapped a six-year-old boy, Edgardo Mortara, from his parent's house when they had learned that a Jewish family's Catholic housekeeper had told friends she had secretly baptized the child years earlier when he was gravely ill.[59] Once a child was baptized, according to the law of the land, it was forbidden from being raised in a Jewish household. Thus, Edgardo was taken to Rome, where he was placed in the House of Catechumens—an institution dedicated to instructing Jewish converts. What followed sparked appeals worldwide to Pius personally to intervene and order the boy's return to his parents. The affair increased discontent. The architect of Italian unification, Count Camillo Cavour, used the affair to agitate against Rome, increasing tension with the papacy's temporal power within Italy. The leader of the Austrian-Hungarian Empire, Emperor Franz Josef, requested that Mortara be returned to his parents, and Napoleon III sought the child's return whose French garrison ironically protected the Vatican, making it possible for the youngster to be held in the first place. Some twenty editorials on the case were published in the *New York Times,* and across Europe and the United States, Protestants were infuriated by the injustice and mobilized against the obscurantism of the Catholic Church. For the pope, it was inconceivable to return the boy to a life of apostasy. He refused to return him and called the boy "son," directing the boy to visit him and raise him personally as a Catholic.[60]

All the impassioned controversy was terrible for the pope's image. The affair contributed to diminishing the Papal power, as it strengthened those nineteenth-century forces seeking liberalism, nationalism, Italian unification, and anti-clericalism. The international and domestic criticism led Pius to use his arsenal of resources embodied in canon law to push back on these geopolitical effects, including papal encyclicals, ex-communication, and syllabi. In 1864, Pope Pius IX announced the Syllabus of Errors outrightly deploring democracy, science, materialism, liberalism, including the separation of Church and state. Since the defeat of Napoleon Bonaparte earlier in the century, the legacy of the French Revolution with its ideological currents continued to challenge the established elites and shape the course of European history. As with the kidnapping, Pius dismissed all criticism and reinforced his view that he alone had been divinely selected to guide the church with the syllabus.

In a last-ditch effort to offset the secular and anticlerical challenges to the Church as well as the simmering internal dissent, Pius IX called all bishops and cardinals to the First Vatican Council to debate the church's role in opposing rationalism. Of the hundreds of leading Catholic theologians able to attend between 1869 and 1870 before the devastation of the Papal State, the aim was to discuss whether a pope's authority had limits. They decided to centralize the ecclesiastical power of the Holy See by declaring the pope's primacy and infallibility[61] concerning faith or morals pertaining to the entire Church according to *Canon Law* 749 §1: "By virtue of his office, the Supreme Pontiff possesses infallibility in teaching when as the supreme pastor and teacher of all the Christian faithful, who strengthens his brothers and sisters in the faith, he proclaims by definitive act that a doctrine of faith or morals is to be held."[62] In all matters of faith and morals, according to the dogma of the 1870 Vatican Council, the pope is infallible when he speaks *ex-cathedra*.[63] His jurisdiction also extends to "all those matters which appertain to the discipline and the law of the Church throughout all the world. He has the power not merely to alter individual canons but even to codify and reform the whole of canon law."[64]

After shedding the last remnants of temporal power following King Victor Emmanuel II's seizure of Rome in 1870, the Vatican would remain deprived of territorial sovereignty for the next fifty-nine years. During this "territorial interregnum," the Holy See transitioned from a small, semi-feudal, and territorial Papal State to pursue the dogmatic issues of the pope's infallibility during the First Vatican Council, refused laws that infringed on the authority of the Church, and chartered new waters in the international order while its sovereignty as it turned out was not adversely affected by the loss of that temporal power. Germany under Chancellor Bismarck attempted to undermine the papacy's power by giving the state the secular power over church authority in the areas of education, marriage, and other details of people's lives. Some years later, such laws were dismantled except for state schools and civil marriage, bringing the *Kulturkampf* to an end. Closer to home, the Italian Parliament passed on May 13, 1871, Italy's Law of Guarantees' assuring Pius IX the freedoms and privileges both home and abroad as some ruler of a state whose representatives would have complete diplomatic immunity, however, subject to the Italian parliament able to modify or abrogate at any time. The pontiff refused by underscoring the preservation of its rights ante-1870 and denying Italy's claim that it could resolve the situation by passing a law at a domestic, national, municipal level.[65] Its international standing was crucial to appear independent from any political power, thus impartial and not merely a "chaplain of the King of Italy."[66] Despite all the assurances by the Italian government, popes largely self-imposed and rhetorically proclaimed themselves, as did Pius IX himself as a "prisoner of the Vatican."[67] Still, the popes continued to communicate with the faithful throughout Europe and beyond[68] until the Lateran Treaty of 1929 settled the Roman Question by establishing Vatican City as an independent, permanently neutral state.

Pius IX's successors Leo XIII (1878–1903) upheld with no uncertain terms the view that Christian civilization was beleaguered by secular humanism and the secular state. He recognized that the Church must resist liberalism and socialism "to preserve the true spiritual nature and dignity of man."[69] Pope Pius X (1903–1914) attacked modernism as "the synthesis of all heresies," criticizing various British and French Catholic scholars that, among other things, believed the Bible should be subject to historical-critical study, that religious dogma develops within history, and sociological concepts can play a valuable role in the study of the history of the Church, which since the Second Vatican Council in 1960 have been generally accepted.[70] Furthermore, Pius X condemned the secular aims of the liberal international world order based on political initiatives to separate state and church and international law to limit religious influence. The Pope's ideological and anti-democratic vows and the Catholic Church's reaction to the rise of modernity "was a state of siege mentality"[71] became the Church's nineteenth-century fortress mentality aligned with the European political forces dating back to the times of the revolutionary spirit end of the eighteenth century as Father Noel Dias, senior lecturer, Faculty of Law at the University of Colombo in Sri Lanka points out:

> The Church at the time in Europe (France) was associated with the ancient regime and seemingly wedded to the monarchy, [it] was antagonistic to the human rights discourse. Pope Pius VI, in his fateful fried *Quod Aliquantum* (March 19, 1791), declared that the Revolutionary Constitution of France was "to annihilate the Catholic religion and with it the obedience to the kings." If one starts from that principle, then the assertion of human rights becomes a "threat" to the Church, and a contrast is set up between "the rights of man" and "the rights of God."[72]

While the Pope was uncompromising on the ideological front in fighting many principles of modern democracy (free press, free speech, democracy, etc.), he and the Holy See came to play a unique guardian role in the international community as a trusted arbitrator and mediator called upon by concerning parties to intervene to secure the peaceful settlement of international disputes. Notwithstanding the question of its status in international law, the Holy See maintained its international juristic personality to become part of the nineteenth-century foundation for international humanitarian law in which States and people began to regulate the conduct of war and the need for greater "responsibility for solidarity as regards humanity."[73] The Holy See also assumed a humanitarian role in the international world order by arbitrating conflicts between Spain and Germany over the Caroline Islands found in the Pacific Ocean in 1895[74] and the significant but unsuccessful effort to prevent the Spanish–American War in 1898 or after World War II the Beagle Channel dispute between Chile and Argentina.[75]

The Pope was so highly regarded for his contributions to world peace that Budapest's 1896 World Peace Conference addressed a special letter to Pope Leo XIII gratefully acknowledging and thanking him for his efforts. In 1899, Tsar Nicholas II of Russia and Queen Wilhelmina of the Netherlands sought the support of the same Pope, requesting the moral help of the Holy See for the success of the Hague Peace Conference. In his reply to Queen Wilhelmina of the Netherlands letter to Leo XIII of May 7, 1899, "We believe that it is a specific part of our task, not only to provide moral help to such undertakings, but also to cooperate in them actively: because their objectives are most noble by nature and intimately linked to our August ministry which, through the divine Founder of the Church and by virtue of age-old tradition, in some way includes the function of mediator for peace."[76]

The dissolution of the Papal States and the opening of the Roman question did not make the Holy See disappear from the international humanitarian scene. Its exclusion from the international conferences marked this troubled period because of the Italian government's opposition to outside interference in supporting the Holy See's return of its territorial sovereignty and canceling the 1871 Guarantee Laws. Arguing that public opinion in Italy would be opposed to any papal representation, the Italian government pressured the great powers to prevent the pope from attending, acknowledging in private that it would be difficult for Russia to exclude the pope. If Italy was to abstain, it could have negative backlashes as Italians supported the proposed Hague conference. In the end, Germany sided with Italy as they too feared that the pope's representation of Catholic Bavarian interests might find international support.[77] In any event, States did not refrain from using their diplomatic relations with the Holy See on various other occasions to support their efforts, mainly to settle international disputes and strengthen the principles and law of humanitarian law dealing with the conduct of war, most strikingly illustrated by the Holy See's participation in the preparations for the Hague Conference in 1899 contributing to international law.

Ironically, popes, after 1870 viewed ever more secularizing liberals, had captured international law aimed to dismantle the Catholic Church and church from public life while underwriting the principles of canon law until Pope Pius X. In 1904, he called for papacy's *Code of Canon Law* to be rearranged to simplify the Holy See's legal architecture and expand the pope's powers. It took almost more than a decade to finish the texts, and on May 19, 1918, it took effect, reflecting the arduous efforts of Catholic theologians and legal scholars to provide Pope Benedict XV with the instrument to engage international law as it was applied by groups opposed to the Church. The *Code of Canon Law* texts presented the roots of international law in medieval Christendom and the brotherhood of humankind. It was portrayed as the preserve of the Catholic Church and to "fire back from the liberals and turn the field of international law into what they thought it should have been all along: a field dominated by Catholic individuals and Catholic prerogatives."[78]

THE HOLY SEE EMERGING AS A SPIRITUAL AND HUMANITARIAN EUROPEAN POWER IN THE TWENTIETH CENTURY TO CHALLENGE THE INTERNATIONAL WORLD ORDER

By the outbreak of World War I, the Holy See had fostered diplomatic relations through reciprocity. Its international personality underscored its spiritual role in the international world order with over a dozen countries, including some major powers—Austria–Hungary, Imperial Russia, and Prussia/Germany.[79] In a 1992 roundtable organized by the Pontifical Commission for History at the Congress of Historical Sciences in Madrid, Prof. Joseph Joblin, SJ, depicts Pope Benedict XV role during World War I as:

> the opportunity to transform the humanitarian concerns of the Church into practical initiatives . . . a real collaboration was established at that time between the warring factions, the Neutrals, the Red Cross and the Holy See. Among all the initiatives of that period, we mention the creation of the Provisional Bureau for Prisoners of War for the gathering and distribution of news of missing and captured soldiers. Started in the beginning of 1915, it handled about 800,000 cases of prisoners or captives. Such efficiency was because the Holy See with its Dioceses constituted a real network of information throughout the world.[80]

Benedict had ensured humanitarian aid for the civilians and prisoners of war, organized prayers for peace, and encouraged a peace-building process. When it came to the post–World War I era, the concern that an entirely secular world was in the making, the instrument of using the concordat was advanced to bind the Holy See and the newly formed countries like Latvia, Poland, Estonia, and Lithuania in Eastern Europe and later with Italy (1929) and Germany (1933). The concordats helped restore the Holy See's role on the international world stage as a bulwark against communism and bedrock of Catholic education, culture, and morality. With such concordats signed, the Holy See greatly expanded everything from making religious instruction in public schools mandatory, giving the Church jurisdiction over a wide range of civil-law matters, addressing the flow of monies from the state to the Church to greater control of press freedom and organizing the local churches.[81]

In November 1918, World War I officially came to an end with such human carnage that no other war had rivaled such destruction of whole generations. Anticlerical revolutionary communism in the Soviet Union heralded the end of any religious authority in that country, as did Wilsonian models for a separation between church and state. In contrast, the Holy See in 1917 under Pope Benedict XV, after receiving the completed revised *Code of Canon Law*, provided an alternative to both Communism and Liberalism calling upon church law to become municipal law and expanding its spiritual role on the European continent. In other words, describing a new world order to attract newly created states sharing a shared vision of humanity and interests based on international law derived from the principles of canon law to become a unifier and animator of international law and its guardian. Out of the ashes of total war, a Christian Europe should be led by the pope utilizing international law as an instrument in complementarity with canon law and not in competition. In this vision, the pope should be the highest authority in contrast to the Peace of Westphalia's secularization of world politics in which there is no higher authority than the sovereignty of each state. In this context, the origin of international law was considered to have secular origins as the basis for the liberal international world order aimed to restrict religious influence in favor of rationalism and broad-religious tolerance. Religion was perceived as a principal source of violence and instability due to intolerance. As the historian Giuliana Chamedes writes, "thus, the religious zealots could be appeased through liberalism."[82]

DUAL PERSONALITIES EMERGE: A COLLISION COURSE IN THE MAKING

Long before the permanent neutral Vatican City State was created, scholars of international law raised many questions provoking serious studies about how the Holy See be a state without territory or how can the pope remain a sovereign after his land had been annexed? The distinguished international lawyer Charles Fenwick in 1929, writes an account about the diversity of opinions held by earlier scholars questionable about the Holy See having the sovereignty of a state.[83] Many international legal scholars agreed that the papacy could not possess an entire legal international personality. Some supporters of the positive school whose understanding of international law was determined by facts rather than theories said that the papacy had lost all international personality since 1870.[84] Other scholars professed that the Holy See had a limited international status drawing attention to the territory left to the pope by the Law of Guarantees. The spiritual authority he exercised over Roman Catholics worldwide was a sufficient basis for a claim of sovereignty. The renowned German jurist Lassa Oppenheim held a middle position that the Holy See transformed from a state "by custom and tacit consent of most states acquire[ing] a quasi-international position"[85] to remain a part of the international world under which it was entitled to be treated "as though she were an International Person," just as the pope was entitled to be treated "as though he were the head of a monarchical State," at the same time, neither was, in fact, the case.[86] Professor of international law Josef Kunz, in 1952, stated that the "pseudo-positivistic prejudice," which equated statehood with international personality was responsible for the negation of a limited personality of the Holy See after 1870. He believed the Holy See, while never a state, had always retained an international legal personality and that the Vatican City is distinct as an international person from the Holy See and is a state but not a sovereign state instead "a vassal state of the Holy See." For him, "historically, the original members of the international community were only the Christian states of Europe and the Holy See. It is this historical development which explains the unique position in international law of the Holy See as the Supreme Head of the Catholic Church."[87]

Although the Holy See had lost the Papal States (that is, the territory), the pope continued to exercise his power of governance over the entire church exercising his legation (*ius legationum*), privileges, and immunities of an international organization in the international arena.[88] The debate about the international personality of the Holy See during the time of the Roman Question is "about the proper status of the Holy See in the international legal order and the legal implications of its participation in international affairs."[89] However, it appears through its role as a unique spiritual power cultivated by its continuing diplomatic relations "alongside the other subjects of international law, namely states and international organisations" to assume one-of-a-kind what Oppenheim calls "anomalous"[90] character referred to in the literature as "sui generis."[91] About statehood, "it is proximate as a state. However, it has no population, apart from resident functionaries, and its sole purpose is to support the Holy See as a religious entity."[92] Some jurists regard the Vatican as a state but fail to meet what might be called the "textbook" criteria for statehood in international law, as articulated in the 1933 Convention on the Rights and Duties of States (Montevideo Convention). In brief, these criteria refer to four dimensions: a permanent population, defined territory, government, and the capacity to enter into international agreements.[93] It currently enjoys diplomatic relations with 183 countries,[94] although it has no fixed population.

Over the past 150 years of Vatican history, two international personalities of the Holy See and the Vatican represented the Catholic Church's interests. At first, "substantive international legal personality remained in operation for the territory-free Holy See (that is to say, the papal mission and its institutions). Legal personality is said to have survived on the basis of a kind of religious legitimacy."[95] The Lateran Accords consists of three parts: a concordat that set forth the terms of the relationship between the Holy See and Italy, a financial convention, and a political treaty restoring the Vatican's territorial integrity,[96] with Italy recognizing the inviolability of the 108.7 acres of the

Vatican City State including fifty-two additional acres of property outside of the Vatican walls granting extraterritorial status to properties that include the papal country residence at Castel Gandolfo as well as other scattered historical buildings under earlier papal control "placed under guarantee" without exterritorial privileges. The pope would then rule as today over a permanently neutral state with an infrastructure with all the features of a functioning state to include its own bank, post office, armed guards, communication center, hospital, and so on. The pope was declared "sacred and inviolable," invested with divine right and having recognition equivalent to a secular monarch, with the cardinals having the privileges as princes by blood. Furthermore, the Italian government acknowledged the validity of church marriage following canon law and that religious education was obligatory for Catholic pupils in primary and secondary schools.[97]

Both the Holy See and eventually the Vatican after the Lateran Treaty embodied a quasi-international persona. They established a unique role in the international order with the Vatican as a permanent neutral whose foreign policy was governed by the Holy See. In return, Church officials agreed to support the government of Prime Minister Benito Mussolini. Additionally, the Holy See was paid 750 million lire in cash—more than $1.3 billion in today's money—and one billion lire in 5 percent negotiable government bonds as compensation for the land annexed to the nation of Italy.[98]

In this way, the Lateran Treaty—also referred to as the Lateran Pacts—impacted Church finances impeding the Holy See and the Vatican to continue over the next ninety-plus years utilizing their international personalities. From June 7, 1929, onward,[99] when the Italian parliament ratified the Lateran Treaty, "the investments of the Vatican . . . moved into the financial markets of the world."[100] By the middle of the 1930s, the Vatican . . . was placed at the centre of worldwide network of banking, and other financial institutions"[101] due to the financial genius Bernadino Nogara whom Pius XI had asked to manage the money received from the treaty. Nogara accepted on two conditions: "That he not be restricted by religious or doctrinal considerations in his investment-making" and "that he be free to invest funds anywhere in the world."[102] When it came to US entry in World War II following the Japanese attack on Pearl Harbor and Hitler Germany declaring war, the Vatican continued being granted dispensation by the Secretary of the Treasury Henry Morgenthau, allowing it to pursue investments in businesses, including life insurance companies, with operations in Nazi-controlled countries due to Vatican's status as a permanently neutral state, which allowed them to continue working in these nations even then as the US was no longer neutral but a belligerent. However, Nogara knew it would be a matter of time before actual transactions under dispensation leave paper trails and potential risks of becoming blacklisted by the Allies. He shored up such an eventuality by drafting a charter to form the Istituto per le Opere di Religione (IOR)—Vatican Bank—that Pius signed on June 27, 1942. The bank was free of all independent audits, operated worldwide without any wartime regulations, paid no taxes, or disclosed annual reports or balance sheets whose practice was to destroy all files every ten years. Efforts by investigators and historians seeking answers have been stymied by the secrecy shrouding the bank's business dealings. Due to the bank's lack of a paper trail, it appears an ideal haven for money plundered from Jews and other wartime victims and to conceal the actual owner of securities or other valuables that would otherwise have been confiscated or illicit to transact violating Trading with the Enemy Act.[103] By the end of the war, the Vatican Bank had become a financial institution, but it is uncertain if it was involved in the Ustaša gold transactions, and instead, other Vatican agencies may have been involved in these alleged transactions. However, that the Vatican used the gold to finance the ratline to foster the escape of Ustaša war criminal leaders is entirely plausible.[104] Explicitly more about the role of the Vatican Bank will be known once the Vatican opens its archives for the postwar period.

CONCLUSION: THE VATICAN AND HOLY SEE DEALING WITH CHALLENGES 1929 TO THE PRESENT

Together, the bishops, Catholic popes, and emissaries supported the Holy See, pursuing cautious diplomacy exemplified by Pope Pius XII's handling of Europe's darkest hours throughout World War II. The well-known Jewish Holocaust historian Michael Marrus, one of three scholars appointed to the 2001 International Catholic–Jewish Historical Commission[105] to investigate the role of Pope Pius XII during the Holocaust, portrays Pius XII as clearly knowing about the mass murder in the east and the deportation convoys of 1942. He was determined to maintain his posture of neutrality, encouraging humanitarian aid by subordinates within the Church but refusing to speak out publicly against the extermination of the Jews, issuing vague appeals against the oppression of unnamed racial and religious groups by the Nazis. With some distinguished exceptions, the Vatican corps of diplomats did not do any better.[106]

In stark contrast, the Vatican/Holy See experiences today in the post–Cold War Era bold evangelism crowned by Pope Francis using the bully pulpit provided by the papacy to help position the Vatican as a neutral broker transforming its brand of discreet papal diplomacy into a vision of diplomatic boldness. Engaged in diplomatic disputes in Venezuela, South Sedan, Lebanon, and Iraq, the Vatican Secretary of State, Cardinal Pietro Parolin, portrays as "positive neutrality" in which "the Holy See does not limit itself to simply looking out the window but contributes to building a dialogue between the parties involved."[107] Furthermore, Pope Francis calls for greater inclusiveness of the human family, extending to refugees, displaced people[108] with uncertainty if it would also spread to the LGBT community.[109]

For the last 150 years, canon and international law competed, thus events like Pope John XXIII giving human rights as the first Pope a central place in his encyclical in *Pacem in Terris*. The encyclical suggests a paradigm shift underscoring that human rights "flow from the very nature of the human person . . . they are universal and inviolable."[110] When Pope John XXIII announced the convocation of the Second Vatican Council II, he aimed to renew the Church in a spirit of (aggiornamento).[111] The scholar Father Thomas Reese wrote that the purpose of Vatican II was "to reorient Catholicism away from its nineteenth-century fortress mentality, to open a new dialogue with the modern world, to look more deeply into the Catholic past in order to prepare for the Catholic future, and to usher in an era of evangelization and renewal."[112] The progressive expectations for renewal afforded accommodation for many conservatives as the spirit of the 1960s was considered a transformation of the Church resembling the Protestant ecclesial spirit of the Church. In pursuance of the pastoral approach taken by Vatican II, the *Code of Canon Law* of 1917 was revised in 1983, enumerating a set of rights and obligations for the laity and clergy extending from freedom of conscience; research freely in the field of theology; make political decisions; the right and even obligation to criticize Church officials; the right of laypersons to participate in the decision making; and the right of women to equality in the Church.[113] Still, canon law would face further challenges and revisions in the new millennium to comply with international law raising the question beyond the scope of this chapter about the operating approach of utilizing both historical natural law and legal jurisprudence approaches with greater intensity to frame the principles of the Church with the evolving social changes in society and scientific understanding boiling down to handling the trend of culture wars in Europe and the United States.

Two divided camps arose in the post-conciliar church. "One followed the actual documents of the council and urged the Church to maintain continuity with Catholic teaching and tradition, and the other was loyal to a "spirit of the council" that just happened to coincide with the cultural fashions that came in its wake,"[114] reminder of how troubled this narrative is in both the spiritual and secular world.

Nevertheless, in many cases, "the hoped-for renewal was hijacked by those for whom renewal meant an accommodation to the spirit of the 1960s, and the transformation of the Church along liberal Protestant lines."[115] The significant tensions facing the Catholic Church in the United States due to the continuing tension between international and canon law as progressive and conservative Catholics utilize them may be best reset by finding the deep-rooted neutrality and tolerance it has called for in its humanitarian vision for peace in the world and its goal to uphold human dignity.

NOTES

1. "The bishop of the Roman Church, in whom continues the office given by the Lord uniquely to Peter, the first of the Apostles, and to be transmitted to his successors, is the head of the college of bishops, the Vicar of Christ, and the pastor of the universal Church on earth. By virtue of his office, he possesses supreme, full, immediate, and universal ordinary power in the Church, which he is always able to exercise freely," *Code of Canon Law*, "Book II: The People of God," Can. 331, last accessed September 1, 2021, at https://www.vatican.va/archive/cod-iuris-canonici/eng/documents/cic_lib2-cann330-367_en.html.

2. Well-known examples of the Roman Catholic Church involved in global diplomacy in the second half of the twentieth century, such as, (1) Pope John XXIII's engagement in a peaceful solution of the Cuban missile crisis (Flamini in Troy, 2016); (2) the Solidarnosc movement, which contributed to Poland's democratization (Byrnes in Troy, 2016); (3) the Philippine people's power revolution, which led to the ousting of dictator Ferdinand Marcos (Astorga; Youngbloodin in Troy, 2016); (4) the Holy See's mediation in the Beagle channel conflict between Argentina and Chile (Laudy; Princen in Troy, 2016); (5) reconciliation efforts in new democracies or countries in transition, such as the Truthand Reconciliation Commission (TRC) in South Africa (Philpott in Troy, 2016); and (6) peace-building fieldwork during the civil war in Mozambique and elsewhere by the Catholic lay community of St. Egidio (Batlogg in Troy, 2016).

3. John L. Kunz, "The Status of the Holy See in International Law," *American Journal of International Law* 46, no. 2 (1952): 308.

4. David Alvarez, "The Holy See and the First Hague Peace Conference (1899)," in *Archivum Historiae Pontificiae* 26 (1988): 433, accessed July 20, 2021, https://www.jstor.org/stable/23564272.

5. "The Lateran Treaty," accessed June 21, 2021, https://www.whitehorsemedia.com/docs/the_lateran_treaty.pdf.

6. "Pope's No. 2: Impartiality Still the Right Choice for the Holy See," *Aleteia*, July 20, 2018, accessed September 6, 2021, at https://aleteia.org/2018/07/20/popes-no-2-impartiality-still-the-right-choice-for-the-holy-see/.

7. United States Conference of Catholic Bishops, "Life and Dignity of the Human Person," accessed September 6, 2021, at https://www.usccb.org/beliefs-and-teachings/what-we-believe/catholic-social-teaching/life-and-dignity-of-the-human-person.

8. Massimo Faggioli, *Joe Biden and Catholicism in the United States* (New London, CT: Bayard, Inc., 2021), 157. Also, Pope Paul VI, Address to the General

Assembly of the United Nations (October 4, 1965), n1; cf. Pope Paul VI, encyclical letter *Populorum Progressio* (March 26, 1967), n13; Pope John Paul II, encyclical letter *Veritatis Splendor* (August 6, 1993), n3; Pope Benedict XVI, Message for World Day of Peace 2010 (January 1, 2010), n4.

9. Courtney Mares, "Pope Francis: Human Dignity Has Political Implications," *Inside the Vatican*, no date, accessed September 11, 2021, at https://insidethevatican.com/magazine/pope-francis-human-dignity-has-political-implications/.

10. Paul R. Rickert, "Legal Positivism: The Leading Legal Theory in America," *Liberty University Helms School of Government Faculty Publications and Presentations* (March 6, 2005, accessed September 10, 2021, at https://digitalcommons.liberty.edu/cgi/viewcontent.cgi?article=1045&context=gov_fac_pubs), 2–4.

11. Robert John Araujo, SJ, "Foreign Sovereign Immunity and the Holy See," *Ave Maria International Law Journal* 1 (Fall 2011): 67–89, at 73, accessed September 4, 2021, at https://avemarialaw-international-law-journal.avemarialaw.edu/Content/iljarticles/2011ilj.pdf.

12. Alan Chong and Jodok Troy, "A Universal Sacred Mission and he Universal Secular Organization: The Holy See and the United Nations," *Politics, Religion, and Ideology* 12, no. 3 (September 2011): 335, accessed July 4, 2021, https://papers.ssrn.com/sol3/papers.cfm?abstract_id=2984379.

13. Faggioli, *Joe Biden and Catholicism in the United States*.

14. Michael Sean Winters, "Massimo Faggioli's Book on Biden and Catholicism Explains Our Critical Moment," *National Catholic Reporter*, January 25, 2021, accessed June 16, 2021, https://www.ncronline.org/news/opinion/distinctly-catholic/massimo-faggiolis-book-biden-and-catholicism-explains-our-critical?site_redirect=1.

15. Peter Steinfels, *A People Adrift: The Crisis of the Roman Catholic Church in America* (New York: Simon & Schuster, 2003), 66.

16. Geoffrey Robertson, *The Case of the Pope: Vatican Accountability for Human Rights Abuse* (London: Penguin, 2010).

17. Kelly Buchanan, "Vatican Criminal Law and Recent Money Laundering Cases," *Custodia Legis Law Librarians of Congress* (blog), May 18, 2021, accessed July 10, 2021, https://blogs.loc.gov/law/2021/05/vatican-criminal-law-and-recent-money-laundering-cases/.

18. "Scholars Say Vatican Holocaust Material Inadequate: Panel of Catholic and Jewish Researchers Says many Questions Remain about Pope Pius XII's Actions," *Beliefnet*, October 25, 2000, accessed August 4, 2021, https://www.beliefnet.com/news/2000/11/scholars-say-vatican-holocaust-material-inadequate.aspx; defending Pope Pius XII and criticizing the forty-seven questions that the 2001 International Catholic-Jewish Historical Commission raised that eventually led to its cessation, see, "Revisiting the October 2000 International Commission Report on Pius XII," *Paul on Pius* (blog), May 10, 2010, accessed August 5, 2021, https://paulonpius.blogspot.com/2010/05/revisiting-october-2000-international.html.

19. Karen Terry et al., *The Nature and Scope of the Problem of Sexual Abuse of Minors by Priests and Deacons*, prepared by the John Jay College of Criminal Justice for the US Conference of Catholic Bishops (Washington DC: USCCB, 2004) last accessed September 9, 2021, at http://www.bishop-accountability.org/reports/2004_02_27_JohnJay/index.html#prev1.

20. Anthony J. Blasi, and Lluis Oviedo (eds.), *The Abuse of Minors in the Catholic Church: Dismantling the Culture of Cover Ups* (New York: Routledge, 2020), 167.

21. *National Catholic Reporter*, "Catholic Dioceses and Orders that Filed for Bankruptcy and other Major Settlements," May 31, 2018, last accessed September 8, 2021, at https://www.ncronline.org/news/accountability/catholic-dioceses-and-orders-filed-bankruptcy-and-other-major-settlements; also, https://www.bishop-accountability.org/bankruptcy.htm.

22. Brendan Daly, "Sexual Abuse and Canon Law," *Compass Review* (September 15, 2009), accessed September 5, 2021 at http://compassreview.org/spring09/6.pdf, 33.

23. Claudia Lauer and Meghan Hoyer, "Almost 1,700 Priests and Clergy Accused of Sex Abuse are Unsupervised," *NBC News*, October 4, 2019, accessed August 4, 2021, https://www.nbcnews.com/news/religion/nearly-1-700-priests-clergy-accused-sex-abuse-are-unsupervised-n1062396; see Ron Dicker, "Priests Accused Of Sexual Abuse Transferred To South America, Report Says," *Huffpost*, September 18, 2015, accessed August 4, 2021, https://www.huffpost.com/entry/priests-accused-of-sexual-abuse-south-america_n_55fc289ce4b08820d9184d73; also, Kieran Tapsell, "'Catastrophic institutional failure' can be fixed," National *Catholic Reporter*, January 9, 2018.

24. Geoffrey Robertson, *The Case of the Pope*, 164.

25. Ibid., 11

26. Kieran Tapsell, "Canon Law on Child Sexual Abuse through the Ages," *ATF Press*, 2014, accessed September 3, 2021, at https://www.catholicsforrenewal.org/Documents%202016/CanonLawOnChildAbuseThruTheAges.pdf.

27. Daly, "Sexual Abuse and Canon Law," 36.

28. Ian B. Waters, "The Law of Secrecy in the Latin Church," *The Canonist* 7, no. 1 (2016): 75–87.

29. Tapsell, "Canon Law on Child Sexual Abuse through the Ages," 10.

30. Ibid., 11.

31. Gabriela Hidalgo, "Recurring Cardinal Sins: How the Holy See and Canon Law Have Perpetuated Child Sexual Abuse by Clergy Members," *Children's Legal Rights Journal* 39, no. 2, article 4 (2019): 151, last accessed September 4, 2021, at https://lawecommons.luc.edu/cgi/viewcontent.cgi?article=1182&context=clrj.

32. "Pope Francis Presides Over the Final Rites of Cardinal Law's Funeral Mass," *America: The Jesuit Review*, December 21, 2017, last accessed September 28, 2021, at https://www.americamagazine.org/faith/2017/12/21/pope-francis-presides-over-final-rites-cardinal-laws-funeral-mass.

33. "The Sexual Abuse of Children in the Roman Catholic Archdiocese of Boston: Executive Summary and Scope of Investigation," Office of Attorney General, Massachusetts, July 23, 2003, last accessed September 10, 2021, at https://www.bishop-accountability.org/resources/resource-files/reports/ReillyExecSum.pdf.

34. Tapsell, "Canon Law on Child Sexual Abuse through the Ages," 15.

35. Cismas, *Religious Actors and International Law*, 158

36. Tapsell, "Canon Law on Child Sexual Abuse through the Ages," 15.

37. Mary McAleese, "Canon Law and the UN Convention on the Rights of the Child," in *Children's Rights and Obligations in Canon Law* (Leiden: Brill–Nijhoff, 2019), 345–458, last accessed July 24, 2021, at https://doi-org.proxycu.wrlc.org/10.1163/9789004411173_005.

38. *Code of Canon Law*, "Book II: The People of God," Can. 331.

39. *Code of Canon Law*, "Book II—Part III: Institutes of Consecrated Life and Societies of Apostolic Life," Can. 590 §1 and §2, accessed August 4, 2021, http://www.ahereford.org/canonlaw/doku.php?id=book2.3. Can. 590 §1 "Institutes of consecrated life, dedicated in a special way to the service of God and of the whole Church, are in a particular manner subject to its supreme authority. §2 "The individuals are bound to obey the Supreme Pontiff as their highest Superior, by their sacred bond of obedience."

40. UN Convention on Abuse of Children III. Specificities in the implementation of the Convention in its Concluding Observations on the Second Periodic Report United Nations CRC/C/VAT/CO/2, January 31, 2014, 2, last accessed August 31, 2021, at https://ccrjustice.org/sites/default/files/attach/2014/12/UN_CRC_ConcludingObservations_CRC.pdf.

41. Vatican Radio, "Holy See Publishes Reply to UN Committee on the Rights of the Child," September 26, 2014, last accessed September 8, 2021, at http://www.archivioradiovaticana.va/storico/2014/09/26/holy_see_publishes_reply_to_un_committee_/en-1107343.

42. Catholic News Agency, "Head of US Bishops After Vatican Abuse Summit: 'Intensify the Dallas Charter,'" National Catholic Register, February 25,

2019, https://www.ncregister.com/news/head-of-us-bishops-after-vatican-abuse-summit-intensify-the-dallas-charter.

43. The *Code of Canon Law* is the legal system that regulates the life of the 1.3-billion-member Catholic Church and operates independently from laws in the secular world. The last time the code was rewritten was in 1983, and before that in 1917, the Associated Press reports. The changes published on Tuesday concern only one of the code's seven sections, or books—the penal law section, or Book VI, and is known as an apostolic constitution with the title, Pascite Gregem Dei, which translates as "Tend the Flock." *See* "Catholic Church Law Tightened to Explicitly Criminalize Sexual Abuse of Adults by Priests, Laity," *Biometrica*, accessed August 1, 2021, at https://www.biometrica.com/catholic-church-law-tightened-to-explicitly-criminalize-sexual-abuse-of-adults-by-priests-laity/.

44. Srivats Lakshman, "Theodore McCarrick: Disgraced Ex-Cardinal Becomes First in US to Face Criminal Charges," *Media Entertainment Worldwide*, Jul 29, 2021, accessed August 5, 2021, at https://meaww.com/former-cardinal-theodore-mccarrick-charged-massachusetts-assault-battery-sex-abuse.

45. John R. Morss, "The International Legal Status of the Vatican/Holy See Complex," *European Journal of International Law* 26, no. 4 (November 2015): 927, https://doi.org/10.1093/ejil/chv062.

46. Joshua Keating, "Vatican Bank Investigated for Money Laundering," *Foreign Policy*, September 21, 2010, last accessed August 2, 2021, https://foreignpolicy.com/2010/09/21/vatican-bank-investigated-for-money-laundering/.

47. Ioana Cismas, *Religious Actors and International Law* (Oxford: Oxford University Press, 2014), 196–97.

48. Alperin v. Vatican Bank, United States District Court, N.D. California, No. C-99-04941 MMC (N.D. Cal. December 27, 2007), accessed July 5, 2021, https://casetext.com/case/alperin-v-vatican-bank-5.

49. On its coat-of-arms, the "U" stands for the name of the Croatian fascists, Ustasha (*ustaše*, "revolutionaries"). However, those living under its terror read it as *ubica*, which means "murderers." Wartime Croatia has been called "one great slaughterhouse."

50. Stuart Eizenstat et al., release of report: *US and Allied Wartime and Postwar Relations and Negotiations With Argentina, Portugal, Spain, Sweden, and Turkey on Looted Gold and German External Assets and US Concerns About the Fate of the Wartime Ustasha Treasury*," US Department of State Archive, accessed August 5, 2021, https://1997-2001.state.gov/policy_remarks/1998/980602_eizenstat_nazigld.html; see Gerald Posner, *God's Bankers: A History of Money and Power at the Vatican* (New York: Simon & Schuster, 2015), 138–54.

51. Doe v. Holy See (State of Vatican City), 793 N.Y.S.2d 565, 565–67 (3d Dep't 2005); Plaintiffs sought certification as a class, representing all victims of priesthood sexual assault in the United States.

52. O'Bryan v. Holy See, 556 F.3d 361 (6th Cir. 2009); O'Bryan v. Holy See, 549 F.3d

431 (6th Cir. 2008); O'Bryan v. Holy See, 471 F. Supp. 2d 784 (W.D. Ky. 2007); Oregon-based case against both the Portland Diocese and the Holy See for the alleged sexual abuse of a parishioner by a priest, Father Andrew Ronan, a onetime Servite priest born in Armagh, Ireland, who was laicized in 1966, after serving both in Ireland and America, and who died in 1992. within the Archdiocese of Portland, Oregon during the late 1950s. The heart of the suit is that every priest in the Catholic Church is a Vatican employee. The case has already made legal history, in that it's the first instance in which an American judge has approved limited requests for discovery, meaning requests for documents and other information, despite the Vatican's status as a sovereign entity under international law.

53. James Fantau, "Rethinking the Sovereign Status of the Holy See: Towards a Greater Equality of States and Greater Protection of Citizens in United States Courts," *Cardozo Journal of International and Comparative Law* 19 (March 1, 2011): 491–92.

54. "Pope Francis Issues Law Reorganizing Vatican Finances," *National Catholic Register*, December 28, 2020, accessed August 2, 2021, https://www.ncregister.com/cna/pope-francis-issues-law-reorganizing-vatican-finances.

55. Valentina Di Donato and Zamira Rahim, "Vatican Bank's Former Chief Found Guilty of Money Laundering, Sentenced to Nearly 9 Years in Prison," *CNN*, January 22, 2021, https://www.msn.com/en-us/news/world/vatican-banks-former-chief-found-guilty-of-money-laundering-sentenced-to-nearly-9-years-in-prison/ar-BB1cYvdt.

56. "Vatican: Opening of the Pope Pius XII Archives," *News*, July 24, 2021, https://fsspx.news/en/news-events/news/vatican-opening-pope-pius-xii-archives-67691.

57. Edward Elton Young Hales, *Pio Nino: A Study in European Politics and Religion in the Nineteenth Century* (New York: P. J. Kennedy, 1954), 71.

58. Owen Chadwick, *A History of the Popes, 1830–1914* (New York: Oxford University Press, 1998), 74–49.

59. David I. Kertzer, *The Kidnapping of Edgardo Mortara* (New York: Alfred A. Knopf, 1997), 59.

60. Gabriella Tzvia Weiniger, "This Week in History: The Mortara Affair," *The Jerusalem Post*, June 23, 2013, last accessed September 9, 2021, at https://www.jpost.com/Jewish-World/Jewish-Features/This-Week-in-History-The-Mortara-Affair-317437.

61. "Catholic Bible 101," accessed July 1, 2021, https://www.catholicbible101.com/papalinfallibility.htm.

The doctrine of infallibility, officially defined at the Vatican I council of 1870, says that when the pope is officially defining church dogma, the Holy Spirit is also. There are three requirements for infallibility to be invoked:

a) The pronouncement must be made by the official successor to Peter.

b) The subject matter must be in the area of faith and morals.

c) The pope must be speaking ex cathedra (from the chair) of Peter, and must be intending to proclaim a doctrine that binds the entire Church to assent.

62. *Code of Canon Law*, "Book III: The Teaching Function of the Church," §1, 749, accessed June 26, 2021, https://www.vatican.va/archive/cod-iuris-canonici/eng/documents/cic_lib3-cann747-755_en.html#BOOK_III; see "Table of Contents," *Code of Canon Law* for other provisions, accessed June 26, 2021, at https://www.vatican.va/archive/cod-iuris-canonici/cic_index_en.html.

63. Peter C. Kent, *The Pope and the Duce: The International Impact of the Lateran Agreements* (London: The Macmillan Press, Ltd., 1981), 4.

64. Robert A. Graham, SJ, *Vatican Diplomacy: A Study of Church and State on the International Plane* (Princeton: Princeton University Press, 1959), 216.

65. See Kurt Martens, "The Position of the Holy See and the Vatican City State in International Relations," *University of Detroit Mercy Law Review* 83, no. 5 (2006): 732–39.

66. John F. Pollard. *Money and the Rise of the Modern Papacy: Financing the Vatican, 1850–1950* (Cambridge: Cambridge University Press, 2005), 11.

67. David I. Kertzer, *Prisoner of the Vatican: The Popes, the Kings, and Garibaldi's Rebels in the Struggle to Rule Modern Italy* (New York: Houghton Mifflin Harcourt, 2006).

68. Kertzer, *Prisoner of the Vatican*, 18.

69. Robert P. Kraynak, "Pope Leo XIII and the Catholic Response to Modernity," *In Defense of Old Europe* (Fall 2007): 531, last accessed September 29, 2021, at https://www.academia.edu/36832893/Pope_Leo_XIII_and_the_Catholic_Response_to_Modernity_pdf.

70. Pollard, *Money and the Rise of the Modern Papacy*, xviii.

71. Thomas Bokenkotter, *A Concise History of the Catholic Church*, revised and expanded edition (New York: Doubleday, 2002), 231.

72. Noel Dias, "Roman Catholic Church & International Law," *Sri Lanka Journal of International Law* 13 (June 2001): 129.

73. Joseph Joblin, SJ, "At the Origins of Humanitarian Law: The Attitude of the Holy See," *L'Osservatore Romano* (weekly edition in English) (August 1999): 3, accessed July 25, 2021 https://www.ewtn.com/catholicism/library/prof-joseph-joblin-sj-4115.

74. Robert Araujo, "The Holy See as International Person and Sovereign and Participant in International Law," in *From Just War to Modern Peace Ethics*, edited by Heinz-Gerhard Justenhoven and William A. Barbieri Jr., 249–74 (Berlin and Boston: De Gruyter, 2012), 254.

75. "Dispute between Argentina and Chile Concerning the Beagle Channel," *United Nations Reports of International Arbitral Awards* 21 (February 18, 1977): 53–264, accessed August 1, 2021, https://legal.un.org/riaa/cases/vol_XXI/53-264.pdf.

76. Alvarez, "The Holy See and the First Hague Peace Conference," 433.

77. Maartje M. Abbenhus, *The Hague Conference and International Politics, 1898–1915* (London: Bloomsbury Academic, 2019), 59.

78. Giuliana Chamedes, *A Twentieth Crusade: The Vatican's Battle to Remake Christian Europe* (Cambridge, MA: Harvard University Press, 2019), 27–29.

79. Between 1870 and 1929, the diplomatic corps accredited to the Vatican was not only not dissolved, but also increased through the years, except for a period just before World War I. There were eighteen permanent diplomatic missions at the Vatican in 1890 dropping to fourteen on the eve of World War and rising to twenty-four in 1921. There were twenty-seven permanent diplomatic missions at the Vatican when the Lateran Treaty was signed in 1929. Luke T. Lee, "Vienna Convention on Consular Relations," *Netherlands International Law Review* 15, no. 2 (1986): 176.

80. Joblin, SJ, "At the Origins of Humanitarian Law."

81. Chamedes, *A Twentieth Crusade*, 7

82. Ibid., 27.

83. Charles G. Fenwick, "The New City of the Vatican," *American Journal of International Law (AJIL)* 23, no. 2 (April 1929): 371, accessed July 1, 2021, https://www.jstor.org/stable/i311947.

84. Morss, "The International Legal Status of the Vatican/Holy See Complex," 931.

85. Robert Jennings and Arthur Watts, *Oppenheim's International Law: Volume 1 Peace*, ninth edition (Oxford: Oxford University Press, 1992), 326.

86. Lassa Francis Lawrence Oppenheim, *International Law: A Treatise Volume 1 Peace*, second edition (New York: Longmans, Green and Co., 1911), 160.

87. Kunz, "The Status of the Holy See in International Law," 309.

88. John Baptist Itaruma, "International Legal Personality of the Holy See last accessed July 14, 2021, https://www.academia.edu/9828824/INTERNATIONAL_LEGAL_PERSONALITY_OF_THE_HOLY_SEE?auto=download&email_work_card=download-paper.

89. Tiyanjana Maluwa, "The Holy See and the Concept of International Legal Personality: Some Reflections," *The Comparative and International Law Journal of South Africa* 19, no. 1 (March 1986): 1, accessed July 2, 2021, http://uniset.ca/microstates2/va_19CompIntlLJSAfr1.pdf.

90. Oppenheim, *International Law: A Treatise*, 150.

91. Maluwa, "The Holy See and the Concept of International Legal Personality."

92. James Crawford, *Brownlie's Principles of Public International Law*, eighth edition (Oxford: Oxford University Press, 2012), 124.

93. "Convention on the Rights and Duties of States 1933," The Avalon Project, Yale Law School, accessed July 23, 2021, https://avalon.law.yale.edu/20th_century/intam03.asp.

94. "Note on the Diplomatic Relations of the Holy See," *Holy See Press Office*, August 2, 2021, https://press.vatican.va/content/salastampa/en/bollettino/pubblico/2021/02/08/210208a.pdf.

95. Morss, "The International Legal Status of the Vatican/Holy See Complex," 938–39.

96. Posner, *God's Bankers*, 48.

97. Susan Zuccotti, *Under His Very Window: The Vatican and the Holocaust in Italy* (New Haven: Yale University Press, 2002), 19.

98. "Lateran Financial Convention (1929): Text," *Concordat Watch*, accessed July 22, 2021, https://www.concordatwatch.eu/topic-39241.834.

99. The Lateran Pacts was signed on February 11, 1929, and the Italian parliament ratified them on June 7, 1929. The treaty recognized Vatican City as an independent state under the sovereignty of the Holy See and from June onward Vatican institutions began to evolve.

100. Pollard. *Money and the Rise of the Modern Papacy*, 149.

101. Ibid., 168.

102. Ibid., 163.

103. Posner, *God's Bankers*, 117–19.

104. Pollard, *Money and the Rise of the Modern Papacy*, 200.

105. The six scholars chosen to serve on the Historical Commission are: Dr. Eva Fleischner, Professor Emerita of Montclair State University in New Jersey; Reverend Gerald P. Fogarty, S.J., William R. Kenan, Jr., Professor of Religious Studies and History, University of Virginia; Dr. Michael R. Marrus, Chancellor Rose and Ray Wolfe Professor of Holocaust Studies and Dean of the School of Graduate Studies, University of Toronto; Reverend John F. Morley, Associate Professor, Department of Religious Studies, Seton Hall University; Dr. Bernard Suchecky, Researcher at the Department of Social Sciences, Free University of Brussels; Dr. Robert S. Wistrich, Professor of History and holder of the Neuberger Chair in Modern Jewish Studies at the Hebrew University in Jerusalem.

106. Michael Marrus, "The Vatican & the Holocaust: Understanding the Vatican During the Nazi Period," Jewish Virtual Library, accessed June 24, 2021, https://www.jewishvirtuallibrary.org/understanding-the-vatican-during-the-nazi-period; see David Dahlin, "Pius XII and the Jews," *The Weekly Standard*, February 26, 2001, for a historiographical account about Pope Pius XII's relationship with the Nazis. Vatican Apostolic Archive (Archivio Apostolico Vaticano) provides access to new records about Pius XII's papacy.

107. See chapter 9 in this book by Massimo Faggioli, *The Liminal Papacy of Pope Francis and a New Context for Vatican Neutrality and Sovereignty*. Cardinal Pietro

Parolin's speech for the ninetieth anniversary of the signing of the Lateran Pacts at LUMSA University, Rome in February 8, 2019, reported in Barbara Castelli, "Cardinal Parolin: Holy See at Forefront Protecting the Human Person," *Vatican News*, accessed July 17, 2021, https://www.vaticannews.va/en/vatican-city/news/2019-02/cardinal-pietro-parolin-holy-see-protecting-human-person.html.

108. Fr. Benedict Mayaki, "Pope Calls for Joint Efforts on Path Towards an Ever Wider 'We,'" *Vatican News*, May 6, 2021, https://www.vaticannews.va/en/pope/news/2021-05/pope-francis-migrants-refugees-wider-we-world-day-message.html.

109. "Full Text: Vatican's Doctrinal Office Response and Note on the Blessing of Same-Sex Unions," *Catholic News Agency*, March 15, 2021, accessed June 8, 2021, https://www.catholicnewsagency.com/news/246855/full-text-vaticans-doctrinal-office-response-and-note-on-the-blessing-of-same-sex-unions; see Rev. Irene Monroe, "Pope Francis Flip-Flops on LGBTQ Church Inclusion," *GBH News*, March 25, 2021, https://www.wgbh.org/news/commentary/2021/03/25/pope-francis-flip-flops-on-lgbtq-church-inclusion-again; also, Leonardo Blair, "Pope Francis Endorses Civil Unions for Same-Sex Couples," *The Christian Post*, October 21, 2020, accessed June 8, 2021, https://www.christianpost.com/news/pope-francis-endorses-civil-unions-for-same-sex-couples.html.

110. Dias, "Roman Catholic Church and International Law," 131.

111. Paul Collins, *From Inquisition to Freedom* (Sydney: Simon & Schuster Australia, 1976), 7.

112. Thomas Reese, "The Catholic Story, Conservative versus Progressive," *National Catholic Reporter*, January 7, 2016, last accessed August 4, 2021, at https://www.ncronline.org/blogs/faith-and-justice/catholic-story-conservative-vs-progressive.

113. Dias, "Roman Catholic Church and International Law," 131.

114. Thomas Reese, "The Catholic Story, Conservative vs. Progressive,"

115. Ibid.

SELECTED BIBLIOGRAPHY

Blasi, Anthony J., and Lluis Oviedo, eds. *The Abuse of Minors in the Catholic Church: Dismantling the Culture of Cover-Ups.* New York and London: Routledge, 2020.

Hidalgo, Gabriela. "Recurring Cardinal Sins: How the Holy See and Canon Law Have Perpetuated Child Sexual Abuse by Clergy Members." *Children's Legal Rights Journal* 39, no. 2 (2019): article 4.

Posner, Gerald. *God's Bankers: A History of Money and Power at the Vatican* New York: Simon & Schuster, 2015.

Robertson, Geoffrey. *The Case of the Pope: Vatican Accountability for Human Rights Abuse* London: Penguin, 2010.

Appendix

Source: Vatican Apostolic Archive (Archivio Apostolico Vaticano), Arch. Nunzio Berlino, buste 103, fasc. 10, "Offese contro il Santo Padre e contro la Chiesa. 1945."

Die Haltung der katholischen Kirche gegenüber Adolf Hitler und die sich daraus ergebende Verantwortung.

Vor der Machtübernahme Adolf Hitlers verhielten sich die deutschen katholischen Bischöfe und Geistlichen gegen Hitler ablehnend. Sie verweigerten den deutschen Katholiken, die der SA oder der Partei beitreten wollten, die Absolution, d.h. sie schlossen sie für den Fall, dass sie ihre Haltung und ihre Gesinnung nicht änderten, aus der kirchlichen Gemeinschaft aus. Viele Katholiken liessen sich dadurch von dem Beitritt zur SA oder zur Partei abhalten.

Die Haltung und Handlungsweise der Bischöfe und Geistlichen entsprach wohl der Haltung und Weisung Roms. Die Beweggründe, die zu dieser Haltung, zur Absolutionsverweigerung führten, konnten nur religiöse und moralische sein. Man befürchtete, die Politik Hitlers werde unchristlich, ja antichristlich sein, zu welcher Befürchtung er in seinem Buche "Mein Kampf" und in seinen Reden genügend Anlass gab. Man denke nur an seinen unchristlichen Antisemitismus und an seine unchristliche Rassentheorie.

Nach der "Machtübernahme" war der Pabst einer der ersten Souveräne, die mit Hitler einen Vertrag abschlossen. Mit Hilfe des Herrn von Papen kam das Koncordat zustande, in welchem der Pabst die Regierung Hitlers als rechtmässig anerkannte und sich von ihm die Anerkennung, Respektierung und den Schutz der katholischen Kirche und ihrer Rechte (nicht zuletzt auch die Zahlung der Gehälter der Bischöfe u. Geistlichen) in Deutschland zusichern liess. Der Pabst gab mit dieser Anerkennung der Regierung Hitlers ein Beispiel. Man könnte vermuten, dieses Beispiel habe auf andere Staaten anregend gewirkt. Jedenfalls erfolgte nun bald auch von ihnen die Anerkennung Hitlers.

Die deutschen katholischen Bischöfe und Geistlichen gaben nach Abschluss des Konkordates ihre ablehnende Haltung auf. Die deutschen Katholiken durften der SA und der Partei unbehindert beitreten. Die katholischen Geistlichen assistierten bei Taufen, Trauungen und Beerdigungen von SA-Leuten und Pgs. Von ihren Häusern und von den Kirchen wehte die Hackenkreuzfahne.

Hitler hatte die Respektierung und den Schutz der katholischen Kirche zugesichert. Und Antisemitismus? Und Rassenpolitik? Reichstagsbrand, Wahlfälschungen, Röhm-Affäre und manches andere? Nun, man glaubte wohl, der Nationalsozialismus gebärde sich nur im Kampf um die Macht und im anfänglichen Überschwang so wild. Er könne gemildert und veredelt werden und das könne am ehesten dadurch bewirkt werden, dass die Katholiken in seine Reihen einträten und dort ihren Einfluss geltend machten. Wir wollen annehmen, man sei dieses guten Glaubens gewesen, obwohl man wohl eher glauben dürfte, der Pabst in seiner politischen Klugheit und bei seinem Wohlunterrichtet sein durch die im Vatikan weilenden diplomatischen Vertreter fast aller Staaten habe das Wesen und die wahren Absichten Adolf Hitlers und seiner Helfer von Anfang an durchschaut, habe aber aus Nützlichkeitsgründen diese bessere Hinsicht hintangestellt.

Jedenfalls: Als bald nach der Machtübernahme die Berliner Kommunisten gegen alles Recht hinter Stacheldraht gesetzt wurden, als die KZ-Lager eingerichtet und im Laufe der Jahrtausende von In- u. Ausländern hineingesperrt, gequält und ermordet wurden, als man die Insassen der Irrenhäuser und Nervenheilanstalten und andere "unproduktive Volksgenossen" aus dem Leben beförderte, als im Warthegau eine regelrechte Verfolgung und Unterdrückung der Katholiken erfolgte, als man dort die Kirchen schloss, die Katholiken entrechtete, viele katholischen Geistliche in die KZ-Lager sperrte, als Hitler in einer öffentlichen Rede die grundsätzliche Ausrottung der jüdischen Rasse verkündete und dann 1938 die Synagogen brannten u. die Judengreuel begannen, als man Österreich und die Tscheckoslowakei gewaltsam angliederte, als man Polen überfiel und "besiegte" und begann, die Polen auszurotten, als man Holland und Belgien und Dänemark und Norwegen überfiel und in diesen Ländern eine Gewalt u. Schreckensherrschaft ausübte, als alles dieses und noch viel mehr geschah, da konnte keiner mehr guten Glaubens sein, da konnte keiner mehr an die Vendlungsmöglichkeit des Nationalsozialismus glauben, vor allem der Pabst nicht, der über alles besser als wir unterrichtet war, da musste der Pabst von der wesenhaften Bosheit Hitlers u. seiner Hilfer überzeugt sein.

Hätte da der Pabst nicht offiziell von Hitler abrücken, den Vertrag mit ihm kündigen sollen? Die Berechtigung zu dieser Kündigung hatte Hitler ihm durch die häufige Verletzung des Vertrages ja gegeben. Hätte da der Pabst nicht die Beziehungen zu Hitler abbrechen, seinen diplomatischen Vertreter aus Deutschland abberufen sollen? Da galt es nicht mehr, die Folgen zu erwägen, die ein solcher Schrift haben könnte. Für die Kirche haben nicht politische, sondern moralische Beweggründe an erster Stelle zu stehen. Und ich darf mich nie unmoralisch verhalten, mag mein Verhalten noch so nachteilige Folgen für mich haben. Da galt es auch nicht, das kleinere von zwei Übeln zu wählen, denn von zwei Übeln, die beide unmoralisch sind, darf ich keines wählen, wie ich mich, vor die Wahl zwischen einem Meineid und einer gewöhnlichen Lüge gestellt, auch nicht für die Lüge, das kleinere Übel, entscheiden darf.

Hätte Jesus die politische Klugheit seines Nachfolgers, des Pabstes besessen, dann hätte er nicht den Führen der jüdisches Volkes, den Schriftgelehrten und Pharisäern, öffentlich ihre Unmoral vorgehalten und sie als Volksverführer gebrandmarkt, sondern hätte auf diplomatischem Wege mit ihnen verhandelt. Dann hätten sie ihn wohl nicht ans Kreuz geschlagen.

Ich weiss wohl, dass deutsche Bischöfe gegen manches, was von Adolf Hitler geschah, in Rundschreiben protestiert haben. Aber diese Rundschreiben gingen nur heimlich von Hand zu Hand und gelangten nicht zur allgemeinen Kenntnis. Ich weiss auch, dass viele katholische Geistliche in die KZ-Lager gekommen sind (in manchen Fällen wegen unzeitgemässer Redewendungen). Bei alledem handelte es sich nicht um offizielle Stellungnahme und Verlautbarungen Roms. Rom hat sich nie offiziell gegen Adolf Hitler und seine Partei erklärt, ist nie offiziell von Adolf Hitler abgerückt, hat nie die Beziehungen zu ihm abgebrochen, hat nie das mit ihm abgescholssene Konkordat gekündigt. Der Gesandte des Vatikans wurde nie aus Deutschland abberufen. Soviel ich weiss, hat der Nuntius bis 1941 (nachher ging es aus technischen Gründen nicht mehr) als Doyen des diplomatischen Korps zu Neujahr Adolf Hitler seine (und damit des Papstes) und des Korps Glückwünsche ausgesprochen.

Ich sagte oben, der Pabst habe durch den Abschluss des Konkordates mit Hitler vielleicht andern Staaten ein anregendes Beispiel gegeben. Sicher haben er und die deutschen Bischöfe und Geistlichen durch ihr Verhalten die deutschen katholiken und wohl auch Nichtkatholiken in ihrer Stellungnahme zu Hitler und seiner Partei weitgehend beeinflusst. Wenn der Pabst mit Hitler ein Konkordat abschloss, wenn er bis zuletzt die Beziehungen zu Hitler aufrecht erhielt, wenn die deutschen Bischöfe und Geistlichen Roms Weisung entsprechend den Beitritt zur SA und zur Partei biz zuletzt für erlaubt erklärten, wie hätte da der gewöhnliche Mann in der Gefolgschaft Adolf Hitlers, in der Bejahung seiner Politik, im Beitritt zz und im Verbleiben in der SA und der Partei ein Unrecht erblicken sollen? Konnte oder musste er nicht aus der Haltung des Pabstes und der Geistlichkeit folgern das, was man Böses von Hitler und den Nazis berichte, müsse doch wohl nicht wahr oder doch nicht so schlimm sein und es handelte sich wohl nur um Verleumdungen und Übertreibungen der ausländischen Propaganda?

Sind die deutschen Pgs, vor allem die katholischen, wenn sie jetzt wegen ihrer Parteizugehörigkeit belangt, ihrer Stellungen, ihres Vermögens, ihrer Einkünfte beraubt werden, nicht berechtigt, zu ihrer Entlastung auf die Haltung des Papstes und der deutschen Bischöfe und Geistlichen hinzuweisen, wodurch sie in ihrem Verhalten beeinflusst worden sind? Ist nicht vor allem der Papst für ihr Unglück mitverantwortlich? Müsste er nicht diese Tatsache jetzt vor aller Welt erklären, um dadurch die verfolgten Pgs. zu entlasten? Zu dieser Erklärung ist der Papst moralisch verpflichtet und er muss sie abgeben, bevor in Nürnberg die Verteidigungsreden beginnen, schon um den treuen Sohn der katholischen Kirche, Herrn von Papen zu entlasten. Man glaubt auch, dass eine solche Erklärung des Papstes in Vorbereitung ist und bald erfolgen wird. Wir wollen abwarten.

Und die deutschen katholischen Bischöfe und Geistlichen? Sie, denen es selbst unter dem früheren Regime im grossen und ganzen erträglich ging, die nicht gedrängt oder gar genötigt wurden, in die SA oder Partei einzutreten, bei denen nicht wie bei den deutschen Beamten die einige wirtschaftliche Existenz und die von Frauen und Kindern auf dem Spiele stand, sie suchen jetzt eine neue politische Linie, um auch für die Zukunft ihre wirtschaftliche Existenz zu sichern. Sie halten sich und ihre Hilfsbeamten bis zu Boten hinunter von allen Lasten, z.B. den schweren Einquartierungslasten, frei. Im übrigen lassen sie den Dingen ihren Lauf und schweigen, wo sie bekennen müssten:

Ein kollektive Schuld, denen Umfang durch nationale Grenzen bestimmt wäre, gibt es nicht. Wenn es eine kollektive Schuld gibt, dann nur im Sinne des Christentums, wonach für menschliche Sünden die ganze Menschheit mit verantwortlich und haftbar ist, zu welcher Erkenntnis auch die geschichtliche Betrachtung führt.

Jedenfalls muss man das, was wir selbst getan haben, um dem Verhängnis zu entgehen, allen Deutschen zugute halten, denn sie konnten noch viel weniger als wir erkennen, wohin der Weg Adolf Hitlers unsere Volk und die ganze Welt führen würde. Was aber heute christliche Völker gegen ihre Glaubensgenossen anderer Nationalität tun, muss zum Untergang des Christentums führen.

Ich hörte vor 14 Tagen eine Predigt Pastor Niemöllers. Es sprach von der deutschen allgemein Schuld, wobei er hätte sagen sollen, wie denn dem einzelnen Privatmann eine Stellungsnahme gegen Hitler möglich gewesen wäre. Aber hauptsächlich klopfte Niemöller an die eigene Brust und betonte seine eigene Unterlassungssünde und die aller evangelischen Geistlichen in Deutschland. (Die katholischen erwähnt er nicht). Er meinte, wenn die evang. Geistlichen in Deutschland (ich glaube, er nannte die Zahl 14,000) einheitlich und geschlossen sich rechtzeitig gegen Hitler und den Nationalsozialismus gestellt hätten, dann wäre es wohl möglich gewesen, dass Hitler hätte alle in die KZ-Lager schleppen und umbringen lassen. Aber dann wären der deutschen Bevölkerung und der ganzen Welt rechtzeitig die Augen aufgegangen und es wäre wohl nicht zum Kriege gekommen.

Wie viel mehr gilt das, was Pastor Niemöller von der evang. Geistlichkeit, die in verschiedene Bekentnisse zersplittert, nicht die Glaubenseinigkeit und nicht die straffe Zentralisation der katholischen Geistlichkeit hat, sagt, von dieser! Eine klare Weisung von Rom hätte genügt, um aus den katholischen Geistlichen eine geschlossene Gegenfront gegen Adolf Hitler aufzustellen. Und, gewiss, es ist möglich, dass Adolf Hitler alle katholischen Geistlichen hätte in die KZ-Lager schleppen und umbringen lassen. Aber dann hätten sie ihr Gewissen salviert. Dann wäre das Wort von dem Weizenkorn, das sterben muss, um Frucht zu bringen, wahr geworden. Und das andere Wort: "Wenn sie mich verfolgt haben, werden sie auch euch verfolgen." Aber davon bin ich überzeugt: ein solches Opfer hätte den Frieden gerettet.

Die Kirche hat das Opfer nicht gebracht und hat sich ihres Herrn u. Meisters nicht würdig gezeigt. Und während nach der Lehre der Kirche Jesus die Sunden der ganzen Welt auf sich genommen hat, müssen diese Sunden der Kirche andere Büssen.

Index

A
ABM Treaty, 230
Abu Dhabi document, 164
Actes et documents du Saint-Siège relatifs à la Seconde Guerre Mondiale (ADSSGM), 86
Administration of the Patrimony of the Apostolic See (APSA), 253
ADSSGM. *See* Actes et documents du Saint-Siège relatifs à la Seconde Guerre Mondiale (ADSSGM)
Advisory Committee of the High Commission for Refugees, 48
Adzhubei, Alexei, 132, 225
African Union, 49
Age of Concordats, 163
Alperin v. the Vatican Bank, 253–4
Alsace-Lorraine, transfer to France, 26–8
America First, xii
Amette, Cardinal, 13
anti-communism
  in Poland, 135
  of Vatican, 121–2, 128–9, 144–6
anti-sanctionists, 70
Antonelli, Giacomo, 40
April Allocution, 4
APSA. *See* Administration of the Patrimony of the Apostolic See (APSA)

Aquinas, Thomas, 130, 226
Archdiocese of Bratislava-Trnava, 28
Archdiocese of Cologne, 30
Archdiocese of Esztergom, xvi, 28
Arkhipov, Vasili, 212
Assad, xviii
Austro-Hungarian Empire, 4
Avramenko, Oleg, 229
Axis powers, 78
Azione Cattolica (Catholic Action), 65

B
Backies, Monsignor Audrys, 232
Baker, James, 232
Balogh, Margit, xvii
Baltia, Herman, 29
Basque Catholics, 78
Belgium, xiii
Belgium, territorial claims of, 29–31
Benedict XV, Pope, xv, xvii, 8, 24, 30, 46, 106, 245, 259–60
  Ad Beatissimi, 9
  allegations against, 10–12
  benevolence and humanitarianism of, 10
  on causes of war, 9
  and just war theory, 13–15
  as "le Pape boche," 9
  as "Maledetto XV," 9

282   *Index*

"Peace Note" of August 1917, 9
   policy of neutrality and impartiality, 10
   Ubi primum, 9
Benedict XVI, Pope, 168, 190–1
Benzler, Willibrord, 27
Bergoglio, Jorge Mario. *See* Francis,
   Pope
Bismarck, Chancellor, 257
Blair, Dennis C., 232
Bourne, Cardinal Francis, 10
Brandt, Willy, 132, 134
Brezhnev, Leonid, 232
Briand, Aristide, 17
Bush, George H. W., 184, 189
Bush, George W., xviii

C
Cahill, xviii
Cardinal Mindszenty, xviii
Casaroli, Agostino, 132–3, 149, 173
   idealistic and optimistic views of
      NPT, 227–9
   negotiation with Soviets on NPT,
      229–31
Castillo, Dennis, 105
Catholic Church, xviii, 23, 130, 194n4,
      203, 226, 262
   approaches to just war theory, xviii,
      13–15, 182, 225–6
   attitude toward Adolf Hitler, 107–11
   clemency for convicted German war
      criminals, 112–15
   distinction between nonproliferation
      and Zero nuclear option, xviii
   followers of, 206–7
   ideological Cold War against
      communism, 122
   in Japan, 89, 96
   relationship between Filipinos,
      Japanese and, 84, *84*
   relationship with Prussia, 4
   of Spain, 87
   theological commitment against
      nuclear weapons, xviii
   view of sovereignty, 205–6

Catholicism, 12, 65, 67, 69–70, 72–3,
      84, 87, 111, 113, 128, 164–8, 172,
      207, 210
Catholic socialism, 130
Catholic Social Teaching (CST), 181,
      226–7
Catholic Women's Religious Corps, 96
Cattolica, Azione, 66, 69, 74
Cavour, Count Camillo, 256
Ceci, Lucia, xvii
Centesimus Annus, 136
Cerretti, Monsignor Bonaventura, 16–17
Chamedes, Giuliana, 121, 124
Chappel, James, 129
Cheli, Cardinal Giovanni, 152
Chiesa, Giacomo Della, 14
Chiesa, Pope Dalla, 43
child abuse by Catholic clergy, 247–51
China–Pakistan nuclear deal, 235
Christian Democracy
   in secular politics, 130
   in Western Europe, 129–30
Christianity, 76
Christian News Service, 113
Christus Dominus, 25
Churchill, Winston, 122
Church magisterium *vs* international
   law, 122–6
Church of Silence, 127–31
Church schism in East Asia, 87
Church's foreign policy, xi
Cicognani, Monsignor Giovanni, 78
Civiltà Cattolica, 75, 77
clemency efforts for convicted German
   war criminals, 112–15
Code of Canon Law
   1917, 25
   1983, 26
Code of Canon Law of 1917, 249,
   259–60, 265
Cold War, 121–8, 133, 136
Communism, xix, 16, 48, 74–6, 78, 115,
   122, 124–7, 131, 136, 144, 235
communist regimes, disintegration of,
   126

Compendium of the Social Doctrine of the Church, 181
Comprehensive Nuclear-Test-Ban Treaty (CTBT), 235
Conciliation Treaty of 1929, 41
Concordat of Worms 1122, 163
Congregation for Extraordinary Ecclesiastical Affairs, 46
Congress of the Comintern (1935), 74
Consalvi, Cardinal Ercole, xv, 3
Convention on the Rights and Duties of States (Montevideo Convention), 1933, 262
Convention with Venezuela of 1964, 49
Cooke, Cardinal Terence, 227
Co-Prosperity Sphere, 92
Cordier, Andrew, 213
Corey, David, 226–7
Cousins, Norman, 213
CSCE. *See* Helsinki Conference on Security and Cooperation in Europe (CSCE), 1975
Csernoch, János Cardinal, 28
CTBT. *See* Comprehensive Nuclear-Test-Ban Treaty (CTBT)
Cuban Missile Crisis, 132, 147, 149, 214–15, 225–6
Curran, Charles E., 226

D
d'Arienzo, Maria, xiv–xv
Day of Faith, 70
Dignitatis Humanae, 47
diocesan boundaries, 25
Diocese of Liège, 30–1
Divini Redemptoris, 76, 125
Dominican Republic of 1954, 49
Dubinine, Juri, 229
Duffy, Eamon, 7

E
Ecclesiam Suam, 134, 149
Eighteen Nation Committee on Disarmament, 225

Einstein, Albert, 211
Emmanuele III, King Vittorio, 23
Emmanuel II, King Victor, 6, 257
Erzberger, Matthias, 11
Etchegaray, Cardinal, 188
Ethiopian Empire, 67
Eupen-Malmedy, territory of, 29–31
Eurocentrism, 47
Evangelii Gaudium, 164
even-handedness, xii
extraneousness, 46

F
Faggioli, Massimo, xi, 206
    The Liminal Papacy of Pope Francis, 203
FAO. *See* Food and Agriculture Organization (FAO)
fascism, 65–6, 70–1, 123
fascist war of conquest, 68
Filipinization of Catholic Church, 87–8, 91
Finnemann, William, 90
First Philippine Republic (1898–1901), 87
Fleming, Suzanne Brown, xiii
Food and Agriculture Organization (FAO), 48
Foreign Sovereign Immunities Act (FSIA), 253
Francis, Pope, xi–xii, 51, 203, 238, 246, 251, 253–4, 264
    activism, 169–72
    activities, 166
    background from Argentina, 165
    Catholicism, view of, 164
    concept of "peripheries," 169
    Fratelli Tutti, 207
    global perspective, 164–5
    global re-alignment, 163–7
    on immorality of nuclear weapons, 204
    interpretation of global history, 164
    interpretation of neutrality and sovereignty, 161

interpretation of Rome's role in global world, 165
liminality and marginality, view of, 167–9
on mercy and neutrality, 170
on nuclear disarmament, 208–9, 234–7
papal diplomacy, 161–2
politics, view of, 166
pontificate of, 162, 164, 168
relations between church and political entities, 163–4, 173
relationship between neutrality and peace, 169–72
rescue of Muslim refugees, 162
role of mediation, 162
role of the church and the war, 171
on social justice, 171–2
understanding of Vatican neutrality's role, 169
vision of neutrality, 170, 173–4
Franco, Francisco, 75
Franco–Prussian War of 1870, xv, 4–5, 16, 254
Fratelli Tutti, 172
Free City of Gdańsk/Danzig, 133
Freedom House, 206
French Catholics, 9
French Revolution, 3
Fritzen, Adolf, 27
FSIA. *See* Foreign Sovereign Immunities Act (FSIA)

G
Gallagher, Paul, 173
Gallagher, SJ, Father Charles, 10
Gandolfo, Castel, 68
Gasparri, Cardinal Pietro, 9, 12–13, 15, 17, 23, 41, 105
Gasperi, Alcide De, 129
Gasquet, Cardinal Aidan, 11
Gaudium et Spes (Joy and Hope), 215–17, 182
Gemelli, Father Agostino, 73
General Assembly (GA) resolution 58/314, 246

Gerlach, Bavarian Monsignor Rudolf, 12
German Catholics, 108
Gioberti, Vincenzo, 64
global stability, 186
Gomá, Isidro, 75
Gorbachev, Mikhail, 208
Graziani, Rodolfo, 72
Great Western Schism, 166
Gregory the XVI, Pope, 255
Gregory VII, Pope, xiv
Grey, Lord, 11
Gromyko, Andrei, 230
Gruppi Universitari Fascisti (Fascist Groups in Italian Universities), 65
Gumbleton, Bishop, 234

H
Hague Convention of 1907, 125
Haig, Alexander, 232
Hamvas, Bishop Endre, 149
Handy, General Thomas, 112
Harada, Ambassador, 98
Hartmann, Cardinal, 8, 11
Helsinki Accords, 1975, 51
Helsinki Conference on Security and Cooperation in Europe (CSCE), 1975, 49–52, 133, 230–1
Helsinki Final Act, 133
Herriot, Édouard, 17
Heung-sik, Lazzaro You, 238
Hiroshima and Nagasaki atomic bombings, 203–4, 210, 216–17
Hitler, Adolf, 67, 106–7
  concordat with, 108–9
  Mein Kampf, 108
  unchristian antisemitism and unchristian race theory, 108–9
Holmes, Allan, 232
Holocaust, 115
Holy See, xix, xv–xvi, xviii, 7–8, 12, 15, 23–4, 26, 28–30, 65, 70, 74, 78, 106, 124, 161, 246, 250–1, 261
  as an observer, 48–9

anti-communism, 121–2
on anti-Jewish laws, 73
under Benedict, 9–15
Canon law and, xiv–xv
as a Cold War mediator, 123, 133
concepts of neutrality and extraneousness, 45, 49–50
concordat revolution, 124
Dicastery on Integral Human Development, 219
diplomatic corps accredited to, 32, 36n35
diplomatic exchange between Belgium and, 30
diplomatic legitimacy to Japan's occupation, 85
diplomatic relations after September 1870, 5
diplomatic relations between Hungary and, 147–51
foreign policy of, xi, 17, 147, 163
Fundamental Agreement with Israel, 1993, xvii
on independence of Slovenia and Croatia, 51
international diplomatic actions, 12, 47–52, 67, 83–4
international position during World War II, 122
legal status of, 40
mediation between Argentina and Chili, 32
mediation of conflict between Spain and Germany, xvii
mediatory role in Ruhr Crisis, 16
milieu and possession goals, 186–7
neutrality approach, 8, 122–6, 135, 179, 184–93. *See also* neutrality
non-recognition principle, 85
Ostpolitik, 48
participation in Helsinki Conference, 49–52
participation in international governmental and nongovernmental organizations, 48–9

policy of neutrality and impartiality, 13–15, 17, 24
political sovereignty, 41–2
protocols for sovereign engagement, 124
relations between Italian State and, 43
relationship between sovereignty and neutrality, 42
relationship between Vatican state and, 43, 44, 45, 53
against Romanov Empire, 4
in secular political affairs, 121
Spanish Civil War and, 74–6
as a spiritual and humanitarian European power, 260–1
Stalin's wartime attitude toward, 122
territorial sovereignty of, xi, xiv–xv, 5, 40–2
Holy See diplomacy, 180–1
on nuclear weapons, 204, 207–20, 225
opposition of wars in Syria and Iraq, 181–93
toward Philippines, 85–6
Howard, Sir Henry, 12
Humani Generis Unitas (Unity of the Human Race), 105
Humanitarian Impact of Nuclear Weapons conferences, 204
Hungarian Pontifical Ecclesiastical Institute in Rome, 150
Hungarian Question, 147
Hungarian revolution of 1956, 147
Hungary, church-state relations, 147–51
Hungary, division of prewar, 28–9
Hussein, Saddam, xviii, 184, 188

I
IAEA. *See* International Atomic Energy Agency (IAEA)
Iberian crisis, 77
ICAN. *See* International Campaign to Abolish Nuclear Weapons (ICAN)
Intermediate Nuclear Forces (INF) Treaty, 208

International Atomic Energy Agency (IAEA), 48
International Campaign to Abolish Nuclear Weapons (ICAN), 237
International Red Cross, 245
Intesa Semplice of 1927, 148
Iran hostage crisis, 1979, 245
Iraqi Christians, 188
Iraq invasion, 2003, 185–9, 193
Iraq invasion of Kuwait, 1991, xviii, 181–5, 193
Iron Curtain, 130–1, 148, 232
Iron Curtain Catholics, 135–6
isolationism, xii
Istituto per le Opere di Religione (IOR), 264
Italian Catholics, 71
Italian war against the Ottoman Empire, 1911–1912, 7
Italo-Ethiopian war (1935–1936), 67–9
Italo–Vatican relations, 12
Italy
  conflict between Church and State in, 71
  decentralization of, 166
  intervention in First World War, 12–13
  relationship between the Holy See and, 67

J
Jantausch, Pavol, xvi
Japanese Religious Section, 94
Joblin, Joseph, 260
John Jay Report, 2004, 247
John XXIII, Pope, 48, 121, 126, 131–2, 134, 145, 147, 149, 163, 211, 214, 216, 226, 265
Josef, Emperor Franz, 6–7, 256
Joyce, James, 207
Julius II, Pope, 3
Jurgens, Constant, 97
just war theory, xviii, 13–15, 182, 225–6

K
Kádár, János, 150–2
Kasper, Cardinal Walter, 187
Kawasaki, Akira, 237
Kellogg-Briand pact, xiii
Ken, Ambassador Harada, 86
Kennan, George, 128
Kennedy, John F., 211–12
Kennedy, Robert, 213
Kent, Peter C., 128
Khrushchev, Nikita, 132, 213–14, 225
Kim Jong Un, 238
Klimo, Arpad von, xvii
König, Cardinal Franz, 149, 152
Kosicki, Piotr, xvii
Kozvrev, Semen, 229
Kozyrev, Andrei, 229–30
Kulturkampf, 4, 6
Kunz, Josef, 262

L
Laghi, Archbishop Pio, 232
Laghi, Cardinal, 188–9
Laïcité, 87
Lateran Accords/Lateran Pacts/Lateran Treaties of 1929, xi, xv, xvii, 17, 23–4, 32, 43, 44, 63, 99, 106, 124, 126, 132, 161, 163, 180, 183, 193, 245, 262–3
  Article 24 of, 24, 44–7, 49–52, 124
  during Great War of 1914 to 1918, 46
  impact on Catholic Church's external relations, 43–4
  neutrality clause in, 40–2
  opportunities and limits of Vatican sovereignty, 64–6
Lateran Concordat, 43–4
Laurel, José P., 83, 96
Law, Cardinal Bernard Francis, 249
Law of 1871, 40
Law of Guarantees, 5, 40–1, 257, 261
League of Nations, 29–30, 35n31, 68–70
Ledechowski, Wlodimir, 11
Ledit, Joseph, 74

Ledóchowski, Wladimir, 74
Lékai, László, 28
Leo XIII, Pope, xiv, 5–8, 19n14, 135, 257–8
  diplomatic strategy, 6–7
  Ralliement, 6
Lettow, Paul, 232
Lettres de Rome, 74–5
liminality, xi, xvii
Limited Test Ban Treaty, 214
Locarno Agreements, 17
L'Osservatore Romano, 8, 71, 131, 183
Lottaz, Pascal, 122, 125, 135
Love, Maryann Cusimano, xviii
Lüthi, Lorenz, 133

M
Maglione, Cardinal, 96
Marella, Archbishop Paolo, 85, 88–90, 93–4, 96
Maritain, Jacques, 77
Marrus, Michael, 264
Martens, Kurt, xvi
Mater et Magistra, 164
Matsumoto, Saho, xviii
Mazzolari, Father Primo, 167
McCloy, John J., 114
Medvedovsky, Povel, 229
Melloni, Alberto, 173
Mendizábal, Alfred, 77
Mercier, Cardinal Desirée, 10
Migliore, Archbishop Celestino, 235
Milani, Father Lorenzo, 167
military alliances, 3
Mindszenty, József Cardinal, 28, 127, 143
  anti-communism of, 144–6
  differences between the Vatican and, 145
  final years, 151–4
  in Hungary, 149–51
  in US legation, 145–7, 154
Mit brennender Sorge, 76
Montevideo Convention, 1933, 180
Monticone, Alberto, 11

Montini, Monsignor Giovanni Battista, 112
Moresnet, 29
Morgenschweis, Carl, 113
Morgenthau, Henry, 263
Mortara, Edgardo, 255–6
Moscow Human Dimension Meeting, 1991, 51
Muckerman, Friedrich, 74
Muench, Aloisius, 112–13
Mussolini, Benito, 9, 23, 41–2, 63, 65, 67, 69, 72, 106, 124, 263
  pro-Soviet policy of early 1930s, 64

N
Nance, James W., 232
Napoleon, Louis, 255
Napoleonic wars, 3
nationalisms, 4–5
National Socialism, xiii, xix, 109, 112
Neuhäusler, Bishop, 114
neutrality, xii–xiv, 46, 107–11, 143, 180, 189
  of Austria, xiii
  bystander, 203
  Church magisterium *vs* international law, 122–6
  Cold War's transformative impact on, 125
  of Finland, xiii
  ideological, 122
  influence on international law, 125
  under international law, xii, 122
  moral *vs* legal, 122, 126
  permanent, xii, 180
  positive, xvii, 161, 172–3, 265
  realist view, xii
  of Switzerland, xiii
  Vatican as neutral actor, xii
  vs normalization, 131–4
  WWII and, xiii
  See also Vatican diplomacy (1870–1929); Vatican's Second World War diplomacy
Neutrality Act, xiii

New START (Strategic Arms Reduction Treaty), 208
Nicholas II of Russia, Tsar, 258
Nimo, John Kwaku, 229
Nixon, President, 146, 153–4
NNWS. *See* nonnuclear-weapon states (NNWS)
Non-aligned movement, xiii
non-alignment, xii
nonnuclear-weapon states (NNWS), 234
normalization of diplomatic relations, 131–4
Norway, xii
nuclear arms treaties, 207
Nuclear Nonproliferation Treaty, 1968, 208–9, 216, 225
 Casaroli idealistic and optimistic views of, 227–9
 North Korea and, 237–8
 post-Cold War period, 234–7
 Vatican negotiation with Soviets, 229–31
nuclear-weapon states (NWS), 234
Nuti, Monsignor, 95

O

O'Connor, Bishop John, 234
O'Doherty, Michael, 84, 90–1, 95
Open Skies Treaty, 208
Operation Barbarossa, 78
Oppenheim, Lassa, 180, 261
Organization for Security and Cooperation in Europe (OSCE), 49, 235
Organization of the Arab League, 49
Oxford Union Debating Society, xiii

P

Pacelli, Cardinal Eugenio, 64, 69, 83, 105
Pacelli, Francesco, 41, 47
Pacem in Terris, 132, 163–4, 214–15, 217, 226
pacifism, xii, xiii
Pact of London, 1915, xxiiin39

Palazzo Venezia, 64
Pan-Slavism, 12
Papacy, xi, 5
papal diplomacy, 161–2
 dualism between papacy and empire, 163–7
Papal Peace Note of 1917, xv, 14
Papal State, 3, 5, 23
 end of, 254–9
 sovereignty of, 40
Papal State, defeat of, 39
Papal States, xi, xiv
Papée, Kazimierz, 133–4
Parolin, Pietro, 44, 161, 208, 246
Partial Nuclear Test Ban Treaty, 230
Patronato Real, 87
Paul I, Pope John, 32
Paul II, Pope John, xii, xviii, 50, 121, 126, 133, 135–6, 162, 183, 188, 192, 216–19, 231–4, 249
Paul VI, Pope, 28, 47–8, 50, 112, 126, 131–3, 143, 150–1, 153, 165, 215–16, 225
 Bull *Episcoporum Poloniae coetus,* 133
PAX, 131
Pax Christi, 217
peace priest movement, 147, 152
peace treaties, 25–6
Pearl Harbor attack, 88–9
Pecci, Cardinal Vincenzo Giacchino, 5
Peloponnesian Wars, xii
permanent neutrality, xi–xii
Philippine–American War (1899–1902), 87
Philippine Catholic Church, 91–2
 humanitarian and spiritual work, 97
Philippine Independent Church in 1902, 87
Philippines, 83
 alliance with Tokyo, 96–8
 Catholic clergy in, 88
 Catholism and nationalism in, 86–8
 as Christian nation, 83–4
 Church activities in, 88–92

freedom of religion, 87
independence of, 96–8
Japanese invasion of, 87–8
Japanese Military Administration (JMA) of, 88, 90–7
land disputes, xvii
pact of alliance with Tokyo, 96–8
US power in, 87
Vatican diplomacy during Japanese occupation in, 83–98
Piani, Guglielmo, 84, 90–4, 96–8
Pius IX, Pope, xiv, xv, 4–5, 39–40, 255
diplomacy, 4–5
Syllabus of Errors, 5
Pius VI, Pope, 3
Pius VII, Pope, 3, 105
Pius X, Pope, 11, 257
pontificate, 7–8, 46
Pius XI, Pope, xii, xvii, 23, 31, 42, 63–7, 70, 72–3, 75–6, 83, 107, 125, 163, 249
diplomatic service, 15
Non Abbiamo Bisogno, 66
opposition to Italian war of conquest, 68
pontificate, 107
Pius XII, Pope, xii, xiii, 24, 46–7, 78, 84, 92, 106, 111–12, 121, 123, 126–7, 131–2, 134, 147, 209–11, 233, 254, 264
anti-communism of, 128
1951 Christmas message, 129
clemency efforts for convicted German war criminals, 112–15
policy of impartiality, 105
pontificate, 107
Planck, Max, 209
Poggi, Luigi, 132
Pohl, Oswald, 113
Pollard, xv
positive neutrality, xvii, 161, 172–3, 265
Puhan, Alfred, 151

Q

Quezon, Manuel L., 83

R

Ratti, Monsignor, 16
Ratti, Pope Achille, 68
Reagan, Ronald, 135, 208, 218, 231–2, 236
Realpolitik notion, xii
Reese, Thomas, 265
Reginbogin, Herbert, xviii, 122, 125, 135
Riberi, Monsignor, 95
Riccardi, Andrea, 129
Rizal, José, 87
Robertson, Geoffrey, 248
Roman Question, xv, 5, 23, 39–41, 43, 163, 262
Rosa, Father Enrico, 77
Ruhr Crisis, 1924, 15–17
Russian Orthodoxy, 6, 12
Russian Sovietism, 77
Ryngaert, Cedric, 180

S

Salis, Count John de, 7
SALT I and II, 230–1
Saltini, Father Zeno, 167
Samorè, Antonio, 132
Sarto, Cardinal Giuseppe, 7–8
Scali, John, 213
Schuman, Robert, 129
Second Hague Conference on the Rights and Duties of Neutral Powers, xii
Second Vatican Council, 25, 47, 131–2, 134, 148, 150, 154, 165, 182, 215, 225, 258, 265
Serédi, Jusztinián György Cardinal, 28
Sevenich, Maria, 111
Shigenori, Togo, 90
Shin Seiki ("New Era"), 84
Silesian dispute, 16
Silvestrini, Bishop Achille, 229
Slipyi, Josyf, 132, 148–9, 211–12, 214
societas iuridice perfecta, xiv, 40
Solidarnoœæ (Solidarity) trade union movement, 135
Soviet-Vatican relations, 229–31

Spanish–American War of 1898, xvii, 87, 258
Spanish Civil War (1936–1939), 63, 70, 73–8
Spellman, Francis Cardinal, 128
Stalin, Joseph, 121, 133
Starkov, Anver, 229
Stehle, Hansjakob, 132
Stehlin, Stewart, 27
Steinberg, David J., 86
Sturzo, Luigi, 77
Syrian Christians, 189–90, 192, 194
Syrian conflict, 2011–2016, 189–94

T
Taguchi, Bishop, 88–9, 92, 94
Taguti, Monsignor, 95
Takami, Archbishop Joseph Mitsuaki, 203
Takefumi, Terada, 89
Tardini, Monsignor Domenico, 69, 71
Tatsuo, Doi, 88–9
Tatsuya, Shimura, 88–9
Tauran, Archbishop Jean-Louis, 186
Temporal Power, 3–5
Testa, Monsignor, 95
Testa, Monsignor Gustavo, 16
Thatcher, Margaret, 135
Third French Republic, 6
Thirty Years War, 3
Thucydides, xii
Thurlow, Setsuko, 237
Tindaro, Cardinal Mariano Rampolla del, 6–8
Tomasi, Archbishop Silvano, 192
Tomoyuki, General Yamashita, 98
tranquilitas ordinas, 206
Treaty for the Prohibition of Nuclear Weapons (TPNW), 204
Treaty of Lausanne, 25
Treaty of London, 1915, 24, 43
Treaty of Neuilly-sur-Seine, 25
Treaty of Saint-Germain-en-Laye, 25
Treaty of Sèvres, 25
Treaty of Trianon, 25, 28–9, 145

Treaty on the Nonproliferation of Nuclear Weapons, 1971, 229
Triple Entente, 24

U
United Nations Committee for the Rights of the Child, 250
United Nations Educational, Scientific, and Cultural Organization (UNESCO), 48–9
United States Conference of Catholic Bishops (USCCB), 247
UN's Conference on Disarmament (CD), 233
Urban II, Pope, xiv
Urbi et Orbi, 183
US Catholic bishops, 234
US–India civil nuclear special deal, 2006, 235
US–Japanese war, 89
US National Archives (NARA), 231

V
Val, Merry del, 7–8
Valk, Hans de, 6
Vatican Bank, 264
  financial corruption case, 252–4
Vatican City, 42, 53, 63
  acceptance of Japanese ambassador, 86
  as an independent state, xi
  anti-Bolshevik campaign, xvi
  approach to neutrality, xv–xix, 67–73
  creation of, 44–5, 261
  diplomacy in Eastern front, 93–6
  diplomatic actions toward Fascist Italy, 85
  German influences in, 10–12
  relations with Imperial Japanese Army, xviii
  relations with Philippine National Church, xviii
  sovereignty of, xiv
  See also Holy See

Vatican diplomacy (1870–1929), xi, 3
  Benedict XV's pontificate, 8
  during Franco-Prussian conflict, 4–5
  in international affairs, xiv–xv
  during July Crisis, 8
  "just war" theory, 13–15
  neutrality in European international relations, 5–6
  "Papal Peace Note," 14
  Pius XI's diplomatic service, 15
  Pius X's pontificate, 7–8
  policy of neutrality and impartiality, 8–10, 16
  relationship with Catholic Austria-Hungary, 6
  relations with Second Reich, 5–7
  during Ruhr Crisis, 15–17
  war crimes and, 10–13
  See also Holy See
Vatican diplomatic policy, xiii
Vatican–French relations, 27
Vatican Office of Information for Prisoners of War, 1939–1947, 107
Vatican *Ostpolitik,* 121, 131–4, 147–51
Vatican's concordats, 106, 126
Vatican's Second World War diplomacy, 83–98
  Catholic support for Japanese actions, 84–5
  communication channels, 85–6, 93–5
  difference between Church realities and, 86, 88–92, 96–8
Venezuelan crisis, 161
Venturi, Jesuit Pietro Tacchi, 69, 73–4
Versailles Peace Conference, 15
Versailles Peace Treaty, 16–17, 25, 31
  Article 32 of, 35n27
  Article 33 of, 35n28
  Article 34 of, 35n29
  Article 51 of, 26–7
  signing of, 27
  transfer of Alsace-Lorraine to France, 26–8
  transfer of Eupen and Malmedy from Germany to Belgium, 29–31
Versailles territorial settlement, 15
Vidal I Barraquer, Cardinal, 76

W

war crimes, 10–13
war in Ethiopia (1935–1936), 63
Warsaw Pact, 49, 230
Warsaw Uprising, 122
Whitmore, Todd, 182
Wilhelmina, Queen, 258
William II of Prussia, King, 4
Wojtyla, Karol Cardinal, 135
World Health Organization, 48
World Meeting of Popular Movements, 171
World Trade Centre attack, 2001, 185
World War II, xiii, 24, 105–6, 122, 124, 126, 205. *See also* Vatican's Second World War diplomacy
WWII Vatican Apostolic Archive (Archivio Apostolico Vaticano), xiii
Wyszyñski, Stefan Cardinal, 134, 148

Y

Yoshigoro, Taguchi, 84

Z

Zágon, Monsignor József, 152
Zivojinovic, Dragan, 10–12

About the Contributors

Dr. Margit Balogh is professor of modern Hungarian history at Eötvös Loránd University. Her research fields include twentieth-century church history, state, and relations between Hungary and the Holy See after 1945. Her publications include *A KALOT és a katolikus társadalompolitika, 1935–1946* (*The KALOT and Catholic Social Policy, 1935–1946*) (1998); *Kardinal József Mindszenty: Ein Leben zwischen kommunistischer Diktatur und Kaltem Krieg* (2014); *Mindszenty József (1892–1975)* (2015); and *Az Apát úr by Göcseji Múzeum* (2019).

Professor Marshall J. Breger is professor of law at the Columbus School of Law, The Catholic University of America. From 1993 to 1995, he was a senior fellow at the Heritage Foundation in Washington, DC. During the George H. W. Bush administration, he served as solicitor of labor, the chief lawyer of the Labor Department with a staff of more than eight hundred. From 1982 to 1984, he served as special assistant to President Reagan and his liaison to the Jewish community. He is the author (with Gary Edles) of *Independent Regulatory Agencies of the United States* (2015). His coauthored book manuscript, *Legal and Political Issues of Holy Places in Jerusalem*, is forthcoming (winter 2021).

Dr. Suzanne Brown-Fleming is director of international academic programs at the United States Holocaust Memorial Museum's Jack, Joseph, and Morton Mandel Center for Advanced Holocaust Studies. Dr. Brown-Fleming's most recent publication, *May Your Holiness Act in the Interest of Protecting Those who Remain Morally Thinking People: Vatican Responses to Antisemitism, 1933*, was part of the Institute for Holocaust Research at Yad

Vashem's *Search and Research* Series (2017). Her first book, *The Holocaust and Catholic Conscience: Cardinal Aloisius Muench and the Guilt Question in Germany*, was published in 2006. Her current research project, *Il Papa Tedesco* (The German Pope): *Eugenio Pacelli and Germany, 1933–1945*, is a study of Pacelli's relationship to Germany, their bishops, leaders, and their people during the Third Reich.

Dr. Luke Cahill is lecturer in international relations at the Department of Politics, Languages, and International Studies at the University of Bath, UK. He holds a PhD in international relations from Bath, an MSc in US politics and contemporary history from the School of Advanced Study, University of London, and a BA in politics and history from University College Dublin. His interests focus on the Holy See, IR Theory, and US Foreign Policy and Diplomatic history.

Dr. Lucia Ceci (1967), PhD, is professor of modern history at the University of Rome Tor Vergata and director of the Roman Center for Jewish Studies. She has published monographs and articles on the relationships between the Catholic Church and politics in Italy and Latin America. Her most recent volume is *The Vatican and Mussolini's Italy* (Friuli Book Prize for Contemporary History, 2016).

Dr. Maryann Cusimano Love is tenured associate professor of international relations in the Politics Department of The Catholic University of America in Washington, DC. She serves as an advisor on international affairs and US foreign policy to the Holy See and the United States Catholic Bishops' International Justice and Peace Committee. Dr. Love is a *New York Times* bestselling author. Her most recent book is *Global Issues* (Rowman & Littlefield, 2020). She is an alumna of Johns Hopkins University (PhD).

Dr. Maria d'Arienzo is professor of ecclesiastical law, canon law, and confessional rights at the Department of Law of the University of Naples "Federico II." She is director of the review *Diritto e Religioni* and an appointed member of the board of directors of the International Jacques Maritain Institute (IIJM). She is also director of the Department of Interfaith Dialogue at the Halal and Shari'a Compliance Academy. Dr. d'Arienzo is the author of four monographs and numerous articles dedicated to the relationship between secularism and religious freedom from a comparative perspective, to the problems concerning the relationship between Islamic law and Western law relating to family law, and to the issue of damages in canon law.

Dr. Massimo Faggioli is professor in the Theology and Religious Studies Department at Villanova University (Philadelphia). He worked in the "John XXIII Foundation for Religious Studies" in Bologna between 1996 and 2008. He was co-chair of the study group "Vatican II Studies" for the American Academy of Religion between 2012 and 2017. He has a column in *La Croix International* and is contributing writer for *Commonweal* magazine and the Italian magazine *Il Regno*. His publications include: *A Council for the Global Church. Receiving Vatican II in History* (2015); *The Rising Laity. Ecclesial Movements since Vatican II* (2016); and *Catholicism and Citizenship: Political Cultures of the Church in the Twenty-First Century* (2017). His latest book is *The Liminal Papacy of Pope Francis: Moving Toward Global Catholicity* (2020).

Dr. Arpad von Klimo is professor at the Catholic University of America in Washington, DC, where he teaches contemporary European history. He was born in Heidelberg, Germany, and studied history, art history, Italian, and economics at the universities of Göttingen, Venice, and graduated from the Free University of Berlin (MA 1992, PhD, habilitation, 2001). His publications include *Remembering Cold Days: The 1942 Massacre of Novi Sad and the Transformation of Hungarian Society until 1989* (2018) and *Hungary since 1945* (2018). He coedited (with Irina Livezeanu) the *Routledge History of East-Central Europe Since 1700* (2017).

Dr. Piotr H. Kosicki is associate professor of history at the University of Maryland, College Park. He holds a PhD in History from Princeton University and specializes in transnational European history and the history of the Roman Catholic Church, with a particular emphasis on ideas, politics, and the international system. He is the author, among others, of *Catholics on the Barricades: Poland, France, and "Revolution," 1891–1956* (2018) and editor/coeditor, among others, of *Christian Democracy Across the Iron Curtain* (2017), *Christian Democracy and the Fall of Communism* (2020), and *Vatican II Behind the Iron Curtain* (2016).

Dr. Pascal Lottaz is assistant professor for neutrality studies at the Waseda Institute for Advanced Study in Tokyo. His research focus is neutrality in world history and Japan's relations with neutral countries during the Second World War. He received his PhD from the National Graduate Institute for Policy Studies (Tokyo) and lectures on international relations at Waseda University and Contemporary European Politics at Temple University, Japan Campus. He is the coeditor of *Notions of Neutralities* (2019).

Dr. Kurt Martens is a Belgian lawyer and professor in the School of Canon Law at The Catholic University of America in Washington, DC. He earned his law and canon law degrees at the Katholieke Universiteit Leuven, Belgium, and is a member of numerous professional organizations serves on the Board of the Consociatio Internationalis Studio Iuris Canonici Promovendo. He is a consultant to the United States Conference of Catholic Bishops Committee on Canonical Affairs (since November 2008). Professor Martens is the editor of *The Jurist* (since 2012), cofounder and coeditor in chief of *Recht, Religie en Samenleving* (*Droit, Religion et Société / Law, Religion and Society*), member of the Comitato Scientifico Internazionale of Ephemerides Iuris Canonici (Studium Generale Marcianum, Venice, Italy), member of the Comitato Scientifico of Monitor Ecclesiasticus, and member of the Comitato Scientifico of Apollinaris. He has published three books, edited nine, and authored almost one hundred scholarly articles on canon law, church and state relations, and religious liberty.

Dr. Saho Matsumoto is the author of *Britain and the Papacy in the Age of Revolution, 1846–1851*, Royal Historical Society Studies in History New Series (2003, in English), based on her PhD thesis for the University of Warwick, UK. Her other publications include the *Vatican Diplomacy and International Organizations* (2019, in Japanese), *History of the Vatican from Pope Pius IX to Pope Francis* (2013, in Japanese). Professor Matsumoto currently teaches in the Department of International Relations at Nihon University, Japan.

Dr. John F. Pollard is fellow of Trinity Hall, Cambridge, a fellow of the Royal Historical Society, and an emeritus professor of modern history at Anglia Polytechnic University. His publications include *The Vatican and Italian Fascism, 1929–1932: A Study in Conflict* (1985), *Papal Diplomacy in the Modern Age*, coedited with Peter Kent (1994), *The Fascist Experience in Italy* (1998), *The Unknown Pope: Benedict XV (1914–1922) and the Pursuit of Peace* (1999), and *Money and the Rise of the Modern Papacy: Financing the Vatican, 1850–1950* (2004).

Dr. Herbert Reginbogin is fellow at The Catholic University of America Institute for Policy Research. He has been a professor of international relations and international law at several institutions of higher learning on both sides of the Atlantic, including Lefke (Cyprus), Bogazici University (Turkey), Cag University (Turkey), Potsdam University (Germany), Touro Law School, (USA), and Kehl University am Rhein (Germany). Dr. Reginbogin's publications include *Notions of Neutrality* (coedited with Pascal Lottaz, 2018),

Permanent Neutrality: A Model for Peace, Security, and Justice (coedited with Lottaz, 2020), *Permanent Neutrality in the Post-Cold War* (coedited with Gaertner and Lottaz, 2022), as well as books and publications in the field of international law, contemporary history, climate, and sustainability over the past twenty years. In addition, he has worked on several high-profile litigation cases and energy security issues in the Eastern Mediterranean, European Union, and the United States regarding international maritime law, international refugee issues, the destabilization of the international world order, and kleptocracy. He is presently working on a new security architecture for US foreign and national security issues and received his Licentiatus Philosophiae/PhD from the University of Bern and his BA from Whittier College.

www.ingramcontent.com/pod-product-compliance
Lightning Source LLC
Chambersburg PA
CBHW021346300426
44114CB00012B/1094